MARTIAL COMPANION

Designer: Steve Danielson
Developer: John W. Curtis III

Project Specific Contributions:

Series Editor: John Curtis;

Content Editor: Coleman Charlton;

Proofreader: Kevin Elliott;

Other Contributions: Don Dennis;

Interior Illustrations: Steven Cavallo, Storn Cook, Fritz Haas, Greg Smith, Adam Wallenta;

Cover Illustration: Romas Kukalis;

Art Direction: Jessica Ney-Grimm;

Assisting Art Direction: Jason O. Hawkins;

Pagemaking: Sherry Robinson;

Cover Graphics: Wendy Frazer;

ICE Staff:

Sales Manager: Deane Begiebing;

Managing Editor: Coleman Charlton;

President: Peter Fenlon;

CEO: Bruce Neidlinger;

Editing, Development, & Production Staff:
John Curtis, Donald Dennis, Jason Hawkins, Wendy Frazer, Bob Mohney, Nick Morawitz, Jessica Ney-Grimm, Michael Reynolds;

Print Buying and Rights Director: Kurt Fischer;

Sales, Customer Service, & Operations Staff:
Becky Blanton, Arthur Brill, Steve Hardy, Olivia H. Johnston, Chad McCully, Dave Platnick, Karina Swanberg, Monica L. Wilson;

Shipping Staff: Dave Morris, Daniel Williams.

Produced and distibuted by IRON CROWN ENTERPRISES, Inc., P.O. Box 1605, Charlottesville, VA 22902
First U.S. Edition 1997   Stock #5602   ISBN 1-55806-313-7
Printed in Canada

CONTENTS

MARTIAL
ARTS
COMPANION

WELCOME

Welcome to *Martial Arts Companion*. This book is designed to allow Gamemasters to incorporate a wider range of martial arts into the *Rolemaster Standard System* (*RMSS*). Inside you will find rules for introducing unarmed combat systems and new martial arts skills. For ease of integration into the Gamemaster's campaign, the optional rules and skills introduced in this book are categorized into the three separate power levels: Core, Heroic, and Fantastic.

When first reading this book, concentrate on reading and understanding the core rules. Any text that is not marked as heroic, or fantastic serves as core or background information, it will be helpful to at least to skim through these sections to get a broad overview of the scope and purpose of this companion.

Pay special attention to the examples covering everything from character creation to combat. After you gain an understanding of the material, create a few sample characters using the core rules before tackling the optional heroic and fantastic rules and options in this companion. Afterwards, feel free to dive into the optional sections of the rules. Each optional ruling has a brief discussion of their impact upon the *RMSS* that should make the job of choosing what options to include (or exclude) in a campaign much easier for the Gamemaster. Some of the key features that are covered by *Martial Arts Companion* include the following:

- History of martial arts
- Guidelines for using martial arts within a campaign
- Two new variant Monk professions, the Taoist and the Zen monk, each with new spell lists
- New and revised background options for martial arts characters
- New and redesigned martial arts skills for the *Rolemaster Standard System*
- Rules for creating your own martial arts style with a point cost system

- Examples of historical martial arts styles
- Introduction of Chi Powers skills to model fantastic feats of martial arts
- Guidelines for using martial arts in combat
- New weapon attack tables
- New critical tables
- New and revised training packages

Sources
Martial Arts: Traditions, History, People. John Concoran and Emil Farkas
The History and Philosophy of Kung Fu. Earl C Medeiros
Classical Bujutsu: The Martial Arts and Ways of Japan, Volume 1. Donn Draeger
Classical Budo: The Martial Arts and Ways of Japan, Volume 2. Donn Draeger
The Fighting Arts. Howard Reid and Micheal Croucher
Zen and Confucius in the Art of Swordmanship. Reinhard Kammer
Asian Fighting Arts. Donn Draeger and Robert Smith
Phoenix-Eye Fist: A Shaolin Fighting Art of South China. Cheong Cheng Leong and Donn Draeger
Recommended Reading
Outlaws of the Marsh, Volumes 1 and 2. Shi Nai'an and Luo Guanzhong
Fox Volant of the Snowy Mountain. Jin Yong
Recommended Viewing
Once Upon a Time in China I, II, III, IV
Last Hero in China
The Swordsman I, II

NOTE

For readability purposes, the book uses the standard masculine pronouns when referring to persons of uncertain gender. In such cases, these pronouns are intended to convey non-gender specific meanings: he/she, her/him, etc. In addition, it is not the main goal of this work to present absolutely correct and historically verifiable information about each martial arts style. Where possible, historical accuracy has been preserved but some of the information regarding special strikes, maneuvers, and abilities of the martial arts practitioners has been created by the author to make each style unique and interesting to play. For those interested in a more in-depth discussion of the historical role of martial arts and deeper knowledge of a certain style, please review the sources and recommended reading list provided in the appendix.

AUTHOR'S NOTE

A special thanks goes out to all the people who have helped to make this product a reality. All the participants on the Rolemaster Internet mailing list have been very helpful. A special thanks goes out to the brave group of Internet play testers—Robert Brott, Nicholas Caldwell, and Kent Krumvieda. I have not met any of you in person, but I have found all of your suggestions and ideas extremely useful. I would also like to thank my parents for all of their support and help in everything I do. A special hello goes out to the Ithaca role playing community, Scott, Laurie, Jim, Diane, Bob, J.P., and Nick. It has been a lot of fun, good luck in Ithaca and beyond! And a final thanks goes out to James Martinez for all the help and support throughout this project and my life—you are the best!

MARTIAL ARTS COMPANION

PART I
CONCEPTS AND PREMISES

PART I CONTENTS

Welcome to *Martial Arts Companion!* This book details rules for creating and running characters that employ martial arts techniques within the *Rolemaster Standard System*. *Martial Arts Companion* uses the standard notation from the following *Rolemaster Standard System* products: *Rolemaster Standard Rules*, *Arms Law*, *Spell Law*, and *Gamemaster Law*. It is also compatible with *Talent Law*, Castles and Ruins, *Weapon Law: Firearms*, *Treasure Companion*, *Arcane Companion*, and Races and Cultures: Underground Races. Within these pages you will find a wealth of information detailing how to use, create, and run martial arts in your campaign. In addition, there is also a great deal of information regarding the historical progression and development of martial arts that may be applicable to any game system.

INTRODUCTION

This book is geared to be a useful reference for both the Gamemaster and the player. As with all companions, the rules detailed within these pages are optional. It is not recommended that the average Gamemaster use every option and rule presented in this companion. In most games, only a certain subset of the rules and guidelines presented in this companion will be used. Players wishing to introduce rules presented in this companion into a game must be aware that their inclusion may upset the game-balance and direction intended by the Gamemaster. In this event, the wishes of the Gamemaster should be respected. Likewise, Gamemasters wishing to include the new rules and options presented in this companion within their games have an obligation to clearly explain to the players the ramifications they present to the players' present and future characters.

This book tries to model the different approaches to martial arts within a consistent framework. To this end, a common set of martial arts rules and skills serve as the foundation for this book. Because of this structure, it is possible to embrace the many complexities of martial arts. It is important, therefore, for the Gamemaster to fully understand the power level of martial arts that he wishes to allow within his campaign. It is equally important that he convey his expectations of the capabilities of martial artists to his players to avoid misunderstandings. With both the players and the Gamemaster starting from a common set of assumptions, a campaign becomes much more stable. There are three power levels in this companion and they are the following:

- **Core Power Level**—The Core power level assumes a near real-world expectation of martial arts. The martial arts are treated as unarmed combat with all the inherent advantages and disadvantage that come with that expectation. The Core power level is well integrated with the entire *RMSS*.

- **Heroic Power Level**—The Heroic power level assumes a slightly larger-than life expectation of martial arts. The martial arts at this level are more effective than they actually are in the real world, allowing players to accomplish extraordinary acts more easily. In most cases, the Heroic power level is the average level at which a role playing campaign is run.

- **Fantastic Power Level**—The Fantastic power level assumes an unrealistic expectation of martial arts. Martial arts are presented as the supreme form of combat and are practiced by the majority of the heroes of the campaign world. Martial arts masters can accomplish supernatural feats through the focus of their inner power. The Fantastic power level is the most potentially imbalancing option with respect to the rest of the *RMSS*.

While players have a wide variety of options to choose from when using this book, it is noteworthy that the mechanisms used for resolving martial arts attacks are quite simple. In summary, *Martial Arts Companion* was created to enhance the enjoyment of Rolemaster players by expanding on and enhancing the martial arts system first introduced in *RMSS*. Furthermore, the assumptions used in creating the rules and guidelines in this book are outlined below to help the Gamemaster understand the foundation from which the rules have been generated.

◆ 1.1 ◆
ASSUMPTIONS

The following is a list of assumptions for this book.

- This book was created to benefit any profession in *RMSS*. Therefore, all martial arts abilities can be used by any profession, albeit at a price.

- This book was created to expand the alternatives available to players having characters who specializing in martial arts. As a result, a system for creating unique martial arts styles was created to emphasize the uniqueness of the martial artist.

- The changes in this companion will imbue the martial arts character with more depth and versatility, which will make this character more interesting to operate. To accomplish this, three changes were instituted:

    1. A consistent and comprehensive framework was developed to incorporate a more detailed martial arts system into *RMSS*.

    2. The range of choices available to martial artists has been increased by the addition of new skills, background options, training packages, and special talents and flaws.

    3. The development point burden on martial arts characters has been lessened to allow them to pursue expertise outside the narrow range of martial arts.

- Finally, the standard *RMSS* combat round system with a 100% limit on activity and three actions per round limit is still being used to resolve combat? Note, however, that variant combat systems used in some *Rolemaster* campaigns may require some modification to complement the rules in this companion. Especially important to recognize are the changes reflected in this companion from previous editions of *Rolemaster*. These are outlined below.

◆ 1.2 ◆
CHANGES

The areas that have changed in *Martial Arts Companion* include professions, guidelines, skills, and weapon attack and critical tables. These are explained below.

1.2.1 · NEW PROFESSIONS

While the Monk profession introduced in *RMSR* remains a valid profession, two new variant professions based on the Monk are introduced. These include the Taoist monk and the Zen monk, both of whom specialize in unarmed combat. These introductions were motivated by the argument of whether the Monk profession was better modeled as an Essence-based or a Mentalism-based spell caster (Charltonian versus Amthorian view). The original Monk profession's spell lists still retain a fair balance between the two variant professions, thus offering the most flexibility to the starting character. However, players now have the option to choose between Monk professions, depending on which heightened attributes they wish their characters to possess.

The Taoist monk is a new Essence-based spell casting martial artist that differs from its *RMSR* predecessor in its ability to manipulate and create elemental forces. The advantage the Taoist monk gains in elemental control is balanced by his lesser effectiveness both at controlling his body and focusing his will when compared to the standard Monk's own ability to master these traits. The Zen monk, a new Mentalism-based spell casting martial artist, on the other hand, is blessed with a superior ability to focus his will and use the power of his mind to influence the perceptions of others that out shadows even that of the standard Monk. However, the Zen monk does not have the standard Monk or Taoist monk abilities at special moving maneuvers.

1.2.2 · GUIDELINES

Some new guidelines dealing with specialized combat situations are detailed in this companion. They cover everything from competing in challenges to fighting on top of a teetering building while it is raining. These guidelines are meant to help the Gamemaster resolve the strange and interesting situations in which players invariably find themselves.

1.2.3 · SKILLS

The most important change to the original martial arts skills found in *RMSR* is the elimination of the four-tiered degree skill system used for martial arts attacks. For simplicity, this has been replaced with a single skill for each general type of attack, of which there are four: martial arts striking, martial arts sweeping, locking holds, and nerve strikes. While the *RMSR*'s original damage threshold system is still present in this book, it is now embedded in the Martial Arts Style skill. The Martial Arts Style skill allows the martial artist to create a specialized unarmed attacking system. The Martial Arts Style skill is also placed in a new skill category under the umbrella Martial Arts Group called the Martial Arts Combat Maneuvers skill category. Many other specialized martial arts skills are included in this skill category. Additional new skills are included in a wide range of skill categories, ranging from General Lore skills to Special Defenses skills. An important addition is the Weapon Style skill to the Combat Maneuvers skill category. The Weapon Style skill allows the user to create unique weapon-using fighting systems, much like the Martial Arts Style skill allows the use to create unique unarmed combat fighting systems.

An optional type of skill called a Chi Powers skill has been introduced to model some of the amazing feats performed by martial artists in history and legend. These skills are found in many different skill categories and are listed in their own section in this book.

1.2.4 · WEAPON ATTACK TABLES AND CRITICAL TABLES

New weapon attack tables offer the martial artist a greater range of choices in traditional martial arts weapons that have as of yet not been created in *Arms Law* format. The additional weapon attack tables for the katana, nunchaku, tetsubo, sai, kris, wakizashi, chigiriki, kusarigama, chain, thorn staff, short stick, dart, spring sword, three-sectioned staff, butterfly knife, and metal whip are listed in this companion. Other specialized martial arts weapons are profiled as well. Furthermore, two additional critical tables, Locking Holds and Nerve Strikes, are introduced as well to offer more effective martial arts attacks.

HISTORICAL MARTIAL ARTS

Part I

Sections
2.0, 2.1

Historical
Martial Arts

The Origins of
Martial Arts

A martial art is an individual fighting style that is systematized and defined in a formal manner. Martial arts require long practice and rigid self-discipline to master. With this discipline comes the mental focus and accuracy necessary for success. Examples of martial arts can be found throughout history and legend from David's smiting of Goliath with his sling to the accounts of ancient Chinese fighting masters. The skills and techniques employed in martial arts are different from those used in warfare. While martial arts are driven by the dictums of accuracy and speed, mass combat or warfare is driven by the dictums of strength and firepower. Whereas the weapons used in warfare are large and heavy and fighting can take days, the combat practiced by the martial artist is free of restraint and swift, with the focused objective of neutralizing the foe as quickly as possible.

◆ 2.1 ◆
THE ORIGINS
OF MARTIAL ARTS

The true beginnings of martial arts are clouded in myth, since most ancient martial arts masters kept little records. Instead, techniques were handed down from master to disciple. Because of a master's untimely death or failure to locate a gifted protégé, many unique martial arts styles and their origins have been lost. It is generally agreed, however, that martial arts first took root in the Asian cultures of the East. Furthermore, it is believed that the religious traditions and medical knowledge practiced in this area were instrumental in developing the forms and style of martial arts we recognize in all the evolved forms of martial arts preset today.

The omnipresent element of inner strength and focus in all martial art forms is attributed to the Eastern practice of meditation and the system of breathing that accompanies it This is believed to empower an individual with the proper relaxation and focused abilities that allow for the proper channeling of strength, coupled with the accuracy and speed, needed to excel in any confrontational situation. In addition, the increased medical knowledge allowed for the identification of those body areas that would sustain the most damage from the punishing strikes perfected through the art of mediation. While martial arts styles are typically classified as hard or soft, both techniques incorporate a small measure of the other.

Before detailing the differences of each style, the following example taken form the animal kingdom might illustrate the contrast between the two opposing styles. Picture a confrontation between a mongoose and a snake. The mongoose jumps quickly from spot to spot, radiating energy as it tests the defenses of the snake with lightning attacks and retreats. The mongoose is clearly displaying the hard style. The snake, on the other hand, waits patiently, giving no indication of when or where it is to strike. It simply sways back and forth before its sudden unexpected attack. This is the essence of the soft style. The differences are further detailed below.

HARD MARTIAL ARTS STYLES

Hard arts typify force opposed by force. In unarmed combat, this force is accomplished by propelling the entire body, or part of it, against the opponent, since added momentum is gained by sending the weight and motion of the entire body after a punch or kick? Various strikes are leveled at the opponent, but the most effective are those whose forces are propelled in a straight line. Blocks that forcefully deflect or stop incoming blows often precede countermoves in a hard style, while the countermove itself rapidly follows the block with direct punches or kicks. This approach is very straightforward and is the basis for many martial arts styles, including karate, Korean tae kwon do, and the hard arts of Chinese kung fu.

To the trained martial artist, however, the hard style does present one flaw. Because of the muscular tension displayed and the momentum of their bodies, the stance of the martial artist can reveal their next intention to their opponent. In addition, while the breathing techniques of the hard arts (focusing breathing to a point between the solar plexus and the upper chest) allow the martial artist to focus his energy into explosive releases, there exists the danger of draining the user of strength. Therefore, in a clash between martial artists using hard styles, there is an emphasis on instinctive and trained reactions using physical strength to quickly end the conflict.

SOFT MARTIAL ARTS STYLES

Circular motion is the forms the basis of the soft arts. Like the snake in the above example, a master of the soft arts is still and relaxed. Unlike the tensed muscles of those martial artists exercising the hard style, a master of the soft arts does not reveal his intentions. In addition, the soft arts masters also seek to use incoming force against itself, instead of opposing the force. For example, the bodily momentum initiated by a striking opponent could be further increased and used against him by simply stepping to one side and pushing the opponent towards the ground. In a clash between two martial artists using soft styles, the emphasis is on using the mind to outwit the opponent.

Correct breathing techniques are very important to the soft arts. Unlike the breathing employed in the hard arts, in the soft arts breathing is initiated low in the body, two inches below the navel, where the center of vital energy or chi is believed to reside. By training the mind to use the muscles of the diaphragm to draw air into the lungs in this manner, it is possible to evoke a tremendous force that radiates from within the body to the extremities, where it can be used to deliver punishing blows to opponents.

◆ 2.2 ◆
THE DEVELOPMENT OF MARTIAL ARTS

The next sections are devoted to the profiling the culture and fighting systems of many different countries of the world. These include Chinese martial arts, European martial arts, Japanese martial arts, Indian martial arts, Indonesian and Malaysian martial arts, Korean martial arts, and Okinawan martial arts. Each region has a brief history of each region and how martial arts developed in that region and interacted with the culture. If a martial arts system is further profiled later in this companion, it is distinguished by its name in bold-faced type.

It is important to realize that martial arts arose in a time when present-day nations were nothing more than mere assortments of independent states or clans, and warfare was small and localized, so that individual fighters attained greater importance due to the small number of troops in conflict. Warfare was ritualized and in some cases settled by single combat. One need only consider the prestige and honor bestowed upon even a slave in Roman times for his expertise as a gladiator to comprehend the allure of this ancient fighting art form.

In the following section, note that the Asian-inspired martial arts are grouped alphabetically by region, whereas the European-inspired martial arts are listed in chronological order.

2.2.1 · ASIAN MARTIAL ARTS

This is a brief discussion of the history of Asian martial arts.

CHINESE MARTIAL ARTS

The great Songshan Shaolin Temple and monastery at the foot of the Songshan Mountains of Central China is the place where Chinese martial arts are believed to have taken root. Although there exists scholarly doubt about the accuracy of this legend, it is widespread among the martial arts community. It is believed that an Indian monk by the name of Bodhidharma arrived to teach the Chinese a new approach to Buddhism that involved intense long periods of meditation, from which the meditative schools of Ch'an in China and Zen in Japan are said to have arisen. One commonly cited story asserts that Bodhidharma stared at the wall of a cave for nine consecutive years. To help the monks of the Temple withstand the long hours of meditation, Bodhidharma taught them exercises and movements to strengthen their bodies, and the Shaolin Temple Boxing technique was born.

THE SHAOLIN TRADITION AND THE RISE OF SECRET SOCIETIES

At the height of its prosperity, the Shaolin Temple had 1,500 monks, 500 of who were fighting monks. They led simple lives, supporting themselves by farming the land they owned. It wasn't until 1674, after 128 of these monks assisted the Ch'ing Emperor in battle, that their highly effective fighting techniques were seen as cause for alarm. This was further heightened when they rejected the titles offered to them by the Emperor in favor of returning to their temple. The Emperor became persuaded that it was dangerous to let such an effective fighting force exist in the center of his empire that he did not fully control. Shortly thereafter, an army led by a renegade Shaolin monk surrounded the temple and burnt it to the ground. It is believe that five of the surviving monks subsequently founded China's infamous secret societies known as the Triads. Thereafter, martial arts became linked with Chinese secret societies.

The first of these to materialize were the White Lotus and White Lily societies. Each society was associated with a specific style of martial arts and would often practice at night during its secret meetings. Like the various secret societies formed afterwards, these two societies were instrumental in helping various factions rise to power, only to be ruthlessly suppressed by the same faction they supported. This antagonistic relationship dotted China's history with ever-changing dynasties in power, since the Chinese government wavered between embracing the advantage of having a large group of highly skilled fighting men in times of need and then feeling the need to suppress the same fighters to guard its power. The preferred martial arts style adopted by these fighters evolved from the Shaolin boxing and is known as the Shaolin kung fu tradition.

KUNG FU

The Shaolin kung fu tradition is divided into two schools, northern and southern. While the two traditions might have evolved from separate schools, most Chinese attribute geography for the manifestation of the northern and southern kung fu styles. Northern China consists mainly of open plains where walking or riding great distances was customary, so that individuals' already developed legs became their main means of attack and defense. Southern China, on the other hand, is riddled with large numbers of waterways, requiring adept rowing and poling skills, which led to greater arm strength. As a result, the southern styles relied on the fists as the main means of attack. The main differences between the northern and southern schools of kung fu will be discussed below, as well as some of the techniques that arose form each school.

Northern Kung fu style

Graceful and smooth movements are characteristic of the northern style of kung fu. In fact, the northern styles provide much of the basis for the martial arts styles used in Peking Opera. Stances are usually very wide and open, and arms are usually fully extended on both attack and defense. Leaps, turns and other sweeping movements are also incorporated in to this style. Movements displayed by animals have influenced the development of certain styles in this school and include: Crane, Dragon, Eagle, Horse, Praying Mantis, and Wing Chun styles among others.

One of the most striking characteristics of the northern styles is their emphasis on kicking. Northern stylists are trained to jump high and deliver one, two, or three kicks to an opponent before landing. Flying sidekicks are also taught, although their original use was to dismount cavalry. Northern styles use long formal sequences of attacks and counters as training aids that cover a wide area of ground. While some locks and grapples are used, most northern styles use strikes and kicks with the arms or legs fully extended. Weapons are also used and include swords, spears, staffs, scimitars, halberds, and war-fans. The forms used with weapon practice are open and graceful, but still effective.

Southern Kung fu style

Maintaining a solid stance and balance is of the utmost importance in the southern style. Like the northern schools, the southern schools also looked to the animal kingdom for inspiration. The southern school, however, developed styles based on the animals' sudden and overpowering attack movements and these include: the Cobra, Monkey, Leopard, Snake, and Tiger styles among others.

Southern-styles fighting are usually done in close quarters and consist of rapid, sequential punches, low kicks, and blocks. There is lighting-speed reaction and action, with great emphasis placed on simultaneous attack and defense. For example, while the left arm may block a punch, the right will slide into the opponent guard and attempt to deliver a blow to the face or chest. The essence of southern-style kung fu lies in the ability to instinctively attack and shower an opponent with blows while avoiding an opponent to grab any limbs. Southern martial artists believe that the speed and power of their attacks will defeat any foe.

Lion Dances

Another unique characteristic of Chinese martial arts schools is the role of the lion dance. The lion is comprised of a highly decorated, stylized lion mask "head" made of paper-mache and a long silk "body" that conceals a second person who helps maneuver the lion. The wearer of the lion mask must be a member of a kung fu school. There are two kinds of lion heads, the young or black lion and the old or multi-colored lion. If a school displays the young lion, it is considered a form of hostility or insult to the other schools of the area.

Traditionally, the lion represents the soul of the kung fu school. During festivals and holidays, the lions from the various schools of the area roam the streets. The lions are tested by various challenges, such as the ability to maneuver past obstacles without breaking the team of the head and body. The performance of the lion serves to reflect the reputation of the school.

2.2.2 · INDIAN MARTIAL ARTS

India has always has a rich history of martial arts and warfare. Like early China, India was separated into many small warring kingdoms. Warfare remained on a small scale with ritualized combat between forces. There does not appear to be a large degree of military specialization like that found in China. Rather the martial arts were taught as part of the complete training for the accomplished noble. India has always had a rich history of individual self-development. One of the most important influences of India was the promulgation of the religion of Buddhism. Buddhism while an important religion in India never achieved the overall influence it gained after it was introduced in China.

Indian martial arts showcase some unique fighting tactics. In silambam, or stick fighting, the attacker will strike the ground first before attacking his opponent. This allows the strike to enter from below as well as confuses the opponent. Single and paired stick forms are studied as well.

Other unique weapons taught in Indian martial arts are the bundi dagger, a grooved double-edged blade; three-directional knives, very useful for blocking attacks and efficient at slashing attacks; and the urumi or spring sword, kept coiled up and when released it is whipped through the air to produce extraordinary noise, dust, and sparks.

The martial art of Kalaripayit was first developed in India. It is a true unarmed combat system that emphasizes evasion of blows followed by hand or foot attacks. The blocks used in this style are mainly circular, seeking to deflect a blow to the side rather than stop it strength to strength. Like Chinese martial arts, the terrain where this art was practiced had a great influence on its form. The kicks used in this style vary depending on whether the Northern or Southern forms are followed. The kicks taught in the Southern style are low and delivered to the front of the body, while in the Northern style the kicks are very high and are often accompanied by acrobatic leaping attacks. In both styles, a great emphasis is placed on evading blows rather than blocking and coming from low stances into kicking or punching attacks. The origin for the difference in styles comes primarily from the terrain. The southern portion of India is hilly and has uncertain footing so attacks involving high leaps and kicks are not pursued because of the danger of losing one's balance. While in northern India, the ground is more level and firm and as a result the more acrobatic attacks could be used without a great fear of losing one's balance.

In fact, many forms taught to students involve movements that begin as a crouch, progress into a leap or a twist, and then end in a crouch that mimics evading a blow, leaping to attack and then evading another blow. A sophisticated system of grappling is taught in both styles, which involves locks, throws, and nerve points. The study of nerve points is called marma-adi and is regarded as a secret art taught only to masters.

2.2.3 · INDONESIAN AND MALAYSIAN MARTIAL ARTS

The region of Indonesia and Malaysia is home to many different types of combat systems. For example, Indonesia's three thousand islands are spread across three thousand miles of ocean encompassing many different kinds of weapon systems – from the Batak of Sumatra's expertise with the blowpipe to the Sea Dayaks of Boreno use of the mandau (long knife).

THE KRIS

The kris is considered to be the national weapon of both Indonesia and Malaysia. It is a double-edged dagger a length of 12 to 16 inches. The blade may be either wavy or straight (with wavy blades being more common). For a full description and combat tables, see Sections 13.0 and 18.0. This weapon is associated with many myths and legends in both cultures. It is said that given the proper incantation water can be drawn from the weapon. A kris is said to be able to kill a designated victim by simply pointing at him. Stories are also told of a kris jumping out of its sheath to protect its owner or rattling within its sheath to warn of danger. The incredible feats associated with the kris are attributed to the supernatural power of the weapon. Each kris is connected to its true owner from the time of the forging of the blade. The tuju (kris sorcery) also allowed the owner to kill a man by stabbing his shadow or his footprints. It has also been said that the kris can control fire by influencing its direction of motion.

All the magical properties attributed to the kris are to be used only in true need and never for display. The selection of a kris is a time-consuming and deliberate action. The fame of the maker of the kris, the pattern of the blade, the number of times the blade has shed blood, and other marks help the prospective owner determine if the blade is right for him.

The kris occupies a central portion in the cultures of this region. In Java during the nineteenth century, criminals were executed by kris and the wearing of the kris was considered a mark of social distinction.

OTHER WEAPONS

Similar to the myths and legends associated with the kris are also stories of the mystical power of the spear. Legends speak of a spear chasing a band of enemies for three miles and killing all but one of them. The Sea Dayak of Borneo wields the mandau, a long single-edged blade similar to the machete. The handle of this weapon was usually adorned with human hair. The scabbard of this blade is brightly colored and is usually also adorned with human or animal hair or teeth.

Missile weapons used in this region revolve around the use of the blowpipe and the bow and arrow. The blowpipe is a common weapon in Java, Sumatra, the Celebes, and Borneo? What made the blowpipe such a dangerous weapon was the poison on the tips of the small missiles. This poison was usually derived from a species of stingray native to the waters of this region.

PENTJAK-SILAT

The national form of defense of Indonesia is pentjak-silat. This combat system appears to have first developed in the Sumatran Minangkabau kingdom in Indonesia. Over the following centuries it spread to the rest of the island of Indonesia. Some scholars say that the inspiration for pentjak-silat is due to the Chinese martial arts that strongly mimicked animal attacks. Local legend says that a peasant woman first discovered this combat system when she watched a tiger and large bird fight to the death.

The word pentjak means "a system of self-defense" and silat as "fencing, to fend off." Pentjak is practiced alone or with a training partner in a carefully controlled exercise, not unlike the Japanese kata forms. An unusual feature of this training exercise is that the use of percussive instruments as background music and training aids are frequently used. This can help the new student learn his timing and focus in this martial art. Silat can also be practiced separately, but it is most commonly practiced against a partner. There are over 150 recorded styles of pentjak-silat. Almost all the pentjak-silat techniques operate on a responsive and adaptive style of fighting. The movements of this system are based on the movements of animals or people. These styles make no use of warming up or preparatory exercises because it recognizes that in combat a person will have no time for these types of exercises.

2.2.4 · JAPANESE MARTIAL ARTS

This is a brief overview of Japanese martial arts.

THE BUGEI AND RYU

Like China, Japan possesses a long history of martial arts tradition. The bugei or martial arts were founded and taught by family organizations called ryu and later by non-bloodline organizations called ryu-ha. Each ryu or ryu-ha had its own unique perspective on the bugei it taught. Scholars have calculated that at one point in history over seven thousand unique ryu and ryu-ha schools existed in Japan. One of the most important ryus in Japanese history is the Tenshin Shoden Katori Shinto ryu. The founder of this ryu, Iizasa Choisai Ienao Sensei, was born in 1387 in Chiba Prefecture, forty miles from present-day Tokyo. As

a young man he became a skilled fighter and served as a retainer to the Chiba family. He took part in many battles and saw the destruction of numerous family lines. When Chiba fell, he retreated to seclusion in the Katori Shrine at the age of 60, where he engaged in daily worship and martial arts training. After a period of one thousand days, Choisai founded the teachings that became known as Tenshin Shoden Katori Shinto Ryu. The prefix "tenshin shoden" means heavenly, true correct tradition and was used because Choisai Sensei believed he had assembled the correct and true teachings. He lived until he was 102 years old and left behind a great body of martial arts and philosophical teachings that were deeply rooted in Zen philosophy. These teachings, in turn, were avidly followed by Japanese professional warriors known as bushi. After the Muromachi period (1392-1573), these warriors were referred to by a more commonly known name: samurai.

THE INFLUENCE OF ZEN ON THE BUSHI/SAMURAI

The feudal Japanese warrior presented a fierce sight. He approached battle with an immovable will and a desire for displaying his combat skills to win personal glory and prove his loyalty to his master. While traditional Buddhism is generally based on compassion and gentleness, bushi were militant warriors. Zen, however, was one of the less militant sects of Buddhism in feudal Japan that survived because most of the bushi followed its teachings? The noted Japanese scholar, D. T. Suzaki, offers this insight:

In Japan, Zen was intimately related from the beginning of its history to the life of the samurai. Although it has never actively incited them to carry on their violent profession, it passively sustained them when they have for whatever reason entered into it. Zen has sustained them in two ways, morally and philosophically. Morally, because Zen is a religion that teaches us to not look backward once the course is decided upon; philosophically, because it treats life and death indifferently.

Zen taught the bushi to become self-reliant, self-denying, and above all, single-minded to the degree that no attachments or fears could sway them from their course. Zen also contributed to the development of the bushi with its concept of mushin no shin or "mind of no-mind." By entering into this state of meditative awareness, the bushi could react without any conscious thought to danger. The concepts of implicit trust in fate, submission to the inevitable and composure in the face of adversity were well ingrained in the bushi. Another factor that heavily influenced the acts of the bushi was the concept of bushido, the way of the warrior?

BUSHIDO

Bushido was developed after centuries of military experience and philosophical influence from other Asian countries. It was never developed as an explicit written code but rather, was communicated directly from leader to follower. Bushido incorporated Confucian ideas such as ancestor respect and filial piety. Furthermore, the rise of the military brought the idea of a bond of loyalty based on honor rather than kinship. A true follower of bushido was said to possess these seven virtues: justice, courage, benevolence, politeness, veracity, honor, and loyalty. It's interesting to note

that amongst all this tradition, superstition managed to play a role in the life of the bushi. This was based on the nine signs or kuji no in.

KUJI NO IN

The nine signs or kuji no in is a practice of a Buddhist sect followed by many Japanese martial artists. Each sign has a name and each corresponds to a special meaning. By making the hand gestures of the nine signs followed by a secret tenth movement, a warrior was said to gain good fortune. The sign name and the corresponding meaning follow.

Rin—Signifies physical strength

Pyo—Is associated with the channeling of energy and is though to deflect objects

To—Achieves harmony and inner peace

Sho—Promotes healing

Kai—Is associated with premonition or foreseeing

Jin—Allows for the opening of one's awareness to the thoughts and intentions of others

Retsu—Is associated with the mastery of time and space

Zai—Signifies control of both will and mind

Zen—Advances enlightenment

To be effective in battle, however, the Japanese warrior could not leave everything to fate. While the nine signs might have been practiced by all bushi, it was the extensive and rigorous training in martial arts or bugei that helped them attain both personal glory the handsome monetary rewards for services rendered. Before listing the bugei that bushi engaged in, it is important to distinguish the bugei, which are martial arts initiated in tenth century Japan, from the budo or martial ways that were developed in twentieth century Japan.

BUGEI VERSUS BUDO

The bugei include the jutsu forms as well as other combat systems. The bugei were developed for maximal effectiveness in a combat situation. The budo, which includes the do forms, such as kendo, judo, karate-do, and iai-do, were developed from the existing bugei and are more concerned with attaining spiritual discipline through which individuals can attain self-perfection. Budo are less combat-oriented and lack the practical aspect of their predecessors. In some cases, the budo have deviated so far from their origins to have almost no value in a combat situation. Unlike budo, however, the bugei are intensely combat-driven fighting systems and include the following:

Ba-jutsu—Horsemanship

Bo-jutsu—Staff art

Chigiriki-jutsu—Technique of using a ball and chain on a short stick

Fuki-baki—Technique of blowing small needles by mouth

Gekigan-jutsu—Technique of using a ball and chain

Genkotsu—Assaulting vital points

Iai-jutsu—Swordsmanship

Jitte-jutsu—Technique using a short metal rod

Jo-jutsu—Stick art

Ju-jutsu—Fighting with minimal use of weapons

Ken-jutsu—Swordsmanship

Kusarigama-jutsu—Technique using a ball, chain, and sickle weapon

Kyu-justu—Bow and arrow technique

Naginata-jutsu—Halberd technique

Sasumata-jutsu—Technique using a forked staff to hold a foe

Shuriken-jutsu—Technique of throwing small bladed weapons

Sodegarami-jutsu—Technique using a barbed pole to catch a foe

So-jutsu—Spear technique

Sumai—Armored grappling

Tessen-jutsu—Technique of using a small iron fan

Tetsubo-jutsu—Technique of using a long iron bar

Uchi-ne—Throwing the arrow by hand

Of all the fighting systems incorporated under bugei, the two most important ones to master were ken-jutsu and iai-jutsu. The reason was the Japanese sword was the most important weapon for any warrior to master.

The Japanese Sword

The bushi carried two blades, the o-dachi or long sword and the ko-dachi or short sword. The dimensions of the swords varied over Japanese history but some generalizations are possible. The long sword had a blade a little over two feet long and was generally a foot longer than the short sword. The blades were one and a quarter inches thick and tapered to a razor edge. The back of the blades sometimes contained a blood grove to make withdrawal from an enemy's body easier and to collect the blood on the blade. The types of swords most commonly associated with the bushi are the katana and wakizasha swords. These are grouped under the tachi swords and are known for their long blades and curved single-edged shape.

A great deal of ritual and customs dealt with the care and handling of these weapons. When confronted with a person with unknown intentions, the bushi kept his long sword close at hand. When kneeling in respect, if a warrior positioned his sword to the right he signaled noble intentions. If on the other hand, the sword was positioned on the left of the kneeling warrior, he signaled hostility or lack of trust of his host. In the house of a friend, the bushi might leave his long sword in the custody of a retainer but he would continue to carry his short sword. The host would keep his swords in easy reach at all times even in his own house. If a guest placed his sword with the handle facing his host, it was considered an insult against the skill of the host. To step over the sword of another as it lay on the ground was also considered to be an insult. The Japanese warrior considered the his sword to be his "soul." To touch or dishonor another's sword in any way was to invite a duel to the death.

The armor of the bushi was equally regarded, as it reflected his worth and prowess in battle; therefore, they were religiously maintained. The armor of the bushi was lightweight to provide the maximum amount of mobility and speed needed

for combat. The armor was typically made of thin sheets of iron, hides, lacquered paper, cloth, and sharkskin. The armor covered the vital areas and was designed not to restrict his movement. Unlike European armor, bushi armor was not designed to withstand powerful direct strikes. Rather, it was designed to survive glancing blows and weak attacks. The breastplate was typically made of overlapping iron plates bound with metal clamps or silken cords. It was decorated with family crests and colors. The helmet of the bushi was a bowl-shaped device made of iron and secured to the head with silk cords. Notable bushi had ornate front pieces attached to their helmets signifying their clan or leadership. The shins were protected by flexible coverings, as were the arms. The body armor as a whole was usually decorated with a strong and impressive color scheme that usually had some significance to the house or clan the warrior was associated.

2.2.5 · KOREAN MARTIAL ARTS

Korea possesses a rich history of martial tradition. The Korean combat systems have traditionally favored empty-handed techniques and missile weapons. The reasons for this development are due to the heavy influence of calvary techniques that used the bow and the relatively late introduction of metallurgy techniques to Korea. Chinese cultural influence played a strong part in the development of Korea's unarmed combat systems. Korean philosophical thought also lead to the ideas that inspired the code of Bushido in Japan.

2.2.6 · OKINAWAN MARTIAL ARTS

Okinawa has always been a center for the exchange of ideas and trade between Japan and China, being situated just off the East China Sea and very close to Japan as well. In the late fifteenth century, a new king arose to power in Okinawa and banned the carrying of weapons by any one not associated with the government to quiet rebellion at the start of his reign. This ban remained in force throughout most of Okinawa's history up to the nineteenth century? These restrictions lead to the development of karate, a rich martial art technique practiced by the native Okinawans. Many new types of weapons were pioneered by Okinawan martial artists due to the restrictions placed upon them, including the nunchaku, sai, kama, and tonfa.

2.2.7 · EUROPEAN MARTIAL ARTS

Traditionally European fighting systems have been less well developed than their Asian counterparts. Where an Asian fighting system may be seen as a "way of life," the European fighting system is seen as a system of mechanical movements or simple recreation. In spite of this, Europe still has some interesting martial arts that have been developed in its rich history.

EARLY HISTORY

The earliest martial disciplines developed in Europe were the events centered on the Greek festivals, the most famous of these being the Olympic games. Some of the events included javelin throwing, boxing, and wrestling? The pancratium was a contest that involved both wrestling and boxing and sometimes ended in the death of one of the combatants. In general these events were seen as public entertainment or a recreational sport, and were not considered to be true fighting systems.

THE MIDDLE AGES

During the Middle Ages, a specialized class of warriors called the knights rose to prominence. The knight could be considered to be the European equivalent of the Asian martial artist. Medieval knights lived by a code in which skill at arms played a central part. Mounted fighting skills formed the core of chivalry. The budding knight primarily learned his skills from within the family. Young nobles practiced their fighting skills every day. The martial skills of the knight were displayed at the tourney. These tournaments could become very dangerous affairs often resulting in deaths.

Knights formed exclusive societies like the Knights Templar and the Knights of Malta. These groups of knights blended their martial skills with religious conviction, not unlike their counterparts in Asia.

THE RENAISSANCE

A codified fighting system for European martial arts did not develop until the end of the Middle Ages and the start of the Renaissance. In the Renaissance era, armor became lighter and fighters began to rely on their skill and agility in combat. The nobles and the new middle class began to practice and learn (or be tutored) the art of self-defense and combat with the blade. The influx of the new middle class lead to the formation of fighting schools that taught them the skills needed for combat. The change from heavy armor cleaving weapons to lighter blades formulated fundamen-

tal changes in fighting strategy. The superiority of the point and quickness asserted itself and the art of fencing was born.

In European history there were many schools of fencing. The earliest and most famous schools came from Spain and Italy. The Italian schools of fencing attempted to simplify the cuts and thrusts of the blade. The Spanish schools of fencing mystified fencing through the inclusion of geometry and natural science. Because of their more practical bent, the Italian schools soon surpassed the Spanish schools of fencing.

The early teachers of fencing did not teach a codified method of fighting, but rather taught secret maneuvers and tricks that they had learned. Like other martial arts masters, the teachers of fencing were secretive, holding back their best tricks and maneuvers for their most worthy (or wealthy) students.

UNARMED FIGHTING SYSTEMS

Unlike the unarmed fighting systems of the East, the unarmed fighting systems of Europe have been viewed more as sports than actual deadly fighting systems. Unlike the Eastern fighting styles, the European unarmed fighting systems have not been closely linked to medicine.

Savate or chausson was developed in France during the 19th century. Of all the European martial arts, savate bears the closest resemblance to the Asian fighting systems. It is believed to be developed from a folk combat art in which punching, kicking, and tripping were permitted. Despite its similarities, it has been confined to recreational uses and it has never been offered as a "way of life" to its practitioners. Savate also taught the use of the walking cane in its unarmed combat techniques.

Part I

**Sections
3.0, 3.1**

Fitting Martial
Arts into Your
Campaign

Integrating
into Current
Campaigns

FITTING MARTIAL ARTS INTO YOUR CAMPAIGN

This section is meant to offer suggestions on how to incorporate martial arts into the campaign. Because the average martial arts specialist character can spend up to half his development points per level in refining his martial arts skills, it is important ensure the player will have ample opportunity for character development and role playing. Each player should have a share of the story and plot of the campaign. For a more in-depth discussion of campaign management and character development, the interested reader should refer to *Gamemaster Law*.

All too often, the martial artist is relegated to the position of an outsider within the campaign structure since he usually comes from an exotic or distant culture. By definition an outsider is disconnected from the normal flow of events. This can make playing martial artists difficult when the campaign setting has a strong influence on the involvement of the players. These circumstances make it easy to fall into the role of observing the campaign rather than participating directly in it. The player of the martial artist should not need to totally rely on his character's combat skills as the only way to interact in the campaign. Some of the ideas and suggestions presented in this section offer ways for the Gamemaster to incorporate martial arts into his campaign without relegating the martial artist to the unenviable position of the outsider.

Sometimes Gamemasters ban martial arts from their campaigns because they simply do not have a good idea on how to integrate martial arts into their current campaign. Section 3.4, which details how to create new martial arts cultures, should give the overworked Gamemaster some ideas for creating new societies that support martial arts. Section 11.5 on player concepts should also give the Gamemaster some story ideas and plot hooks that can be used to allow the martial arts character to be integrated with the current gaming group. There are some more general topics that concern the overall campaign theme and campaign metabolism that need to be addressed as well. This section will attempt to answer some of the complexities that arise when including martial arts into a current campaign setting.

◆ 3.1 ◆
INTEGRATING INTO CURRENT CAMPAIGNS

Depending on the general campaign theme, the Gamemaster can incorporate martial arts in a variety of ways into the campaign. It can be very beneficial to have the martial artist integrated into the campaign in some other manner than fighting or hired muscle. Here are some common general campaign themes and ideas on how to incorporate martial arts into them.

FREE-FORM ADVENTURE CAMPAIGNS

Free-form adventure campaigns are the most common type of campaign. In this type of campaign, player actions determine more of the plot than Gamemaster scheming. The Gamemaster tailors his campaign style to play to his player's desires and goals. In this type of campaign, martial arts can become an easy fit. The martial artist simply brings another set of skills to the player group that can help them accomplish their goals. Other than creating the cultural background for the martial artist (if none existed in the campaign before this), the Gamemaster does not have to do very much more than manage the group as before.

MYSTERY CAMPAIGNS

Mystery campaigns are a little more rare than other types of campaigns as they require a significant amount of advance preparation by the Gamemaster to ensure that the campaign flows smoothly. In most cases, mystery campaigns revolve around many non-combat skills. This can put the dedicated martial artist at a disadvantage since he must spend more development points than most other types of characters to have effective combat skills. In the case of mystery campaigns, it is might be best to have the martial artist's homeland located fairly nearby. The reasoning behind this is that, in order for the martial artist to have equal story leverage with the other characters in the party, it will probably be necessary to have the martial artist's order or organization involved in the mystery to some degree. Another possible avenue is to have the martial artist have personal contacts with important figures in the involved mystery. Perhaps the martial artist once served as their bodyguard or taught them martial arts at some point in the campaign. In this way, the martial artist can use his contacts or his organization to help the party solve the mystery. In the case of the mystery campaign where the martial artist's order or organization plays a role, it is very important that the Gamemaster put a fair amount of time into creating the organization, culture, or order from which the martial artist learned his skills. It is not always necessary for the order or organization to be directly involved with the campaign-spanning mystery; they may only have a piece of the puzzle. For example, the martial artist's order or organization could simply point towards the involvement of another martial order or organization that is truly involved.

POLITICAL CAMPAIGNS

Political campaigns are probably the rarest type of campaign as they take the most effort in terms of world creation and plotting on the part of the Gamemaster. Like mystery campaigns, political campaigns revolve around non-combat skills. Intrigue skills and role playing become important for every character whose player wishes to have the character fully involved in this aspect of the campaign. Many of the suggestions outlined for mystery campaigns

can be followed for political campaigns. In some ways, a martial artist is out-of-place in political campaigns, since many political campaigns de-emphasize combat. Since a martial artist must spend a significant portion of his development points to keep his combat skills effective, it may be more appropriate to play another profession like a Rogue or Thief. However, with a little extra effort by the Gamemaster, this does not have to be the case. Again we turn to the order or organization that trained the martial artist, perhaps the martial artist can gain real power by challenging his superiors to ritual combat to take their position in the organization. By linking the martial artist with the political power of his organization, he can compete on an equal basis with the other players. Or perhaps the martial artist can serve as the bodyguard to a powerful NPC that can afford him access to the NPC's resources and backing. Perhaps the current campaign setting allows dueling and challenges and the martial artist is a feared duelist who is employed by other powerful organizations to further their own interests? The possibilities are endless if the Gamemaster and player should sit down before the start of the campaign and discuss how this character can fit into the overall campaign theme.

QUEST CAMPAIGNS

Quest campaigns are probably the most common campaign type encountered next to the Free-Form campaign. Quest campaigns have the benefit of focused structure and common goals. The martial artist's combat skills can be useful as the party attempts to overcome obstacles that hinder their success. It is also important to have the martial artist's culture or organization involved in the overall quest plot line. The martial artist's contacts and knowledge of his organization and culture should prove important to the eventual success of the party's quest. Some of the ideas listed in the mystery and political campaign types may prove useful in quest campaigns as well.

These suggestions are of course not only for martial artists. Other professions and character types should also be integrated into the campaign structure similarly.

◆ 3.2 ◆
COMMON CHARACTER THEMES

When designing a campaign for the players it is important to carefully consider each player's goals and integrate these goals into the campaign structure. Ideally each player will have certain goals for his character that can tie in with other player goals to move the campaign forward with minimal effort by the Gamemaster.

There are several character themes that are particularly appropriate to martial artists. These themes would make good individual goals for martial artists within the campaign structure. Players are of course encouraged to make up their own individual goals whenever possible. Section 11.5 on character concepts may offer some additional ideas for character goals.

SELF-ENLIGHTENMENT

A typical goal for a martial artist character is the goal of self-enlightenment and inner peace. The martial artist attempts to attain a tranquil state of mind where his actions flow without conscious direction. This state of mind leads to inner peace and tranquillity.

SELF-MASTERY

A related goal to self-enlightenment is the goal of self-mastery for martial artists. Self-mastery involves the martial artist controlling his body's natural responses to threats and pain. The most important goal for a martial artist striving for self-mastery is the development of an iron will and determination that will allow him to achieve his goals.

MARTIAL PROWESS

Another common goal for martial artist characters is the goal of martial prowess. The martial artist's goal is to become the most talented practitioner of his martial arts style or weapon style in the world. He wishes to meet and defeat all other martial arts masters of different schools and traditions to prove his mastery.

◆ 3.3 ◆
CHALLENGES AND FINDING TEACHERS

In a martial arts campaign, there should be plenty of opportunity for players to interact with local and foreign martial arts champions in contests and exhibitions. If the Gamemaster takes the time to develop some rivalries between martial arts schools and annual martial arts contests for insertion into the campaign, he will be rewarded well in terms of player feedback and participation.

Historically, challenges were a central part of a martial arts master's existence and could not be refused. The challenger could stipulate whether an armed or unarmed match was desired and the host had to accept. Further, the guest could decide whether the match would end in mere defeat or death? Although a master could not refuse a challenge, if the challenger was a stranger of unproved merit, he could be referred to a senior student. Often masters would do so for the opportunity to study the challenger's style and technique. The chief reasons for having senior students accept challenges from unknowns were to avoid fights with brash young inferior fighters. If such a challenger did fight the resident master and lost, he would often leave with a phrase such as "two years" or "five years"—indicating how long he would train before returning for another bout. Due to the prevalence of challenges, many masters would keep the ultimate secrets of their martial arts to themselves for fear of being challenged by their own students.

Challenges can be inserted into the campaign to provide many plot lines and plot hooks for martial artists. Perhaps the characters are senior students of a respected master, and as a result are continuously challenged by local toughs who wish to improve their reputations. An interesting variant plot line would be having a character's teacher lose to an ill-mannered braggart. The master mysteriously became ill

Part I

Sections
3.2, 3.3

Common
Character
Themes

Challenges
and Finding
Teachers

before the match, but decided to continue with the fight. His illness got worse during the match and he was defeated easily. The braggart then set about starting his own school and bad mouthing the character and his fellow students. The master's students might suspect foul play and investigate the situation on their own.

Annual contests are also a great source for campaign ideas and memorable moments. Perhaps the players wish to have their characters enter the famous martial arts tournament. Will they succeed and defeat all challengers or will they fail and bring shame to their school? Some of the ideas in Section 14.7, which details cinematic combat, might be useful for staging ideas. Perhaps the contest is held on wooden scaffolding twenty feet above the ground so the spectators can see the combatants and the fighters are in constant danger of falling to the ground.

An interesting role playing option available to martial artists is the task of finding a master to teach them martial arts skills. The Gamemaster may make the players act out the process, or he may say that they find and establish a relationship with a teacher and take the role playing from there. The martial arts teacher can provide a great NPC for campaigns, not only as a source of training, but a source for the Gamemaster to introduce new plot lines.

Historically, one of the most difficult challenges facing a prospective student of a martial arts style was finding a master to accept him as a student. Most masters taught only a few students at a time, and those that accepted students usually taught very slowly. Usually, if a new student was accepted, he would be taught by to a senior student for years, until it was decided that he had learned enough to benefit from the master's instruction. Many masters followed the dictum, "never tell too plainly," when teaching their students. Often the concept they were trying to teach would be clouded in metaphor and double-meanings. There were several reasons behind this inefficient teaching style. Master's often followed traditional teaching methods, teaching their students as they were taught. A master could be hiding his lack of true knowledge of a style behind a cloak of secrecy and ill-defined techniques. The master might simply be ill-natured or unwilling to teach his secrets to his students. Because many students ended up challenging their masters, this fear was not unwarranted. Many martial arts styles died with their final masters because of this need for secrecy.

◆ 3.4 ◆
CREATING CULTURES

The Gamemaster is encouraged to create his own special cultures and societies for his campaign world that have their own unique martial arts. This section offers some examples for creating your own societies and how to model martial arts within them. For a more general discussion of how to create fantasy worlds and societies, refer to *Gamemaster Law*. For more information on the historical development of martial arts and how martial arts interacted with the cultures in which they developed, please see Section 2.0.

When introducing martial artists into your campaign, it is necessary to decide where their skills originated if these skills are not normal to the current campaign setting. To make sure that the campaign feels authentic, it is necessary to develop some extra background for the campaign to explain the martial artist's place within it. Even if there is a pre-existing culture or society that will be a good fit, it is still recommended that the Gamemaster take time to answer the questions in this section.

The easiest way to determine how the martial arts interact with a new culture or society is to ask some simple questions, like the following.

WHAT IS THE HISTORY OF MARTIAL ARTS IN THIS CULTURE?

Does the culture or society have a rich heritage of martial arts? This question asks whether martial arts existed for most of the culture or society's existence? Depending on the answer, the Gamemaster gains an immediate understanding of what level of martial arts might exist.

What group or organization was first involved in martial arts in this culture? Why were martial arts developed? Answering this question helps to cement the place of martial arts in a society. For example, martial arts could have been developed as a response to oppression from the ruling classes, or it could have developed after challenges and dueling became widespread in the society. Another possibility is that martial arts could have developed for another reason altogether (e.g., strengthening exercises) and later evolved into fighting arts.

WHAT MARTIAL ARTS SKILLS ARE TAUGHT IN THIS CULTURE?

What type of martial arts does this culture specialize in? This question asks whether the culture focuses on a specific type of martial arts. For example, a culture could focus more on martial arts involving weapons than unarmed combat, or the reverse.

Does this culture have knowledge of rare martial arts skills, like the Chi Powers skills, or other Restricted martial arts skills? It is suggested that one region not have access to all the martial arts skills in the campaign world, or if such a region does exist, that martial arts skills be taught in other regions and cultures as well. Following this suggestion offers a little more diversity and depth to the created society.

How are martial arts taught in this culture? This question really involves several decisions that must be answered before this question can be fully addressed. Are martial arts taught to everyone in the culture or are they taught to a subset of people in the culture? To pass the skills and knowledge necessary for the continued evolution of martial arts there must be some way to train other students who will later become masters. This training can follow many different avenues. The Gamemaster can decide that there exists one primary organization that trains most of the martial artists in the culture? Or the Gamemaster can decide that there are many independent organizations that train their members in the martial arts. It is even possible to say that the primary teaching method for martial arts revolves around individual teacher/student relationships.

WHAT ARE UNIQUE FEATURES OF THIS CULTURE'S KNOWLEDGE OF MARTIAL ARTS?

Does this culture have knowledge of certain martial arts skills that are not readily available to other cultures and societies? For example, is this the only culture that has knowledge of Chi Powers skills? Does this culture have a bias against certain types of skills? For example, the culture could have a bias against Maneuvering in Heavy Armor skills or Missile Weapon skills. Does this culture specialize in certain types of martial arts skills? For example, a culture that specializes in Weapon Style skills could have their Basic Weapon Style skill style point range from 0 to 35 rather than the standard 0 to 30 style point range. For some examples where martial arts skills are specialized in specific cultures, see Section 16.1.

WHAT IS THE PLACE OF MARTIAL ARTS IN THIS CULTURE?

What is the place of martial arts in the culture? If the ruling class developed advanced martial arts skills, these skills will be most likely held in higher regard than if the common people (usually in response to oppression from the ruling class) developed the same skills.

Does this culture honor and recognize martial arts? This is an important question that helps to define the place of martial arts within the society. If most of the martial arts skills were developed by the ruling class, then it is more likely that martial arts will hold some position of honor and respect within the society. If most of the martial arts skills were developed by the general populace of the culture, then it may be likely that martial arts are suppressed as a challenge to the noble's power.

Depending on the culture's view of martial arts, what types of career paths are available to martial artists? Can a martial artist open his own school of martial arts and make a comfortable living? Can a martial artist make a living as an instructor and martial arts consultant? Must the martial artist always be working (as a bodyguard, warrior, etc.) to make a living?

What are the place of challenges and contests in this culture? If the society allows challenges to decide points of law or dispute, then the role of martial arts in the society becomes very important. Also if challenges are legal, then martial arts become a survival skill for the social class that is most involved in challenges. When the Gamemaster decides the place of challenges in the new culture, he should also think about any forms or conventions that are also associated with a challenge. Are challenges only performed with certain weapons? Are there restrictions on who can challenge whom? When is a challenge illegal or unlawful?

◆ 3.5 ◆ POWER LEVELS

It is important for the Gamemaster to fully understand the power level of martial arts that he wishes to allow within his campaign. It is equally important that he convey his expectations of the capabilities of martial artists to his players so there is no chance for misunderstanding. With both the players and the Gamemaster starting from a common set of assumptions, a campaign becomes much more stable.

3.5.1 · CORE

The Core power level assumes a near real-world expectation of martial arts. The martial arts are treated as unarmed combat with all the inherent advantages and disadvantage that come with that expectation. The Core power level is well integrated with the entire *RMSS*. The basic components of the Core power level are as follows.

• The Adrenal Defense skill is redefined to require a 40% activity action in the round it is used;

• New Essence-based and Mentalism-based Monk variant professions are introduced;

• The new Martial Arts Combat Maneuvers skill category is added;

• The new martial arts skills listed in Section 7.0 are added;

• The optional rules listed as Core may be used if desired.

3.5.2 · HEROIC

The Heroic power level assumes a slightly larger-than-life expectation of martial arts. The martial arts are treated as a little more effective than they actually are in the real world. The Heroic power level lets players accomplish extraordinary acts more easily. In most cases, the Heroic power level is the average level at which a role playing campaign is run. The basic components of the Heroic power level are as follows.

• The inclusion of the new background options and talent and flaws;

• The inclusion of the new training packages listed in this companion;

• The special techniques associated with some martial arts styles and weapon styles may be used;

• The optional rules listed as Heroic may be used if desired.

3.5.3 · FANTASTIC

The Fantastic power level assumes an unrealistic expectation of martial arts. Martial arts are presented as the supreme form of combat and are practiced by the majority of the heroes of the campaign world. Martial arts masters can accomplish supernatural feats through the focus of their inner power. The basic components of the Fantastic power level are as follows.

• The inclusion of Chi Powers skills, as described in Section 10.0;

• The widespread use of the Cinematic Combat options, as described in Section 14.7;

• Basic Weapon Style skills and Basic Martial Arts Styles skills are treated as Everyman skills for all professions;

• Advanced Weapon Style skills and Advanced Martial Arts Styles skills are treated as non-Restricted skills for all professions;

• The optional rules listed as Fantastic may be used if desired.

It is important to recognize that the Fantastic power level is the most potentially unbalancing option with respect to the rest of the *RMSS*. Inclusion of the options given for this power level will create some imbalances in the system as the role of martial arts skills achieves a greater prominence over other types of skills.

PART II
THE RULES

Who can use this companion? Make no mistake here, the rules and skills detailed within are applicable to all professions available to players. There is absolutely no reason why a Healer or a Thief can not also become an accomplished martial artist. This fact underscores one of the greatest strengths about the design of the *Rolemaster* system: anything is possible!

PART II CONTENTS

MARTIAL
ARTS
COMPANION

THE NOTATION

Certain selections of text in *Martial Arts Companion* contain an additional identifier: Core, Heroic, or Fantastic. These headings have been inserted to help Gamemasters keep a consistent power level when using martial arts in their campaigns. Those sections that do not have any additional headings present general information that is useful for any one of the three power levels. The actual criteria of the headings are explained below:

CORE

Most of the information in this companion can be considered as part of the core rules for martial arts. The Core sections encompass the basic framework of martial arts as they are presented in this companion, and are necessary for this companion to be used effectively. The Core rules encompass most of the revised skills, professions, martial arts styles, weapon styles, and combat rules. With a little modification, the Core rules can be also used to run martial arts in modern campaigns. Refer to the section 15.0 on running martial arts in modern settings for more information.

HEROIC

The Heroic sections introduce many of the common options used in *Rolemaster* campaigns such as training packages, background options, and talents and flaws. The heroic sections should be used in addition to the core companion rules. Additional information is provided for incorporating Heroic style martial arts in current campaigns in Section 3.5.2. The heroic martial arts campaign is likely to be the most common type of campaign chosen by Gamemasters.

FANTASTIC

The Fantastic sections present a high-powered version of the martial arts in fantasy campaigns with the inclusion of Chi Powers skills. The chi powers are high-powered skills that allow the martial artist to accomplish incredible feats. The Fantastic sections should be used in addition to the Core and Heroic rulings. Additional information is provided to the Gamemaster for running high-powered martial arts in a campaign without disrupting game balance. Refer to Section 3.5.3 for more details.

USING THIS COMPANION WITH ROLEMASTER PRODUCTS

The rules presented in *Martial Arts Companion* should be considered for use as the Gamemaster sees fit. Every effort has been made to present a balanced set of rules, but as always the Gamemaster is the final judge of what he will include in his campaign.

◆ 5.1 ◆
THE ROLEMASTER STANDARD RULES

Martial Arts Companion makes some additions and a few significant changes to the *Rolemaster Standard Rules*.

PROFESSIONS

The Everyman and Occupational skills for the Warrior monk and Monk professions have undergone changes. In addition, the Monk profession has two new variant professions, the Taoist monk (an Essence-based monk) and Zen monk (a Mentalism-based monk). Each new profession has a set of new base spell lists. Refer to Section 6.2 for further details on the new and changed professions. Players must choose which type of monk to play (Monk, Taoist monk, or Zen monk) when choosing this type of profession.

APPRENTICE DEVELOPMENT

Martial Arts Companion presents new training packages for characters that are training in the martial arts. In addition, some of the training packages presented in the *Rolemaster Standard Rules* have been revised for inclusion in this companion. Refer to Section 18.0 for more details on the new training packages.

SKILLS

Martial Arts Companion presents new and revised skills within several existing skill categories and introduces a new skill category, Martial Arts Combat Maneuvers. The following skill categories or groups have either had skills added or have had skills within them modified: Combat Maneuvers, Lore Group, Martial Arts Group, Self Control, Special Attacks, and Special Defenses. Section 7.0 presents the new skills in detail.

RULES

Martial Arts Companion presents some new rules and options for characters using martial arts in combat situations in the game. Section 14.0 presents rules for running martial arts in combat.

◆ 5.2 ◆
SPELL LAW

Martial Arts Companion presents several new spell lists as well as revised versions of the *Spell Law* Monk spell lists. All the new and revised spell lists have been printed in Section 20.0.

◆ 5.3 ◆
ARMS LAW

Martial Arts Companion provides many descriptions of new martial arts weapons. Each martial arts weapon described is given either a corresponding attack table from *Arms* or an entirely new weapon attack table. Sections 13.0 and 18.0 includes both all the martial arts weapon descriptions and the new weapon attack tables.

◆ 5.4 ◆
GAMEMASTER LAW

Martial Arts Companion reviews the play balance discussion first presented in *Gamemaster Law* between the Fighter and Warrior monk professions in light of the changes made to martial arts rules in this companion. Section 17.0 addresses this discussion in full. In addition there is a wealth of information presented throughout this companion to help the Gamemaster create new cultures, societies, and organizations that use martial arts, as well as integrate martial arts into the overall campaign structure.

◆ 5.5 ◆
TALENT LAW

Martial Arts Companion presents new talents and flaws, designed to be used with *Talent Law*. Random tables are also included for readers who do not have *Talent Law*. Refer to Section 11.0 for more details.

◆ 5.6 ◆
BLACK OPS AND PULP ADVENTURES

Martial Arts Companion details rules and guidelines for running martial arts in a modern or pulp setting. Section 15.0 explores this concept more fully.

◆ 5.7 ◆
RACES AND CULTURES: UNDERGROUND RACES

Martial Arts Companion includes a section on using martial arts with racial special attacks (e.g., horns, claws, etc.).

◆ 5.8 ◆
OTHER RMSS BOOKS

Martial Arts Companion does not present any special rules for integrating martial arts and firearms (*Weapon Law: Firearms*), any special rules for Arcane magic (*Arcane Companion*), any special rules for alchemy (*Treasure Companion*), or any special rules for castle life (*Castles and Ruins*).

PROFESSIONS

Part II

Sections 6.0, 6.1, 6.2, 6.3

Professions

Revised Development Point Skill Costs

Unchanged Professions

New and Modified Professions

Martial Arts Companion introduces two new variant Monk professions: the Taoist monk (an Essence-based monk) and Zen monk (a Mentalism-based monk). This companion also changes some of the existing professions slightly through the modifications of some of the skill category costs, as well as offering a host of new and revised skills and other options for martial arts.

To paraphrase a certain English playwright, "The character is the thing." Never has this statement been truer than in the case of role playing games. Players wishing to create characters skilled in the martial arts will find a host of new options and capabilities to explore that will add depth and enjoyment to any campaign. Once again, all professions can benefit from the new rules and skills within these pages.

◆ 6.1 ◆
REVISED DEVELOPMENT POINT SKILL COSTS

The chart on page 25 presents the revised development point costs for all the professions introduced into *RMSS*. The two changes presented in this chart are the inclusion of a new skill category called Martial Arts Combat Maneuvers and the revision of the Special Defenses skill category costs for all professions. The Combat Maneuvers, Martial Arts Strikes, Martial Arts Sweeps, Self Control, and Special Attacks skill categories are included for ease of reference even though their costs have not changed, since there are many new and revised skills introduced in these skill categories.

◆ 6.2 ◆
UNCHANGED PROFESSIONS

All professions not specifically mentioned in Section 6.3 remain unchanged except for the inclusion of the new Martial Arts Combat Maneuvers skill category and the revision of the Special Defenses skill category costs. Each profession can use any of the skills presented within this companion as they would any skill presented in the *RMSR* without any additional restrictions or qualifiers.

◆ 6.3 ◆
NEW AND MODIFIED PROFESSIONS

A new concept presented in this companion is the idea of variant professions. A variant profession is a profession that is closely related to an existing *RMSS* profession but with a unique twist or bent that makes it different. This book introduces two variant Monk professions—the Taoist monk and the Zen monk. The concepts behind these two variant professions share some similarities with the original Monk profession presented in *RMSR*.

The original concept of the Taoist monk springs from Chinese philosophical thought. Taoism provided great influence on the development of Chinese martial arts. The doctrine of Tao is one of naturalism. Taoism teaches that the only means of attaining a full life is through the observation of nature and living according to the ways of nature. In Taoism, nothing should be done contrary to the natural order of the world. There are also two supporting doctrines of Taoism, first stated by its founder Lao Tzu. The first doctrine is the concept of the "Uncarved Block." The "Uncarved Block" represents man in his original state of existence, unpolluted by concerns of the world or hatred. Taoism strives to return man to his unconditioned natural state. The other doctrine is the concept of non-action. Non-action does not imply doing nothing, rather it implies taking no action against natural law. This doctrine shows that force is futile in some circumstances and it is sometimes better to yield to strength than to be destroyed by striving against it. The Taoist monk profession deals more with the natural world and elemental forces than the original *RMSR* Monk profession. Many of the spells used in the base lists of this profession take their inspiration from the natural world.

The original concept of the Zen monk springs from Japanese philosophical thought. Meditative Buddhis? or Zen provided a great influence on the development of Japanese martial arts. The doctrine of Zen teaches the practitioner to become self-reliant, self-denying, and above all to be single-minded to such a degree that no attachments or fears could sway him from his course. Zen also introduced the concept of mushin no shin or "mind of no-mind." Also important to the concept of the Zen monk is the tradition of Shingon Buddhism in Japanese society that uses mystical incantations and practices to accomplish incredible feats. It is the attributed powers of this obscure and secretive sect of Buddhism that provides much of the inspiration for the Zen monk's base lists.

It is possible to have all three professions within a campaign; each profession has its own unique focus and approach to the martial arts and life that should make them easily distinguishable. The original *RMSS* Monk profession remains the most flexible of the three professions. The Taoist monk profession focuses more on the elements and the natural world. The Taoist monk can also create mystical effects that can not be attributed solely to self-discipline or willpower. The Zen monk profession focuses on mental discipline and willpower that allows the user to transcend the limitations of his body and influence the perceptions of others.

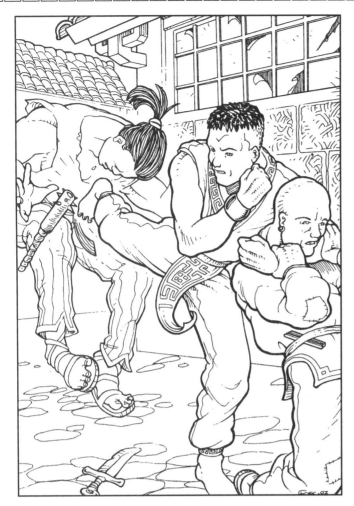

6.3.1 · FIGHTER

Fighters are non-spell users who will find it relatively easy to develop a variety of different weapons and to wear heavier types of armor. They are less skilled in maneuvering and manipulating mechanical devices such as locks and traps (although they are still superior to most spell users in these areas). They have the greatest difficulty learning anything connected with spells.

Prime Stats: Constitution and Strength

FIGHTER SPELL LISTS

The Fighter has no base lists, though he may learn (at a high development point cost) spells from his chosen realm of magic.

SKILL CLASSIFICATION NOTES

Everyman Skills: Situational Awareness: Combat, Leadership, Frenzy, Boxing, Wrestling, and any one non-Restricted Combat Maneuver

Occupational Skills: none

Restricted Skills: Channeling (if the character's chosen realm is not Channeling), all skills in the Martial Arts Combat Maneuvers skill category

6.3.2 · WARRIOR MONK

Warrior Monks are non-spell users who are experts at maneuvering and martial arts. Warrior Monks may learn to use normal weapons, although not as easily as others in the realm of Arms. Rather they prefer to utilize unarmed combat.

Prime Stats: Quickness and Self Discipline

WARRIOR MONK SPELL LISTS

The Warrior monk has no base lists, though he may learn (at a high development point cost) spells from his chosen realm of magic.

SKILL CLASSIFICATION NOTES

Everyman Skills: Sense Ambush, choice of one non-Restricted Combat Maneuver skill or one non-Restricted Martial Arts Combat Maneuver skill

Occupational Skills: none

Restricted Skills: Boxing, Wrestling, Channeling (if the character's chosen realm is not channeling)

6.3.3 · MONK

Monks are semi spell users who combine the realm of Essence with the realm of Arms. Their base spells deal with personal movement, the control of their own body, and mind while their arms capabilities are concentrated in unarmored, unarmed combat.

Prime Stats: Self Discipline and Empathy

MONK SPELL LISTS

The Monk has six base spell lists found below. Full descriptions of these lists can be found in *Spell Law* (pages 111-116). For a slightly higher development cost, he may also develop Open Essence spell lists. Other spell lists may be developed, but will cost a larger number of development points.

Body Reins: Allowing the caster to perform abnormal feats (e.g., breathe underwater).

Body Renewal: Increasing the healing rate of the caster's body.

Evasions: Allowing the caster to make incredible evasive maneuvers.

Mind Over Matter: Hardening the caster's body, resulting in more lethal blows and tougher defense.

Monk's Bridge: Allowing the caster to move in unusual fashions.

Monk's Sense: Enhancing the caster's senses.

SKILL CLASSIFICATION NOTES

Everyman Skills: Time Sense and choice of one non-Restricted Martial Arts Combat Maneuvers skill

Occupational Skills: Meditation

Restricted Skills: Channeling

6.3.4 · TAOIST MONK

Taoist monks or Essence-based Monks are semi spell users who combine the realm of Essence with the realm of Arms. Their base spells deal with personal movement, the control of their own body, and the natural world while their arms capabilities are concentrated in unarmored, unarmed combat. A Taoist monk is reclusive and disdains much of the comforts of civilization, seeking to gain enlightenment through the observation of the natural world. A Taoist monk will tend to specialize in unarmed combat styles that mimic the attacks of animals.

"All life should be as the blade of grass in the wind, effortless, smooth, natural. The blade of grass does not resist but bends with the wind. Thus should life be lived."

Prime Stats: Self Discipline and Empathy

TAOIST MONK SPELL LISTS

The Taoist monk or Essence-based Monk has six base spell lists found below. The full description of these lists may be found in Section 20.1. For a slightly higher development cost, the he may also develop Open Essence spell lists. Full descriptions of these lists can be found in *Spell Law* (pages 111-116). Other spell lists may be developed, but will cost a larger number of development points.

Body Renewal: Increasing the healing rate of the caster's body.

Evasions: Allowing the caster to make incredible evasive maneuvers.

Inner Eye: Enhancing the senses of the caster and the ability to sense magical phenomena.

Haas'97

Nature's Forms: Allowing the caster to change his body and take on characteristics of the natural world.

Nature's Harmony: Allowing the caster to influence the natural world.

Monk's Bridge: Allowing the caster to move in unusual ways.

PROFESSION BONUSES

Athletic • Gymnastics	+5	Outdoor Group	+5
Awareness Group	+5	Power Awareness	+5
Body Development	+5	Self Control	+10
Martial Arts Group	+10	Weapon Group	+5

SKILLS AND SKILL CATEGORIES

Armor • Heavy	11	Power Awareness	3/7
Armor • Light	9	Power Manipulation	6/12
Armor • Medium	10	Power Point Development	8
Artistic • Active	2/4	Science • Basic	2/5
Artistic • Passive	2/5	Science • Specialized	8
Athletic • Brawn	3/7	Self Control	2/4
Athletic • Endurance	2/7	Special Attacks	5
Athletic • Gymnastic	1/5	Special Defenses	6
Awareness • Perception	4/14	Subterfuge • Attack	8
Awareness • Searching	2/6	Subterfuge • Mechanics	4
Awareness • Senses	3/7	Subterfuge • Stealth	2/7
Body Development	4/14	Technical • General	3/7
Combat Maneuvers	5/12	Technical • Professional	8
Communications	3/3/3	Technical • Vocational	5/12
Crafts	4/10	Urban	4
Directed Spells	9	Weapon • Category 1	5
Influence	2/6	Weapon • Category 2	8
Lore • General	1/3	Weapon • Category 3	8
Lore • Magical	3/6	Weapon • Category 4	8
Lore • Obscure	3/7	Weapon • Category 5	15
Lore • Technical	2/6	Weapon • Category 6	15
Martial Arts Combat Man	4/9	Weapon • Category 7	15
Martial Arts • Strikes	2/5		
Martial Arts • Sweeps	2/5		
Outdoor • Animal	2/7		
Outdoor • Environmental	2/5		

The weapon categories are: 1-H Concussion, 1-H Firearms, 1-H Edged, 2-Handed Firearms, 2-Handed, Missile, Missile Artillery, Polearms, and Thrown. The player should assign one of the cateogires to each of the weapon categories shown above.

Everyman Skills: Time Sense and choice of one non-Restricted Martial Arts Combat Maneuvers skill

Occupational Skills: Meditation

Restricted Skills: Channeling

SPELL DEVELOPMENT*

Base List (all)	6/6/6	Closed List (1-5)	10/10
Open List (1-10)	8/8	Closed List (6-10)	12
Open List (11-15)	12	Closed List (11-15)	25
Open List (16-20)	18	Closed List (16-20)	40
Open List (21+)	25	Closed List (21+)	60

*: When playing in a pulp campaign, this skill is only allowed if the GM is running a High Magic campaign.

TRAINING PACKAGES

See Section 17.0 for a listing of TP costs for this profession.

6.3.5 · ZEN MONK

Zen monks or Mentalism-based Monks are semi spell users who combine the realm of Mentalism with the realm of Arms. Their base spells deal with personal movement and the control of their own body and mind, while their arms capabilities are concentrated in unarmored, unarmed combat. The Zen monk uses his incredible mental focus and concentration to accomplish his incredible feats. The Zen monk gains his incredible powers of self-mastery through long sessions of practice and mediation.

"Do not focus on your defeating your enemy, remain calm and he will defeat himself."

Prime Stats: Self Discipline and Presence

ZEN MONK SPELL LISTS

The Zen monk has six base lists. The full description of these lists may be found in Section 20.2. For a slightly higher development cost, he may also develop Open Mentalism spell lists. Full descriptions of these lists can be found in *Spell Law* (pages 137-146). Other spell lists may be developed, but will cost a larger number of development points.

Body Renewal: Increasing the healing rate of the caster's body.

Evasions: Allowing the caster to make incredible evasive maneuvers.

Body Control: Allowing the caster to alter his appearance and perform special attacks.

Monk's Awareness: Enhancing the senses of the caster and the ability to sense the thoughts of others.

Mind's Illumination: Allowing the caster to unlock the power of his mind.

Monk's Focus: Allowing the caster to resist pain and focus his physical and inner strength.

PROFESSION BONUSES

Athletic • Gymnastics	+5	Power Awareness	+5
Awareness Group	+5	Self Control	+10
Body Development	+5	Subterfuge Stealth	+5
Martial Arts Group	+10	Weapon Group	+5

SKILLS AND SKILL CATEGORIES

Armor • Heavy	11	Power Awareness	3/7
Armor • Light	9	Power Manipulation	6/12
Armor • Medium	10	Power Point Development	8
Artistic • Active	2/5	Science • Basic	2/5
Artistic • Passive	2/4	Science • Specialized	8
Athletic • Brawn	3/7	Self Control	2/4
Athletic • Endurance	2/7	Special Attacks	5
Athletic • Gymnastic	1/5	Special Defenses	6
Awareness • Perception	4/12	Subterfuge • Attack	8
Awareness • Searching	2/6	Subterfuge • Mechanics	4
Awareness • Senses	2/6	Subterfuge • Stealth	2/7
Body Development	4/14	Technical • General	3/7
Combat Maneuvers	5/12	Technical • Professional	8
Communications	3/3/3	Technical • Vocational	5/12
Crafts	4/10	Urban	3/7
Directed Spells	10	Weapon • Category 1	6
Influence	2/7	Weapon • Category 2	8
Lore • General	1/3	Weapon • Category 3	8
Lore • Magical	3/6	Weapon • Category 4	8
Lore • Obscure	3/7	Weapon • Category 5	15
Lore • Technical	2/6	Weapon • Category 6	15
Martial Arts Combat Man	4/9	Weapon • Category 7	15
Martial Arts • Strikes	2/5		
Martial Arts • Sweeps	2/5		
Outdoor • Animal	2/7		
Outdoor • Environmental	2/7		

The weapon categories are: 1-H Concussion, 1-H Firearms, 1-H Edged, 2-Handed Firearms, 2-Handed, Missile, Missile Artillery, Polearms, and Thrown. The player should assign one of the cateogires to each of the weapon categories shown above.

Everyman Skills: Time Sense and choice of one non-Restricted Martial Arts Combat Maneuver

Occupational Skills: Meditation

Restricted Skills: Channeling

SPELL DEVELOPMENT*

Base List (all)	6/6/6	Closed List (1-5)	10/10
Open List (1-10)	8/8	Closed List (6-10)	12
Open List (11-15)	12	Closed List (11-15)	25
Open List (16-20)	18	Closed List (16-20)	40
Open List (21+)	25	Closed List (21+)	60

*: When playing in a pulp campaign, this skill is only allowed if the GM is running a High Magic campaign.

TRAINING PACKAGES

See Section 17.0 for a listing of TP costs for this profession.

Part II

Section 6.3

New and
Modified
Professions

New/Revised
Skills Cost
Table T–6.1

NEW/REVISED SKILLS COST TABLE T-6.1

Profession	Combat Maneuvers	MA Strikes and Sweeps	MA Combat Maneuvers	Self Control	Special Attacks	Special Defenses
Rolemaster Standard Rules						
Fighter	3/9	3/5	5/12	2/6	2/6	25
Thief	4/12	3/7	5	2/6	2/8	25
Rogue	4/10	3/7	5	2/9	2/7	25
Warrior Monk	4/9	1/3	3/8	1/3	2/10	4/9
Layman	4/12	3	6	2/7	5/11	20
Magician	18	9	18	6	15	30
Illusionist	18	9	18	6	15	30
Cleric	10	6	12	5	10	30
Animist	10	6	12	5	10	30
Mentalist	14	3	6	3	12	18
Lay Healer	14	3	6	3	12	18
Healer	18	6	12	2/7	15	18
Sorcerer	18	9	18	5	15	30
Mystic	18	6	12	5	15	18
Ranger	5/12	4	8	2/7	3/9	30
Paladin	4/10	6	12	2/7	2/8	30
Monk	5/12	2/5	4/9	2/4	5	6
Dabbler	6/14	4	8	2/7	6	30
Bard	6/14	3	6	2/7	6	15
Magent	6/14	3	6	2/6	4	15
Arcane Companion						
Arcanist	18	9	18	5	18	30
Wizard	18	9	18	5	18	30
Chaotic	5/12	5	9	6	8	25
Magehunter	4/12	3	6	2/6	4/9	20
Treasure Companion						
Channeling Alchemist	10	6	12	5	10	30
Essence Alchemist	18	9	18	6	15	30
Mentalism Alchemist	14	3	6	3/9	12	18
Black Ops						
Academic	7	4	8	4/10	7	25
Fighter (Modern)	3/9	3/7	5/12	2/6	2/6	25
Layman (Modern)	4/12	3	6	2/7	5/11	20
Rogue (Modern)	4/10	3/7	5	2/6	2/7	25
Scientist	11	6	14	4/12	10	25
Technician	5/12	4	8	2/7	6/12	25
Thief (Modern)	4/12	3/7	5	2/6	2/8	25
Warrior Monk (Modern)	4/9	1/3	3/8	1/3	2/10	4/9
Martial Arts Companion						
Taoist monk	5/12	2/5	4/9	2/4	5	6
Zen monk	5/12	2/5	4/9	2/4	5	6
Pulp Adventures						
Academic (Pulp)	7	4	8	4/10	7	25
Fighter (Pulp)	3/9	3/7	5/12	2/6	2/6	25
Layman (Pulp)	4/12	3	6	2/7	5/11	20
Noble Savage	5/12	3	6/12	2/6	3/9	20
Rogue (Pulp)	4/10	3/7	5	2/6	2/7	25
Technician (Pulp)	5/12	4	8	2/7	6/12	25
Thief (Pulp)	4/12	3/7	5	2/6	2/8	25
Warrior Monk (Pulp)	4/9	1/3	3/8	1/3	2/10	4/9
Healer (Pulp)	18	6	12	2/7	15	18
Sorcerer (Pulp)	18	9	18	5	15	30
Mystic (Pulp)	18	6	12	5	15	18
Ranger (Pulp)	5/12	4	8	2/7	3/9	30
Monk (Pulp)	5/12	2/5	4/9	2/4	5	6
Bard (Pulp)	6/14	3	6	2/7	6	15

SKILLS

Part II

**Sections
7.0, 7.1, 7.2**

Skills

Overview

Combat
Maneuvers

The new and revised martial arts skills form the foundation of this companion. It is important that the Gamemaster gain a firm understanding of the contents of this section, as these skills will change the skill selection strategy of players who wish to develop characters proficient in the martial arts.

Between the first and second printing of *RMSR*, there was an important change in the definition of Everyman, Occupational, and Restricted skills. For those readers that do not have the second printing, the changes are briefly summarized below:

In the *RMSS*, skills are classified as Normal, Everyman, Occupational, or Restricted. Normal skills are developed per the standard rules outlined in *RMSS*. Each rank purchased with development points by the character translates to a single new rank in the skill. Everyman, Occupational, and Restricted skills are handled differently. For Everyman skills, each rank developed in that skill actually results in two skill ranks. For Occupational skills, each rank developed in that skill actually results in three skill ranks. For skills classified as Restricted, every two ranks developed in that skill actually results in a single skill rank. Note that developed skill ranks are those "purchased" with development points (i.e., not gained through training packages, adolescence, etc.).

◆ 7.1 ◆
OVERVIEW

Listed here is the overview of the affected skill categories and skills. In each following section, each category is shown with all of the new skills that belong to that category (old skills are not listed).

COMBAT MANEUVERS

New skills are introduced in this skill category, as well as some skills are slightly revised to accommodate the new rules presented in this companion. The new skills introduced are Blind Fighting, Weapon Style (Basic), and Weapon Style (Advanced). The revised skills are Missile Deflecting, Tumbling Evasion, and Two-Weapon Combat.

LORE SKILL GROUP

A few new skills are introduced in this skill group. The new skills in Lore General are Martial Styles Lore and Weapon Styles Lore. The new skill in Lore Obscure is Vital Points Lore.

MARTIAL ARTS COMBAT MANEUVERS

This new skill category introduces some new skills. The new skills introduced are Adrenal Deflecting, Adrenal Evasion, Blind Fighting, Martial Arts Style (Basic), and Martial Arts Style (Advanced).

MARTIAL ARTS SKILL GROUP

This skill group is drastically different from its original presentation in *RMSR*. Aside from the addition of the Martial Arts Combat Maneuvers skill category, the four separate Degree skills for Martial Arts Strikes and Martial

Arts Sweeps have been replaced with a single skill for each type of attack. The Nerve Strikes skill is introduced in the Martial Arts Strikes skill category and the Locking Holds skill is introduced in the Martial Arts Sweeps skill category.

SPECIAL ATTACKS

Some new skills are introduced in this skill category. The new skills are introduced are Feint and Racial Attacks. In addition, the Disarm Foe skill is revised according to the new method for resolving special attacks, which is further explained in Section 14.3.

SPECIAL DEFENSES

This skill category presents a single new skill—Adrenal Resistance. In addition, Adrenal Defense and Adrenal Toughness have been revised according to the rules presented in this companion.

CHI POWERS SKILLS

Chi Powers skills comprise an optional set of skills that allow the practitioner to transcend the limitations of his body to accomplish supernatural feats. As such, not all chi powers skills may be suitable for all campaigns. Chi Powers skills are presented separately in Section 10.0.

◆ 7.2 ◆
COMBAT MANEUVERS

Standard Skills: Weapon Style (Basic),
Two-Weapon Fighting

Restricted Skills: Blind Fighting, Missile Deflecting, Tumbling Evasion, Weapon Style (Advanced)

Applicable Stat Bonuses: Ag/Qu/SD

Skill Rank Progression: Combined

Skill Category Progression: 0 • 0 • 0 • 0 • 0

Group: None

Classification: Static Maneuver, Special, and OB

BLIND FIGHTING

The Blind Fighting skill allows its practitioner to overcome some of the penalties associated with not being able to see one's opponent. This skill trains the practitioner to use senses other than sight during combat. Normally a character will have at least a -100 modifier to his OB if he is fighting an opponent he cannot see. A successful Blind Fighting static maneuver can be used to offset the OB penalty for not being able to see one's opponent. To determine the effect of such an attempt, roll (open-ended) and add the Blind Fighting skill bonus. Then refer to the Maneuver/Movement Table (T-4.1) using the "Extremely Hard" column. If the result is a number, that number is used to offset the current penalty for vision. Successful use of this skill will never increase the wielder's OB; it can only offset penalties due to not being able to see one's opponent. A failure result when attempting this skill will result in the character not being able to take any action this round. An extraordinary success when attempting this skill will allow the character to completely offset the penalty for not being able to see his opponent. {SD}

MISSILE DEFLECTING

This skill provides a bonus for using the body or a weapon or a shield to deflect or even catch a thrown weapon or missile directed at the user. To determine the effect of such an attempt, roll (open-ended) and add the Missile Deflecting skill bonus. Then refer to the Maneuver/ Movement Table (T-4.1) using the "Extremely Hard" column against thrown weapons or the "Sheer Folly" column against missile weapons. If the result is a number, it is subtracted from the weapon's attack roll (in addition to the normal DB). If the missile or thrown object misses, the character has a chance of catching the item. Roll d100 (open-ended) and add the modification received earlier from the Movement/Maneuver Table; if the result is over 100, the item has been caught; if desired. The Missile Deflecting skill requires a 100% activity action. The roll is modified by -20 for each additional missile that the character wishes to try to deflect that round. Resolve each missile attack separately. {SD}

TUMBLING EVASION

This skill provides a bonus for evading attacks by using tumbling maneuvers. The skill rank (not the skill rank bonus) is added to the tumbler's DB for all other attacks. The Tumbling Evasion maneuver is resolved during the round it is actively used and it requires a 60% activity action. {Ag}

TWO-WEAPON FIGHTING

This skill allows a combatant to fight with two weapons simultaneously. He is allowed to make two weapon attacks for each melee attack action, and may engage two opponents providing neither opponent is receiving any positional combat modifiers for their OB (e.g., if either opponent is receiving a +15 bonus for Flank Attack or a +20 bonus for Rear Attack the attacker would not be able to strike both opponents in the same round).

Two Weapon Fighting skills must be developed for each two-weapon combination (e.g., shortsword/handaxe, rapier/dagger, etc.). The OB for each weapon attack is equal to the skill bonus for the Two-Weapon Fighting skill for the combination of those two weapons or one of the individual weapon OBs, whichever is the lesser bonus.

Against 1 Opponent: There is no negative attack modification against one opponent.

Against 2 Opponents: There is a -20 modification to both attacks.

Parrying or Special Attacks: The user must reduce both weapon OBs by the same amount (i.e., the amount of his parry or special attack). Against one opponent, the user increases his DB by the amount of his parry. Against two opponents, the amount of his parry must be split between the two opponents as the user sees fit.

Using the off-hand: The two-weapon combination is developed for a specific weapon and hand combination. For example, a Rogue trained in a rapier/dagger combination might have decided to use the rapier left-handed and the dagger in his right. Switching either weapon to the other hand incurs the normal -20 penalty for using the off-hand for each weapon. {St}

WEAPON STYLE (ADVANCED)

This skill allows the wielder to become more skilled in combat with his chosen weapon. The Advanced Weapon Style skill incorporates the most difficult combat techniques. The Advanced Weapon Style skill bonus represents the offensive bonus of the character while using his weapon in the manner prescribed by the weapon style. Each weapon style must be developed separately. Refer to Section 8.0 for more on weapon styles. {Ag}

WEAPON STYLE (BASIC)

This skill allows the wielder to become more proficient at fighting with his chosen weapon. The Basic Weapon Style skill incorporates very effective combat techniques. The Basic Weapon Style skill bonus represents the offensive bonus of the character while using his weapon in the manner prescribed by the weapon style. Each weapon style must be developed separately. Refer to Section 8.0 for more on weapon styles. {Ag}

Part II

Sections 7.3,
7.4, 7.5

Lore • General

Lore • Obscure

Martial Arts •
Combat
Maneuvers

◆ 7.3 ◆
LORE · GENERAL

Standard Skills: Martial Arts Style Lore,
Weapon Style Lore

Restricted Skills: none

Applicable Stat Bonuses: Me/Re/Me

Skill Rank Progression: Standard

Skill Category Progression: Standard

Group: Lore

Classification: Static Maneuver

MARTIAL ARTS STYLE LORE

This skill provides a bonus for recognizing a particular martial arts style. This skill allows the user to anticipate the most common types of attacks of a martial arts style, as well as recognize the respected masters of martial arts styles. Successful lore static maneuvers may allow the user to anticipate attacks of a person using a martial arts style. A successful Martial Arts Style Lore static maneuver will give the character a special +2 bonus to his initiative roll for the duration of the combat providing the opponent continues to use the same martial arts style. This skill requires 25% activity action in the round that it is attempted. Obscure, secret, or forgotten martial arts styles will impose a negative modifier on the use of this skill. {Me}

WEAPON STYLE LORE

This skill provides a bonus for recognizing a particular weapon style. This skill allows the user to anticipate the most common types of attacks of a weapon style as well as recognize the respected masters of weapon styles. Successful lore static maneuvers may allow the user to anticipate attacks of a person using a weapon style. A successful Weapon Style Lore static maneuver will give a special +2 bonus to the initiative roll for the duration of the combat, provided the opponent continues to use the same weapon style. This skill requires 25% activity action in the round that it is attempted. Obscure, secret, or forgotten weapon styles will impose a negative modifier on the use of this skill. {Me}

◆ 7.4 ◆
LORE · OBSCURE

Standard Skills: Vital Points Lore

Restricted Skills: none

Applicable Stat Bonuses: Me/Re/Me

Skill Rank Progression: Standard

Skill Category Progression: Standard

Group: Lore

Classification: Static Maneuver

VITAL POINTS LORE

This skill provides a bonus for recognizing the vital points of attack on a foe. This knowledge is very specialized and is often guarded jealously. The study of vital points is very complex and takes into account the time of day, season, and emotional state of the target in some of the more advanced and esoteric techniques. This skill must be taken for each general type of foe (i.e., humanoid, reptile, etc.). A successful Vital Points Lore static maneuver against an

opponent can allow the practitioner to modify his next critical roll by 2 points during melee combat in the current or following round. This skill requires a 25% activity action in the round that it is attempted. {Me}

◆ 7.5 ◆
MARTIAL ARTS · COMBAT MANEUVERS

Standard Skills: Adrenal Deflecting,
Martial Arts Style (Basic), Adrenal Evasion

Restricted Skills: Martial Arts Style (Advanced),
Blind Fighting

Applicable Stat Bonuses: Ag/Qu/SD

Skill Rank Progression: Combined

Skill Category Progression: 0 • 0 • 0 • 0 • 0

Group: Martial Arts

Classification: Static Maneuver, Special, and OB

ADRENAL DEFLECTING

This skill provides a bonus for using the body, weapon, or a shield to deflect or even catch a thrown weapon or missile directed at the user. To determine the effect of such an attempt, roll (open-ended) and add the Adrenal Deflecting skill bonus. Then refer to the Maneuver/Movement Table, T-4.1, in the Rolemaster Standard Rules book, using the "Extremely Hard" column against thrown weapons and the "Sheer Folly" column against missile weapons. If the result is a number, it is subtracted from the weapon's attack roll (in addition to the normal DB). If the missile or thrown object

misses, the character has a chance of catching the item. Roll d100 (open-ended) and add the modification received earlier from the Movement/Maneuver Table; if the result is over 100, the item has been caught; if desired. Every Adrenal Deflecting attempt requires 60% activity action. The roll is modified by -20 for each additional missile to be deflected that round. Each missile attack must be resolved separately. {SD}

ADRENAL EVASION

This skill provides a bonus for evading a single attack by using a tumbling maneuver. To determine the effect of such an attempt, roll (open-ended) and add the Adrenal Evasion skill bonus. Then refer to the Maneuver/Movement Table, T-4.1, in the *Rolemaster Standard Rules*, using the "Hard" column against melee and thrown weapons and the "Extremely Hard" column versus missile weapons. If the result is a number, it is subtracted from the attack's roll (in addition to the normal DB). The skill rank (not the skill rank bonus) is added to the tumbler's DB for all other attacks. The Adrenal Evasion skill is rolled for during the round it is actively used and it requires 60% activity action. {Ag}

BLIND FIGHTING

This skill trains the practitioner to use senses other than sight during combat. Normally a character will have at least a -100 modifier to his OB if he is fighting an opponent he can not see. A successful Blind Fighting static maneuver can be used to offset the OB penalty for not being able to see one's opponent. To determine the effect of such an attempt, roll (open-ended) and add the Blind Fighting skill bonus. Then refer to the Maneuver/Movement Table (T-4.1) using the "Extremely Hard" column. If the result is a number, that number is used to offset the current penalty for vision. Successful use of this skill will never increase the wielder's OB, it can only offset penalties due to not being able to see one's opponent. A failure result when attempting this skill will result in the character not being able to take any action this round. An extraordinary success when attempting this skill will allow the character to completely offset the penalty for not being able to see his opponent. {SD}

MARTIAL ARTS STYLE (ADVANCED)

This skill allows the user to become more skilled at a specific type of unarmed combat. The Advanced Martial Arts Style skill represents the most difficult unarmed combat techniques. The Advanced Martial Arts Style skill bonus represents the offensive bonus of the character while using his martial arts attacks in the manner prescribed by the martial arts style. Each individual martial arts style must be developed separately. Refer to Section 9.0 for more information on martial arts styles. {Ag}

MARTIAL ARTS STYLE (BASIC)

This skill allows the user to become more proficient at a specific type of unarmed combat. The Basic Martial Arts Style skill represents very effective unarmed combat techniques. The Basic Martial Arts Style skill bonus represents the offensive bonus of the character while using his martial arts attacks in the manner prescribed by the martial arts style. Each individual martial arts style must be developed separately. Refer to Section 9.0 for more information on martial arts styles. {Ag}

◆ 7.6 ◆
MARTIAL ARTS STRIKES

Standard Skills: Boxing, Martial Arts Striking
Restricted Skills: Nerve Strikes
Applicable Stat Bonuses: St/Ag/St
Skill Rank Progression: Normal
Skill Category Progression: Normal
Group: Martial Arts
Classification: Offensive Bonus

BOXING

The Boxing skill represents using one's fists to strike at an opponent's upper body and torso, while protecting oneself from similar blows. This skill uses the Arms Law Martial Arts Strikes Attack Table and may not exceed the Degree 1 damage threshold. {St}

Optional Rule [Core]: If hard or spiked protective coverings (e.g., the Roman cestus) are worn, use the Degree 2 damage threshold on the Martial Arts Strikes Attack Table.

MARTIAL ARTS STRIKING

This skill represents the attacking forms of the "hard" martial arts. This skill uses the *Arms Law* Martial Arts Strikes Attack Table and may not exceed the Degree 1 damage threshold. Accompanied by a Weapon Style skill or Martial Arts Style skill, this skill can exceed the Degree 1 limitation. All criticals should be rolled on the Martial Arts Strikes Critical Table. {St}

MARTIAL ARTS SWEEPING

This skill represents the attacking forms of the "soft" martial arts. This skill uses the *Arms Law* Martial Arts Sweeps Attack Table and may not exceed the Degree 1 damage threshold. This skill accompanied by a Weapon Style skill or Martial Arts skill can exceed these limitations. All criticals should be rolled on the Martial Arts Sweeps Critical Table. {Ag}

Optional Rule [Core]: If the character has 10 or more skill ranks, he can use the Degree 2 damage threshold on the Martial Arts Sweeps Table rather than the Degree 1 damage threshold, but he must suffer a special –20 modifier.

WRESTLING

This is the skill of using one's arms and legs to grapple an opponent and immobilize him. Note that it is not normally intended to be injurious to either partner, though injury may result. This skill may be used to immobilize an opponent who does not wish to be immobilized, but it is assumed that injury is not the intent. Attacks are resolved on the *Arms Law* Martial Arts Sweeps Attack Table and may not exceed the Degree 1 damage threshold on the Martial Arts Sweeps Attack Table. All criticals are resolved as Grappling criticals. {SD}

Optional Rule [Core]: *If the wrestler's body size is considerably larger than his opponent's, he may use the Degree 2 threshold on the Martial Arts Sweeps Attack Table. If the wrestler's body size is considerably smaller than his opponents, he suffers a special modifier of -20 to his OB and he must use the Degree 1 damage threshold on the Martial Arts Sweeps Attack Table.*

Optional Rule [Core]: If the character has 10 or more skill ranks, he can use the Degree 2 damage threshold on the Martial Arts Strikes Attack Table rather than the Degree 1 damage threshold, but he must suffer a special -20 modifier.

NERVE STRIKES

This skill provides an offensive bonus to strike an opponent precisely at a vulnerable nerve cluster. Depending on the resolution of the attack, the opponent can be put in extreme pain, temporary paralyzed, or even killed. This skill uses the *Arms Law* Martial Arts Strikes Attack Table with the Nerve Strikes Critical Table substituted for the Martial Arts Strikes Critical Table. This skill may not exceed the Degree 1 damage threshold unless a Weapon Style skill or Martial Arts Style skill that allows the user to exceed this limitation accompanies it. {Ag}

◆ 7.7 ◆
MARTIAL ARTS SWEEPS

Standard Skills: Martial Arts Sweeping, Wrestling

Restricted Skills: Locking Holds

Applicable Stat Bonuses: Ag/St/Ag

Skill Rank Progression: Normal

Skill Category Progression: Normal

Group: Martial Arts

Classification: Offensive Bonus

LOCKING HOLDS

This skill provides an offensive bonus to render an opponent helpless with an immobilizing technique. This technique is usually only effective while the martial artist is applying constant force and pressure to maintain the locking hold. This skill uses the Arms Law Martial Arts Sweeps Attack Table with the Locking Holds Critical Table substituted for the Martial Arts Sweeps Critical Table. This skill may not exceed the Degree 1 damage threshold unless a Weapon Style skill or Martial Arts Style skill that allows the user to exceed this limitation accompanies it. {Ag}

◆ 7.8 ◆
SPECIAL ATTACKS

Standard Skills: Disarm Foe (Armed), Disarm Foe (Unarmed), Feint (Armed), Feint (Unarmed)

Restricted: Racial Attack

Applicable Stat Bonuses: St/Ag/SD

Skill Rank Progression: Combined

Skill Category Progression: 0 • 0 • 0 • 0 • 0

Group: None

Classification: Static Maneuver and Offensive Bonus

See Section 14.3 for details on how to use special attacks during a combat round.

DISARM FOE (ARMED)

This skill provides a bonus to remove a foe's weapon with your weapon. If the disarming skill check is successful, the opponent will drop his weapon. Depending on how successful the character is in his disarming attempt, the Gamemaster may decide to let the player decide where the disarmed weapon will go. To determine the success of the disarming attempt, make a static maneuver and add the character's skill bonus. The opponent's total usable OB (e.g., his OB before delegating parry or special attacks) with his weapon is taken as a negative modifier to the static maneuver. There are four separate skills for the user to develop, representing weapon categories against which a character can be trained: 1-Handed, 2-Handed, Pole Arm, and Two-Weapon Combination. {Ag}

DISARM FOE (UNARMED)

This skill provides a bonus to remove a foe's weapon while unarmed. If the disarming skill check is successful, the opponent will drop his weapon. Depending on how successful the character is in his disarming attempt, the Gamemaster may decide to let the player decide where the disarmed weapon will go. To determine the success of the disarming attempt, make a static maneuver and add the character's skill bonus. The opponent's total usable OB (e.g., his OB before delegating parry or special attacks) with his weapon is taken as a negative modifier to the static maneuver. There are four separate skills for the user to develop, representing weapon categories against which a character can be trained: 1-Handed, 2-Handed, Pole Arm, and Two-Weapon Combination. {Ag}

FEINT (ARMED)

This skill provides a bonus to trick your opponent to react to a false melee attack and weaken his defenses. A successful feint maneuver may result in a temporary reduction in the total DB of the target. To determine the success of the feint attempt, take the amount of the character's Feint skill bonus committed to the attack and make a static maneuver roll. The opponent's total usable OB (e.g., his OB before delegating parry or special attacks) is subtracted from this roll. Then refer to the Maneuver/Movement Table T-4.1, in *Rolemaster Standard Rules*, using the "Extremely Hard" column. If the result is a number, this number is subtracted from the target's normal DB.

A Feint maneuver may negate some or all of a target's DB due to shield bonus (including magical shields), parrying actions, skills that increase the DB of the target, or the target's Quickness modifier. Any positional DB or inherent DB of a target will not be reduced by a Feint maneuver. Examples of positional DB are fighting from higher ground or being behind some sort of cover. An inherent DB could be general magical protection or high quality armor, both of which cannot be affected by a feigned attack.

If the Feint maneuver is successful, half of the OB committed for the feint is regained for the normal melee attack. If the feint fails, all OB shifted to the feinting maneuver is lost for this round. However, the player must still make his attack action. {Qu}

If the character develops Situational Awareness: Feinting, he may apply this skill bonus against Feinting attacks made against him in addition to any other modifiers.

FEINT (UNARMED)

This skill provides a bonus to trick your opponent to react to a false melee attack and weaken his defenses. A successful Feint maneuver may result in a temporary reduction in the total DB of the target. To determine the success of the Feint attempt, take the character's Feint skill bonus committed to the attack and make a static maneuver roll. The opponent's total usable OB (e.g., his OB before delegating parry or special attacks) is subtracted from this roll. Then refer to the Maneuver/Movement Table T-4.1, in *Rolemaster Standard Rules*, using the "Extremely Hard" column. If the result is a number, this can be used to negate some of the target's DB.

A Feint maneuver may negate some or all of a target's DB due to shield bonus (including magical shields), parrying actions, skills that increase the DB of the target, or the target's Quickness modifier. Any positional DB or inherent DB of a target will not be reduced by a Feint maneuver. Examples of positional DB are fighting from higher ground or being behind some sort of cover. An inherent DB could be general magical protection or high quality armor, both of which cannot be affected by a feigned attack.

If the Feint maneuver is successful, half of the OB committed for the feint is regained for the normal melee attack. If the feint fails, all OB shifted to the feinting maneuver is lost for this round. However, the player must still make his attack action. {Qu}

If the character develops Situational Awareness: Feinting, he may apply this skill bonus against Feinting attacks made against him in addition to any other modifiers.

RACIAL ATTACKS

This skill provides a bonus to use a natural weapon attack available to the character. The bonus of this skill is treated in all ways like a normal OB for purposes of attacking, parrying, using other special attacks, etc. Examples of natural weapon attack are horn attacks, claw attacks, tail lashes, or even biting attacks. Generally, all races with a special racial attack may learn this skill as an Everyman skill regardless of profession. The relative strength and effectiveness of each racial attack will vary by race and must be determined by the Gamemaster. See Sections 8.0 and 9.0 for more details on how to integrate racial attacks into weapon styles and martial arts styles.

◆ 7.9 ◆
SPECIAL DEFENSES

Standard Skills: Adrenal Defense

Restricted Skills: Adrenal Toughness,
Adrenal Resistance

Applicable Stat Bonuses: None

Skill Rank Progression: Combined

Skill Category Progression: 0 • 0 • 0 • 0 • 0

Group: None

Classification: Special

ADRENAL DEFENSE

The Adrenal Defense skill allows the user to avoid attacks with missile or melee weapons during combat. The skill bonus of the defender is added to his DB versus melee attacks. Against missile attacks the skill bonus is halved and added to his DB. To use Adrenal Defense, an individual must be aware that he is under attack. In addition, the character must not be wearing armor and can not have a shield or large object in his hands. To represent the division of concentration necessary to avoid multiple attacks targeted at the user in the same round, Adrenal Defense requires 40% activity action in the combat round. {None}

This Adrenal Defense activity does count as one of the three allowable actions in a tactical round (this restriction may be negated by using the proper Weapon Style or Martial Arts Style skill). The 40% activity required for Adrenal Defense does apply against the 100% activity limit for the round (this restriction may be lessened by using the proper Weapon Style or Martial Arts Style skill).

ADRENAL RESISTANCE

The Adrenal Resistance skill enhances a character's inner strength to resist negative modifiers due to pain or wounds. To determine the penalty that can be offset, make an open-ended roll, adding this skill bonus, and all other applicable modifiers. Take the resulting number and refer to the "Extremely Hard" column of the Maneuver/Movement Table T-4.1, in Rolemaster *Standard Rules*. If the result is a number, it can be used to reduce any negative modifiers due to the pain from concussion hit loss or wounds by the amount shown. This skill requires a 20% preparation action in the round it is attempted, and the effects last up to an entire hour. Note that the Gamemaster may decide in the case of using this skill to resist pain from extremely serious wounds that there may be a risk of further aggravating the injury. {None}

This skill requires a 10% activity action each round it is used, regardless of the amount of negative modifiers from wounds offset. The Adrenal Resistance activity does not count against the three-action limit in a tactical round. The 10% activity action required for this skill does apply against the 100% activity limit for a given round.

ADRENAL TOUGHNESS

The Adrenal Toughness skill allows the user to toughen his body to withstand blows that would otherwise inflict damage. This skill requires taking a 20% preparation action in the round immediately prior to the use of this skill (or during the snap action phase of the same round). Then the character must make a static maneuver modified by the skill bonus. If successful, the individual may reduce the severity of any critical by one during the next round or the remainder of the current round. (In the case of an 'A' critical, the critical is modified by -20). In addition, any self-inflicted critical stemming from the individual striking a surface or object with his hand or foot is nullified completely. {None}

WEAPON STYLES

Part II

**Sections
8.0, 8.1, 8.2**

Weapon
Styles

Overview

Creating a
Weapon Style

Nothing broke the silence except the hissing of blades and the sharp exhalation of breath as the pack of thugs circled their prey warily. The old swordsman held his blade aloft as he stood his ground before his numerous adversaries. He moved in a slowly turning circle, keeping his foes from attacking directly at his back, and he rotated his blade through the seven positions of guard. The young toughs were armed with a variety of weapons from swords to clubs to chains, and several suffered in silence the pain from their wounds that were inflicted when they had first rushed the old man.

The crash of arms echoed once again down the deserted street and the faint sound of the city guard's alarm could be heard approaching. The city guard would be here soon. The old man's face remained calm as his six foes rushed at him simultaneously, trying to bring down their prey before the advent of the guard. The old man pivoted smoothly to his left, leaving empty air for the most impetuous of his attackers. His blade then shimmered in the air, a solid arc of metal, as it cut through the arm of the bravo holding a spiked club who had moved to attack from the side. The two thugs armed with swords found themselves holding their stomachs as the old man ducked low under the hissing attack of the chain-wielding man and spun low under their guard, bringing his blade around in a deadly arc.

Momentary silence was broken by the sound of weapons dropping to the ground and feet racing down the cobblestone street. The old man raised himself from his crouching position and calmly cleaned his weapon as he watched the bandits attempt to flee from the newly arrived city guard. They would not get far and he would know the reason for this attack soon enough. They were new to this city or very well paid fools, since no sane man would attempt to ambush the weapons master of the royal guard unless he did not value his life.

◆ 8.1 ◆
OVERVIEW

The Weapon Style skills are a new concept presented in this companion. Each Weapon Style skill offers a set of unique capabilities and benefits to the practitioner in combat. The additional training required by the weapon style allows its user to become more efficient and economical in the use of his weapon.

The weapon stylist's advanced training in the use of his weapon allows him to exceed certain limitations that restrict the common practitioner of his specific weapon. For example, a weapon stylist can have a reduced fumble range or bonus to melee initiative as a benefit of his training.

The mechanics of using weapon styles are the same as any other Combat Maneuver skill. When in combat, the weapon stylist will always use the lesser of his Weapon Style skill OB or his Weapon skill OB. As long as the weapon stylist is using his Weapon Style skill, he can receive the special benefits conferred by this skill.

Any modifiers that directly affect a character's OB will also affect his Weapon Style skill OB (except professional category bonuses that only affect Weapon skills). Allowable OB modifiers to weapon styles include spells, item bonuses (assuming it is the primary weapon of the style), and some skill bonuses (e.g., a +10 OB bonus due to a successful Adrenal Strength maneuver).

Any bonuses that a weapon style confers upon a character are only applicable while the character is actively using that style (i.e., the character is attacking using the weapon style). If a player decides to not use his Weapon Style skill to attack, none of the benefits of that weapon style will be available even if the player chooses to use the weapon associated with that particular weapon style. See Section 14.2.1 for further discussion.

◆ 8.2 ◆
CREATING
A WEAPON STYLE

Gamemasters are encouraged to create their own weapon styles for use in their games. The rules and guidelines detailed here will help to make the process easier and provide game balance. Weapon styles are created using a point-based system. These points are referred to as "style points" and they are only used during the creation of the weapon style skill. After a weapon style is created it will either be classified as a Basic or Advanced Weapon Style skill (based on its total style point cost). Section 8.3 presents some examples of created weapon styles.

• Basic Weapon Styles can range from 0 to 30 style points.

• Advanced Weapon Styles range can from over 31 to up to 60 style points. It is not advised to create a weapon style that uses more than 60 style points.

STEPS OF CREATION

The first step in creating a new weapon style is choosing the general focus of the weapon style. The style can be based on can be an individual weapon, a group of related weapons, or a weapon category. The broader the range of weapons the style includes, the more expensive the weapon style will be to learn. In addition, the type of weapon chosen will dictate some of the options available for the weapon style. If the weapon style is based upon a two-handed weapon, any options that require the practitioner to have a hand free will not be available within this specific weapon style. Choose one of the following weapon categories as the primary focus of the new weapon style.

• One-handed Edged or One-handed Concussion
  Weapon Categories
    Allowed choices for the weapon style: Standard options; Melee weapon options; One hand free options

• Two-handed or Pole Arm Weapon Categories
    Allowed choices for the weapon style: Standard options; Melee weapon options

• Missile Weapon Category

Allowed choices for the weapon style: Standard options; Missile weapon options

• Thrown Weapon Category

Allowed choices for the weapon style: Standard options; Thrown weapon options; One hand free options

• Artillery Weapon Category

It is not possible to create a weapon style with the Artillery Weapon category.

8.2.1 · STANDARD OPTIONS

This section presents a series of charts that show the costs for the various standard options that are available. If a cost shows as a dash ("—"), that option may not be selected.

BASE WEAPON STYLE COST

	Melee	Missile	Thrown
Single weapon	5	5	5
Related weapons	10	10	10
Category of weapons	20	20	20

Single Weapon—The weapon style uses a single specific weapon.

Related Weapons—The weapon style uses a specific group of related weapons (i.e., all club-like weapons).

Category of Weapons—The weapon style uses an entire weapon category (e.g., 1H Edged Weapons, 1H Concussion Weapons, 2H Weapons, Pole Arms, Missile Weapons, or Thrown Weapons, etc.).

COST FOR MODIFYING INITIATIVE ROLLS

	Melee	Missile	Thrown
+1 to initiative rolls	5	10	10
+2 to initiative rolls	10	15	15
+4 to initiative rolls	15	—	—

COST FOR REDUCING FUMBLE RANGE

	Melee	Missile	Thrown
-1 to fumble range	5	10	10
-2 to fumble range	10	—	15
-3 to fumble range	15	—	—

Note: The minimum fumble range that may be gained through this ability is 01-02.

COST FOR REDUCING RANGE PENALTIES

	Melee	Missile	Thrown
-10 to range penalties	10	10	10
-20 to range penalties	—	20	20
-30 to range penalties	—	30	—

Note: A range penalty cannot be brought above +0.

COST FOR MODIFYING CRITICAL ROLLS

	Melee	Missile	Thrown
±1 to the critical roll	15	30	30
±2 to the critical roll	30	—	—
±3 to the critical roll	50	—	—

Note: Modification is chosen by the attacker after the critical roll is made.

COST FOR BONUS TO SPECIAL ATTACKS

	Melee	Missile	Thrown
+10 bonus to skill	5	5	5
+15 bonus to skill	10	10	10

Note: The bonus applies to one specific skill in the Special Attacks skill category while using this weapon style.

COST FOR BONUS TO SELF CONTROL

	Melee	Missile	Thrown
+5 bonus to skill	10	10	10
+10 bonus to skill	15	15	15

Note: The bonus applies to one specific skill in the Self Control skill category while using this weapon style.

COST FOR BONUS TO NON-RESTRICTED SKILL

	Melee	Missile	Thrown
+5 bonus to skill	5	5	5
+10 bonus to skill	10	10	10

Note: This bonus applies to one other specific skill that is not classified as Restricted (excluding skills in the Special Defense skill category) while using this weapon style.

COST FOR BONUS TO RESTRICTED SKILL

	Melee	Missile	Thrown
+5 bonus to skill	10	10	10
+10 bonus to skill	15	15	15

Note: This bonus applies to one other specific skill that is classified as Restricted (excluding skills in the Special Defense skill category) while using this weapon style.

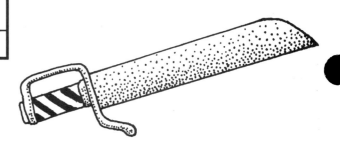

8.2.2 · MELEE WEAPON OPTIONS

This list shows other options that are available when "building" weapon styles that use melee weapons. All the advantages gained from these options are only available when a character is using his weapon style. The style point cost is shown in brackets ("[]" after each entry).

Adrenal Defense, Greater—The character has specialized in integrating his Adrenal Defense techniques within his weapon style. The character may ignore restrictions for objects in his hands while using Adrenal Defense if he is using weapons associated with this weapon style. In addition, an Adrenal Defense maneuver only requires 10% activity and it does not count against the three actions per round limit (though he must still allocate no more than 100% activity to all of his actions). [30 points]

Adrenal Defense, Lesser—The character has specialized in integrating his weapon attacks within his Adrenal Defense techniques. The character may ignore restrictions for objects in his hands while using Adrenal Defense if he is using weapons associated with this weapon style. Additionally, an Adrenal Defense maneuver only requires 30% activity and it does not count against the three actions per round limit (though he must still allocate no more than 100% activity to all of his actions). [10 points]

All-Around Attack—The character can make attacks against foes who have a positional modifier (such as flank or rear) against him without changing his facing or position. The OB is penalized by double the positional bonus of the opponent (i.e., attacking a foe to the rear results in a –50 OB modifier). [15 points]

All-Around Defense—The character can choose to negate one positional bonus that a foe has against him during a combat round by taking a 10% action. [15 points]

Weapon-Breaker—The character has learned to incorporate special maneuvers into his attacks that are designed to cause his opponents' weapons to break. Any foe fighting the character has his breakage numbers increased by one for the duration of the combat (e.g., if the weapon's breakage numbers are normally 1 through 5 they will be 1 through 6 while the foe is fighting this character). In addition, the foe must modify the weapon strength rolls by –10. [10 points]

8.2.3 · MISSILE WEAPON OPTIONS

This list shows other options that are available when "building" weapon styles that use missile weapons. All the advantages gained from these options are only available when a character is using his weapon style. The style point cost is shown in brackets ("[]" after each entry).

Movement—Movement penalties to OB are halved while using this weapon. For example, if using this weapon, a character may move using a 40% action and only suffer a -20 to his OB with the weapon. [10 points]

Reloading, Lesser—The reload action for this missile weapon takes 10% less activity (to a minimum of 20%). [10 points]

Reloading, Greater—The reload action for this missile weapon takes 20% less activity (to a minimum of 20%). [20 points]

8.2.4 · THROWN WEAPON OPTIONS

This list shows other options that are available when "building" weapon styles that use thrown weapons. All the advantages gained from these options are only available when a character is using his weapon style. The style point cost is shown in brackets ("[]" after each entry.

Movement—Movement penalties to OB are halved while using this weapon. For example, if using this weapon, a character may move using a 40% action and only suffer a -20 to his OB with the weapon. [10 points]

8.2.5 · OTHER OPTIONS

This list shows other options that are available when "building" weapon styles. All the advantages gained from these options are only available when a character is using his weapon style. The style point cost is shown in brackets "[]" after each entry.

Additional Melee Weapon Attack—This weapon style allows two distinct weapon strikes per attack action. Through extensive training the character can use a one-handed weapon in your off-hand along whenever the character uses his weapon style. The cost for this option is triple the base weapon style cost for the secondary weapon type (see Section 8.2.1). Skill with this weapon must be developed separately as a normal weapon skill. When a character takes an attack action, he makes an attack roll for each weapon with the restrictions shown below. [varies]

#1) The OB for each weapon attack is the lesser of the Weapon Style skill bonus or the skill bonus for the weapon.

#2) Any penalty for parrying or special attacks must modify both weapon OBs equally. If the character is attacking two separate foes, the amount of OB dedicated for the parry or special attack may be split between them.

#3) The character can strike one opponent with both attacks at no extra penalty.

#4) The character can attack two separate opponents as long as neither of the opponents is receiving a positional bonus against the character. The character must take a –20 modifier to both weapon OBs (this is applied after restriction #1).

Example: If a weapon style includes additional attacks with a mace held in the off-hand, the cost for this option would be 15 style points (5 x 3). The character could choose to attack with each weapon against the same opponent or to attack two separate opponents with a special –20 modifier.

Paired Weapon Attack—This weapon style allows enhanced combat strikes by using two weapons. Unlike the additional melee attack option, the paired weapon attack does not allow an extra strike but makes each strike more deadly. For purposes of determining the melee OB for the single attack, the lesser of the Weapon Style skill bonus and the primary weapon OB is used.

Any attack that delivers a critical will do an additional critical of two levels less severity (using the same dice roll). If the normal critical result is an 'A' critical, the secondary critical is treated as an 'A' critical modified by -40 (modified rolls less than zero result in no effect). If

MARTIAL
ARTS
COMPANION

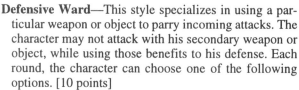

the normal critical result is a 'B' critical, the secondary critical is resolved as an 'A' critical modified by -20 (modified rolls less than zero result in no effect). The type of additional critical delivered should be determined by the GM (but is normally the most common type for the paired weapons). When fighting creatures that take Large or Super Large criticals, no additional critical is delivered. The cost for this option is double the base weapon cost of the secondary weapon. [varies]

Additional Unarmed Attack—This weapon style specializes in using strikes, kicks, and other unarmed fighting techniques while in melee combat. The unarmed attack skill must be developed separately. The cost for this additional attack is 10 points for a Degree 1 damage threshold and 15 points for a Degree 2 damage threshold (damage thresholds cannot be taken higher than Degree 2). When this style is created, the type of unarmed attack (either Striking or Sweeping) must be chosen. When a character, takes an attack action, the restrictions shown below must also be observed. [10 or 15 points]

#1) The OB for the unarmed attack is the lesser of the Weapon Style skill bonus or the skill bonus for the unarmed attacking skill.

#2) Any OB penalty for parrying or special attacks must modify both attacks equally. If the character is attacking two separate foes, the amount of OB dedicated the parry or special attack may be split between them.

#3) The character can strike one opponent with both attacks at no penalty.

#4) The character can attack two separate opponents as long as neither opponent has a positional bonus against him. In addition, he must take a -20 modifier to both his weapon OB and unarmed attack OB.

Additional Thrown Weapon Attack—This weapon style specializes in thrown weapons in melee combat. The thrown weapon skill must be developed separately. The cost for this additional attack is triple the base cost of the thrown weapon attack. When a character takes an attack option, the restrictions shown below must also be met. [varies]

#1) The OB for the thrown weapon is the lesser of the weapon style bonus or the skill bonus for the thrown weapon.

#2) Any penalty for parrying or special attacks must modify both weapon OBs equally. If the character is attacking two separate foes, the amount of OB dedicated to the parry or special attack may be split between them.

#3) The character can strike one opponent with both attacks at no penalty.

#4) The character can attack two separate opponents as long as neither of the opponents has a positional bonus against him. In addition, he must take a -20 modifier to both weapon OBs.

Example: *If the weapon style includes an additional thrown weapon attack that includes all short knives, the cost for this option would be 30 (10 x 3).*

Defensive Ward—This style specializes in using a particular weapon or object to parry incoming attacks. The character may not attack with his secondary weapon or object, while using those benefits to his defense. Each round, the character can choose one of the following options. [10 points]

#1) Increase the normal DB from his secondary weapon by 10 against one opponent (e.g., a normal shield would give +30 DB instead of +20).

#2) Affect an additional opponent with his DB due to his parrying item. The additional opponent cannot have a positional bonus on the character.

Example: *A weapon style that incorporates a main-gauche as a defensive weapon could use the passive DB of the main gauche against two opponents or he could use it with an additional +10 DB against one opponent.*

Shield Training—This style specializes in using a shield to its maximum potential during combat. One type of shield must be picked when this option is chosen. Available shield types are target (this includes all "buckler"-sized shields), normal, full, and wall shields. Each round, the character can choose one of the following options. [20 points]

#1) He can increase his shield DB against one opponent by 15.

#2) He can affect an additional opponent with his shield DB. The additional opponent cannot have a positional bonus on the character. This option cannot be chosen with a style that uses wall shields.

Example: *A weapon style that incorporates the use of a full shield could increase its DB by 15 against one opponent, or use his normal shield bonus against two opponents.*

#3) He can make a Shield Bash attack on the Ram/Butt Attack Table. The maximum result is limited by the Small damage threshold (target shields also suffer an OB penalty of -20 to reflect their small size and weight). The weapon skill for the shield must be developed separately as a one-handed concussion weapon.

SAMPLE WEAPON STYLES SUMMARY CHART		
Weapon Style Name	**Type of Weapon Style Skill**	**Total Style Point Cost**
Japanese Weapon Styles		
Bo-jutsu	Basic Weapon Style	30
Iai-jutsu	Advanced Weapon Style	55
Ken-jutsu	Advanced Weapon Style	60
Kusarigama-jutsu	Advanced Weapon Style	35
Kyu-jutsu	Advanced Weapon Style	35
Naginata-jutsu	Basic Weapon Style	20
Shuriken-jutsu	Basic Weapon Style	25
So-jutsu	Basic Weapon Style	30
Tetsubo-jutsu	Basic Weapon Style	30
Tessen-jutsu	Basic Weapon Style	20
European Weapon Styles		
Classic Fencing	Advanced Weapon Style	35
Italian Fencing	Basic Weapon Style	20

◆ 8.3 ◆
SAMPLE WEAPON STYLES

Here are some sample weapon styles that illustrate how the weapon styles work. While these sample weapon styles draw inspiration from historical weapon systems, they are only approximate models of the historical systems. For the historical evolution of weapon styles, see Section 2.0.

The format of the each weapon style example is as follows:

- Name of Weapon Style
- Whether the weapon style is Basic or Advanced, followed by the total style points used to create the weapon style (in brackets, "[]").
- A description of the weapon style's origins and history follows this information. Also included are some of the more common combat techniques that the style uses.
- A list of skills that a character will probably want to develop along with this weapon style. These skills are not "required" but will probably be desired to take full advantage of the style.
- A breakdown of the abilities and costs for the weapon style (costs are shown in brackets, "[]"). These abilities are listed as "Core" because they define the style and should be used with all power levels.

8.3.1 · JAPANESE WEAPON STYLES

Japanese weapon fighting systems were highly developed throughout the history of this small island nation. As a result, the style points ranges for Japanese weapon styles may be changed from the original ranges given for the skills in Section 8.1.

Optional Rule [Core]: When designing Japanese weapon styles, Basic Weapon Styles range from 0 to 35 style points and Advanced Weapon Styles range from 36 to 45 style points.

BO-JUTSU (QUARTERSTAFF)

Basic Weapon Style [30 style points]

Description—This weapon style specializes in the use of the staff as a weapon. The wooden staff, while inelegant compared to the sword, was nevertheless an effective weapon in combat and could not be neglected by the bushi (warrior class) in feudal Japan. The standard length of staff for training was the six foot staff that was also known as the rokushaku-bo.

While the art of bo-jutsu focuses on tactics that can be used to subdue an aggressive swordsman, it is also useful against other types of weapons. The training concentrates on methods of blocking, parrying, and thrusting against an opponent. The wielder is also taught to use the longer range of his weapon to keep foes at bay and to prevent foes from closing the range to a point where the staff becomes ineffective.

Formal training in the use of the staff as a weapon was taught in over three hundred different traditions in feudal Japan. For more information on the historical development of the Japanese martial arts, see Section 2.4

Recommended Skills—Bo (Quarterstaff) weapon skill

Weapon Style Abilities [Core]—Bo (Quarterstaff) melee attack [5 points]; +2 bonus to initiative [10 points]; All-around defense [15 points]

IAI-JUTSU (SWORD)

Advanced Weapon Style [55 style points]

Description—Iai-jutsu is the Japanese art of sword fighting that seeks to perfect the single deadly stroke of a sword. The essence of this system is the focus on lightning speed and unwavering accuracy with the single goal of cutting down an enemy with one stroke. Much of the training involves defensive maneuvers to protect the adept from unexpected attack. Unlike many other Japanese martial arts, much of the training for this style is done as a solo exercise. Because this style seeks to prepare the wielder to react to unexpected attacks, much of the training begins from a low crouching position to simulate combat that starts from a sitting position.

There are four distinct areas of emphasis in the art of iai-jutsu. The first is the nukitsuke, or draw; the second is the kiritsuke, or cutting action; the third is the chiburi, or removal of blood from the blade; and the fourth is the noto, or return of the blade to the scabbard.

This discipline teaches the swordsman to evade multiple attacks from the front, side, and rear. The adept of this weapon style spends several hours each day practicing his draws and attacks with his blade. A central goal of this style is to reach a state of meditative awareness in which the adept can react instantly to any attack. Over four hundred formal traditions taught the art of iai-jutsu in feudal Japan. See Section 2.4 for more information on the historical development of Japanese martial arts.

Recommended Skills—Katana weapon skill, Quickdraw, Meditation, Alertness, Sense Ambush, Adrenal Defense

Weapon Style Abilities [Core]—Lesser Adrenal Defense [10 points]; Katana melee attack [5 points]; Reduce fumble range by 3 (to minimum fumble range of 01-02) [15 points]; +10 bonus to Quickdraw maneuvers [10 points]; All-around defense [15 points]

KEN-JUTSU (SWORD)

Advanced Weapon Style [60 style points]

Description—Ken-jutsu is the Japanese art of offensive sword fighting. In feudal Japan, the slightest error in combat with a skilled opponent meant death. To survive in a sword fight to the death, the Japanese warrior codified and practiced many strikes and counters that he might encounter in a duel. After time, these techniques were standardized and incorporated into a growing canon of swordsmanship. Most individual schools of ken-jutsu practiced a policy of secrecy regarding their attacking techniques to preserve an advantage over their competitors. The result of this practice was that individual swordsmen seeking to improve their skills would travel from school to school in feudal Japan, fighting with other students and learning what new techniques they could in the case of a defeat.

Ken-jutsu is an extremely deadly and focused fighting style. Techniques in ken-jutsu involve cutting (kiri) and thrusting (tsuri). Like most Japanese martial arts, training was always done in natural terrain against opponents to mimic combat conditions.

Some ken-jutsu styles taught two-sword combat. At the height of the warring states period in Japan, there were over seventeen hundred distinct styles of ken-jutsu. See Section 2.4 for more information on the development of Japanese martial arts.

Recommended Skills—Katana weapon skill, Meditation

Weapon Style Abilities [Core]—Katana melee attack [5 points]; All-around attack [15 points]; +2 bonus to initiative [10 points]; +2 to all critical rolls inflicted [30 points]

KUSARIGAMA-JUTSU (SICKLE AND CHAIN)

Advanced Weapon Style [35 style points]

Description—The kusarigama is several weapons in one. It is at once a bladed weapon, a stick weapon, and a flail. The user of a kusari-gama can slash or cut the enemy with his blade, entangle him with his chain, club him with his hardwood handle, and strike him with the iron weight at the end of the chain. The use of this weapon required expert skill and patience to overcome better-armed opponents. The most important skill taught is the ensnaring or maki technique. The wielder was taught to entangle his opponent at the moment of his attack. The versatility of this dangerous weapon required extensive training and practice to learn properly. See Section 2.4 for more information on the development of Japanese martial arts.

Recommended Skills—Kursarigama weapon skill, Disarm Foe

Weapon Style Abilities [Core]—Kusari-gama melee attack [5 points]; +15 bonus to Disarm Foe (1H-edged) attempts [10 points]; Reduce kusari-gama fumble range by 3 (to minimum fumble range of 01-02) [10 points]; +2 bonus to initiative [10 points]

KYU-JUTSU (LONG BOW)

Advanced Weapon Style [35 style points]

Description—Kyu-jutsu is the Japanese art of bowmanship. The longbow has long had an important place in Japanese history. At the end of the tenth century, Masatsugo Zensho formalized techniques for the bow and arrow. The dai-kyu or traditional bow used by Japanese archers possessed an asymmetrical shape; up to two-thirds of the bow's length was above the archer's left hand. The bow itself was made of a combination of wood and bamboo toughened by fire treatment. The bow's great length required several men to string it successfully. Three- and four-men bows were the most common type of bows used by archers. The arrows used by Japanese archers while of a uniform three feet in length, possessed several different types of heads depending on their use. Some arrows made noise as they flew and were used to either terrorize the enemy or as signals. Other arrows were specifically designed to penetrate armor or to cut through cords.

The yugamae, or correct posture, was of the utmost importance in the battlefield effectiveness of the Japanese bowman. The bowman was trained to unify with his target and his bow to release his arrows with the maximum accuracy. The mechanical movements of reloading the bow and drawing the bow were formalized and practiced often so that they became unconscious actions of the bowman. In addition, the archer was trained in sustained long distance shooting to pin enemy forces down.

See Section 2.4 for more information on the development of the Japanese martial arts.

Recommended Skills—Dai-kyu missile weapon skill, Meditation

Weapon Style Abilities [Core]—Dai-kyu missile attack [5 points]; Reduce dai-kyu range penalties by 10 [10 points]; Reduce dai-kyu reloading time by 20% [20 points]

NAGINATA-JUTSU (HALBERD)

Basic Weapon Style [20 style points]

Description—In Japan, the naginata (similar to a halberd) became an effective weapon against mounted or unmounted foes in the hands of an expert. In open terrain, the naginata was an excellent weapon because its reach allowed the warrior to keep his foe at bay while at the same time launching attacks against him. In combat, the wielder of the naginata used short slashes and circular movements to harry and attack his foe. As with most Japanese weapon systems, training with the naginata was on open terrain to simulate battlefield conditions. However in wooded or close terrain, the naginata became much less useful. See Section 2.4 for more information on the development of Japanese martial arts.

Recommended Skills—Naginata weapon skill

Weapon Style Abilities [Core]—Naginata melee attack [5 points]; +4 bonus to initiative [15 points]

SHURIKEN-JUTSU (THROWING WEAPONS)

Basic Weapon Style [25 style points]

Description—This weapon style specializes in learning how to throw shuriken (Japanese throwing weapons) accurately and quickly at a target. This weapon style incorporates special throwing techniques to ensure more accurate results. Shuriken range in appearance from iron bolts that can be thrown for greater range and penetration to the familiar bladed star that can be thrown for a greater chance to hit the target.

This weapon style also covers the techniques for readying a shuriken secretly for a quick attack against an unsuspecting opponent. The wielder uses his own body to shield the preparation of the weapon, until his foe is within range and then he unleashes with a deadly attack. The master of shuriken-jutsu is taught to throw quickly and accurately at the vulnerable parts of the body rarely covered by armor: the face and neck.

Typically this weapon style is taught as part of training in the art of the ninja (the ninja were spies and assassins in feudal Japan). For more information on the historical development of the Japanese martial arts, refer to Section 2.4.

Recommended Skills—Thrown Shuriken weapon skill, Missile Deflecting, Quickdraw

Weapon Style Abilities [Core]—Shuriken thrown attack [5 points]; Reduced shuriken range penalties by 10 [10 points]; +10 bonus to Quickdraw maneuvers [10 points]

SO-JUTSU (SPEAR)

Basic Weapon Style [30 style points]

Description—The yari or spear is one of the oldest weapons used in Japan and figures prominently in the religious and cultural traditions of Japan. The spear did not initially come into wide favor with the bushi, or professional warrior since they associated the sword and kenjutsu with their rank and station in life. However, the warrior-priests of Japan known as so-hei embraced the weapon and developed sophisticated techniques using the spear.

The warrior using the yari, or spear, trained to become skilled with his thrusts (tsuki) and in maintaining the correct combat distance for the effective use of the spear. The spear was used from the ground or horseback in most cases. A benefit of the training in the use of the spear was that the warrior became very skilled in anticipating tactics of his foes and in closing the engagement distance so that he could use his primary weapon (usually a sword).

Only after the Muromachi period in feudal Japan was the spear welcomed by the bushi class and taught formally in schools. Some four hundred formal traditions taught the use of the spear by the end of Japan's feudal era. See Section 2.4 for more information on the development of Japanese martial arts.

Recommended Skills—Yari weapon skill, Feint, Adrenal Defense

Weapon Style Abilities [Core]—Lesser Adrenal Defense [10 points]; Yari melee attack [5 points]; +10 bonus to Feint maneuvers [5 points]; +2 bonus to initiative [10 points]

MARTIAL ARTS COMPANION

TETSUBO-JUTSU (IRON STAFF)

Basic Weapon Style [30 style points]

Description—The tetsubo was a solid iron bar used in much the same manner as a staff. The tetsubo was of varying lengths and shapes. It often had a circular or hexagonal cross-section. The bar would taper from one end to the narrower handle. This weapon required immense physical strength to wield properly and could be dangerous to the wielder if not treated with respect. The art of tetsubo-jutsu concentrated on using (and maintaining) the tremendous force generated by swinging the staff while attacking.

   The drawback to this weapon was that its immense weight could be a liability to the wielder if faced with a quicker opponent. The wielder had to swing his weapon very rapidly to prevent quicker opponents from taking advantage of openings in his defense. See Section 16.3 for more information on the development of Japanese martial arts.

Recommended Skills—Tetsubo weapon skill, Adrenal Strength

Weapon Style Abilities [Core]—Tetsubo melee attack [5 points]; +10 bonus to Adrenal Strength maneuvers [10 points]; Reduce tetsubo fumble range by 3 (to the minimum fumble range of 01-02) [15 points]

TESSEN-JUTSU (IRON FAN)

Basic Weapon Style [20 style points]

Description—This weapon style specialized in the use of the fan as a weapon. In feudal Japanese society, the fan was considered part of the dress and equipment of the professional warrior. In some social situations, a warrior might be required to leave his swords with his host, but with a fan (tessen) carried in his sash he was never totally unarmed. If need required it, the warrior could defend himself with his tessen from attackers. In actuality, the fan referred to by this weapon style only appeared to be the classical fragile fan; in fact, the actual fan used by practitioners of this weapon style was different. The tessen came in two types. The first type only appeared to be a fan, as it could not be opened. The second type could be opened. In both cases, iron was used to construct the tessen to give it the strength and durability it needed to survive combat. The solid (or unopenable) tessen was the more popular type to use since it had greater strength.

   In combat the tessen was used in much the same manner as a short stick. It was used to block incoming attacks and retaliate with poking attacks against vital points. The wielder of this style carefully selected sashikata (or the proper way of wearing the tessen) to have it instantly available if need arose. Training with the tessen involved learning how to block attacks (uke), parry incoming attacks (nagashi), striking (uchi), and thrusting (tsuki). However, the tessen was primarily viewed as a defensive weapon, for use only when the warrior's true weapons were not available.

   Almost one hundred different traditions formalized the use of the tessen in combat in feudal Japan. For more information on the historical development of the Japanese martial arts, see Section 2.4.

Recommended Skills—Tessen weapon skill, Quickdraw

Weapon Style Abilities [Core]—Tessen (Iron Fan) melee attack [5 points]; +1 bonus to initiative [5 points]; +10 bonus to Quickdraw maneuvers [10 points]

8.3.2 · EUROPEAN WEAPON STYLES

   European cultures did not develop fighting systems to as high a degree as Asian cultures. As a result, the style points ranges for European weapon styles may be reduced from the original ranges given for the skills in Section 8.1. Though European weapon styles are more highly developed than their European martial arts styles, they still fall below the average level of sophistication of Eastern weapon fighting systems.

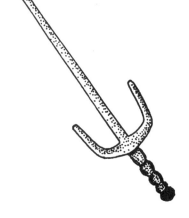

Optional Rule [Core]: When designing European weapon styles, Basic Weapon Styles range from 0 to 25 style points and Advanced Weapon Styles range from 26 to 45 style points.

CLASSIC FENCING

Advanced Weapon Style [35 style points]

Description—Many fencing schools arose in Italy, France, and Spain to teach the effective use of the blade. While different fencing styles did exist during the golden age of fencing, they also shared many traits. The common stance for single rapier fencing is to present only the weapon arm and side of your body to your opponent to limit his targets for attack. The use of the point, rather than the edge is also emphasized. Fencing emphasizes straight-line attacks with the target being the face or stomach of the opponent. The later fencing techniques introduced the lunge, a quick strike made by extending the arm as the lead foot extends out and bends to attack your opponent from a greater range. Unlike Olympic fencing, combat fencing is a much more cautious affair. The true winner is he who strikes without being hit in return, not just he who strikes first without regard for personal safety. See Section 2.7 for more on the development of European martial arts.

Recommended Skills—Rapier weapon attack, Feinting, Disarm Foe (1H Weapons)

Weapon Style Abilities [Core]—Lesser Adrenal Defense [10 points]; Rapier melee attack [5 points]; +2 to Initiative rolls [10 points]; +10 OB Bonus to Feint [5 points]; +10 OB Bonus to Disarm Foe (1H Edged) [5 points]

ITALIAN FENCING
(WITH DAGGER OR CLOAK)

Basic Weapon Style [20 style points]

Description—Many fencing schools arose in Europe to teach the effective use of the blade. Some of the first fencing schools were opened in Italy. Common with Italian fencing masters was the teaching of techniques for using a secondary object in the off-hand to parry attacks. When fencing with a dagger in the off-hand, the dagger was used as a defensive weapon to parry the thrusting attacks of the opponent rather than an additional offensive attack as might be first thought. In fact, the object carried in the off-hand was not always a dagger, in some cases a cloak or buckler was used instead. The reasoning behind this teaching was direct and simple. The blade had the longest reach and as such should be used for attacking the opponent. It was considered unwise to maneuver close enough to your opponent to thrust a dagger into his ribs when you could do the same from a much greater range with the blade. The use of these items in combat was to parry incoming attacks so that the blade would be free to attack in turn. Fighting cloaks were made out of stiff material and were smaller than normal cloaks of the period. The cape was be sturdy enough to withstand the abuse of being cut or thrust with a rapier. Typically the cape was held either by the collar or at one edge close to the hem. The cloak could be used offensively to entangle a blade or twirled or flicked at your opponent to confuse them. The bucklers were likewise very small shields that were primarily used defensively though a wielder could punch a foe with a buckler. See Section 2.7 for more on the development of European martial arts.

Recommended Skills—Rapier weapon skill, Feinting, Disarm Foe (1H Weapons)

Weapon Style Abilities [Core]—Rapier melee attack [5 points]; Defensive ward (using a dagger or a cloak to parry incoming attacks) [10 points]; +1 to initiative [5 points]

Part II

Sections
9.0, 9.1, 9.2

Martial Arts
Styles

Overview

Creating a
Martial Arts
Style

9.0
MARTIAL ARTS STYLES

The slow rhythmic beating of the drum began as the two masters bowed to each other from opposite sides of the rough dirt ring. Arrayed in a semi-circle behind their masters, their students held banners and signs proclaiming the strength and power of their schools. One master was a slender young man in a white robe embroidered with wading and flying cranes. I later learned his name was Chu Ho and that he was the youngest man to be awarded the rank of master of the Imperial Tiger style in over forty years and as such he was known as the Young Master to his friends. His face appeared impassive as he stared at his adversary across the ring. The other master, an older man in an ornate but threadbare robe stood motionless on the other side of the ring. I later learned his name was Hsieh Fu and that he was known as the Iron Palm in the martial arts world.

Their students yelled and clamored behind their masters, urging each to victory. I narrowly avoided being caught in a fight between some of the more impetuous students from each side. Luckily another bystander intervened and calmed the students down. When I looked back at the ring, the masters were circling slowly around each other as the pace of the drumbeats began to increase.

Suddenly Chu Ho moved closer to Hsieh Fu and launched a lightning-like volley of hand strikes aimed at his head and throat that I recognized from the teachings of my master as the feared Seven Claws of the Tiger attack. Hsieh Fu ducked back and raised his arms to deflect most of the blows, but one slipped through and hit him on the side of the head. Momentarily dazed by the blow Hsieh Fu let his attention waver for an instant and the younger Chu Ho sensed his advantage. Chu Ho crouched low and unleashed a viscous spinning kick against the older master's legs. Hsieh Fu was knocked down on his side, but he used his motion to tumble away from Chu Ho. Chu Ho followed the path of the older master's retreat, stamping and striking at the rolling form that was barely out of his reach.

Somehow the Young Master made a mistake; perhaps he was following too closely or became overeager sensing his foe's imminent defeat. In any case, he launched his trademark Seven Claws of the Tiger attack once more against Hsieh Fu. At the same instant, Hsieh Fu reversed his roll and tumbled inside the Young Master's defenses. Hsieh Fu then unleashed a twisting and spinning kick from the ground that simultaneously knocked the Young Master back a few steps and put Hsieh Fu back on his feet. Before Chu Ho could guard himself, Hsieh Fu closed with him again and launched one blow into the center of the Young Master's chest. Chu Ho flew fifteen feet back from the center of the ring into the suddenly quiet group of his students. I now recalled why Hsieh Fu was called the Iron Palm in the world of martial arts.

Hsieh Fu bowed again to the judges and the unconscious Chu Fu before striding out of the ring. Half the crowd followed him and his students back to his small school at the outskirts of the city. I think that this week, Hsieh's school of martial arts will be getting a record number of new students.

—From the Writings of Chiang Shun

◆ 9.1 ◆
OVERVIEW

The Martial Arts Style skills are a new concept presented in this companion. Each Martial Arts Style skill represents a set of unique capabilities and benefits to the user in combat. Training in a martial arts style allows its user to become more efficient and economical with his unarmed attacks.

The martial artist's advanced training in unarmed combat allows him to exceed certain limitations to which the common unarmed combatant is bound. For example, a martial artist could have improved attack skills or a bonus to initiative as a benefit of his training.

The mechanics of using martial arts styles are the same as any other Martial Arts Combat Maneuvers skill. When in combat, the martial artist will always use the lesser of his Martial Arts Style skill OB or the appropriate unarmed martial arts attack OB. As long as the martial artist uses his Martial Arts Style skill, he can receive the special benefits conferred by this skill.

Any modifiers that directly affect a character's unarmed combat OB will also effect his Martial Arts Style skill OB. Allowable OB modifiers to martial arts styles include spells and skill bonuses that affect OB (e.g., a +10 OB bonus from a successful Adrenal Strength maneuver).

Any bonuses that a martial arts style confers upon a character are only applicable while the character is actively using that style (i.e., the character is attacking using the martial arts style). If a player decides to not use his Martial Arts Style skill to attack, none of the benefits of the martial arts style can be used. See Section 14.2.1 for further discussion.

◆ 9.2 ◆
CREATING A
MARTIAL ARTS STYLE

Gamemasters are encouraged to create their own martial arts styles for use in their games. The rules and guidelines detailed here will help to make the process easier and more game-balanced. Martial arts styles are created using a point-based system. These points are referred to as style points and they are only used during the creation of the Martial Arts Style skill. After a martial arts style is created, it will either be classified as a Basic or Advanced Martial Arts Style skill (based on its total style point cost).

• Basic Martial Arts Style skills range from 0 to 30 style points.

• Advanced Martial Arts Style skills range from 31 to up to 60 style points. It is not advised to create a martial arts style that uses more than 60 style points.

STEPS OF CREATION

The first step in creating a martial arts style is deciding what types of martial arts attacks will be available in the style. The martial arts style can be based on several different degrees of martial arts attacking techniques. The more techniques that a martial arts style encompasses, the more expensive the martial arts style will be to learn. Section 9.3 provides some examples of created martial arts styles.

9.2.1 · STANDARD OPTIONS

This section presents a series of charts that show the costs for the various standard options that are available. If a cost shows as a dash ("—"), that option may not be selected.

BASE COST
MARTIAL ARTS STYLE COST
0 points ..... Allow up to 2 degrees of attacks [maximum damage threshold of Degree 2]
5 points ..... Allow up to 5 degrees of attacks [maximum damage threshold of Degree 3]
10 points ... Allow up to 7 degrees of attacks [maximum damage threshold of Degree 4]
20 points ... Allow up to 11 degrees of attacks [maximum damage threshold of Degree 4]

The degree thresholds may be associated with any of the following skills: Martial Arts Striking, Martial Arts Sweeping, Nerve Strikes, and Locking Holds (in any combination; so if a character is taking 7 degrees of attacks, he could take 4 in Martial Arts Striking, 2 in Martial Arts Sweeping, and 1 in Locking Holds). The damage threshold for Nerve Strikes must be less than or equal to the damage threshold for Martial Arts Striking and the damage thresholds for Locking Holds must also be less than or equal to the damage thresholds for Martial Arts Sweeping. The martial arts attacks are cumulative, so if a player wishes to allow Degree 3 Martial Arts Striking attacks he can also use the Degree 1 and Degree 2 damage thresholds if he wishes.

Optional Rule [Core]: If the Gamemaster desires, he can allow a player to receive a special +5 modification to OB for each damage threshold below the maximum for his style that he decides to use in an attack.

COST FOR
MODIFYING INITIATIVE ROLLS
5 points ..... +1 initiative bonus
10 points ... +2 initiative bonus
15 points ... +4 initiative bonus

COST FOR
BONUS TO SPECIAL ATTACKS
5 points ..... +5 OB to one Special Attacks skill
10 points ... +10 OB to one Special Attacks skill

COST FOR
BONUS TO SELF CONTROL
5 points ..... +10 bonus to one Self Control skill
10 points ... +15 bonus to one Self Control skill

COST FOR
BONUS TO NON-RESTRICTED SKILLS
5 points ..... +5 bonus to one specific skill that is not classified as Restricted (excluding skills in the Special Defenses skill category)
10 points ... +10 bonus to one specific skill that is not classified as Restricted (excluding skills in the Special Defenses skill category)

COST FOR
BONUS TO RESTRICTED SKILLS
[10] .... +5 bonus to one specific skill that is classified as Restricted.
[15] .... +10 bonus to one specific skill that is classified as Restricted.

9.2.2 · ADRENAL DEFENSE OPTIONS

This list shows options that are available when "building" martial arts styles that use the Adrenal Defense skill. All the advantages gained from these options are only available when a character is using his martial arts style. The style point cost is shown in brackets ("[]" after each entry).

Adrenal Defense, Greater—The martial artist has specialized in integrating his Adrenal Defense techniques within his martial arts style. The martial artist may ignore restrictions for objects in his hands while using Adrenal Defense if he is using weapons associated with this martial arts style. In addition, an Adrenal Defense maneuver only requires 10% activity and it does not count against the three actions per round limit (though he must still allocate no more than 100% activity to all of his actions). [20 points]

Adrenal Defense, Lesser—The martial artist has specialized in integrating his martial arts attacks within his Adrenal Defense techniques. The martial artist may ignore restrictions for objects in his hands while using Adrenal Defense if he is using weapons associated with this martial arts style. Additionally, an Adrenal Defense maneuver only requires 30% activity and it does not count against the three actions per round limit (though he must still allocate no more than 100% activity to all of his actions). [10 points]

9.2.3 · SPECIAL OPTIONS

This list shows special options that are available when "building" martial arts styles. All the advantages gained from these options are only available when a character is using his martial arts style. The style point cost is shown in brackets ("[]" after each entry).

Additional Strike—The martial artist can make an additional martial arts strike during his attack action. The cost for this option varies according to the highest damage threshold in the martial arts style. A Degree 1 attack costs 5 style points, a Degree 2 attack costs 10 style points, a Degree 3 attack costs 15 style points, and a Degree 4 attack costs 20 style points. Each of the restrictions listed below must be followed to use this ability. [5, 10, 15, or 20 points]

#1) The OB for both strikes is the lesser of the Martial Arts Style skill OB or the martial arts attack skill OB used in either strike.

#2) If the martial artist attacks one opponent with both attacks, there no modification to either attack.

#3) If the martial artist attempts to attack two separate opponents, each attack suffers a -20 to the attack roll. The martial artist may attack two separate opponents as long as neither is receiving any positional bonus (note that the All-Around Attack ability can eliminate this requirement).

#4) If the martial artist decides to parry or attempt a special attack, he must reduce that OB for each attack by the amount of OB dedicated to his parry or special attack. Against one opponent, a parry simply increases his DB, against two opponents he may split his parry as he sees fit.

All-Around Attack—The martial artist can make attacks against foes who have a positional modifier (such as flank or rear) against him without changing his facing or position. The OB is penalized by double the positional bonus of the opponent (i.e., attacking a foe to the rear you results in a –50 OB modifier). [10 points]

All-Around Defense—The weapon stylist can choose to negate one positional bonus that a foe has against him during a combat round by taking a 10% action. [10 points]

Weapon Kata—The martial artist can use a weapon with his martial arts style. A weapon kata represents a weapon attack that is taught as part of the martial arts style attack. The martial artist uses either his Martial Arts Style skill OB or his martial arts attack skill OB, whichever is the lesser of the two, with an additional -20 modifier as his total OB using the weapon. The martial arts style must include at least a Degree 2 martial arts attack skill to include this option (Degree 3 if the weapon requires two hands to wield or if the kata uses two-weapons kata or paired weapon kata). The martial artist uses the normal fumble range for his weapon while he is using the weapon kata (unless modified by the martial arts style). The weapon's normal attack table is used to determine the result of the strike (instead of the martial arts attack tables). Any criticals delivered are the determined normally for the weapon. Refer to Section 9.2.4 for more options for weapon katas. [5 points]

9.2.4 · WEAPON KATA OPTIONS

These options only apply if the martial arts style has the Weapon Kata option and while the martial artist is using his weapon along with martial arts style. These options do not apply to normal unarmed attacks made with a martial arts style incorporating weapon katas. The style point cost is shown in brackets "[]" after each entry.

COST FOR REDUCING FUMBLE RANGE

5 points ..... Reduce fumble range by 1

10 points ... Reduce fumble range by 2

Note: Fumble ranges cannot be reduced by 01-02 with this option.

COST FOR MODIFYING CRITICAL ROLLS

15 points ... ±1 to the critical roll.

30 points ... ±2 to the critical roll.

Note: Modification is chosen by the attacker after the critical roll is made.

SPECIAL WEAPON KATA OPTIONS

Two-weapon Kata—The martial artist has learned how to fight with paired weapons while using his weapon katas. Both weapons must be included as weapon katas for the martial arts style being used. In addition, the martial artist must abide by all restrictions for two-weapon combat. [15 points]

#1) The OB for each weapon kata attack is the lesser of the Martial Arts Style skill OB or the martial arts attacking skill OB. The -20 modifier to OB due to weapon katas still applies.

#2) There is no modification for attempting two attacks against the same opponent.

#3) If the martial artist attempts to attack two separate opponents there is an additional -20 modifier to both attack rolls. The martial artist may attack two separate opponents as long as neither is receiving any positional bonus (note that the All-Around Attack ability can eliminate this requirement).

#4) If the martial artist decides to parry or attempt a special attack, he must reduce the OB for each attack by the amount of OB dedicated to his parry or special attack. Against one opponent, a parry simply increases his DB, against two opponents he may split his parry as he sees fit.

Paired Weapon Kata—The martial artist has trained to fight with identical paired weapons using his weapon kata. Unlike the Two-Weapon Kata option, this does not allow the martial artist two separate strikes; instead, the one attack is more lethal.

Any attack that delivers a critical will do an additional critical of two levels less severity (using the same dice roll). If the normal critical result is an 'A' critical, the secondary critical is treated as an 'A' critical modified by -40 (modified rolls less than zero result in no effect). If the normal critical result is a 'B' critical, the critical, the secondary critical is resolved as an 'A' critical modified by -20 (modified rolls less than zero result in no effect). The type of additional critical delivered should be determined by the GM (but is normally the most common type for the paired weapons). When fighting creatures that take Large or Super Large criticals, no additional critical is delivered. [5 points]

Weapon-Breaker—The martial artist has learned to incorporate special maneuvers into his attacks that are designed to cause his opponent's weapons to break. Any foe fighting the martial artist while the martial artist is using his weapon kata has his breakage numbers increased by one for the duration of the combat (e.g., if the weapon's breakage numbers are normally 1 through 5 they will be 1 through 6 while the foe is fighting the martial artist). The foe must also modify weapon strength rolls by –10. [10 points]

9.2.5 · SPECIAL MANEUVERS

Special maneuvers are a Heroic option for martial arts in his campaign. For each martial arts style, there can be a number of assorted special maneuvers reflecting special attacks, defenses, or techniques associated with the particular martial arts style. The creation of special maneuvers is left to the Gamemaster's imagination, but a few caveats should apply.

For Basic Martial Arts Styles, there should be at most one special maneuver available. For Advanced Martial Arts Styles, there should be no more than three special maneuvers available. Including too many special maneuvers in a martial arts style will tend to dilute the focus of the style, and impose unnecessary bookkeeping on both the Gamemaster and players. Special maneuvers should add uniqueness and flavor to a martial arts style, but not overshadow it.

If a special maneuver has an effect that is similar or better than an already existing skill, it should be balanced in one of two ways. Either the special maneuver should rely on the bonus of the similar skill, or it should have a more limited applicability.

◆ 9.3 ◆
EXAMPLE
MARTIAL ARTS STYLES

Here are some martial arts styles that illustrate how martial arts styles may be developed. While these styles draw inspiration from actual martial arts styles, they are only approximate models of historical systems. For a historical evolution of martial arts styles, please see Section 2.0.

The format of the each martial arts style example is as follows:

• Name of Martial Arts Style

• Whether the martial arts style is Basic or Advanced, followed by the total style points used to create the weapon style (in brackets, "[]").

SAMPLE MARTIAL ARTS STYLES		
MA Style Name	**Type of MA Style Skill**	**Total Style Point Cost**
Chinese Martial Arts Styles		
Choy Lee Fut Style	Basic Martial Arts Style	25
Cobra Style	Basic Martial Arts Style	30
Cotton Fist Style	Basic Martial Arts Style	10
Crane Style	Advanced Martial Arts Style	55
Dragon Style	Advanced Martial Arts Style	60
Eight Drunken Fairies	Advanced Martial Arts Style	40
Hsing-i Style	Advanced Martial Arts Style	35
King Cobra Style	Basic Martial Arts Style	25
Iron Robe Style	Advanced Martial Arts Style	50
Monkey Style	Basic Martial Arts Style	30
Pa Kua Chu'an Style	Advanced Martial Arts Style	50
Praying Mantis Style	Advanced Martial Arts Style	55
Snake Style	Advanced Martial Arts Style	60
Tiger Style	Basic Martial Arts Style	30
Two Instruments Style	Basic Martial Arts Style	30
Wing Chun Style	Basic Martial Arts Style	15
Indonesian Martial Arts Styles		
Baru Pentjak-Silat	Basic Martial Arts Style	25
Harmimau Pentjak-Silat	Basic Martial Arts Style	30
Kumango Pentjak-Silat	Basic Martial Arts Style	30
Japanese Martial Arts Styles		
Ju-jutsu	Basic Martial Arts Style	15
Nin-jutsu	Basic Martial Arts Style	30
Sumai	Basic Martial Arts Style	25
Korean Martial Arts Styles		
Hwarang-do	Advanced Martial Arts Style	60
Tae Kwon Do	Basic Martial Arts Style	30
Okinawan Martial Arts Styles		
Karate	Basic Martial Arts Style	30
European Martial Arts Styles		
Savate	Basic Martial Arts Style	15

• A description of the martial arts style's origins and history follows this information. Also included are some of the more common combat techniques that the style uses.

• A list of skills that a character will probably want to develop along with this martial arts style. These skills are not "required" but will probably be desired to take full advantage of the style.

• A breakdown of the abilities and costs for the martial arts style (costs are shown in brackets, "[]"). The abilities are listed as "Core" because they define the style and should be used with all power levels.

• Finally, any special maneuvers or techniques used by the martial arts style are listed as well as any special skills that might be learnt by practitioners of the martial arts style. These abilities should only be used in games of Heroic or Fantastic power levels.

9.3.1 · CHINESE MARTIAL ARTS STYLES

The Chinese martial arts have a rich history of excellence. The introduction in Section 2.0 as well as the historical information on Chinese martial arts in Section 2.1 serve as a good background for this section. If desired some of the style points ranges for Chinese martial arts styles may be changed from the original ranges given for the skills in Section 9.1.

Optional Rule [Core]: When designing Chinese martial arts styles, Basic Martial Arts Styles range from 0 to 35 style points and Advanced Martial Arts Styles range from 36 to 60 style points.

CHOY LEE FUT STYLE
(SOUTHERN EXTERNAL STYLE)

Basic Martial Arts Style [25 style points]

Description—The Choy Lee Fut style was developed during the nineteenth century in China. It started as primarily a Southern style and it later spread to Northern China. This style was originally taught to secret rebel societies trying to overthrow the Manchu Dynasty in the nineteenth century. Therefore this style was developed with a desire to teach the basics of martial arts to its students in the shortest possible amount of time. The Choy Lee Fut style focuses on aggressive punching and kicking attacks until the opponent is conquered. This style uses long-range attacks to defeat foes quickly. It is best known for its knuckle jabs, uppercuts, and roundhouse swings. High and low kicks are used, as well as several types of kicks with 360 degree spins are featured as well. The Choy Lee Fut stylist tries to throw an opponent off-balance by moving directly at him all the while throwing hard strikes. Many of the moves of a fighter using this martial art look strikingly similar to techniques of Western boxing. See Section 2.1 for more information on the historical development of Chinese martial arts.

Recommended Skills—Martial Arts Striking, Martial Arts Sweeping, Adrenal Defense

Martial Arts Abilities [Core]—Lesser Adrenal Defense [10 points]; Degree 3 Martial Arts Striking attacks and Degree 2 Martial Arts Sweeping attacks [5 points]; +2 to initiative rolls [10 points]

Special Maneuvers—None

COBRA STYLE
(SOUTHERN INTERNAL STYLE)

Basic Martial Arts Style [30 style points]

Description—The Cobra style is an ancient Chinese martial art. It is designed to be totally defensive in nature, modeled after a cobra lying in the grass. A master of the Cobra style will not execute acrobatic defensive maneuvers; rather he will expend as little energy as possible to avoid attacks. Most attacks against the stylist will be sidestepped rather than blocked directly. The attacks of the Cobra stylist are relentless and deadly when they are finally executed. These quick and deadly attacks are focused on the eyes and throat with hand strikes. It is said that Cobra stylists have developed deadly dim mak techniques that allow them to kill or maim with merely a touch.

The basic stance of the Cobra style is a defensive one, with the adept keeping his stance low to the ground and raising his hands and arms near his chest. This position mimics a cobra rising from the ground with an outspread hood. A variant of the Cobra style is the King Cobra style. See Section 2.1 for more information on the historical development of Chinese martial arts.

Recommended Skills—Martial Arts Striking, Adrenal Defense, Contortions, Nerve Strikes

Martial Arts Abilities [Core]—Lesser Adrenal Defense [10 points]; Degree 3 Martial Arts Striking attacks and Degree 2 Nerve Strikes attacks [5 points]; +10 OB bonus to all Feint maneuvers [5 points]; +1 to initiative rolls [5 points]; Dagger weapon kata [5 points]

Special Abilities—This style has a signature attack (the Strike of the Cobra). In addition, if the GM is allowing Chi Power skills, this style allows access to Chi Power: Distance Strike.

Strike of the Cobra—*The Cobra style teaches the martial artist to strike without mercy when his foe is hurt. If the Cobra stylist inflicts a critical against his opponent, he gains a special +10 bonus (non-cumulative) to his OB for his next attack against that same opponent.*

COTTON FIST STYLE
(NORTHERN INTERNAL STYLE)

Basic Martial Arts Style [10 style points]

Description—The Cotton Fist style is a northern style of Chinese kung fu. The name of this martial art conveys weakness, softness and slowness. This style is taught to its students very slowly. A saying about this style is "Cotton Fist, ten years stay at home," means that a student will need to practice for ten years to be able to defend himself. The cotton fist emphasizes soft training and perfection of movement. While this style is not perfect for the goal of self-defense, it is important in teaching the mental aspects of martial arts.

Recommended Skills—Martial Arts Sweeping, Adrenal Defense, Meditation

Martial Arts Abilities [Core]—Lesser Adrenal Defense [10 points]; Degree 2 Martial Arts Sweeping attack [0 points]

Special Abilities—If the GM is allowing Chi Power skills, this style should allow access to either Chi Powers: Falling Leaf or Chi Powers: Sticking Hands.

CRANE STYLE
(SOUTHERN EXTERNAL STYLE)

Advanced Martial Arts Style [55 style points]

Description—The Crane style is an ancient Chinese martial art whose movements originally were formed to develop both muscular control and spiritual strength. The Crane style emphasizes rapid footwork and evasive techniques, coupled with relentless attacks. While the Crane style is considered to be the most beautiful of all Chinese Kung Fu martial arts styles, it is also one of the most complex with over ten thousand movements contained in ten basic form sets.

Folklore states that the Crane style was developed after a monk observed a fight between an ape and a white crane. Initially the monk expected the ape with its greater physical strength to easily crush the crane. But the white crane managed to avoid the powerful attacks of the ape and inflict accurate painful blows with its beak. The crane maintained its perfect composure as it used its short wings for balance and the long-range attack of its beak against the larger ape. Finally the ape retreated back to the forest after being severely hurt and the unharmed white crane resumed the protection of its eggs.

In combat, the Crane stylist will almost arrogantly disdain any physical contact with an opponent, instead opting for a single fierce blow, usually delivered from long range. The elusive footwork of the Crane stylist serves to help him avoid the attacks of his opponent. In most cases, a forceful opponent will be thrown off balance by such evasion as he strikes air. Once the opponent has lost his balance by missing his target, the Crane stylist will be ready to strike at the weakest point exposed by his off-balance foe. If a Crane stylist instead chose to physically block an incoming attack with strength, his foe could use the block to stabilize himself and deliver an immediate counter-attack. By concentrating on avoiding blows, the Crane stylist can rob an opponent of his trained block and counter-punch techniques.

The basic stance of the Crane style is the royal pecking form. The Crane stylist raises both arms up parallel to his body and forms the shape of a crane's beak with his hands. One foot of the stylist is kept raised to quickly strike or block. This stance actually mimics the warning posture of the true white crane. Should the strike of a Crane stylist miss, he will always attempt to retreat and set up another long-range strike rather than close with his opponent and grapple. Variants of the Crane style are the Black Crane and the Imperial Crane styles. The Black Crane style emphasizes footwork and the basic hand and foot strikes while the Imperial Crane style emphasizes the use of weapons within the traditional Crane style. See Section 2.1 for more information on the historical development of Chinese martial arts.

Recommended Skills—Martial Arts Striking, Martial Arts Sweeping, Nerve Strikes, Adrenal Defense, Feint

Martial Arts Abilities [Core]—Greater Adrenal Defense [20 points]; Degree 4 Martial Arts Striking attacks, Degree 4 Martial Arts Sweeping attacks, and Degree 3 Nerve Strikes attacks [20 points]; +10 OB bonus to Feint maneuvers [10 points]; Broadsword weapon kata [5 points]

Special Abilities—This style has a special maneuver (Wading in the Reeds) and a special attack (Beak of the Crane). In addition, if the GM is allowing Chi Powers skills, this style allows access to either Chi Powers: No Shadow Attack or Chi Powers: Continuous Strikes.

> **Wading in the Reeds**—*The Crane stylist practices elusive footwork to prepare attacks. When an attack completely misses a Crane stylist (i.e., no hits or criticals are delivered), the stylist gains a special +15 modification to his OB if he chooses to attack the foe that missed in the next combat round.*

> **Beak of the Crane**—*The Crane stylist learns how to focus his energy to deliver punishing blows to his opponent. If the martial artist takes a 15% preparation action in a given round, he may attack during the following combat round with a special +15 modification to his OB.*

DRAGON STYLE
(NORTHERN INTERNAL STYLE)

Advanced Martial Arts Style [60 style points]

Description—The Dragon style is an ancient Chinese martial art originally designed to develop alertness and concentration. This martial arts style emphasizes controlled breathing with powerful attacking movements. The Dragon stylist uses flowing movements that explode into powerful strikes using entire force of his body. The Dragon style uses continuous advancing and retreating motions, like the movements of a serpent to prevent the opponent from landing a solid blow. The powerful hissing sound emitted by the stylist is a product of his concentrated breathing and focusing of energy.

The Dragon stylist trains his hands to have powerful grasping strength to grab or twist limbs with great force. The grip of an advanced Dragon stylist is said to be almost unbreakable. In addition, the legs are used to deliver powerful lashing kicks. The Dragon style emphasizes simultaneous attack and defense techniques during combat. While one hand is attacking, the other hand is held at guard, ready to grab or twist an attacker's incoming limb.

In defense, the Dragon stylist withdraws before a strike, absorbing its power and retaliating only when he believes his foe has over-extended himself. The dragon crouch is the basic blocking technique of the Dragon style. The stylist crouches low with his hands set in the dragon claw form and positioned in front of him. In all the varied forms of this style, the martial artist's eyes appear to look directly outward like the eyes of a reptile, no matter how much his head moves about. See Section 2.1 for more information on the historical development of Chinese martial arts.

Recommended Skills—Martial Arts Striking, Martial Arts Sweeping, Locking Holds, Adrenal Defense, Meditation

Martial Arts Abilities [Core]—Greater Adrenal Defense [20 points]; Degree 3 Martial Arts Sweeping attack, Degree 2 Locking Holds attack, Degree 2 Martial Arts Striking attack [10 points]; Quarterstaff weapon kata [5 points]; Metal whip weapon kata [5 points]; Broadsword weapon kata [5 points]; Reduce weapon fumble range by 2 for all kata weapons (to minimum fumble range of 01-02) [10 points]; +10 bonus to all Adrenal Strength maneuvers [5 points]

Special Abilities—This style has two special attacks (Lash of the Dragon and Claws of the Dragon). In addition, all Adrenal Strength maneuvers only take a 10% preparation action. Finally, if the GM is allowing Chi Power skills, this style should allow access to either Chi Powers: Cloth Lance, Chi Powers: Fists of Iron, or Chi Powers: Resist Pain.

Lash of the Dragon—*By rapidly spinning a length of cloth (at least a six-foot length of cloth), the Dragon stylist can attack on the Whip Attack Table with a -20 modification to his normal OB.*

Claws of the Dragon—*The Dragon stylist can choose to attack on the Medium Claw Attack Table instead of his normal Martial Arts Striking Attack Table. The martial artist suffers a special –20 modifier to his OB while using the Medium Claw Attack Table and the Martial Artist must use the lesser of his Martial Arts Striking skill OB or his Dragon style skill OB for the attack.*

EIGHT DRUNKEN FAIRIES
(NORTHERN EXTERNAL STYLE)

Advanced Martial Arts Style [40 style points]

Description—The Eight Drunken Fairies or Drunken Boxing style is a very deceptive martial arts style. While using the techniques of the Drunken Boxing style, the martial artist appears to stagger and lurch without any control over his body. In actuality, the martial artist is in complete control of himself at all times during this display. The apparently uncontrolled movements of the adept of this style serve to distract and bewilder his opponent, allowing the martial artist to strike unexpectedly.

The Drunken Boxing style uses equal amounts of striking and locking attacks. Many of the striking techniques involve punching, but some unique kicks are included as well. It is difficult to master without superb balance and coordination, but it is a quite effective style in combat.

Recommended Skills—Adrenal Defense, Martial Arts Striking, Martial Arts Sweeping, Adrenal Strength

Martial Arts Abilities [Core]—Greater Adrenal Defense [20 points]; Degree 3 Martial Arts Striking attacks and Degree 2 Martial Arts Sweeping attacks [5 points]; +1 to all initiative rolls [5 points]; +15 bonus to Adrenal Strength maneuvers [10 points]

Special Abilities—This style has a special attack (the Drunken Fist) and a special defense (the Drunken Stagger). In addition, all Adrenal Strength maneuvers only take a 10% preparation action (this does not affect the Drunken Fist attack). Finally, if the GM is allowing Chi Power skills, this style should allow access to either Chi Powers: Rise of the Phoenix, Chi Powers: Fists of Iron, or Chi Powers: Resist Pain.

Drunken Fist—*By focusing his internal energy and striking an opponent, a master of the Drunken Boxing style can do triple normal concussion damage to his foe. To successfully accomplish this feat, a special Adrenal Strength maneuver must be made with a 40% preparation action. If the maneuver is successful, the next round the martial artist can attack with a +10 OB modifier and do triple concussion damage.*

Drunken Stagger—*By moving in unpredictable patterns, an adept of the Drunken Boxing style learns how to launch unexpected attacks against his opponent. If an adept takes a special -20 modifier to his OB, his attack happens in such an unexpected manner that his opponent will lose half of his DB against the attack.*

HSING-I STYLE
(NORTHERN EXTERNAL STYLE)

Advanced Martial Arts Style [35 style points]

Description—The Hsing-i style is an ancient Chinese martial art that has also been called Hsing-i Lu-ho Ch'uan or I Ch'uan. Most records suggest that Hsing-i was created in the mid-sixteenth century in Shanghai, China. Hsing-i is composed of five basic movements. Beyond these basic five movements, Hsing-i has an additional twelve sets of movements based on animals—Dragon, Tiger, Monkey, Horse, Water-skimmer (insect), Cock, Hawk, Snake, Eagle, Bear, Swallow, and Leopard. Hsing-i uses linear movements with strong fundamental balance. When attacking, an adept strikes like a wave crashing on the shore—rising, striking, falling, and overturning.

The five basic postures correspond to the five basic elements in Chinese philosophy—fire, water, metal, wood, and earth. The fire stance is an explosive posture from which attacks can be launched with either hand or foot. The metal stance is defensive and can be used easily to block an opponent's attack. The water stance is a very stable, wide stance in which the adept can attack with his fists. The wood stance is a very low stance that is flexible enough for the adept both to be protected from attack and able to attack. The earth stance is a wide stance that allows the adept to deflect attacks easily.

The practitioner of Hsing-i uses punches, low strikes, and stances similar to those of the Shaolin hard martial arts. Like the hard schools of martial arts, the student is also taught to advance in a straight line; however, the Hsing-i body posture is unusual, as the shoulders are kept rounded and many low stances are used. In this martial arts style, blocking is through circular motions that seek to deflect incoming attacks rather than directly opposing them. In addition, the practitioner mimics the actions of an animal much more closely than in hard schools that are based on animal attacks. The true master of Hsing-i learns how to see into the forms of the various animal styles and grasp their essences. This intuition can then be used to read the intent of the opponent. At the highest level of mastery, the Hsing-i stylist will be free of form and thought and be able to react instinctively to any threat. This state of mind is called "no form, no meaning."

There exist several similar branches of this style that espouse philosophic and stylistic differences. The Wang Hsiang-chai branch teaches that the postures are not as important as the focus of the will. The Sun Lu-t'ang branch simplifies and merges many of the basic movements and forms to provide a less complicated martial art. See Section 2.1 for more information on the historical development of Chinese martial arts.

Recommended Skills—Martial Arts Striking, Martial Arts Sweeping, Locking Holds skill, Adrenal Defense, Adrenal Speed, Meditation

Martial Arts Abilities [Core]—Lesser Adrenal Defense [10 points]; Degree 3 Martial Arts Striking attack, Degree 3 Martial Arts Sweeping attack, and Degree 1 Locking Holds attack [10 points]; +15 bonus to Adrenal Speed [10 points]; +1 to initiative [5 points]

Special Abilities—This style has a special technique (State of No Mind). In addition, all Adrenal Speed maneuvers only take a 10% preparation action. Finally, if the GM is allowing, Chi Power skills, this style should allow access to either Chi Powers: Light Feet, Chi Powers: Sense Weakness, or Chi Powers: Fantastic Leap.

> **State of No Mind**—*The Hsing-i stylist learns how to anticipate the attacks of his opponents. Any successful Martial Arts Style Lore or Weapon Style Lore static maneuver results in twice the normal combat bonus (because of the stylist's superior ability to read the intentions of his attackers).*

KING COBRA STYLE
(NORTHERN EXTERNAL STYLE)

Basic Martial Arts Style [25 style points]

Description—The King Cobra style is a variant style of the Cobra style (see above). The unarmed attacks and movements of this fighting system are very similar to the Cobra style. Where the King Cobra style differs is in its heavier reliance on weapons. This style also teaches its students how to prepare and use poisons (such as snake venom) in combat to disable their foes. Throwing knives and daggers are often used by adepts of this martial arts style.

Recommended Skills—Adrenal Defense, Martial Arts Striking, Martial Arts Sweeping, Thrown Dagger attack skill, Poison Lore, Using/Removing Poison

Martial Arts Abilities [Core]—Lesser Adrenal Defense [10 points]; Degree 3 Martial Arts Striking attacks and Degree 2 Nerve Strikes attacks [5 points]; Dagger weapon kata [5 points]; Paired-weapon dagger kata [5 points]

Special Abilities—This style has a special attack (the Spit of the Cobra). In addition, if the GM is allowing Chi Power skills, this style allows access to Chi Powers: Poison Fist.

> **Spit of the Cobra**—*The King Cobra stylist learns how to integrate his thrown weapon attacks into his martial art. The stylist can make an additional thrown weapon attack during his normal attacking action if he has a weapon ready. This additional attack would be subject to all the normal restrictions outlined in the "Additional Thrown Weapon Attack" option profiled in Section 8.2 under One Hand Free Options.*

IRON ROBE STYLE
(NORTHERN EXTERNAL STYLE)

Advanced Martial Arts Style [50 style points]

Description—The Iron Robe martial arts style is a very disciplined and difficult style to learn. The student spends many years learning how strengthen his body against attacks from all directions and ignore pain. This style of martial arts requires the student to subject himself to intense physical pain to learn how to control his reactions and still function in combat. Offensively this style relies on strong hand and foot attacks, and very few locking or throwing techniques are used. Adepts of this style rely upon their defensive skills and the ability to outlast their opponents to win challenges.

The name of this style comes from the ability of the adept to absorb blows that would seriously injure or even kill an unarmed man. An adept of the iron robe style does not fear weapons and would never resort to armor, as it would imply that he did not think his martial arts abilities were enough to protect himself from harm.

Recommended Skills—Martial Arts Striking, Martial Arts Sweeping, Adrenal Defense, Adrenal Strength, Stunned Maneuvering, and Chi Power: Resist Pain (if Chi Powers skills are used)

Martial Arts Abilities [Core]—Lesser Adrenal Defense [10 points]; Degree 4 Martial Arts Striking attacks and Degree 3 Martial Arts Sweeping attacks [10 points]; +15 bonus to Stunned Maneuvering [10 points]; +10 bonus to Adrenal Strength [5 points]; +10 bonus to Adrenal Toughness [15 points]

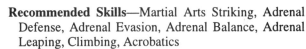

Special Abilities—This style has a special maneuver (Inner Air) and a special attack (the Toppling Kick). In addition, all Adrenal Strength and Adrenal Toughness maneuvers take only a 10% preparation activity to use (this has no effect on the Inner Air maneuver). Finally, if the GM is allowing Chi Power skills, the style should allow either the Chi Powers: Invincible Stance, Chi Powers: Invulnerability, or Chi Powers: Rise of the Phoenix skills.

Inner Air—*With a successful Adrenal Toughness maneuver using a 40% preparation action, the Iron Robe adept may reduce any one critical by two levels. An 'A' critical is resolved as an 'A' critical with a special modification of -40 (with modified rolls of less than 01 resulting in no extra damage). A 'B' critical is resolved as an 'A' critical with a special modification of -20 (with modified rolls of less than 01 resulting in no extra damage).*

Toppling Kick—*The Iron Robe stylist can attack with a unique spinning kick that rises from the ground to strike an opponent. The stylist gains a special +2 modifier to initiative if he uses this attack, but he must also suffer a special -10 modifier to his OB.*

MONKEY STYLE
(SOUTHERN EXTERNAL STYLE)

Basic Martial Arts Style [30 style points]

Description—The Monkey style is a Chinese martial art that traces its origins back to the early twentieth century in Peking, China. It is said that the Monkey style was created when Kua See, Chinese fighting expert, killed an officer when he resisted being drafted into the Manchu army. Kua See surrendered to police and was placed in jail in Peking. At that time, Chinese authorities used monkeys as "watchdogs." If a prisoner broke out, the monkeys sounded a loud chattering alarm that alerted the prison guards. Kua See began to study the movements of his simian jailers over the course of his ten years of imprisonment and ended up designing a fighting style.

The appearance of the Monkey style is very deceptive. It appears comical at times, but is actually an extremely effective martial arts style. The Monkey style specializes in attacking from the ground using techniques that are physically very demanding. A Monkey stylist learns how to handle falls and unleash powerful kicks from a prone position. Spinning and twisting movements are used to conceal the a target of an attack. Hand attacks are modeled after the clawing and scratching hand attacks of a monkey. Unlike many Chinese martial arts, the Monkey style uses very low defensive crouches to avoid attacks and aggressive leaps when attacking.

The Monkey style uses a basic defensive stance in which the stylist is ready to roll away from attacks against him. Several different variants of the Monkey style exist: Stone Monkey style, Wooden Monkey style, and Drunken Monkey style. Of the three, the Drunken Monkey style is the most exotic. In the Drunken Monkey style the practitioner fakes drunken staggers and weaves, all the while ready to unleash a surprise attack. See Section 2.1 for more information on the development of Chinese martial arts.

Recommended Skills—Martial Arts Striking, Adrenal Defense, Adrenal Evasion, Adrenal Balance, Adrenal Leaping, Climbing, Acrobatics

Martial Arts Abilities [Core]—Greater Adrenal Defense [20 points]; Degree 2 Martial Arts Striking attacks [0 points]; +10 bonus to Adrenal Evasion maneuvers [10 points]

Special Abilities—This style has two special maneuvers (the Monkey's Leap and the Monkey's Evasion). Also, if the GM is allowing Chi Power skills, this style allows either the Chi Powers: Fantastic Leap, Chi Powers: Leaping Strike, or Chi Powers: Lizard's Climb skill.

Monkey's Leap—*The Monkey stylist can attack while leaping towards or away from his foe. The result of this maneuver is that the Monkey may also position himself up to 10' away, suffering only a -20 modifier to his OB. A Monkey stylist could use this maneuver to attack and then scale a wall for instance. If the maneuver is successful, the stylist's DB is doubled against one foe.*

Monkey's Evasion—*With a successful Adrenal Evasion maneuver against an attacker, the Monkey stylist gains a +15 flank positional bonus for his next round if he so desires (this is in addition to the normal benefits gained from Adrenal Evasion). The stylist can gain this positional bonus on any target within normal attack range when he starts his Adrenal Evasion maneuver. The Monkey stylist can also choose as a result of this maneuver to position himself up to 10' away from one opponent.*

PA KUA CHU'AN STYLE
(SOUTHERN INTERNAL STYLE)

Advanced Martial Arts Style [50 style points]

Description—The Pa Kua Chu'an style is an ancient Chinese martial arts style. The name of the style literally means the "eight trigrams." Legend holds that an emperor of China, Fu His (2,953-2,838 BC), invented the eight symbolic trigrams after pondering the scarred markings on the back of a tortoise shell. These trigrams were later incorporated into the I Ching. The eight trigrams figuratively express the evolution of nature and its cyclical changes – representing heaven, earth, metal, wood, water, fire, soil, and man. The Pa Kua stylist attains mastery of his art through the practice of the eight fundamental postures of the martial arts style. These postures are based on an ingenious inspiration of applying various animal forms to the eight trigrams. Each fundamental posture demonstrates the key actions of the dragon, snake, stork, hawk, lion, monkey, and bear.

Just as life's expressions are found in the eight trigrams of the I Ching, a Pa Kua adept asserts that all possible bodily movements are found within the eight fundamental postures. This is practiced by "walking the circle," the principle exercise leading to the perfection of Pa Kua Ch'uan. This martial art does not contain specific fighting techniques like most other martial arts styles. Instead, Pa Kua Ch'uan is a system of defense designed to avoid aggression though constant movement. The master may perform elusive circular gyrations that allow him to circle behind his attacker for a fraction of a second, sufficient time to fell his attacker with a single blow of the palm. The stylist's internal energy is focused into his palm strike, enough to stun even the most hardy foe.

The chief stance of this style involves "walking the circle." The Pa Kua stylist uses his footwork to walk and rotate his body while going through the complicated hand movements of the style. Fighting a skilled practitioner of this style can be very bewildering as your opponent will seem to spin away out of your field of vision before you can strike him. See Section 2.1 for more information on the development of Chinese martial arts.

Recommended Skills—Martial Arts Striking, Nerve Strikes, Adrenal Defense, Subduing, Meditation

Martial Arts Abilities [Core]—Greater Adrenal Defense [20 points]; Degree 4 Martial Arts Striking attack and Degree 3 Nerve Strikes attack [10 points]; All-Around Defense [10 points]; +10 OB bonus to Subduing attacks [10 points]

Special Abilities—This style has a special maneuver (Walking the Circle) and a special attack (Stunning Strike). Also, if the GM is allowing Chi Power skills, this style allows access to either the Chi Powers: Buddha's Palm or Chi Powers: Distance Strike.

Walking the Circle—*The Pa Kua adept continuously trains to avoid and sidestep blows. His elusive footwork allows him to negate positional bonus modifiers that foes have against him per combat round by taking a 10% activity action during the combat round. This ability can be used against up to two foes per round.*

Stunning Strike—*By focusing his energy into one precise blow, a Pa Kua stylist can stun an opponent. When attempting a Subduing attack, the stylist can receive a special +2 modification to a critical roll (if any).*

PRAYING MANTIS STYLE
(EXTERNAL STYLE)

Advanced Martial Arts Style [55 style points]

Description—The Praying Mantis style is a Chinese martial arts style said to be created 350 years ago by a Chinese fighting master named Wang Lang. The story goes that Wang Lang was a skilled fighter who traveled to the Shaolin Temple to challenge its monks in combat but he suffered several humiliating defeats at the hands of the monks. While he was mediating upon his failures, he observed a fragile-looking praying mantis engaged in combat with a much larger cicada. Wang decided to capture the insect and use its defensive and offensive movements as the basis for a new fighting style. Wang observed that the insect could defend itself from attacks from all directions. Armed with his bewildering array of insect moves, Wang overwhelmingly defeated the senior monks of the Shaolin Temple. Wang's Praying Mantis school of martial arts became one of the most prominent schools of martial arts in China during his lifetime.

The Praying Mantis style is a very effective close-combat fighting style. A Praying Mantis stylist does not attempt long-range attacks against his foe, instead he remains in a defensive position until he has closed the distance to his foe. The style teaches the practitioner to launch powerful short-range blows with little preparation or room for motion. Like many Chinese martial arts, the Praying Mantis adept always keeps one hand free to defend at all times. There are few pure blocking movements in the Praying Mantis style. The stylist is taught to strike at an incoming limb while deflecting it or to rely upon elusive footwork to avoid the blow. Once the stylist has closed with his foe, he can then unleash a devastating series of short-range blows. The style primarily uses elbow and hand strikes since these types of attacks are very effective in close quarters. Some waist high kicks are also taught, but they are not primary attacks in of this style.

The on-guard position of the Praying Mantis style mimics the actual insect's fighting position, with the hands resembling the poised feelers. The original Praying Mantis style is called the Seven Stars style (so named for its footwork pattern). Variants of the original style are the Six Harmonies style that incorporates softer and more circular movements, and the Eight Steps style, which alters the footwork pattern of the original style. See Section 2.1 for more information on the historical development of Chinese martial arts.

Recommended Skills—Martial Arts Striking, Martial Arts Sweeping, Locking Holds, Adrenal Defense, Adrenal Speed

Martial Arts Abilities [Core]—Greater Adrenal Defense [20 points]; Degree 3 Martial Arts Striking attack, Degree 2 Martial Arts Sweeping attack, and Degree 2 Locking Holds attack [10 points]; +10 bonus to Adrenal Speed maneuvers [5 points]; Three-sectioned staff weapon kata [5 points]; Broadsword weapon kata [5 points]

Special Abilities—This style has a special attack (the Mantis Punch) and a special defense (Stance of the Mantis). In addition, any Adrenal Speed maneuvers only take a 10% preparation action. Finally, if the GM is allowing Chi Power skills, this style allows access to either the Chi Powers: Sticking Touch or Chi Powers: No Shadow Attack skills.

Mantis Punch—*The Praying Mantis adept learns how to focus his energy to deliver several precise strikes within one punching attack. The result of this attack is that the opponent will also take an Unbalancing critical of two levels less severity than any critical inflicted by an attack table (same roll). While using this ability, a special modifier of -20 is applied to the OB of the Mantis stylist (to represent the increased control and focus required for executing this technique successfully).*

Stance of the Mantis—*The Praying Mantis stylist learns how to use his martial arts expertise to maneuver and attack in very close confined spaces. The stylist suffers half the normal penalty for fighting within a cramped or enclosed space (see Section 14.6). In addition, as a result of this close inward stance, all Martial Arts Sweeping attacks against the martial artist suffer an additional -20 modifier due to the stylist's understanding of stances.*

SNAKE STYLE
(SOUTHERN EXTERNAL STYLE)

Advanced Martial Arts Style [60 style points]

Description—The Snake style is an ancient Chinese martial art originally developed to help practitioners develop endurance and concentration. It is also an effective fighting art. The Snake style emphasizes controlled breathing and flowing movements that incorporate elaborate finger and hand movements. The movements or forms of the Snake style actually resemble the motions of

a snake. In comparison to the Cobra style, the Snake style is much more expressive. The adept will coil his body and twist his arms to mimic the motions of the snake. Like the Cobra style, the main attack of the Snake style is hand attacks that strike at the weak points of an opponent, like the throat or eyes. The defensive postures also emphasize avoiding attacks rather than blocking.

When an attacker strikes at the Snake stylist, the Snake stylist is taught to strike the attacker's limb as it comes into range or to quickly sidestep the attack and deliver a pin-point strike of his own. A Snake stylist will almost never trade blows with an opponent. Rather he is taught to attack and retreat to avoid counterstrikes. There are several variants of the Snake style but common to all of these styles are precise strikes and twisting arm motions intended to disguise the true target of the attack.

Unlike flashier martial arts, there are few preparatory stances or threatening gestures in this style. Rather, the Snake stylist will avoid and sidestep attacks until an opportunity presents itself and then quickly and ferociously attack at a weak point. The lack of flamboyant or threatening moves in this martial arts style can be seen as a strength; a foe will not know what style of martial artist he is facing until it is most likely too late. See Section 2.1 for more information on the historical development of Chinese martial arts.

Recommended Skills—Martial Arts Striking, Nerve Strikes, Adrenal Defense, Contortions

Martial Arts Abilities [Core]—Greater Adrenal Defense [20 points]; Degree 4 Martial Arts Striking attacks and Degree 3 Nerve Strikes attacks [10 points]; Additional martial arts attack [20 points]; +1 to initiative [5 points]; Dagger weapon kata [5 points]

Special Abilities—This style has a special attack (Hidden Strike) and a special maneuver (Snake Rising from the Grass). Also, if the GM is allowing Chi Power skills, this style allows access to the Chi Powers: Poison Fist skill.

Hidden Strike—The Snake stylist has spent years learning how to disguise the true target of his attacks. If the martial artist has taken a 20% preparation action in the previous round, he may attempt to make a "Very Hard" static maneuver to mislead his opponent about the true target of his strike this round

(against another Snake stylist, the difficulty of this maneuver roll is "Absurd"). If successful, he will gain +6 initiative and +15 OB against the foe.

Snake Rising From the Grass—*The Snake stylist can use this maneuver to regain his feet from a prone position with only a 25% activity action. This maneuver is treated as a "Hard" Moving Maneuver. Failure means that the martial artist must expend the normal 50% activity action to regain his feet.*

TIGER STYLE
(SOUTHERN EXTERNAL STYLE)

Basic Martial Arts Style [30 style points]

Description—The Tiger style is an ancient Chinese martial art originally developed to strengthen the bones, tendons, and muscles. The Tiger style is a brutal attacking style that uses both powerful kicks and clawing motions. The Tiger stylist is taught to fight ferociously, attacking any unguarded portion of his opponent.

The Tiger style concentrates on hand attacks and powerful kicks. The main hand attack is called the claw of the tiger. The Tiger stylist also practices using his hands to disarm or hold his enemy's weapons to unleash powerful kicking attacks. These attacks emphasize strength and muscular tension in the martial artist.

The Tiger style uses an upright stance with the hands set in the claw of the tiger form. There are many variants of the Tiger style that have been developed throughout the years. Some of the most common variants are the Leopard style, White Tiger style, Imperial Tiger style, and Drunken Tiger style. See Section 2.1 for more information on the historical development of Chinese martial arts.

Recommended Skills—Martial Arts Striking, Martial Arts Sweeping, Adrenal Defense, Disarm Foe (Unarmed), Adrenal Strength

Martial Arts Abilities [Core]—Lesser Adrenal Defense [10 points]; Degree 3 Martial Arts Striking attack and Degree 2 Martial Arts Sweeping attack [5 points]; +10 bonus to Adrenal Strength maneuvers [5 points]; +10 OB bonus to Disarm Foe (1H-edged) maneuvers [10 points]

Special Abilities—This style has a special attack (Claw of the Tiger). In addition, all Adrenal Strength maneuvers only take a 10% preparation round. Finally, if the GM is allowing Chi Power skills, this style allows access to the Chi Powers: Leaping Strike and Chi Powers: Continuous Strikes skills.

Claw of the Tiger—*The Tiger stylist may choose to attack on the Claw Attack Table (with a Medium damage threshold) instead of the Martial Arts Striking Attack Table while attacking with this style. The martial artist suffers a special -20 modifier to his OB while using the Claw Attack Table and the Martial Artist must use the lesser of his Martial Arts Striking skill OB or his Tiger Martial Arts Style OB.*

TWO INSTRUMENTS BOXING
(NORTHERN INTERNAL STYLE)

Basic Martial Arts Style [30 style points]

Description—This martial art was developed in China and it takes its name from the mechanics it uses to attack. This martial art stresses the use of double attacks that use the

momentum and speed generated by each other to overwhelm the defenses of an opponent. The almost rhythmic nature of the timing of the strikes leads to the name of "Two Instruments" to describe this boxing style. Despite the very aggressive foundation behind the striking techniques used in this style, it remains an internal style that focuses on the use inner energy to provide power behind the blows. A skilled adept of this art can generate an exhausting array of attacks without seeming winded through the judicious use of his inner energy. Refer to Section 2.1 for more information on the historical development of Chinese martial arts.

Recommended Skills—Martial Arts Striking, Martial Arts Sweeping, Adrenal Defense

Martial Arts Abilities [Core]—Lesser Adrenal Defense [10 points]; Degree 3 Martial Arts Striking attacks and Degree 2 Martial Arts Sweeping attacks [5 points]; Additional strike (up to Degree 3) [15 points]

Special Abilities—If the GM is allowing Chi Power skills, this style allows access to either the Chi Powers: Fists of Iron skill or the Chi Powers: No Shadow Attack skill.

WING CHUN (NORTHERN EXTERNAL STYLE)

Basic Martial Arts Style [15 style points]

Description—The Wing Chun style was first developed over two hundred years ago. The story behind the founding of this martial art is very interesting. The originator of this style is a woman named Yim Wing Chun who was the daughter of a food merchant. She was very beautiful and due to be wed to her love Leong Bok Chao. A powerful warlord heard of her beauty and demanded that she become one of his wives. Faced with the threat of death, her father agreed to the match. Wing Chun was shocked at the news but became resigned to her fate, she did not want to see her father or her true love die trying to defy the warlord. Fate intervened at this point, Wing Chun encountered Ng Mui a Shaolin nun who had been taught the fighting arts of the crane and the dragon. When Ng Mui heard the unfortunate Wing Chun's story, she decided to help the girl. The nun counseled the young girl to delay the wedding by a year and start to undergo training in the martial arts. Due to the turmoil in the country at that time, the warlord accepted a delay of a year to break the existing betrothal to her true love, Leong Bok Chao. Wing Chun trained hard in the arts that Ng Mui taught her. For her part, Ng Mui simplified and streamlined the existing martial arts she already knew into this new system. After a year the warlord appeared to claim his bride, the father explained that Wing Chun had studied martial arts since she was young and would refuse to marry any man that could not defeat her in unarmed combat. Sure of his strength the warlord agreed to the challenge. His impulsive rush towards Wing Chun resulted in his defeat and he left in shame. Wing Chun married her true love and the martial art of Wing Chun was born.

There are three basic forms in this martial arts style. The first consists of simple arm blocks and strikes. The second form consists of more advanced blocking techniques that seek to deflect an opponent's attacks rather than match them strength to strength. The basic low kicks of the martial art are introduced as well. The last form teaches the use of finger strikes and other hand forms in

attacks. This form also introduces more footwork including more low kicks and stances. While this martial art may seem very simple to the novice, the experienced martial artist can admire its elegant simplicity.

Recommended Skills—Martial Arts Striking, Martial Arts Sweeping, Adrenal Defense

Martial Arts Abilities [Core]—Lesser Adrenal Defense [10 points]; Degree 3 Martial Arts Striking attacks and Degree 2 Martial Arts Sweeping attacks [5 points]

9.3.2 · INDONESIAN MARTIAL ARTS

Indonesia has a rich tradition of martial arts based on the system of fighting called pentjak-silat. All of pentjak-silat is evasive. Its normal responses to an attack are quick deceptive movements that seek to avoid direct contact with the opponent's strikes. Nearly all the movements taught in this style of combat may be performed unchanged, either empty-handed or armed. The kris and parang (machete) are blades often used with this fighting system. The pentjak-silat stylist is alert and reactive to attacks. All pentjak-silat styles are practiced with rhythmic music that serves to heighten the atmosphere during training sessions. Most pentjak-silat movements are based on the movements of animals. The pentjak-silat stylist does not go through warming-up exercises, it is structured so the stylist can react without an opportunity to warm-up. To achieve this degree of readiness, the stylist practices and trains to achieve flexibility and strength. When sparring, the pentjak-silat stylist is taught to view his partner as his "enemy" in preparation for actual combat. This martial art has more than twenty separate hand forms. Some of the more esoteric hand forms have descriptive names like the arrowhead fist, the beak hand, the tiger's claw fist, and the crane fist. Full-arm extensions during striking are rarely done. The pentjak-silat stylist is wary of locking his arm in a straight line, preferring to stop before his arm is fully extended.

BARU PENTJAK-SILAT

Basic Martial Arts Style [25 style points]

Description—This style of pentjak-silat developed in the coastal area of Sumatra that has firm ground. The Baru stylist concentrates on developing and maintaining secure footholds while fighting. Often during combat, the stylist will dig his feet into the ground to offer a firm foothold. By using his strong footholds, the stylist can attack with great speed and power. This martial arts style uses a good balance of leg and arm tactics to attack opponents. For more information on the history of Indonesian development of martial arts, see Section 2.3.

Recommended Skills—Martial Arts Striking, Martial Arts Sweeping, Adrenal Defense, Adrenal Strength

Martial Arts Abilities [Core]—Lesser Adrenal Defense [10 points]; Degree 4 Martial Arts Striking attacks and Degree 3 Martial Arts Sweeping attacks [10 points]; +10 bonus to Adrenal Strength maneuvers [5 points]; Kris weapon kata [5 points]

Special Abilities—If the GM is allowing Chi Power skills, this style allows access to the Chi Powers: No Shadow Attack skill.

Harmimau Pentjak-Silat

Basic Martial Arts Style [30 style points]

Description—The uneven and slippery ground found in the region of Sumatra has had a great influence on the development of this martial art. The Harimau (or tiger) fighter considers an upright posture during combat as ineffective it is easily to lose one's balance on the slippery ground. The stylist prefers to get close to the ground. In some cases the stylist hugs the ground, using his legs, arms, and his back, side, or belly for support. The fighter practices attacking from this low posture with powerful kicks and other attacks. He may also spring up quickly at his enemy, surprising him with powerful clawing attacks. For more information on the history of Indonesian development of martial arts, see Section 2.3.

Recommended Skills—Martial Arts Striking, Martial Arts Sweeping,, Adrenal Defense, Adrenal Balance

Martial Arts Abilities [Core]—Lesser Adrenal Defense [10 points]; Degree 3 Martial Arts Striking attacks and Degree 2 Martial Arts Sweeping attacks [5 points]; +10 bonus to all Adrenal Balance maneuvers [5 points]; +1 to initiative [5 points]; Kris weapon kata [5 points]

Special Abilities—This style has one special maneuver (Balance of the Tiger). In addition, if the GM is allowing Chi Power skills, this style allows access to the skills Chi Powers: Leaping Strike and Chi Powers: Light Feet.

> **Balance of the Tiger:** *The Harimau stylist suffers half the normal penalty for fighting on slippery or unstable surfaces (see Section 14.6). In addition any Unbalancing criticals suffered by the stylist while he is using this martial arts style are reduced by one level of severity. If he receives an 'A' Unbalancing critical, resolve as an 'A' critical with a special modification of -20 (modified dice less than 01 result in no extra damage).*

Kumango Pentjak-Silat

Basic Martial Arts Style [30 style points]

Description—The loose and sandy soil found in the region of Sumatra has strongly influenced the development of this martial art. This version of pentjak-silat prefers to use an upright stance. This style uses an effective balance of arm and leg attacks, but often arm strikes only serve to distract the opponent, setting him up for a powerful kick. Stylists sometimes slap a free hand against a thigh or throw sand to distract their foe. The skillful footwork found in this style sets up the powerful leg strikes found in this system. The almost rhythmic movements of this style can lull the opponent to underestimate the fighting skill of the adept. For more information on the history of Indonesian development of martial arts, see Section 2.3.

Recommended Skills—Martial Arts Striking, Martial Arts Sweeping, Adrenal Defense

Martial Arts Abilities [Core]—Greater Adrenal Defense [20 points]; Degree 3 Martial Arts Striking attacks and Degree 2 Martial Arts Sweeping attacks [5 points]; Kris weapon kata [5 points]

Special Abilities—If the GM is allowing Chi Power skills, this style allows access to the skill Chi Powers: Light Feet.

9.3.3 · JAPANESE MARTIAL ARTS

This is an overview of a sampling of Japanese martial arts styles.

Ju-jutsu

Basic Martial Arts Style [15 style points]

Description—Ju-jutsu is an ancient Japanese martial art that stresses unarmed techniques. Ju-jutsu includes methods of kicking, striking, throwing, and joint-locking. From within the ju-jutsu forms came the systemized development of striking vital points called atemi. This Japanese system of classifying vital points remained less developed than the Chinese methods due to the restriction of these techniques to the warrior class, which predominately focused its energies on swordmanship. Many different versions of ju-jutsu exist, but they are all considered more defensive than offensive. For more aggressive attacks, most Japanese warriors would use other forms of martial arts. See Section 2.4 for more information on the development of historical Japanese martial arts.

Recommended Skills—Martial Arts Striking, Martial Arts Sweeping, Adrenal Defense

Martial Arts Abilities [Core]—Lesser Adrenal Defense [10 points]; Degree 3 Martial Arts Sweeping attacks and Degree 2 Martial Arts Striking attacks [5 points]; +1 initiative while using this style [5 points]

Nin-jutsu

Basic Martial Arts Style [30 style points]

Description—The ancient art of Nin-jutsu covers a wide array of techniques and styles. The focus of the style is reflected in the traditional role of the ninja, who was a trained spy in Japanese feudal society. The ninja used his skills to accomplish his missions, which usually involved spying or sabotage. Nin-jutsu also taught hand-to-hand combat techniques. A ninja was trained early in life to master the many skills required in his training. The first phases of training emphasized balance, mental toughness, endurance, and athletic abilities such as swimming, jumping, and climbing. In later phases, the ninja began to learn to use weapons and practice unarmed combat. Most ninjas were taught the use of the sword, staff, spear, chain, and the shuriken. The final phases of training involved the arts of disguise, camouflage, poison, and map-making. Ninjas were taught to be self-reliant and to act independently over long periods of time.

The unarmed combat of the ninja focused on learning how to deliver punishing attacks to unarmored foes and how to escape capture from more heavily armored guards. Most of the stances and attacks taught to a ninja were very practical and direct. Koppokitsu or bone-breaking techniques were also taught at the advanced levels of training within this martial arts style. See Section 2.4 for more information on the historical development of Japanese martial arts.

Recommended Skills—Martial Arts Striking, Martial Arts Sweeping, Nerve Strikes, Adrenal Defense, Adrenal Strength, Stalking and Hiding, Climbing, Swimming, Contortions, Adrenal Leaping, Adrenal Concentration, Adrenal Balance, Poison Lore, Disguise, Thrown Weapons, Ambush, Sense Ambush

Martial Arts Abilities [Core]—Lesser Adrenal Defense [10 points]; Degree 3 Martial Arts Striking attacks, Degree 2 Nerve Strikes attacks, and Degree 2 Martial Arts Sweeping attacks [10 points]; +10 bonus to Adrenal Evasion maneuvers [10 points]

Special Abilities—This style has a special maneuver that is signature technique (Yodo Aruki). In addition, if the GM is allowing Chi Power skills, this style allows access to the skills of Chi Powers: Falling Leaf, Chi Powers: Hold Breath, Chi Powers: Light Feet, Chi Powers: Lizard's Climb, and Chi Powers: Resist Elements.

Yodo Aruki ("Sideways Walking")—*The ninja learns how to walk quickly with unique steps and foot motions to avoid easy tracking by guards. Those unfamiliar with these techniques suffer -30 to any Tracking maneuvers made against the ninja.*

SUMAI

Basic Martial Arts Style [25 style points]

Description—The art of sumai is an ancient Japanese form of wrestling that is today known as Sumo. Sumo also relies on close quarter grappling but is much less dangerous than its ancient precursor. Sumai uses grappling in conjunction with kicking, butting, and striking attacks. The sumai attacks are based on strength and weight rather than many martial arts techniques that emphasize speed and mobility. Sumai is designed to knock one's opponent to the ground where they may be trampled. The martial artist uses his hips and legs to throw his opponent off balance, then immobilizing or dispatching his foe with a small blade slipped into the gaps of the armor. Sumai is practiced standing with an emphasis on wide, powerful stances. See Section 2.4 for more information on the historical development of Japanese martial arts.

Recommended Skills—Martial Arts Striking, Martial Arts Sweeping, Adrenal Strength, Adrenal Toughness, Stunned Maneuvering

Martial Arts Abilities [Core]—Degree 3 Martial Arts Sweeping attacks and Degree 2 Martial Arts Striking attacks [5 points]; +10 bonus to Adrenal Strength [5 points]; +15 bonus to Stunned Maneuvering [10 points]; +5 bonus to Adrenal Toughness maneuvers [10 points]

Special Abilities—This style has a special defense (Rooted in Earth). In addition, all Adrenal Strength and Adrenal Toughness maneuvers take only a 10% preparation action. Finally, if the GM is allowing Chi Power skills, this style allows access to the skills of Chi Powers: Resist Pain and Chi Powers, Invulnerability.

Rooted in Earth—*The Sumai stylist has learned to keep his balance and stance no matter how fierce the blows against him. As a result, all successful Adrenal Toughness maneuvers may reduce any Grappling or Unbalancing criticals against the adept by two levels of severity.*

9.3.4 · KOREAN MARTIAL ARTS

Korean martial arts have traditionally focused on empty-handed techniques for fighting. The unarmed fighting systems listed here represent only a small sampling of Korean martial arts. For some more information on Korea, refer to Section 2.5.

HWARANG-DO

Advanced Martial Arts Style [60 style points]

Description—Hwarang-do is an ancient Korean martial art. It is also a healing art. The original system was conceived by a Buddhist priest and taught to the young members of the royal family and other nobles. Collectively these men were known as the hwarang, their ranks included famous generals and leaders who inspired the rest of the country with their deeds. The name hwarang-do means "way of the flowering manhood" and its members followed a code of ethics that promoted loyalty to country and parents, trust and brotherhood between friends, courage, and justice. During the Yi Dynasty, the teaching of this art was discouraged and its masters and practitioners retreated to remote monasteries in the mountains to continue their teachings. This continued until 1960 when the first public school was opened in Korea.

The study of this martial art encompasses the development of inner energy through meditation and breathing. The fighting techniques of this system are complex, involving thousands of different combinations. For example, over three hundred separate styles of kicks are taught. More advanced training teaches the use of pressure points and joint locking. The adept of this style also strives to develop his inner energy to increase his awareness of his surroundings. Also important in this martial art is the study of the healing arts. Since the practitioner of hwarang-do is required to have an advanced knowledge of the human body to use some of the advanced attacking techniques, he also studies the ways to heal the body. Herbal medicine, bone setting, acupuncture, and other traditional medicines are taught to the hwarang-do adept. For more information on Korea and Korean martial arts, refer to Section 2.5.

Recommended Skills—Martial Arts Striking, Martial Arts Sweeping, Nerve Strikes, Locking Holds, Adrenal Defense, Adrenal Strength, Meditation, First Aid, Prepare/Use Herbs

Martial Arts Abilities [Core]—Greater Adrenal Defense [20 points]; Degree 4 Martial Arts Striking attacks, Degree 3 Nerve Strikes attacks, Degree 2 Martial Arts Sweeping attacks, and Degree 2 Locking Holds attacks [20 points]; All-Around Attack [10 points]; +10 bonus to all Adrenal Strength maneuvers [5 points]; Broadsword weapon kata [5 points]

Special Abilities—If the GM is allowing Chi Power skills, this style allows access to the skills Chi Powers: Buddha's Palm, Chi Powers: Sense Weakness, and Chi Powers: Resist Elements.

Tae Kwon Do

Basic Martial Arts Style [30 style points]

Description—Tae kwon do is a martial art that emphasizes using the entire body to attack. Punching, jumping kicks, blocks, and dodges are all used in this martial art. Training consists of practicing the attack and defense forms and hardening the body. This unarmed combat system still survives to present day. For more information on Korea and Korean martial arts, refer to Section 2.5.

Recommended Skills—Martial Arts Striking, Martial Arts Sweeping, Nerve Strikes, Adrenal Defense, Adrenal Leaping

Martial Arts Abilities [Core]—Lesser Adrenal Defense [10 points]; Degree 4 Martial Arts Striking attacks, Degree 2 Martial Arts Sweeping attacks, and Degree 1 Nerve Strikes attacks [10 points]; +1 initiative bonus [5 points]; +10 bonus to all Adrenal Leaping maneuvers [5 points]

Special Abilities—If the GM is allowing Chi Power skills, this style allows access to the skill of Chi Powers: Leaping Strike.

9.3.5 · OKINAWAN MARTIAL ARTS

Okinawa has a long history of martial arts. It is ideally situated between mainland China and Japan and as a result has benefited from ideas and techniques from both countries.

Karate

Basic Martial Arts Style [30 style points]

Description—Karate is an aggressive martial art that seeks to disable an opponent as quickly as possible. Karate emphasizes kicks and strikes in extensive training to improve strength, speed, and flexibility. Primarily front and side kicks are emphasized, though flying or jumping kicks are also taught. Blocking techniques emphasize deflecting strikes or stopping them directly to set the opponent up for a fierce counter-attack. Many unique weapons have also been introduced into forms of karate, some of which include the nunchaku, sai, tonfa, and kama. See Section 2.6 for information on Okinawan martial arts.

Recommended Skills—Martial Arts Striking, Martial Arts Sweeping, Nerve Strikes, Adrenal Defense

Martial Arts Abilities [Core]—Lesser Adrenal Defense [10 points]; Degree 4 Martial Arts Striking attacks, Degree 2 Martial Arts Sweeping attacks, and Degree 1 Nerve Strikes attacks [10 points]; Nunchaku weapon kata [5 points]; Reduce nunchaku fumble range by 1 [5 points]

9.3.6 · EUROPEAN MARTIAL ARTS

European cultures did not develop fighting systems to as high a degree as Asian cultures. As a result, the style points ranges for European martial arts styles may be reduced from the original ranges given for the skills in Section 9.1.

Optional Rule [Core]: When designing European martial arts styles, Basic Martial Arts Styles range from 0 to 20 style points and Advanced Martial Arts Styles range from 21 to 40 style points.

Savate

Basic Martial Arts Style [15 style points]

Description—Savate is a French form of unarmed combat that focuses on leg and foot attacks. The influence of English style boxing eventually added some more effective hand strikes. This martial art was not followed as a primary form of combat. It was seen as a gentleman's sport that was used for exercise, sparring, and self-defense when a weapon was not available. This martial art also incorporated the use of the gentleman's walking cane or stick into its attack and defense techniques.

Recommended Skills—Martial Arts Striking, Feint

Martial Arts Abilities [Core]—Degree 2 Martial Arts Striking attacks [0 points]; +10 OB bonus to Feint maneuvers while using this style [10 points]; Club weapon kata while using this style [5 points]

CHI POWERS SKILLS

Part II

Sections 10.0, 10.1, 10.2, 10.3, 10.4

Chi Powers Skills

Creating Your Own

Magical Effects

Methods of Training

Chi Powers Skills

The Chi Powers skills are an optional set of skills for use with this companion. The purpose of Chi Powers skills is to represent the incredible feats that have been associated with martial artists. The Chi Powers skills are presented in three levels of power Core, Heroic, and Fantastic. Not all the Chi Powers skills may be appropriate for the Gamemaster's game (each Gamemaster should evaluate each skill to determine its fate in his world).

◆ 10.1 ◆
CREATING YOUR OWN

If a player or Gamemaster wishes to develop new Chi Powers skills, keep in mind several guidelines that were used in the creation of all the Chi Powers skills presented in this companion. No Chi Powers skills give automatic combat capabilities to unskilled practitioners. These skills are used in concert with other combat skills that the wielder possesses. All Chi Powers skills require a significant investment in time and effort to learn. No Chi Powers skill should create a spell effect that is greater than an average 10th level spell presented in *Spell Law*.

◆ 10.2 ◆
MAGICAL EFFECTS

A Chi Powers skill is developed after instruction in the secret techniques needed to cultivate the specific power, and then is further developed by the student undergoing a rigorous training regimen that may take many years to complete. The effects of Chi Powers skills should be considered as magical in nature and thus should be detectable by users of magic or possibly even with Power Perception static maneuvers.

◆ 10.3 ◆
METHODS OF TRAINING

The following two examples are taken from actual training methods used by martial artists in ancient China for the development of incredible skills. In ancient China there are recorded descriptions of the training practices followed by martial artists to develop their chi powers, the time required for complete mastery of a single technique could be anywhere from five to twenty years of continuous training. This brief section is designed to give the Gamemaster some ideas of how characters in his campaign might train to develop Chi Powers. The word kung used in the titles of these samples is Chinese and loosely means "method of training." Both of the examples given show ways that characters might develop the Chi Powers: Distance Strike skill. See Section 2.1 for further information on the historical development of Chinese martial arts.

10.3.1 · RED SAND PALM KUNG

The Red Sand Palm Kung allows the adept to make motions of striking an opponent with his palm from a distance and directly injure his target through the force of the adept's Chi. In most cases, death will result in a matter of weeks.

Initially the training begins with a basin of very fine red sand. The student trains by scooping up the fine sand with both of his hands and closing his palms together while he attempts to crush the grains of sand. The student will practice this exercise for hours every day until, after years of continuous training, the student can cause the fine sand to move without touching it while holding his hands at a distance of several inches. The student would then repeat this training with coarser sand until he could achieve the same results at a distance of roughly one foot. Next the student would replace the sand with small iron beads and follow the same process. After success was achieved with the beads, larger iron balls would be placed in the basin. When a student is finally able to cause an iron ball to jump out of the basin by merely rubbing his palms sharply over the basin, he will have achieved mastery of this skill. At this point, the new adept can now focus his power to injure an opponent from a distance.

10.3.2 · ONE FINGER KUNG

The One Finger Kung seeks to achieve effects similar to the Red Sand Palm Kung. In this form of training, the student begins by attempting to move a large iron bell by pressing it with one finger. After continuous practice, the student is soon able to make the iron bell move with only the lightest touch. The next goal of the student is to practice this exercise until he can make the iron bell move from a distance of several feet by merely pointing at it with his finger. The final stage of the bell training involves the student practicing until he can cause the clapper to ring inside the iron bell without the bell moving.

The next stage of training involves attempting to extinguish the flame of a lighted candle from a distance of ten to twenty feet away. When the student can accomplish this feat, a glass lantern with a lit candle inside is substituted for the final phase of training. When the student reaches a level of mastery at which he can extinguish the candle without breaking the glass of the lantern, he will have achieved mastery of this skill. At this advanced level of skill, an opponent can be injured even if a door or other obstacle stood in one's way.

◆ 10.4 ◆
CHI POWERS SKILLS

Each new Chi Powers skill is detailed in this section. Following the skill name, the recommended power level (Core, Heroic, or Fantastic) for each skill is shown in brackets. These are suggestions for the Gamemaster and may not be suitable for all campaigns. Only the new Chi Powers skills are shown in each category.

10.4.1 · LORE OBSCURE

Standard Skills: Chi Powers Lore
Restricted Skills: None
Applicable Stat Bonuses: Me/Re/Me
Skill Rank Progression: Standard
Skill Category Progression: Standard
Group: Lore
Classification: Static Maneuver

CHI POWERS LORE [CORE]

This skill provides a bonus for recognizing and knowing the capabilities of chi powers. In addition, this skill also illuminates some of the esoteric training techniques used to develop chi powers. Successful use of this skill will allow the user to be able to observe whether chi powers are being used. {Me}

10.4.2 · MARTIAL ARTS COMBAT MANEUVERS

Standard Skills: Chi Powers: Cloth Lance, Chi Powers: Leaping Strike
Restricted Skills: Chi Powers: Sticking Touch
Applicable Stat Bonuses: Ag/Qu/SD
Skill Rank Progression: Combined
Skill Category Progression: 0 • 0 • 0 • 0 • 0
Group: Martial Arts
Classification: Static Maneuver, Special, and OB

CHI POWERS: CLOTH LANCE [HEROIC]

The character learns how to spin a wet ten-foot length of cloth rapidly enough to serve as a weapon. The tightly wound cloth can serve as a staff. The wielder of the cloth lance can attack on the Quarterstaff attack table. The wielder can also release the tension in the cloth to attack on the Three-Sectioned Staff attack table. {Ag}

CHI POWERS: LEAPING STRIKE [HEROIC]

The character learns how to focus his internal energy to make incredible leaping and tumbling attacks. Upon a successful use of this skill, the character may cover up to 30' through a series of leaps and rolls and attack an opponent with no penalty to his OB. This skill requires a 20% preparation action in the previous round. {Ag}

CHI POWERS: STICKING TOUCH [HEROIC]

The character learns to synchronize his movements with his target's actions. A successful static maneuver will allow the character to move in concert with his opponent's every move. Any attempt by the character to stay in contact with his opponent is considered to automatically be successful. If his opponent moves in a way that the character physically cannot move, the sticking touch is broken. {Em}

10.4.3 · SELF CONTROL

Standard Skills: Chi Powers: Hold Breath, Chi Powers: No Shadow Attack, Chi Powers: Resist Elements, Chi Powers: Resist Pain
Restricted Skills: Chi Powers: Falling Leaf, Chi Powers: Fantastic Leap, Chi Powers: Light Feet, Chi Powers: Lizard's Climb, Chi Powers: Sense Weakness
Applicable Stat Bonuses: SD/Pr/SD
Skill Rank Progression: Standard
Skill Category Progression: Standard
Group: None
Classification: Static Maneuver

CHI POWERS: FALLING LEAF [HEROIC]

The character learns to focus the power of his mind to accomplish incredible feats of levitation. A successful static maneuver will allow the character to reduce the severity of a fall by his skill bonus times two in feet. The severity of a fall may never be reduced below that of a 1' fall. A 20% activity action is required the round after the fall to recover (assuming the character is alive and conscious). {Em}

Example: *If a character has a bonus of +45 and makes a successful static maneuver to use this skill, he may take 90' off the distance of any fall. If the character is facing a fall of 110', he may treat it as a fall of 20' (110-90). If the character is facing a fall of 12', he may treat it as a fall of only 1' (the minimum distance a fall can be reduced to with this skill).*

CHI POWERS: FANTASTIC LEAP [HEROIC]

The character learns to focus his power to accomplish incredible leaps. A successful static maneuver allows the user to leap up to 20' horizontally or 15' vertically. This skill requires a 20% preparation action in the previous round. {Ag}

CHI POWERS: HOLD BREATH [CORE]

Normally, a character can hold his breath for 5 rounds plus his temporary Constitution stat (not bonus) divided by 10. Thus, a character with a 90 temporary Constitution stat can hold his breath for 14 rounds (or just around two and a half minutes). The character can make a static maneuver to increase the amount of time he can hold his breath. If the maneuver is successful, he can hold his breath up to twice as long as normal. This skill requires a 20% preparation action in the round prior to holding breath. {SD}

CHI POWERS: LIGHT FEET [CORE]

The character learns to focus the power of his mind to make his steps light and quick. A successful static maneuver will allow the character to run on snow, sand, or a similar unstable surface without a movement penalty due to terrain. Also, the character can avoid any applicable penalties associated with fighting on these types of terrain. {Ag}

CHI POWERS: LIZARD'S CLIMB [CORE]

The character learns to climb vertical walls with his back facing the wall. A successful static maneuver allows the user to make a Climbing maneuver with only half the normal activity required. This skill requires a 20% preparation action in the round prior to climbing. {SD}

CHI POWERS: NO SHADOW ATTACK [HEROIC]

The character learns how to focus his internal energy to deliver lightning-quick attacks to his opponent. A successful static maneuver allows the character to roll an additional die for initiative. The character may choose which die to use for his initiative roll. This skill requires a 10% preparation action in the previous round. {Qu}

CHI POWERS: RESIST ELEMENTS [CORE]

The character can ignore effects of normal heat and cold through the use of this skill. In addition, the character can make a static maneuver to gain a bonus of +20 to RRs versus magical fire and cold attacks. To gain this benefit, this skill requires active concentration by the character (e.g., a 50% action) while it is being used. The character will expend exhaustion at double the normal rate while using this skill (when exhausted, this skill cannot be used). Examples of normal ranges of heat and cold that can be resisted through the use of this skill would be walking on hot coals or ignoring the effects of near zero temperatures. {SD}

CHI POWERS: RESIST PAIN [HEROIC]

The character can make a static maneuver to ignore the effects of pain. If the maneuver is successful, the character may ignore any penalties from loss of concussion hits for 10 minutes per point of Constitution bonus (with a minimum of 10 minutes). This skill requires a 20% preparation action in the previous round. {SD}

CHI POWERS: SENSE WEAKNESS [FANTASTIC]

The character learns to sense weak spots in his opponent's defenses. A 40% preparation action is required to attempt to sense the vulnerable spot. A successful static maneuver will allow the character to possibly inflict more damage on a successful attack in the following round. The character may re-roll any one critical inflicted in an attack made in the following round. If the critical is re-rolled, the character must abide by the result of the second roll {In}

10.4.4 · SPECIAL ATTACKS

Standard Skills: Chi Powers: Continuous Strikes

Restricted Skills: Chi Powers: Buddha's Palm, Chi Powers: Distance Strike, Chi Powers: Fists of Iron, Chi Powers: Elemental Fist, Chi Powers: Poison Fist

Applicable Stat Bonuses: St/Ag/SD

Skill Rank Progression: Combined

Skill Category Progression: 0 • 0 • 0 • 0 • 0

Group: None

Classification: Static Maneuver and Offensive Bonus

CHI POWERS: BUDDHA'S PALM [FANTASTIC]

The character learns how to focus the internal energy of his body to strike an opponent with this deadly attack. This skill requires a 30% preparation round to focus and marshal the internal energy needed. Upon a successful static maneuver, the character may severely disrupt an opponent's internal energy. If, in the following round, the character makes a successful unarmed attack, his opponent receives a special negative modifier to all Chi Powers and Self Control maneuvers. For each level of critical inflicted by the martial arts attack, a special -20 modifier is applied to the opponent (e.g., a 'C' critical would result in a special –60 modifier to the opponent). This negative penalty reduces by 10 points per round after it is first inflicted (to a minimum of 0). {None}

CHI POWERS: CONTINUOUS STRIKES [HEROIC]

The character learns how to use his inner energy to lengthen the duration of his attacks. This skill requires a 60% preparation action. On the round after this preparation (with a successful static maneuver), the minimum percentage activity needed for a melee attack is halved (to 30% for melee attacks and 15% for missile attacks). {Qu}

CHI POWERS: DISTANCE STRIKE [FANTASTIC]

The character learns to project the force of his attacks without making physical contact with his opponent. If the static maneuver is successful, the character may make a normal melee attack with his chosen melee weapon or martial arts attack. The opponent may not parry this strike (but all other defensive bonuses apply). See the chart below for other modifiers. This skill requires a 40% preparation action in the previous round. {Em}

DISTANCE STRIKE MODIFIERS	
Range to target	-2 per 1'
Striking through an interposing object	-70

CHI POWERS: ELEMENTAL FIST [FANTASTIC]

The character learns to summon the power of the elements while attacking. A successful static maneuver allows the user to inflict an additional elemental critical (Cold, Heat, Electricity, or Impact) of equal severity each time he attacks with an unarmed attack. This skill requires a 40% preparation action in the previous round. This skill must be developed separately for each type of element. {Em}

CHI POWERS: FISTS OF IRON [HEROIC]

The character learns how to focus the power of his mind into his attacks. A successful static maneuver allows the user to resolve all unarmed martial arts attacks during that combat round on the Mace Attack Table. This skill requires a 20% preparation action in the previous round. The damage threshold of the Degree being used by the martial artist also modifies his OB (as shown in the chart below). {Pr}

FISTS OF IRON MODIFIERS
Degree 1 attack OB ....-60
Degree 2 attack OB ....-40
Degree 3 attack OB ....-20
Degree 4 attack OB ....-0

CHI POWERS: POISON FIST [FANTASTIC]

The character learns how to channel his inner power to deliver punishing damage to an opponent. This skill requires a special 30% preparation round to focus the internal energy necessary. Upon a successful static maneuver, the character's next unarmed attack in the following round will cause his opponent to suffer a debilitating injury. The opponent suffers a special -10 modifier to all skills and maneuvers for each level of critical inflicted by the un-

armed attack (e.g., a 'C' critical would result in a special –30 modifier to the opponent). This negative penalty remains for one round for each concussion hit of damage delivered with the attack. This skill does not effect magical creatures or opponents with the Large or Super Large critical type. {Em}

10.4.5 · SPECIAL DEFENSES

Standard Skills: Chi Powers: Invincible Stance

Restricted Skills: Chi Powers: Invulnerability,
   Chi Powers: Rise of the Phoenix

Applicable Stat Bonuses: St/Ag/SD

Skill Rank Progression: Combined

Skill Category Progression: 0 • 0 • 0 • 0 • 0

Group: None

Classification: Static Maneuver and Offensive Bonus

CHI POWERS: INVINCIBLE STANCE [FANTASTIC]

The character that masters this skill learns how to use his own inner power to resist the effects of other Chi Powers skills. Any Chi Powers skill that someone attempts to use against him, suffers a special penalty equal to the number of skill ranks the character possesses in this skill. {None}

CHI POWERS: INVULNERABILITY [FANTASTIC]

This skill allows the character to focus his inner energy to resist attacks. The type of attack that this skill resists must be chosen when this skill is first developed (e.g., Edged weapons, Concussion weapons, Unarmed attacks, etc.). The character can harden his body to this type of attack through practice and inner strength. This skill requires taking a 20% preparation action in the round immediately prior to the use of this skill (or during the snap action phase of the same round). Then the character must make a static maneuver. If successful, the individual may half the concussion damage delivered from the attack and reduce the severity of any critical by two levels of severity. If the critical result is an 'A' critical, treat it as an 'A' critical modified by -40 (modified rolls less than zero result in no effect). If the critical result is a 'B' critical, resolve it as an 'A' critical modified by -20 (modified rolls less than zero result in no effect). {None}

CHI POWERS: RISE OF THE PHOENIX [FANTASTIC]

The character learns how to summon the power and strength of the legendary phoenix into his body. This skill requires a special 40% preparation action in the round immediately prior to the use of this skill (or during the snap action phase of the same round). Upon a successful static maneuver, the character may temporarily ignore the effects of any one critical that he has received. The character may delay the effect of this critical for up to two rounds per point of Self Discipline stat bonus (with a minimum of two rounds).

CHARACTER CREATION

Part II

**Sections
11.0, 11.1,
11.2, 11.3**

Character
Creation

What Remains
Unchanged

Adolescence
Skill
Development

Background
Options

This section outlines the new options available for character creation in *RMSS* using this companion. Some guidelines for including martial arts skills in the Adolescent development stage are briefly stated. For those players who wish to use new talents and flaws, new tables are introduced that focus on the martial arts. Some character concepts that fit well into martial arts are briefly profiled to spark player or Gamemaster imaginations. In addition a number of random tables for generation of martial arts organizations and teachers are included in the next section to make the Gamemaster's job even easier.

◆ 11.1 ◆
WHAT REMAINS UNCHANGED

The stats, potential stats, and stat bonuses use the same generation rules as presented in *RMSS*. The determination of race and culture remains the same as presented in *RMSS*. The determination of profession remains the same as in *RMSS*.

EXAMPLE

Melissa is generating a new character for a campaign. Having just read through the contents of this companion, she decides that she wishes to make a Warrior Monk character. This campaign is using the point total character creation method, and Melissa has 660 points available to spend. Melissa chooses to play a Common Man culture in the campaign world that is known for its knowledge of martial arts. Noting that the prime requisites for the Warrior monk are Quickness and Self Discipline, Melissa decides to spend her points as follows (potentials are in brackets, followed by total modification for stats):

Stat	Value	Stat Mod	Racial Mod		Total Mod
Ag	90 [95]	+5		=	+5
Co	75 [92]	+2		=	+2
Me	65 [84]			=	0
Re	55 [82]			=	0
SD	90 [100]	+5	+2	=	+7
Em	25 [64]	-2		=	-2
In	35 [68]			=	0
Pr	55 [94]			=	0
Qu	92 [93]	+6		=	+6
St	76 [89]	+2	+2	=	+4

Melissa has the foundations of a strong character here. Melissa decides her Warrior monk character will be known as Ming Te, the Ginger Blossom.

◆ 11.2 ◆
ADOLESCENCE SKILL DEVELOPMENT

With the advent of many new martial arts skills in this companion, players and Gamemasters may wish to allow a certain race or culture to gain martial arts skills during adolescence to reflect a race's or culture's preoccupation

with martial arts. This is acceptable as long as only non-Restricted skills are taken. Remember during adolescence development that characters are assumed to be products of their race and culture and not of their profession. Therefore any martial arts skills granted during adolescent development are representative of the expertise of the race or culture in its entirety. A balanced solution is to allow a race or culture with a high degree of integration with the martial arts to gain martial arts skills as hobby ranks.

EXAMPLE (continued)

Melissa decides that her character, Ming Te, comes from a region in the campaign world that has a great knowledge of the martial arts. The Gamemaster decides to model her character's culture as a Ruralman culture with the following additional standard hobby skills: Meditation, Martial Arts Strikes, Martial Arts Sweeps, Basic Martial Arts Style, Adrenal Concentration, Adrenal Leaping, and Martial Arts Lore.

Melissa has 12 hobby ranks to spend and she decides to spend them as follows: Acrobatics 1, Climbing 1, Cooking 1, Dancing 1, Stalking 1, Swimming 1, Weapon Skill 1, Martial Arts Strikes 2, Martial Arts Sweeps 1, Basic Martial Arts Style 1, Martial Arts Lore 1.

◆ 11.3 ◆
BACKGROUND OPTIONS

Some new background options are available to characters created using this companion.

11.3.1 · STANDARD BACKGROUND OPTIONS

In addition to the normal background options as listed in RMSR, there are a number of new background options available to the martial artist. A player can choose to roll on the Martial Arts Talents Chart instead of the normal talent tables provided in *RMSR*. See Section 11.3.3 and 11.3.4 for the Martial Arts Talents and Flaws charts.

If you decide to use the *Talent Law* point-based system instead of *RMSR*'s background options, Talent point costs are also included for each new talent and flaw included in this companion.

11.3.2 · TRAINING PACKAGES

For one background option (or 10 Talent Points if using *Talent Law*), the character may choose to purchase a single training package at half cost. The training package will be learned in half the normal amount of time as well. This is a one-time bonus; if the training package is purchased again, it must be purchased at full cost and will require the full amount of time to learn. See Section 18.0 for the new training packages introduced in this companion.

11.3.3 · MARTIAL ARTS TALENTS CHART

Roll on this chart (or use the point totals in brackets if using *Talent Law*). If the player is not using *Talent Law*, treat the talents listed here as Major Talents for purposes of determining the cost of the talent in background options.

11.3.4 · MARTIAL ARTS FLAWS CHART

Roll on this chart, or use the point totals if you are using *Talent Law*.

SPECIAL NOTE ABOUT FLAWS

If players have picked flaws that do not actually restrict their characters in any real way, the Gamemaster should feel free to have the player roll for another flaw or choose one for them. There is nothing wrong with allowing players to change flaws during the course of the campaign, but a flaw should always be detrimental to a character in some "real" way. The flaws listed here correspond to Major Flaws if *Talent Law* is not being used.

EXAMPLE (continued)

Melissa has 6 background options to spend (or 60 talent points if using Talent Law). She chooses to spend her points as follows?

She spends three background points to select the Inner Chi talent and rolls for her randomly selected flaw that turns out to be the Family Enemy flaw. She spends a background option to gain extra languages since her character will be from a foreign culture compared to the rest of the party. She spends another background option to gain a special +5 bonus in the Martial Arts Combat Maneuvers skill category. Her last background option she spends to half the cost and time of the Martial Arts Opera Performer training package.

◆ 11.4 ◆
APPRENTICESHIP

Apprenticeship character development remains unchanged from *RMSS*. This companion includes new training packages for characters who wish to specialize in the martial arts.

TRAINING PACKAGES

The martial artist can use any of the standard training packages presented in *RMSR* except for the Martial Artist and Weapon Master training packages, which have been revised in this companion. See Section 18.0 for the new training packages introduced in this companion.

MARTIAL
ARTS
COMPANION

MARTIAL ARTS TALENTS CHART	
01-10	**Respected Teacher**—You were taught by a respected teacher. Most other practitioners in the martial arts world will give you respect because of his reputation. [5 points]
11-24	**Good School**—You come from a good school of martial arts that is well respected. You will be able to call upon your fellow graduates of the school for help if you are in need. [5 points]
25-32	**Heir to Secrets**—You are the next in line to learn the secret maneuvers of your martial arts style (or weapon style) from your master. If the style is Basic, you gain a special one-time bonus of 10 skill ranks in your style skill. If the style is Advanced, you gain a one-time bonus of only 5 skill ranks in your style skill. [25 points]
33-40	**Natural Talent**—You gain a special bonus of +10 to any one martial arts or weapon style (your choice). [5 points]
41-48	**Natural Gift**—You may learn one Basic Martial Arts or Basic Weapon Style skill as an Everyman skill or you may treat one Advanced Martial Arts or Advanced Weapon Style skill as a non-Restricted skill. [10 points]
49-57	**Secret Scrolls**—You gain a special bonus of +20 to one Combat Maneuvers or Martial Arts Combat Maneuvers skill due to secret training knowledge that you possess. [7 points]
58-65	**Smooth Footwork**—You were taught early on that footwork is the most important component of a martial arts or weapon style. As a result, you may move up to 20% of your base movement rate each round with no penalty to your OB. [7 points]
66-77	**Powerful Strikes**—You are immensely strong and have a focused will. You have a special bonus of +10 to all Adrenal Strength maneuvers. On a successful Adrenal Strength maneuver, you may inflict triple damage instead of double damage. [7 points]
78-82	**Inner Chi**—Your Chi Powers skills are highly developed. You gain a special bonus of +20 to all Chi Powers skills in the Self Control skill category. You may also pick two Chi Powers from the Self Control skill category and develop them as non-Restricted skills. [12 points]
83-89	**Kung Training**—You have received extensive physical training. You gain a special bonus of +10 to Adrenal Leaping, Adrenal Landing, Adrenal Balance, Adrenal Strength, and Adrenal Speed static maneuvers because of your intense physical training. [5 points]
90-100	**Family Martial Art**—Your family is associated with a particular martial arts or weapon style. You may learn this style without paying fees associated with teachers. You also gain a special bonus of +20 while using your family's martial arts or weapon style. [9 points]

MARTIAL ARTS FLAWS CHART

01–07 **The Challenged**—You are constantly challenged by other students of martial arts who believe stories about your prowess to be overrated. The challenges will become more frequent the longer you stay in one area, as other students will travel to your location. In addition, the challenges will be more frequent in more highly populated areas. At least once per session, the Gamemaster should have a challenge occur. [-5 points]

08-14 **Lesser Requirement**—To use your martial arts or weapon style, a minor restriction must be obeyed. Failure to meet this requirement will result in a -15 modifier to the martial arts or weapon style bonus until the situation is rectified. An example of a lesser requirement could be a three to five hours of practice each day. [-5 points]

15-21 **Dirty Fighter**—You have gained a reputation as an unscrupulous fighter who uses dirty tricks. Whether this is true or not, you will have to be on guard against these types of tricks being used against you. As a result of your suspicion, you suffer a –1 to all initiatives. Your reputation makes people doubt your words. This may result in opponents ganging up on your character in supposedly fair fights, or using poison against you, surprise attacks, etc. [-5 points]

22-25 **Poor Stance**—All attacks using any martial arts or weapon styles are modified by -10 due to your poor understanding of the fundamental attacking stances of the styles. [-5 points]

26-31 **Disdain**—You have great disdain for any single weapon category (excepting the Missile Artillery weapon category). This weapon category is treated as a Restricted category for you and you treat wielders of weapons from this category with open contempt. [5 points]

32-36 **Opposing School**—An opposing martial arts or weapon style chosen by the Gamemaster exists that is very effective against your martial arts or weapon style. When facing an opponent using this opposing style, you have a special -20 modifier to your martial arts or weapon style for the duration of the combat. [-5 points]

37-44 **Family Enemy**—Your family has a very skilled enemy who hails from an opposing school of martial arts style or weapon style. Your foe will seek to hinder and ruin you at every turn. [-5 points]

45-49 **Outlawed Martial Art**—Your favorite martial arts or weapon style is outlawed in the land. Combatants caught using this style are placed under immediate arrest and may face death at the hands of the government. You must practice and train in your martial arts or weapon style in secret. [-3 points]

50-54 **Weak Chi**—All Chi Powers skill maneuvers are modified by –20 due to your lack of inner Chi. [-5 points]

55-59 **Bloodlust**—When you enter any type of combat, you find yourself starting to lose control. Every round you are in combat there is a cumulative 5% chance that you will seek to kill your opponent no matter what the initial conditions of the match were. [-5 points]

60-65 **Secret Society**—You are a member of a secret society that is suppressed by the government. You owe your training and skills to the other members of the secret society and are sworn to support the cause of your society with your life. If you are discovered as a member of this society, you will be imprisoned or possibly executed. [-10 points]

66-71 **Weak Wrists/Feet**—You have a good understanding of your martial arts or weapon style but you are hampered by your physical attributes. Your weak wrists or feet result in a special –20 modifier to any martial arts or weapon style and a –10 modifier to any moving maneuver you attempt. [-10 points]

72-78 **Secret Flaw**—All of your techniques in your martial arts styles or weapon styles have a secret flaw. If a foe realizes one of your flaws, he will gain a special +20 OB against you while you are using martial arts styles or weapons styles. You may not eliminate this flaw through training or further development. [-7 points]

79-84 **Secret Weakness**—You have a secret weak point, that, if struck, incapacitates you. If a natural 13 is rolled for any critical result against you, you will become unconscious for 10 hours in addition to the critical result. [-15 points]

85-90 **Demanding Master**—You have a demanding teacher who has pressured you into accepting onerous tasks for him. Failure to respect the wishes of your teacher will lead to a bad reputation in the martial arts world as well as the anger of the teacher's other students. [-3 points]

91-95 **Missile Disdain**—The Missile and Thrown Weapon skill categories are treated as Restricted skill categories for you and you scorn those fighters who use such "weak" weapons. [-7 points]

96-100 **Flawed Stance**—All of your martial arts or weapon style attacks that result in a critical are reduced by one level because of your lack of understanding the techniques of attack (an 'E' to 'D', 'D' to 'C', … and all 'A' criticals are modified by –20). [-10 points]

◆ 11.5 ◆
YOUR ROLE

It is very important to determine a character's role within the campaign. The ideas presented in this section do not target how to use the rules or skills to your best advantage when creating a character who uses martial arts. Rather, they concentrate on creating good character concepts that will be fun to play campaign. Here are some sample character concepts for martial artists. They are meant to serve as inspiration for player characters as well as non-player characters (NPCs).

THE HEALER

When you first started training in the martial arts, you were interested in learning how to make yourself more powerful. Finally after years of training, you have reached one of the highest levels of accomplishment in your chosen martial art. However, you no longer have the desire to fight others to prove your strength and power. The more you learned about the natural functions of the body and how to heal it, the more fascinated you became. Your master recognized your interest and began to teach you the deeper secrets of the body. Your calm and unruffled demeanor hides a great martial arts talent, but you are more interested in avoiding combat than showing your prowess.

> **Quote:** *"I am sorry I had to do that to you but you would not listen. Sit still and I will get some medicine to fix your arm—at least it is a clean break. Whoever taught you to lunge with a knife in that manner?"*

The healer is an interesting type of character concept to play. It couples the aggressive nature of the martial arts skills presented in this companion with an enlightened restraint. This character concept allows for a lot of fun role playing opportunities. Interestingly enough, traditionally skilled martial arts masters were also the local doctors of their communities due to their advanced knowledge of the body.

THE COWARD

Since you were little you have always been afraid of others and confrontation. Admitting your fear to yourself, you then set out to become the best fighter you could possibly become. You never act in a manner to give offense, even though your martial arts skills are very advanced. If you are forced to defend yourself, you attack without mercy until your foes have fallen. Most of your opponents do not last long, victims of both your skill and their overconfidence.

> **Quote:** *"<whap, whap, thump ... thud> Now do you realize that you should have just taken my money and left me alone?"*

The coward is a challenging type of character concept to play. In most cases, it is not a suitable character concept for players, as they will be constantly seeking danger throughout the campaign. As a NPC, this character concept comes into its own and can be a very intriguing addition to the campaign. Having the players trying to maneuver the immensely more skilled but cowardly NPC into helping them fulfill a quest can lead to many exciting role playing sessions.

THE YOUNG STUDENT

You have just finished several years of apprenticeship with a demanding master. You have decided to set out to see the world and to use your martial arts skills. You are confident in your abilities, but your confidence is tempered by the memory of how easily your master can still defeat you.

> **Quote:** *"Well I had to follow my master around for three years before he would teach me anything. I'd better be good by now."*

The young student is a typical character concept for martial arts. Since most starting characters will be just learning the more advanced martial arts, this character concept fits in well with the level of skill of the character. This is a very flexible character concept with many possible variations. Anyone choosing this character concept should ask themselves several questions: Did the young student part on good terms with his master? Why is the student deciding to leave the shelter of his tutor now? Were there other students of the master training with him? Did the student get along with them or was there a bitter conflict? These and similar questions will help establish a strong character background.

THE YOUNG MASTER

You are a child prodigy of martial arts. You have trained in the martial arts since you were born and have gained great fame as a child martial artist. Now that you are an adult, you have become an accredited master of your particular style over the objections of some who cry that you are too young. You strive to be respectful to your fellow masters, but someone always seems willing to test your "mastery."

> **Quote:** *"The young reed bends with the wind, the old tree breaks under the strain."*

The young master is an interesting character concept for martial artists. The player who wishes to use this concept for their character must be willing to invest either background options or development points to make sure that a high level of proficiency in the martial arts is obtained. Like some of the other character concepts presented already, this concept carries within it the seeds for campaign ideas and plots. Perhaps the other older masters of his martial arts style wish to humiliate the character, or they seek to use his youthful naivete for their own ends. In either case, some interesting gaming sessions could be generated from this concept.

THE STREET PERFORMER

You are a skilled showman or perhaps a martial artist down on his luck. Whatever the case, you make your living by demonstrating your martial arts talents in the streets. If you are skilled, the spectators throw you money. You soon learned that the demonstration of the more showy maneuvers of your style gained greater wealth than other more effective maneuvers. As a result you tend to fight in a showy or flashy way that is disdained by some purists but is still very effective.

> **Quote:** *"Allow me demonstrate my humble skills. You will be witness to the first time this daring feat has been attempted since the tragic death of my former master many years ago."*

The street performer is a very interesting character concept for martial artists. The character gets to use his martial arts skills and display his prowess in an arena other than combat. The player should describe what his character is doing to earn his money as a performer, because it can lead to interesting role playing and character development. Players who choose to follow this character concept should also probably receive a more flamboyant description of their character's combat actions during gaming sessions. Interesting plots can develop from this character concept. Perhaps the character wishes to be respected as a traditional martial artist after a time. What must he do to earn the respect of the other masters? Another option could be the existence of a Performers Guild that has secret connections to other organizations and its own shadowy motives. This concept should generate a lot of player interaction within the party as the various players role-play their reactions to the street performer's talents.

THE SECRETIVE MASTER

You are the inheritor of a secret style of martial arts. Perhaps it is a style taught by your family or a secret society. You have sworn never to reveal it to outsiders. As a result, you have studied another more common type of martial arts to use in public places. Your secret mastery means that you can never claim the respect and accolades due to a master of the martial arts, but it is a small price to pay for the knowledge you have gained.

Quote: *"Now we that are finally alone, I can unleash my Shooting Stars Fist technique? I hope you will be able to appreciate my mastery before you die."*

The secretive master is an interesting character concept for martial artists. This character concept may appeal to players who like to have a secret agenda or players who like starting out with the deck stacked against them. It is also can create interesting NPCs for long-term campaigns. This concept allows for a lot of plot development that can be shared between the player and the Gamemaster as they decide why the weapon style or martial arts style is being kept secret. Perhaps it is secret because it is associated with an organization or group of people thought long dead that was once a threat to the established order. Or maybe the style is a secret art of a powerful organization; to accidentally reveal its secrets publicly would result in death for the offender. In any case, this concept lends itself to long-term plot threads as the Gamemaster reveals the reasons behind the secrecy of this martial art. It is important that this concept be honored if a player wishes to develop this type of character. If the Gamemaster does not have the time or the inspiration to weave this plot line into the ongoing campaign, the player is better off using a different character concept.

THE HEADSTRONG SHOWOFF

You have never listened to the words of your master, who always cautioned you to act with restraint and respect. You know that you are the best and you are not afraid to prove it. Those who will not fight you are cowards who fear the public humiliation of being defeated in public. You are a master at provoking a fight, when you wish, to prove your mastery in the martial arts.

Quote: *"Your style is as pathetic and weak as you are yourself. I am young and strong and my martial arts skills are superior to yours. If you admit that your skills are inferior to mine, I will not fight you since I was always taught to respect my elders. Well, I await your answer, old man!"*

The headstrong showoff is a very dynamic character concept for martial artists. This concept, if chosen by a character, will most likely propel the entire player group careening from one misadventure to another. The headstrong showoff is like a bull trapped in a china closet. If a Gamemaster is running a tightly scripted campaign, this is probably not a wise concept to encourage characters to play. This concept will keep the group involved in the thick of things and the Gamemaster on his toes. An interesting variant to play on this character concept is the showoff who finally realizes that he is not the best. How does the character react to this realization? Does he feel fear, shame, acceptance, anger, etc., and does he change his outlook on life or continue on the same path?

THE VENGEFUL STUDENT

Your best friend or family was killed before your eyes, only you managed to escape a similar fate. You were helpless to save them, as you lacked any combat skills. Since that fateful day, you have sworn to avenge their deaths by slaying their murderers. To reach your goal, you have obsessively trained in martial arts so that you can take your vengeance personally.

Quote: *"You killed my family, now prepare to die…"*

The vengeful student is a classic character concept for martial artists. This concept provides strong motivation for their narrow focus in the martial arts as well as a strong emotional background to the character history. Good role playing can lead to the other members of the party taking up the character's quest for vengeance. It is relatively easy for a Gamemaster to integrate this plot thread into his campaign. If the character succeeds in avenging his family or friends, it can be a climactic cap to a long campaign. For the health of a long-term campaign, however, it is important that this character grow beyond this rather narrow concept to a more fully three-dimensional character.

◆ 11.6 ◆
FINAL CHARACTER PREPARATION

To add the final touches to a newly created character, take a look in some of the other sections of this companion. Perhaps the character specializes in the use of a unique weapon. Section 13.0 details many new weapons used almost exclusively in martial arts styles. If your character has a special history, some of the options for talents and flaws in this section may be useful in fleshing him out. Other helpful areas include Section 12.0, which details some of the training methods used in learning martial arts and Section 2.0, which describes the historical development of martial arts throughout the world.

EXAMPLE (continued)

Melissa and the Gamemaster talk about her character in the context of the campaign. The Gamemaster informs Melissa that she is from a distant nation since the current campaign setting has had little martial arts in it up to this point. Melissa decides that her character was a performing actor/acrobat in a traveling troupe from her homeland. The troupe ran afoul of both the law and the local criminal powers and was forced to leave. Melissa's character could not be reached in time and she is left penniless in a foreign land.

Melissa decides that her character will be very refined and cultured and designs her martial arts style (with the Gamemaster's approval) to be elegant and graceful as well. Melissa decides to call her martial arts style the Silken Ribbon. After the martial arts style is defined and Melissa's starting equipment is chosen, she is ready to play in the campaign.

MARTIAL ARTS IN THE CAMPAIGN

Part II

Sections
12.0, 12.1

Martail Arts
in the
Campaign

Finding a
Teacher

A martial artist learns his skills through intensive training and tutoring. One of the most interesting things that a Gamemaster can bring into a martial arts campaign is the introduction of the methods and resources needed to become proficient in martial arts. Adding this degree of detail and information brings depth and verisimilitude to the campaign.

◆ 12.1 ◆
FINDING A TEACHER

If a player wishes a character to learn a certain martial arts skill, he must find a teacher to instruct him. The success of finding a teacher depends on the location of the character, the local attitude to martial arts in general, and the difficulty of the martial arts skill. For more information on creating cultures and organizations that support martial arts see Section 3.0 and read further in this section.

If the Gamemaster wishes to let random chance determine whether the character will find a qualified teacher, consult the following chart to determine success:

Roll 1d100 (open-ended) and apply the following modifications. Consult the chart below to determine the result of finding a teacher.

MODIFICATIONS TO FINDING A TEACHER

Basic Martial Arts Style or Weapon Style	0
Advanced Martial Arts Style or Weapon Style	-20
The martial arts skill is normally a Restricted skill	-20
Popular style (as decided by the GM)	+10 to +40
Large urban area (i.e. a city)	+15
Culture / society that discourages martial arts (GM's discretion)	+5 to +20
Small urban or large rural area	-5 to -20
Very rural area	-20 to -40
Culture / society that does not promote martial arts	-40
Outlawed martial arts or weapon style	-50

TYPE OF TEACHER

01-40	Organization
41-100	Individual teacher

FINDING A TEACHER CHART

-26 or less   **Spectacular Failure**

You search high and low and fail to find a teacher or school willing to teach you your desired martial art. You do, however, succeed in finding the attentions of the local authorities (or a powerful underworld organization) that brands you a dangerous subversive and imprisons you without a trail. You languish in prison for 1-10 (high open-ended roll) months before you are finally freed.

-25 to 25   **Absolute Failure**

You fail miserably. You lose a fair amount of money in the pursuit of your teacher.

26 to 75   **Failure**

You fail to find any qualified teachers. The local martial artists do not think anyone in this region practices the martial art that you desire to learn. Perhaps you should try elsewhere.

UM 66   **Unusual Event**

You are taken in by a fraud who teaches you useless lessons in exchange for your hard-earned money. You discover the scheme after several months, but you do not catch the criminal. You only learned a lesson in caution.

76 to 90   **Partial Success**

You do not find a teacher of the exact martial arts skill that you were looking for but, you do find a skilled teacher.

UM 100   **Unusual Success**

You find a great teacher who is able to teach you your desired martial arts skill as well as several other skills that you are interested in. The teacher takes a personal interest in your training and considers you a friend.

91 to 110   **Near Success**

You find a teacher able to teach you your desired martial arts skill, but he does not have the time to teach you. He gives you some other names in this region and adjoining regions to try. You may roll again on this table if you desire with a special +10 modifier.

111 to 175   **Success**

You find a qualified teacher willing and able to teach you the desired martial arts skill.

176 or more   **Absolute Success**

A legendary teacher of your desired martial art agrees to take you on as his student. When determining whether a martial arts style or weapon style is a Basic or Advanced skill, you may treat the style as if it costs ten fewer style points. This represents the superior teaching methods of your new instructor.

Individuals that train a character in the use of his martial arts skills have a very important influence on the character's life. In terms of game mechanics, a player who has a character that specializes in martial arts skills can easily spend approximately 30% to 60% of his available development points each level on his martial arts skills. It is then becomes equally important to attempt to make sure that some of the character's role playing and campaign involvement will stem from his martial arts skills.

Here are some charts to determine some random characteristics about the character's past, present or future martial arts teachers and organizations.

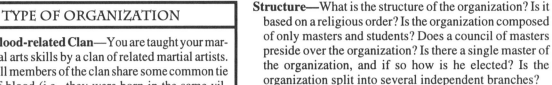

TYPE OF ORGANIZATION

01-10	**Blood-related Clan**—You are taught your martial arts skills by a clan of related martial artists. All members of the clan share some common tie of blood (i.e., they were born in the same village, descended from the original members of some secret organization, etc.).
11-20	**Family**—You are taught your martial arts skills by members of your family. Your family may have a secret martial arts or weapon style that you have been taught as well.
21-40	**School**—You are taught your martial arts skills by a loose organization of martial arts students, headed by a chief instructor. The school usually accepts monetary payment for training, but you may have worked out a special deal with the instructors (GM's choice).
41-65	**Religious Order**—You are taught your martial arts skills by a religious organization. You were also taught the precepts and beliefs of the religious order. You have been taught to support the order and your brothers in the order at all costs.
66-80	**Secret Society**—You are taught your martial arts skill by a secret society. You have been taught the beliefs and goals of the secret society. You know several other secret society members within your region and you know you can turn to them for aid.
81-100	**Clan**—You are taught your martial arts skills by a clan of martial artists. All members of this group share a common bond of love for the martial arts, coupled with respect for the organization's goals. Loyalty and respect are expected among clan members.

OTHER DETAILS

A few other decisions flesh out an organization that teaches martial arts skills. Among other things, the Gamemaster must decide how large the organization is, what are its goals, its structure, and any other interests the organization may have.

Popularity—Is the organization popular? Has it recently won a famous challenge from a rival school, or been granted some favor by a powerful figure? Is the organization losing popularity, has it lost an important challenge, or has it been involved in a scandal? Is the organization relatively unknown, is it a secret organization or newly founded?

> **Example:** *Melissa and the Gamemaster talk some more about the background of her character, Ming Te.*

Goals—What are goals of the organization? Is the organization serving as a front for another secret organization or clan? Does the organization have political motives? Does the organization serve a religious movement? Is the organization out to simple gain money and political power? Does the organization strive to uphold a rigid moral or religious code of ethics?

Structure—What is the structure of the organization? Is it based on a religious order? Is the organization composed of only masters and students? Does a council of masters preside over the organization? Is there a single master of the organization, and if so how is he elected? Is the organization split into several independent branches?

Wealth—How wealthy is the organization? Is it impoverished? Is it moderately wealthy with several training halls and many members? Is it wealthy with branches in many cities and access to ready cash? How does the organization raise its money? Does the organization have funding from another source, does it have membership dues, or does it have other revenue generating means?

Advancement—How do you advance within the organization? Is advancement through seniority of the student or of the master of the student? Is advancement handled through popular acclaim or vote, and if so who is allowed to vote? Is advancement handled through formal challenges, and if so what are the regulations regarding challenges?

Other interests—Does the organization have any other interests besides promoting martial arts? For example the organization could be involved in banking, challenges, providing instructors, providing bodyguards, providing mercenaries, producing duelists, acting as the enforcement arm of another organization, training assassins, training doctors, or providing arbitrators.

Recent Events—What recent events have occurred to the organization since characters have become involved with it? Has there been a scandal (political, religious, law, or moral)? Has a split or schism occurred in the ranks of the organization recently? Has the organization had a sudden loss or gain of popular favor, and if so what occurred? Are there upcoming martial arts competitions that will involve the organization?

MASTER'S BACKGROUND

Gamemasters may use the following chart to create a background for NPC martial artists or teachers with whom the characters interact during the campaign. This can make the Gamemaster's job a little easier by removing some of the burden of creation.

MASTER'S BACKGROUND CHART

01-02 Fake Credentials—Your master is a fake with very little real knowledge of the martial arts. You soon discover this, but you are not yet sure why he is posing as a martial arts instructor.

03-06 Secret Society Member—Your master is a member of a secret society that has been outlawed by the current government. He will try to recruit you into the secret society as a new member.

07-10 Drunkard—Your master is a drunkard. He will go on drunken binges, getting into fights and creating a nuisance of himself, every time he is under a great deal of stress. On any given night, there is a 15% chance that he is drinking, whether alone or in a tavern or pub.

11–13 Chi Knowledge—Your master has knowledge of Chi Powers skills. He may teach you the Chi Master training package if you so desire.

14–17 Challenger—Your master strives constantly to challenge others to prove his martial arts skills are superior. He often requires you to challenge other master's students. You do not have many friends in the martial arts world.

18–20 Secretive—Your master carries secrecy to an extreme. You must practice in a closed room with him and he is constantly checking for spies looking to steal his secrets. Progress with this master is 50% slower than normal due to his excessive precautions and reluctance to part with his secret knowledge of the martial arts.

21–24 Hermit—Your master is a hermit. To learn martial arts skills from him, you must travel to a remote rural location where he lives to learn his skills.

25–28 Partial Knowledge—Your master only taught you the initial forms of your martial arts skill. You cannot learn any Restricted martial arts skills from this teacher. In addition, your teacher docs not know any martial arts skills beyond 10 ranks.

29–31 Paranoid—Your master is a skilled practitioner of the martial arts, but he is extremely paranoid that others are out to steal his secrets or do him harm. You must constantly reassure your master that you are not plotting against him. Your master has strictly forbidden you from talking with other martial artists.

32–35 Poor Teacher—Your master is a very poor teacher. He is impatient and does not explain himself. Progress under this master takes twice as long as normal due to his poor teaching techniques.

36–38 Rival School—Your master has a rival school that challenges his teachings. If you are learning a martial arts style or a weapon style, this rival school also teaches an opposing martial arts style or weapon style.

39–42 Disgraced—Your master has committed some action in his past that has permanently disgraced his reputation. Some of his dishonor carries to you since you are his student. Your master hopes you can repair the wrong that he did.

43–45 Hidden Knowledge—Your master possesses hidden knowledge of a martial arts skill. Your master can teach you martial arts skills thought lost (i.e., an ancient martial arts or weapon style or a martial arts skill not normally allowed in this culture).

46–49 Retired Soldier—Your master has had a long career in the military. You may make use of some of his military contacts if necessary.

50–53 Former Bodyguard—Your master used to be a highly respected (in specialized circles) bodyguard. You may make use of some of his contacts in bodyguard guilds and the underworld.

54-57 Highly Respected—Your master is universally respected for his wisdom and strength. Being his student, you are accorded some of the same respect.

58–60 Excellent Teacher—Your master is an excellent teacher. You may learn your martial arts skills at half the normal rate.

61–63 Full Knowledge—Your master has complete knowledge of his chosen martial arts and weapon styles. He knows all the secret maneuvers and special attacks associated with them as well.

64–66 Enemies—Your master has made some very powerful enemies in the course of his life. As his student, you have inherited their enmity. They may seek to strike at your master through you – be warned!

67-70 Vengeful—Your master is vengeful. If anyone does him wrong, he will attempt to exact revenge no matter the cost.

71-72 Blood-Guilt—Your master suffers from guilt due to all the enemies he killed in his youth. Your master will not take another life, even if it costs him his own. Unfortunately, your master's enemies are not so restricted.

73-75 Cursed—Your master is cursed. The exact nature of the curse is up to the Gamemaster.

76–78 Impoverished—Your master is very poor. Your training facilities are substandard.

79-81 Debtor—Your master owes a large debt to another organization or person. He has trained you in secret to prevent you from incurring any of his debt. You want to help your master in any way possible.

82-84 Outlaw—Your master is an outlaw. As his student, you are branded an outlaw by the government as well.

85–86 Wandering Monk—Your master is a wandering monk. He teaches you your martial arts skills on the road.

87–90 Wealthy Patron—Your master has a wealthy patron that keeps him well supplied. You are indebted to this wealthy patron as well.

91–95 Rival Students—Your master has several more advanced students who consider you a dangerous rival. They make life hard for you and try to have you dismissed.

96-100 Many Students—Your master has many students (twice the normal number for this culture/organization) and you must constantly compete for his attention.

MARTIAL
ARTS
COMPANION

◆ 12.2 ◆
TRAINING METHODS

While there are many historical methods used to help train martial artists ranging from running with weights to leaping in and out of pits or training on top of small round wooden pillars, all of these methods share some common factors. The training method seeks to develop the martial artist physically through exercise, and emotionally and intellectually through sparring and set forms.

EXERCISE

Exercise is one of the most important training methods. Martial arts require a high degree of flexibility and strength from their practitioners. Much of the exercise and training methods used in martial arts styles focus on making the student more limber and flexible. Examples in history ranged from tying weights to one's body while exercising to practicing atop of small structures to promote balance, to hardening the body by striking objects repeatedly.

SPARRING

Most martial arts styles teach their more advanced students through sparring, or controlled fighting with another student. Sparring allows the student to prepare himself for actual combat in a safe environment. The student becomes comfortable with striking an opponent and being struck to prevent fear from freezing his reactions in an actual combat situation. In addition sparring helps the student understand the reasons and methods behind his martial arts techniques through experience.

SET FORMS

Included in many martial arts styles are several set forms (katas). A set form is a predefined series of movements, strikes, and counter-strikes using the martial arts style that a student can practice on his own. The set forms allow the student to gain confidence in his ability and instill trained reactions to certain types of attacks. Through extensive use of set forms, the student can react to attacks without thinking because he has practiced counters so often that they have become instinctive.

ANCIENT TRAINING METHODS

The following methods are ancient training methods once used in China for practitioners of the martial arts. It is hoped that these examples will stimulate Gamemasters and players to create their own unique training methods for their martial arts.

Climbing Wall Kung—With this training, a skilled adept can with his back against a wall, move freely on the wall through the strength of his heels and elbows. Like a lizard the adept will be able to use the small cracks and protrusions on the wall to scale it. The student first practices lying on his back and moving with only the strength and coordination of his heels and elbows. Then a training wall with protruding bricks and ledges is built and the student practices climbing it with only his elbows and heels. After the student has mastered this, the protrusions are reduced and weight is added to the student's body. After many years of practice, the student will be able to scale a wall with the easy and dexterity of a lizard.

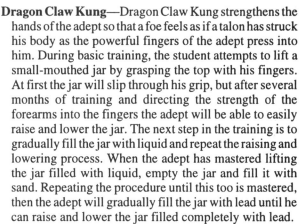

Dragon Claw Kung—Dragon Claw Kung strengthens the hands of the adept so that a foe feels as if a talon has struck his body as the powerful fingers of the adept press into him. During basic training, the student attempts to lift a small-mouthed jar by grasping the top with his fingers. At first the jar will slip through his grip, but after several months of training and directing the strength of the forearms into the fingers the adept will be able to easily raise and lower the jar. The next step in the training is to gradually fill the jar with liquid and repeat the raising and lowering process. When the adept has mastered lifting the jar filled with liquid, empty the jar and fill it with sand. Repeating the procedure until this too is mastered, then the adept will gradually fill the jar with lead until he can raise and lower the jar filled completely with lead.

In advanced training, the adept puts the jar aside and practices the same hooking finger grip empty-handed with dynamic tension. Each morning the adept will practice this motion as if he was trying to grasp the sun. At its ultimate pinnacle, "birds flying across the sky will fall as if shot with arrows at a stretch of gripping fingers. Wild horses can be managed as if bridled on the reins in one's hands."

Hing Kung—With this training, a student learns to step as lightly as a butterfly. The training begins by filling a one-hundred pound earthen vessel with water. The student practices walking around on the edge of the vessel without upsetting it. After this exercise is mastered, the student then ties some weights to his body and repeats the exercise. When the student can step around the vessel without spilling a drop, he begins to lessen the amount of water in the vessel while at the same time increasing the weight on his body. He continues to practice until he can successfully walk around the edge of the nearly empty vessel while carrying weights equal to his body weight. The next phase of the training involves replacing the earthen vessel with a reed basket filled with rocks. Once again the student continues to practice, all the while, removing rocks from the basket until the student can walk around the edge of the empty basket without upsetting it.

In advanced training, the student begins to practice to walk on sand. Using small-grained sand, the student lays down a path one foot deep, three feet wide, and ten feet long. The sand path is then covered with rice paper and the student practices walking along it. When the student can walk the length of the path without causing the fragile paper to rip, the paper is removed and the student practices walking on the sand until not even a footprint can be seen.

Iron Forearm Kung—The Iron Forearm Kung is one of the simplest training methods to master. The arm training begins by striking the inner and outer forearms against a wooden post or pole. As the arms become stronger, the student can begin hitting harder and for a longer duration of time. After six months of training, the student will begin practicing against a sturdy tree with coarse bark. This portion of the training will continue for two years, after which the student will have gained immense strength in his forearms. The next phase of the training involves hitting smooth rocks with the forearms. After the student becomes used to this training, substitute uneven rocks. When the student can shatter rocks with his iron-hard forearms, his training is complete.

Iron Sweeper Kung—The Iron Sweeper Kung develops the strength and toughness of the student's legs. The student begins by practicing the low Horse Stance each day, which develops the leg muscles. After several years of strengthening the legs, the student begins to practice low kicks against a wooden post driven into the earth. Each day the student practices leg sweeps against the pole until he breaks it. Another larger wooden pole is driven into the ground, and the student practices his leg sweeps against it until it too breaks. The final phase of the training involves the student practicing against a large tree, until by dint of continual battering he is able to strike the tree with enough force to bring the tree swaying and cause the leaves to fall.

Leaping Kung—The student begins by digging a hole two feet deep and three feet wide. Standing in this trench, the student practices leaping out to ground level. Every two weeks, additional weights are added to the body and the trench is dug an inch deeper. After continuing for several years, the adept will be able to leap out of a trench seven feet deep with over ten pounds of weights attached to his body. Then the adept will be able to jump across a chasm or leap to the top of a small building with ease.

Speed Running Kung—Initially the adept attaches lead weights to the ankles and then practices running in open fields until winded. The adept will continue to increase the weights on his ankles every two weeks. After several years, he will be able to run ten miles while wearing the weights. Eventually the student will practice running up and down hillsides. After removing the weights, the adept will feel as light as a butterfly.

Water Dividing Kung—Water Dividing Kung concentrates strength in the backs of the palms and arms. The adept begins by burying a dozen ten-foot long bamboo poles vertically three feet in the ground. Then the student ties a rope in and around the upper part of the poles, in effect creating a wall. The disciple then starts to practice by pushing both hands through the center of the bamboo row, then spreads him arms outward. As practice increases, a small gap will appear. Eventually the disciple will be able to bend open the bamboo poles and walk to the other side. When this is accomplished, the adept will add additional poles on each side and repeat this training until twenty poles can be pushed apart with ease. Should an unruly crowd ever detain an adept or block his passage, his Water Dividing Strength will have the force to part the mob as an earthquake splits the ground.

Wooden Man Kung—The Wooden Man Kung involves practicing strikes against a wooden structure that resembles a man. The student begins by practicing slowly, emphasizing the accuracy of his strikes. As the student becomes more accurate, he begins to strike in faster and more complicated patterns moving around the wooden dummy as he attacks from all angles. After several months of practice, the student will be able to strike the dummy with fast and accurate blows that will become second nature to him in an actual fight with an opponent.

◆ 12.3 ◆
REPUTATION

An important part of running a martial arts campaign is the role that reputation plays in the campaign world. In the world of martial arts, reputation has carried heavy weight. For example, the various martial arts styles are differentiated by their reputation of effectiveness. A teacher with a good reputation as a skilled fighter will draw many more students than a teacher with a poor reputation as a fighter. Fighters with a high reputation in their martial arts skills may draw more challenges. Reputation allows the character to be known by other martial arts practitioners who may then decide to help or hinder the character based on his reputation.

REPUTATION IN THE CAMPAIGN

Reputation should not be measured as a statistic during the campaign. The Gamemaster should keep a rough rule of thumb approximation of the character's reputation in the martial arts. There are several factors to consider when assigning a reputation to a character in a campaign, but the some of the guidelines presented below can make the job easier.

WHO TAUGHT THEM

The principle teacher or organization that trained the character in the use of his martial arts skills plays an important role in a starting character's reputation. The starting character's reputation should be higher than normal if he is taught by a teacher or organization with a high reputation, or lower than normal if the opposite case holds true. However, the true measure of a character's reputation is in his actions.

MARTIAL
ARTS
COMPANION

GAINING AND LOSING REPUTATION

Martial artists can gain and lose reputation by participating in challenges and tournaments against other martial artists. A martial artist who continually refuses challenges will lose reputation as will a martial artist who indiscriminately challenges opponents. A martial artist who continually wins challenges and tournaments will gain reputation as a skilled martial artist.

SIGNATURE MOVES, DEFENSES, OR ATTACKS

Have the player of the martial arts character outline some special signature moves, defenses or attacks that his character is especially skilled at performing. The action does not have to be explicitly tied to a specific game mechanic, unless desired. For example, a martial artist could be famous for his Crossing Fists technique when attacking (Martial Arts Strikes) or he could be famous for his Arrow Cutting Technique (Adrenal Deflecting). There is a two-fold purpose for having the player do this. First, it offers the Gamemaster some details regarding the character that he can easily work into the campaign, and second it causes the player to think a little more deeply about his martial arts character.

◆ 12.4 ◆
CHALLENGES

Challenges occupy an important place in the martial arts world. Through the mechanism of challenges, martial artists attempt to prove that their particular martial arts style or training is superior to another. Challenges can make the campaign more interesting for players who have created characters that specialize in the martial arts.

MOTIVATIONS FOR CHALLENGES

The most common motivation for entering a contest or accepting a challenge is the desire to build up one's reputation. In most cases, a martial artist makes his living through his skill at arms, and success in these types of contests helps to improve his job prospects. Perhaps the martial artist wishes to prove his martial arts style is superior to all others and become a famous martial artist. Challenges can also be motivated by the desire to revenge oneself on a hated enemy by defeating him in a public arena.

TYPES OF CHALLENGES

There are many types of challenges ranging from informal duels in the street to very structured tournaments involving hundreds of martial artists. Important things for the Gamemaster to consider are the place of challenges in the society and the rules and regulations that govern challenges. If challenges are illegal, then players run the risk of breaking the law or being thrown in jail by issuing one. A little forethought on the legality and regulations of challenges can make a campaign very interesting. For example if losing in a challenge results in exile or loss of life, characters will be much more wary about offending other martial artist.

RESOLUTION

Depending on the situation, challenges can be resolved in a number of ways. A challenge can be until the first blow, first blood, death, until an opponent gives up, or it can also involve the environment (e.g., first person to be pushed out of the ring loses). See Section 14.6 for more information on how to resolve these types of challenges and some ideas for creating interesting challenges for players.

MARTIAL ARTS WEAPONS

The use and development of weapons has always been linked with martial arts. Certain styles of martial arts may emphasize the use of weaponry more than others, but most martial arts styles have some association with weaponry. The types of weapons used with martial arts have varied wildly, depending on the location and time period in which the martial art developed.

Of all the of the historical martial arts styles of the world, the Chinese martial arts styles are famous for their wide and inventive use of weaponry. One example of a Chinese martial arts style that formulated the efficient use of bizarre weapons is Choy-Li-Fut which taught the use of the smoking pipe and wooden bench as weapons. Of course, martial arts also encourage the use of more obvious weapons such as the sword, spear, or staff.

There are literally hundreds of different types of martial arts weapons that have been used with various martial arts styles throughout history. Presented here are some of the most popular martial arts weapons, as well as some of the more obscure weapons to inspire the imagination of the reader. In the case where multiple attack tables are listed for the same weapon, the wielder may choose before he strikes which attack table to use on his opponent. In all cases, the wielder needs only to develop a single skill with the specific weapon in order to use it, no matter how many different attack tables the weapon may use.

A common theme among the martial arts weapons listed in this section is their limited effectiveness against fully armored opponents. Traditionally, these weapons were designed to be used against other martial arts masters who wore light or no armor. Many of the unusual weapons listed required great skill to use, and as a result a martial artist using one of these unusual weapons was in effect advertising his martial arts prowess and expertise. Little effort was expended in learning to use very large smashing weapons, as the encumbrance of such weapons did not play to the strengths of a martial artist - speed and mobility.

◆ 13.1 ◆
USING WITH ARMS LAW

Most of the weapons presented below are done so in an abbreviated format from the full attack table format presented in *Arms Law*. Instead, each weapon has a description (and a brief listing of its vital statistics needed for *Arms Law* is given in the Appendix). For those weapons that could not use an existing *Arms Law* attack table, new attack tables are given to represent their capabilities. This information will supersede any information already printed on the Weapon Statistics Chart (p. 138, *Arms Law*).

Note: *The new attack tables and statistics can be found in the Appendix. What is presented below are simply descriptions of the weapons.*

◆ 13.2 ◆
WEAPON DESCRIPTIONS

This section contains a complete listing of all martial arts weapons that are covered by this book.

13.2.1 · CONCUSSION WEAPONS

This sub-section contains descriptions of all weapons that deliver their damage by "bashing" their victim (this includes both one-handed and two-handed weapons).

HAMMER, COPPER

The copper hammer is a Chinese weapon used in certain styles of martial arts. The copper hammer has a short handle attached to a large round copper ball. This weapon is usually paired with another for use in combat. The heavy blows delivered by this weapon can be devastating to an unarmored opponent.

JITTE

The jitte is a weapon that originated in feudal Japan. The jitte consists of a fifteen-inch iron rod mounted on a long hilt with a square hook jutting from the rod where it meets the hilt. The jitte was used by law enforcement officers in feudal Japan for whom it was also a symbol of their position. The jitte was created to disarm swordwielding samurai, and an entire array of sophisticated combat techniques were developed by the practitioners of this weapon. In the hands of a master, the jitte can easily break a steel blade or rip it from the hands of the unsuspecting owner.

Note: *The wielder of the jitte has a special +15 bonus to Disarm Foe-Armed skill maneuvers.*

NUNCHAKU

The nunchaku is a unique weapon first developed in Okinawa. The nunchaku consists of two pieces of hardwood connected by a short rope. The length of each piece of wood ranges from twelve to fourteen inches. The connecting rope can be anywhere from one to five inches long. In combat the wielder of the nunchaku wraps the nunchaku around his body to generate high speeds and then strikes his opponent with blinding speed with the extreme end of one of the hardwood segments. The crushing force generated by this weapon is immense when applied with skill. Commonly, the nunchaku is used with both hands, but skilled practitioners can use the nunchaku with only one hand.

Note: *The nunchaku is normally developed as a 2-Handed weapon, but can be developed as a 1-H Concussion weapon. If wielded as a one-handed weapon, the wielder suffers a special −20 OB modifier to represent the decreased effectiveness of the weapon.*

RING, METAL

The metal ring is an unusual weapon used in some styles of Chinese martial arts. This weapon is actually a large two-to four-foot-diameter metal ring. The ring was used in a deceptive manner to catch a foe's weapon or weapon arm and disarm him. The metal circumference of the ring was also useful in parrying attacks against the wielder. The ring could be used offensively as a crushing implement, but its primary focus was as a defensive weapon.

Note: *The wielder of the ring has a special +15 bonus to Disarm Foe-Armed skill maneuvers.*

STAFF, THORN

The thorn staff is a weapon that was first used in Chinese martial arts. The name thorn staff is actually misleading as the thorn staff was actually a two- to three-foot rod ending in a hilt much like a sword handle. The "thorns" in this case are sharp one-or two-inch metal slivers pressed into the rod portion of the weapon. Against an unarmored opponent, a blow from this weapon can inflict painful scraping wounds. Even against armored opponents, the heavy core of the thorn staff generates crushing blows not unlike a mace.

STAFF, BO

The bo staff is a universal weapon found in many different martial arts styles in both Japan and China. The staff measures some six feet in length and is usually made of wood. The ease of use of this weapon coupled with its inexpensive nature make this a popular weapon with martial artists.

STAFF, JO

The jo staff is a shorter version of the bo staff. It is designed to be more easily maneuverable due to its lighter weight and shorter length. The jo staff was used widely in feudal Japan by the warrior classes.

STAFF, THREE-SECTIONED

The three-sectioned staff is a weapon first developed in China. The three-sectioned staff is actually made up of three equal pieces of hardwood ranging from two to three feet in length each. The pieces are connected by metal links or a cord two to five inches long. In combat this weapon can be used to attack not unlike a flail, with the free end of the staff striking the opponent. This weapon is also useful in trapping opponent's weapons between the sections of the staff.

Note: *The wielder of the three-sectioned staff has a special +10 bonus to Disarm Foe-Armed skill maneuvers.*

TETSUBO

The tetsubo is a heavy iron staff approximately six feet in length. Tetsubo is the Japanese name for this weapon, which has many counterparts in other Asian countries. The

staff typically has either a circular or hexagonal cross-section and a flaring shape that is widest at the striking end and narrowest at the handle. This weapon requires immense physical strength to use effectively.

Note: *The user of this weapon must have a Strength stat bonus of +5 or greater in order to use this weapon effectively. If the Strength stat bonus is less than +5, this skill should be classified as Restricted.*

TONFA

The tonfa is a weapon first developed for use in martial arts in Okinawa. Originally peasants used the tonfa in their daily work but the martial artists of the island soon developed it as a weapon. The tonfa resembles a rectangular wooden block measuring one and a half feet in length and four inches in width. The tonfa has a short wooden handle near one end of the rectangular block that sticks perpendicularly from the broad plane of the weapon. The tonfa is held with the broad rectangular surface parallel to the forearm and a short section of several inches projecting beyond the fist. The tonfa is useful both as a blocking weapon and an attacking weapon.

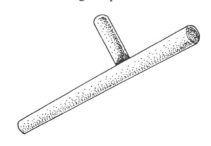

13.2.2 · BLADES

This sub-section contains descriptions of all weapons that deliver their damage by "slicing" their victim (this includes both one-handed and two-handed weapons).

KAMA

The kama is a weapon originally developed in Okinawa. Nominally a rice harvesting implement, the kama became a dangerous weapon in the hands of the Okinawan martial artists. The kama consists of a hardwood handle with a short edged blade set perpendicularly to the handle. The kama can be used in combat either singly or in sets. In short range combat, the kama is particularly deadly, as it could be used to chop, block, hook, or slash an opponent.

KATANA

The katana is a long, curved single edged sword developed in feudal Japan. The blade of the kanata is three to four feet in length. The katana was usually wielded by members of the samurai class in Japan and was considered a symbol of both their status and honor. The katana's hilt is long enough for two hands and it is primarily made of wood and covered with decorative silk cords. The tsuba or guard of the katana is typically made of metal and decorated with beautiful detail work. The secrets of the master swordsmiths who manufactured the katanas were jealously guarded from competitors. The katana is legendary for its strength and sharpness.

Note: *Normally, the katana is a developed as a 2-handed weapon. However, it may be developed instead as a 1-handed Edged weapon. If a katana is used one-handed, the wielder suffers a special penalty of -20 to his OB.*

KNIFE, BUTTERFLY

The butterfky knife is a Chinese weapon that originated in the Southern provinces of China. Butterfly knives are modeled after the chopping cleavers used by butchers. Usually the knives are used in pairs. The shape of the butterfly knife is distinctive, with a flat, heavy, wide, single-edged blade and a curved handle to protect the fingers of the wielder.

KNIFE, CIRCULAR

The circular knife is a distinctive Chinese weapon consisting of a two-to three-foot wooden rod with a long, single-edged, curved blade spanning from end to end. The circular knife is used with both hands and can be a disorienting weapon for the uninitiated foe to face. Typical attacks using this weapon involve sweeping and spinning strikes to take advantage of the very long blade surface.

KNIFE, WILLOW LEAF

The willow leaf knife is a thin curved single-edged knife that is used with several Chinese martial arts. The typical length of the blade of this weapon is just over two feet long. This weapon very closely resembles the scimitar in both appearance and effectiveness.

KRIS

The kris is an extremely long double-edged blade from Indonesia and Malaysia. The kris has a unique wavy blade shape that widens as the blade approaches the hilt. The more waves the blade of a kris possesses, the deadlier it is supposed to be in combat, as a wavy blade can cause a larger wound and slips more easily in between the ribs of a foe. Many stories surround the mystical properties of these blades; it is said that a kris is lethal even when stabbed in the shadow or footprint of a foe.

SAI

The sai is a weapon that was simultaneously developed in many countries in the Eastern Hemisphere, but it was first formalized in several fighting styles in Okinawa. The sai is a short metal weapon with a blunt rod fifteen to twenty inches in length, flanked by two broad tines projecting forward about five inches. The sai is usually paired with another. In combat the sai is primarily used defensively. The blunt rod serves to channel attacks down towards the tines, where the weapon can be trapped and snared. Typically the wielder of the sai carries an extra sai as a reserve.

Note: *The wielder of the sai has a special +10 bonus to Disarm Foe-Armed skill maneuvers.*

SWORD, CHINESE

The Chinese sword is the most common sword design found in ancient China. The Chinese sword is a straight, double-edged sword with a blade two to three feet in length. Typically the hilt of the sword is wrapped with silk and a long tassel is attached to the end of the hilt. The hilt or guard of the sword is minimal and the sword presents a streamlined appearance.

SWORD, NINE-RING

The nine-ring sword is a wide blade used in some Chinese martial arts. The descriptive name of the sword comes from the series of nine small metal rings attached to the upper, non-edged side of the blade near the tip of the sword. These rings are useful in catching an opponent's blade, as well as creating a lot of noise to warn others that a fight is occurring.

Note: *The wielder of the nine-ring sword has a special +5 bonus to Disarm Foe-Armed skill maneuvers.*

SWORD, SPRING

The spring sword or urumi is an ancient Indian weapon. This weapon consists of about four steel bands each one to two inches wide and six feet long attached to a sword handle. Both edges of each steel band are very sharp. The spring sword is kept coiled up when not in use, and when it is released it is capable of producing extraordinary noise, dust, and sparks as it is whipped through the air. It can be used to create a defensive screen by rapid circular movements of the wielder. An adept can safely bring the spring sword to a stop by wrapping it around his waist.

WAKIZASHI

The waskizashi was the most common sword used in feudal Japan. The waskizashi has a curved, single-edged blade that is roughly two feet long. A wider range of people in feudal Japan could use the waskizashi compared to the range of people that could use the kanata. This weapon was made using the same superior swordcrafting techniques of the Japanese swordsmiths used for the katana.

13.2.3 · CHAINS

This sub-section contains descriptions of all weapons that deliver their damage at a slightly extended range by using a chain to extend their reach. Skill with this type of weapon is developed in the Thrown Weapons skill category (though the weapon is not actually thrown).

CHIGIRIKI

The chigiriki is a feudal Japanese weapon that consists of a staff with an attached metal chain that is three to ten feet long ending in a metal weight. The chain can be used to ensnare a weapon or even disarm an opponent by wrapping the chain around their weapon and then jerking the weapon out of his hands. The metal weight can also deliver punishing blows to an opponent. In addition, the wielder can close with an entangled opponent and make strikes with the wooden ends of the staff.

Note: *The wielder of the chigiriki has a special +10 bonus to Disarm Foe-Armed skill maneuvers.*

KUSARI-GAMA

The kusari-gama is a feudal Japanese weapon that, like the chigiriki, incorporats an iron chain. Instead of a using a wooden staff, the kusari-gama is a short sickle attached to a three to ten foot metal chain that ends in a metal weight. The chain is often used to ensnare an opponent in order for the wielder of the kusari-gama to safely close the range and use his razor-sharp sickle on the helpless foe. This type of weapon was favored by the ninja in feudal Japan and required much skill to use.

Note: *The wielder of the kursari-gama has a special +15 bonus to Disarm Foe-Armed skill maneuvers.*

MANRIKI-GUSARI

The manriki-gusari is yet another chain-based weapon developed in feudal Japan. It is a metal chain approximately two feet in length with weights on either end. This chain weapon was invented to disarm an opponent without spilling blood. The chain can also be used to immobilize, hobble, or even choke an opponent. By holding the chain taut between the hands, the user can block sword strikes. Similar types of chain weapons were developed in other countries using the same principles of attack and defense.

Note: *The wielder of the manriki-gusari has a special +5 bonus to Disarm Foe-Armed skill maneuvers.*

13.2.4 · POLE ARMS

This sub-section contains descriptions of all weapons that are all long and generally have a wooden shaft (e.g., a spear, etc.).

FORK, TIGER

The tiger fork is a weapon that was originally used to kill tigers in China. The tiger fork resembles a large trident with wide curving outer tines. These tines prevented a tiger from charging up the fork, much like the tines on an European boar spear. Lighter versions of the tiger fork were also used in certain Chinese martial art styles.

NAGINATA

The naginata is a weapon that developed in feudal Japan. The naginata has a thick, curved, single-edged blade nearly three feet in length attached to a slightly longer staff. The naginata became a very popular weapon in Japan due to its versatility, it could be used for both thrusting and slashing. The naginata can be used to make sweeping attacks at exposed portions of the foe. The short handle length allows the wielder to make many short chopping or thrusting strikes against his foe. Only the most determined, or foolhardy, warrior can penetrate the swirling defense of a skilled practitioner of the naginata.

NINE-DRAGON TRIDENT

The nine-dragon trident is a weapon developed for use in certain styles of Chinese martial arts. The nine-dragon trident is an immense weapon weighing near twenty pounds and extending nearly six feet in length. The immense weight of this weapon comes from the many blades and hooks mounted on its end. The nine-dragon trident can be used to strike or sweep an opponent. In addition, the trident can be used to disarm a foe with a corkscrewing motion after a blade strikes against one of its many protruding hooks at the end of the weapon.

Note: *The wielder of the nine-dragon trident has a special +15 bonus to Disarm Foe-Armed skill maneuvers.*

YARI

The yari is the principle spear used in feudal Japan. The yari is a little over six feet in length, and it is tipped with a straight, double-edged blade. This weapon is primarily designed to be a thrusting weapon rather than a thrown weapon.

13.2.5 · MISSILE WEAPONS

This sub-section contains descriptions of all weapons that deliver their damage by striking their victims from a distance. All of these weapons require "ammunition" of some type (usually arrows) and the ammunition is fired through a mechanical process (e.g.., a bow propels the arrow, etc.).

DAI-KYU

The dai-kyu is a very large Japanese bow. Unlike Western bows, the dai-kyu is asymmetrical with the handle placed on the lower one-third of the bow so that the upper portion of the bow is much longer. The reason for this design is to allow this bow to be used while on horseback or while the archer is kneeling. The typical dai-kyu is approximately seven feet long. As a result, this bow produces more power than the typical longbow.

Note: *The time required to string this bow is double that of a normal long bow. In addition, the percentage activity needed to fire this bow is increased by 10% (from 30-60% to 40-70%).*

HAN-KYU

The han-kyu is a small, compact bow developed in feudal Japan. The kan-kyu is designed to be concealed in clothing and as small as possible. The ninja clans of feudal Japan developed this bow in order to conceal their weapons when in disguise.

13.2.6 · THROWN WEAPONS

This sub-section contains descriptions of all weapons that deliver their damage at a distance but do not use a mechanical device to propel the weapon (using the thrower's skill alone).

CLAW, FLYING

The flying claw is a weapon used in certain types of Chinese martial arts. The flying claw consists of a metal weight, stylized to resemble a claw, attached to a long cord or light metal chain. The flying claw is used to ensnare an opponent and draw him off balance in order to leave him vulnerable to other attacks.

Note: *A 60% activity action is needed to reload (rewind) this weapon for another attack.*

DART, ROPE

The rope dart is a weapon used in some styles of Chinese martial arts. The rope dart consists of a long rope or light metal chain that has a metal dart at one end. The wielder of the metal dart uses specialized maneuvers to wind the rope around his body, and then to unwind it at a high velocity to shoot the metal dart at his enemy.

Note: *A 60% activity action is needed to reload (rewind) this weapon.*

DART, THROWN

Small thrown darts are used in various styles of martial arts. Typically the darts are concealed from the opponent until the last moment and then hurled at the face and eyes. Traditionally, darts are hidden in the sleeves of a garment. Most martial arts masters look upon these weapons with disdain, as they imply that the wielder's martial arts skills are too weak to be used in melee combat.

SHURIKEN

The shuriken is a type of throwing dart developed in feudal Japan. Shuriken come in many shapes and styles. The most accurate types of shuriken are those shaped like long narrow darts. Other styles of throwing darts were developed with three to ten points, leading to the popularly known "star shuriken." Star shuriken do not have high penetrating power and thus are aimed at the face and the throat in order to slow an attacker.

13.2.7 · UNUSUAL WEAPONS

This sub-section contains descriptions of all weapons that are unusual in nature, perhaps not normally thought of as weapons, or operate slightly differently than most weapons.

FAN

The fan is a popular accessory that is also used as a weapon in some Chinese martial arts. One reason for its popularity is that in Chinese society, a fan could be carried without comment. A man's fan was carried in the waistband or sleeve and it contained 9, 16, 20, or 24 ribs. The fan can be used closed to deliver precise blows to an opponent and then opened to confuse and distract the opponent. An opened fan can also be used to momentarily screen the sight

of a foe in order to launch sneak attacks. A variant of this weapon is the iron fan, developed in Japan. The iron fan lived up to its descriptive name, as it had sharp iron blades for ribs (treat weapon strength as 65 – 76).

FINGERNAIL RAZORS

The fingernail razors are a special weapons used in some Chinese martial arts. They resemble small, sharpened, metal razors, which are inserted underneath the fingernails. They are typically used in to make a surprise attack.

Note: *If an attack from this weapon results in a bleeding wound, the bleeding is increased by one point per round. It is also possible to coat the razors with a poison, but this could prove as dangerous to the wielder as the foe. Any attack that results in a critical transmits the poison, but the wielder has a 5% chance of poisoning himself each round.*

FLUTE

The flute is a musical instrument that is also used as a weapon in some Chinese martial arts. It was thought that the music of the flute helped the wielder to channel his inner power or chi. In practice, the flute is wielded in much the same manner as a short stick with an emphasis on thrusting attacks with the end of the flute.

SHUKO

The shuko is a weapon developed by the ninja in feudal Japan. The shuko are worn over the hands and have metal plates with four spikes extending from the palm. Usually the shuko were used to aid in climbing, but they could also be used to make raking attacks with the palm spikes.

Note: *The individual wearing shuko while climbing gains a special bonus of +15 to Climbing skill maneuvers. Martial Arts striking attacks while wearing the shuko can be resolved on the Claw Attack Table (maximum of Small results) if desired.*

WHIP, NINE-SECTION

The nine-section whip is a weapon developed in ancient China. It consists of nine flattened metal links, each three- to five-inches in length attached together. The farthest link from the handle of the whip has a sharp point. This weapon is employed in combat by snapping the sharpened metal link at a foe. The heavier weight of the metal links allowed for more force to be generated than by a standard hide whip.

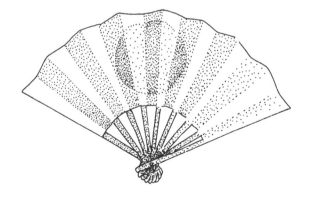

RULES

Part II

**Sections
14.0, 14.1**

Rules

The Tactical
Round

This section integrates the rules and options presented in this book into the *RMSS* rules for combat. These rules are offered as suggestions to Gamemasters, but as always Gamemasters are the final judge of what to include or discard in their campaign.

◆ 14.1 ◆
THE TACTICAL ROUND

This is a brief overview of the tactical round discussion presented in the *RMSR* Sections 18 through 26. This overview is meant to show how the options presented in this companion are to be integrated with Rolemaster. It is assumed that the reader has a firm understanding of the fundamental concepts presented in *RMSR* covering combat and the brief overview presented here is only for the purpose of clarity.

When it is necessary to impose a tactical sequence on events, the *RMSR* uses ten second rounds. Within each round, a character can attempt different actions that take a different amount of the 100% total activity available in that round. In the course of normal events, the sum of a character's actions cannot exceed 100% activity for a round, and a character cannot normally exceed three actions in a round.

14.1.1 · SEQUENCING ACTIONS

Actions are normally performed in the following order during a round (unless a character cancels his action or has previously declared an opportunity action).

1) Action Declaration Phase—All players declare the actions of their characters. Each player may declare an action in each action phase as long as they abide by their total activity percentage limitation in the round. Normally this limitation is 100% activity in one round.

2) Initiative Determination Phase—Initiative is determined in the combat round by rolling two ten-sided dice and adding the character's Quickness stat bonus, plus any additional modifiers. Actions in each action phase of the round are resolved in highest initiative result order.

3) Snap Action Phase—Snap actions are resolved in the order of initiative results and are modified by -20. A movement action may not take more than 20% of the character's movement rate.

4) Normal Action Phase—Normal actions are resolved in the order of initiative results. A movement action may not take more than 50% of the character's movement rate.

5) Deliberate Action Phase—Deliberate actions are resolved in the order of initiative results and are modified by +10. A movement action may not take more than 80% of the character's movement rate.

14.1.2 · UNUSED ACTIVITY

At the end of the deliberate action phase, any unused activity (up to a maximum of 80%) may be used as movement that is resolved simultaneously with all other moving individuals after all of the deliberate actions have been resolved.

14.1.3 · OPPORTUNITY ACTIONS

A player may decide to have his character enter an opportunity state when his chance for action arrives. As soon as a character enters an opportunity state, the rest of his activity for that round is canceled. The opportunity action may then be resolved during any action phase after it has been declared. The character may not perform any other action until his opportunity action is resolved or canceled. However, the character may use up to 20% activity at the end of the deliberate action phase for movement.

14.1.4 · CANCELING ACTIONS

Any time before his actions are resolved, a player may decide to cancel the remaining actions of his character. If the canceled actions total less than 60% of his activity, the character may move 10% of his normal movement as a deliberate action. If the canceled actions total more than 60% of activity, the character may choose one of the following:

• Move 50% of his normal movement as a deliberate action.

• Engage in melee as a deliberate action with an additional -60 OB modification.

• Make a maneuver as a deliberate action modified by an additional -60.

14.1.5 · THE ACTIONS

This is a summary of actions that may be taken in a tactical round.

ATTACK ACTIONS

In *RMSR*, the ability of a combatant is measured by his skill in his chosen form of attack. The total of this skill is referred to as the offensive bonus (OB). The entire *RMSR* combat system is predicated on the fact that the OB of a combatant represents the total skill of the individual in combat with that weapon and is available for both offense and defense. Traditionally part of the OB is sacrificed into a parrying action to avoid blows.

• A Full Melee attack requires 60% to a 100% activity action.

• A Press and Melee attack or a React and Melee attack requires an 80% to 100% activity action.

If the melee attack is attempted with less than a 100% activity action, a negative modifier equal to the percentage below 100% activity is applied to the attacker's total OB. A character cannot attack with less than the indicated minimum.

• A missile attack requires a 30% to 60% activity action.

If the missile attack is attempted with less than 60% activity action, a negative modifier equal to the percentage below 60% activity is applied to the attacker's total OB. A character cannot attack with less than the indicated minimum.

PREPARATION ACTIONS

Certain types of skills require a preparation action during the round. A preparation action requires a great deal of mental focus and concentration and as a result, a character is limited to one preparation action per round. Examples of skills or situations requiring preparation actions include preparing spells and preparing Adrenal or Chi Powers skills.

OTHER ACTIONS

Other actions allowed in the round include spell casting, static maneuvers, moving maneuvers, and movement. Please refer to the appropriate section in *RMSR* for further details.

◆ 14.2 ◆
SPECIAL MECHANICS

This section offers a brief overview of the special mechanics used to resolve the new skills presented in this companion, as well as suggestions for running martial arts combats.

14.2.1 · STYLE COMBAT BONUSES

It is very important for the players and Gamemaster to understand in what order modifiers should be applied to skill bonuses, especially when using martial arts or weapon styles, to avoid confusion when using this book, follow this simple procedure to determine the final OB bonus.

- Choose the martial arts or weapon style attack to be used;
- Determine what attack form within the style will be used;
- Take the lesser of the two bonuses (style or attack form) and use this as the OB for the attack action;
- Apply any modifications to this OB due to positional bonuses, environment, spells, items, wounds, or other factors as determined by the Gamemaster;
- This is the final OB to be used for the attack action, which can now be dealt with normally.

Example: *Yang Chung, the Fierce Tiger, is a skilled adept of the Leaping Blade style with a total style OB of +85 and a broadsword OB of +110. Currently Yang Chung is fighting a pack of bandits who have ambushed his caravan. Yang Chung is at -20 due to being thrown off his horse when his horse panicked. Seeing a bandit near him, Yang Chung moves to engage his foe.*

Yang Chung's player announces he is going to use his Leaping Blade style and attack the bandit who is threatening him. To figure out the bonuses, let's take things one step at a time. The attack form within the weapon style is the broadsword. Since his weapon style OB is less than his broadsword OB, we will use the weapon style bonus as the OB for the attack. Now it is time to apply any modifiers to the current OB. Yang Chung has a special –20 modifier due to being thrown off his horse. He has no special bonuses due to spells, items, or position. Thus the total OB for his attack is +65 (85 - 20). As with any attack action, Yang Chung's player can decide to further reduce his OB by parrying his opponent's attack.

14.2.2 · WHEN IS A STYLE BEING USED?

It is very important for the player and the Gamemaster to agree when the bonuses from a Martial Arts Style or Weapon Style skill can be applied. The basic rule of thumb is shown below.

- The bonuses from a Martial Arts Style or Weapon Style skill are only considered active if the character is actively attacking an opponent using the style.

The reasoning behind this ruling is simple and direct. These skills are considered a special form of combat that integrates several different types of skills within his attacking techniques.

Most of the benefits that can be gained by using a martial arts style or weapon style really only apply to combat, but

there are some benefits that can be considered applicable outside of melee combat and may come into question during play.

COMBAT RELATED BENEFITS

Most of the benefits conferred by a Martial Arts Style or Weapon Style skill can be considered combat related benefits. Examples of combat related benefits include (but are not limited to):

- Lesser and Greater Adrenal Defense
- Initiative bonuses
- Fumble range reduction
- Critical modifications
- Range penalty reduction
- Special Attacks skill bonuses
- Special Defenses skill bonuses

To further clarify the situation, consider some more examples with the one of the heroes of this companion, Yang Chung, also known as the Fierce Tiger. This character is using the Leaping Blade style, which incorporates Lesser Adrenal Defense, broadsword attacks, and initiative bonuses.

Example 1: *Yang Chung is still embroiled in his life or death struggle with the pack of bandits. If Yang Chung attacks using his Leaping Blade style, he gains all of the benefits of his Weapon Style skill this round. If Yang Chung decides to make normal melee attacks using his higher broadsword OB, he loses all benefits associated with his Leaping Blade weapon style for this round. This is very clear-cut and as a result it is the easiest situation to adjudicate.*

Example 2: *Having successfully leaped across the stream, Yang Chung begins to taunt the bandits. Several bandits attempt to duplicate his feat, but they fall short and are caught in the strong current of the river. One bandit, more levelheaded than his fellows readies his crossbow and aims at Yang Chung who is standing across the river. Yang Chung's player decides it is time to beat a hasty retreat, and decides to have Yang Chung attempt to move away from the bandits towards the sheltering cover of the forest while using his Adrenal Defense skill against the missile attack. If the Yang Chung was attacking with his Leaping Blade style, he could use his Adrenal Defense skill with only a 30% action and he would gain a special +2 bonus to his initiative. Yang Chung's player argues that he should not be penalized in this case simply because he has no one to attack.*

Question—In the above examples, should the player be allowed to have his Adrenal Defense action considered a 30% action?

Answer—No. The Adrenal Defense action should be considered a 40% action for the following reason. The Lesser and Greater Adrenal Defense options available with Martial Arts Styles and Weapon Styles skills allow a reduction in the required Adrenal Defense activity because the style skill allows the attacking action to be combined with the Adrenal Defense action. The Weapon Style or Martial Arts Style skill allows for improved coordination between the two skills. In one sense the Adrenal Defense skill is always a 40% action, but certain weapon and martial arts styles allow some part of that action to be incorporated into an attack with no penalty.

Question—In the above examples, should the player be allowed to use his special initiative bonus?

Answer—No. The initiative bonus is part of the attacking technique of the style. In a real sense the bonus only applies against the foe that the stylist is attacking since he will be committing the majority of his activity for that round to his attacking action. The initiative bonus conferred by Weapon Style or Martial Arts Style skills is due to the elusive positioning and feinting movements built into the system that momentarily confuse and distract the opponent.

NON-COMBAT RELATED BENEFITS

Some of the benefits conferred by a Martial Arts Style or Weapon Style skill can be considered non-combat related benefits. Examples of non-combat related benefits include:

- Adrenal skill bonuses
- Other skill bonuses, such as bonuses to Missile Deflecting or Adrenal Evasion

For example if the Leaping Blade style gave a special +10 bonus to all Missile Deflecting maneuvers, this bonus would be active if the style was actively being used. However Missile Deflecting is a 100% activity action in the round it is being used. It would be impossible to attack and use Missile Deflecting in the same round, assuming a normal 100% activity.

In the case of this and related examples, the special bonus conferred by the style is allowed even though the practitioner of the style is not actively attacking. However, the total skill bonus (including the special bonus from the style itself) cannot be higher than the style skill that conferred that bonus.

Example 3: *The Leaping Blade style also offers a special +10 bonus to all Missile Deflecting maneuvers. Yang Chung's player argues that he should be able to use his special bonus to Missile Deflecting, even though he can not also attack with his style this round. The Gamemaster agrees that this is reasonable and calculates the bonus that Yang Chung will receive. His normal bonus for Missile Deflecting is +80. The special bonus conferred by his style is +10, but his total style skill is only +85. Thus his revised Missile Deflecting skill is +85 which is then modified by –20 because Yang Chung fell off his horse at the beginning of the combat and injured himself. Yang Chung can use his Missile Deflecting skill in this case with a +65 bonus (85 – 20).*

◆ 14.3 ◆
USING SKILLS IN COMBAT

This section discusses the use of typical skills that a martial artist will use during combat and gives guidelines for the Gamemaster to resolve any questions that might arise.

14.3.1 · UNARMED ATTACKS AND PARRYING

It is important to note that *RMSR* assumes that martial artists do not suffer any disadvantage in fighting opponents with weapons. A martial artist can parry attacks from weapons without penalty. He is assumed to be able to use terrain, footwork, and body positioning to be able to avoid incoming blows. The same argument also applied to animal attacks – the martial artist is not at any special disadvantage when parrying animal attacks.

14.3.2 · STATIC MANEUVERS

Static maneuvers are allowed within combat situations. The only restriction is that there is a special -20 modifier to represent the added difficulty of attempting a typically non-combat static maneuver that generally requires some concentration during combat. This modifier would also apply to Chi Powers and Self Control skills that are usually attempted during combat. This ruling takes precedence over the first and second *RMSR* printings (this rule is actually errata for these printings).

14.3.3 · COMBAT MANEUVERS

This sub-section discusses the various combat maneuvers that a character might want to perform in a combat round.

WEAPON STYLES

Both Basic and Advanced Weapon Style skill are used during a character's attacking action. Only one weapon style at a time can be used in a combat round. The advantage in using a weapon style is that the stylist gains the unique benefits of his style for that round. See Section 14.2 for further discussion on using weapons styles during combat.

MISSILE DEFLECTING

The Missile Deflecting skill requires a 100% activity action during the round. While engaging in Missile Deflecting, the combatant is considered to be carefully watching and gauging the flight of all missiles towards him. The difficulty of the Missile Deflecting maneuver is directly proportional to the number of missiles the character attempts to deflect in a given round. If the character has a

large object that would be useful in parrying missiles, the Gamemaster may assign a bonus to the attempt (e.g., a shield might give a +20 bonus and a small pot might give a +5 bonus). In the case of a Failure result, the character loses the benefit of any DB due to Quickness. In the case of an Extraordinary success, the character is assumed to safely deflect the missiles.

TUMBLING EVASION

The Tumbling Evasion skill requires a 60% activity action in the round it is attempted. This action represents the character performing his evasion techniques. The character attempting Tumbling Evasion may not have any large objects in his hands or be encumbered (suffering from a Moving Maneuver Penalty) while he is performing the maneuver. If the maneuver is successful, the Gamemaster should let the player position his character where he desires (as long as it is within 10' from where the Tumbling Evasion maneuver was attempted). In the case of a Failure

result, the character loses the benefit of any DB due to Quickness. In the case of an Extraordinary success, the character is assumed to automatically avoid any one attack directed at him this round (choose before results are rolled).

14.3.4 · MARTIAL ARTS COMBAT MANEUVERS

This sub-section discusses the various martial arts combat maneuvers that a character might want to perform in a combat round.

MARTIAL ARTS STYLES

Both Basic and Advanced Martial Arts Styles are considered to be used in a character's attacking action. Only one martial arts style at a time can be used in a combat round. The advantage in using a martial arts style is that the martial artist gains the unique benefits of his style for that round. See Section 14.2 for further discussion on using martial arts styles during combat.

MARTIAL
ARTS
COMPANION

Optional Rule [Heroic]—Martial artists can attempt to use higher attack forms within their own style. If the martial artist tries to use a martial arts attack with a higher damage threshold than the current martial arts style he is using, he may use the more sophisticated attacking technique with an additional -20 modifier for every Degree he is exceeding the style's limitation. The martial artist is still constrained by his Martial Arts Style skill bonus when determining his available OB.

> **Example:** *Shih Yung, the Stone General is a master at the Iron Robe Advanced Martial Arts Style with a total style OB of +70 and an expert at Martial Arts Sweeping with an OB of +65. While using his style, he wishes to use a Degree 3 Martial Arts Sweeping attack against his foe. Since the Iron Robe style only incorporates Degree 2 Martial Arts Sweeping attacks into its style, Shih Yung will have an additional –20 modifier to his OB. Now Shih Yung's total bonus to attempt this attack will be +45 (take the lesser of the style OB and the sweeping OB, then apply any negative modifiers).*

ADRENAL DEFLECTING

Adrenal Deflecting requires a 60% activity action during the round it is attempted. While engaging in Adrenal Deflecting, the combatant is considered to be carefully watching and gauging the flight of all missiles towards him. The difficulty of the Adrenal Deflecting maneuver is directly proportional to the number of missiles the character attempts to deflect in a given round. If the character has a large object that would be useful in parrying missiles, the Gamemaster may assign a bonus to the attempt (e.g., a shield might give a +20 bonus and a small pot might give a +5 bonus). In the case of a Failure result, the character loses the benefit of any DB due to Quickness. In the case of an Extraordinary success, the character is assumed to safely deflect the missiles.

ADRENAL EVASION

The Adrenal Evasion maneuver requires a 60% activity action in the round it is attempted. The character attempting Adrenal Evasion may not have any large objects in his hands or be encumbered while he is performing the maneuver. If the maneuver is successful, the Gamemaster should let the player position his character where he desires as long as it is within 10' from where the Adrenal Evasion maneuver was attempted. In the case of a Failure result, the character loses the benefit of any DB due to Quickness. In the case of an Extraordinary success, the character is assumed to avoid any two attacks directed at him this round (choose before results are rolled).

14.3.5 · SELF CONTROL

This sub-section discusses the various skills in the Self Control skill category that a character might want to perform in a combat round.

ADRENAL SKILLS

There is no penalty for attempting back-to-back Adrenal skills. As long as the player allocates the 20% activity required for preparation time during the round, he may

attempt an Adrenal skill during the following round. The roll for success of the adrenal skill in the next round comes at the end of the Deliberate Phase of the current preparation round. Please note that only one preparation action may be taken each round.

Optional Rule [Core]—Gamemasters may wish to add additional restrictions on attempting the Adrenal skills back-to-back (i.e., round-to-round). This restriction may be justified by stating that these types of skills require a good deal of internal energy to be expended that exerts a considerable strain upon the user if he does not get a chance to "rest". This can be modeled in game terms by adding an additional -10 modifier to the static maneuver for each consecutive round that these types of skills are being used.

> **Example:** *Shih Yung has performed the following skills in consecutive rounds: Adrenal Strength, Adrenal Speed, and Adrenal Speed. His player now wishes to attempt another Adrenal Speed static maneuver and the Gamemaster informs him that he will suffer an additional –30 modifier to his attempt since he has performed these type of skills for the three prior rounds.*

Optional Rule [Heroic]—Gamemasters may wish to allow characters to carry the effects from an Adrenal maneuver to carry over from round to round. If the Gamemaster allows this, the character should make a new static maneuver every round (using the Adrenal skill). This skill roll suffers from a special penalty of -10 per round beyond the first round (this is cumulative; so carrying Adrenal Speed to a second round is a -10; a third round will be -20; a fourth round will be -30; etc.).

STUNNED MANEUVERING

A successful Stunned Maneuvering skill will allow the wielder to attempt a non-attack action. The Stunned Maneuvering skill is declared in addition to the maneuver attempted and is resolved at the start of the Action Phase the maneuver was declared in. The maneuver will take place in the normal initiative sequence of actions.

14.3.6 · SPECIAL ATTACKS

Each Special Attacks skill represents the ability of the character to do something unusual during his attacking action. Most Special Attacks skills are resolved in combat the following way:

- It is assumed, unless stated otherwise, that the Special Attacks skill is available to all weapons of the same general type listed in the skill description (e.g., Disarm Foe-Armed (Polearm) would apply to all weapons in the Polearm category).

- The character must take an attack action to use his Special Attacks skill.

- If the Special Attacks skill has a higher bonus than the OB of the skill used to deliver the special attack, the Special Attacks skill bonus is limited to the skill OB. This means a character cannot be more skilled with a special attack than he is with the weapon he is using to deliver the special attack.

his Feint skill bonus remains at +80. Hsio decides to allocate all 80 points (the maximum he can) to his Feint attempt of the remaining 40 points of his broadsword OB, Hsio places all 40 into defense and attempts a +0 OB attack.

The chances for success of each maneuver are as follows: the Laughing Swordsman has a modifier of –90 to his disarming attempt (his 30 Disarm Foe skill bonus minus Hsio Tung's total useable OB of 120). If the Laughing Swordsman succeeds, his opponent will be at his mercy; Hsio Tung has a modifier of +15 to his feinting attempt (his 80 Feint skill bonus minus the Laughing Swordsman's total useable OB of 65). If Hsio Tung succeeds, he will be able to nullify some or all of the Laughing Swordsman's defenses and he will receive a +40 bonus to his weapon OB (he will get half of the points he put into the Feint maneuver back if he succeeds). If either combatant fails his maneuver, he must still attack.

RACIAL ATTACKS

A racial attack is generally considered an Everyman skill for the race that use them. Racial attacks might include a tail bash, bite attack, claw attacks, etc. Racial attacks can be incorporated into Martial Arts Styles or Weapon Styles skills. Treat a racial weapon attack with a Small damage threshold as the point cost equivalent to a martial arts Degree 1 attack and a racial weapon attack with a Medium damage threshold as the point cost equivalent to a martial arts Degree 2 attack. Normally, Racial Attack skills cannot progress above Medium damage (or Degree 2 effectiveness).

14.3.7 · SPECIAL DEFENSES

This sub-section discusses the various skills in the Special Defenses skill category that a character might want to perform in a combat round.

ADRENAL DEFENSE

Adrenal Defense is quite possibly the most important skill for a martial artist to develop. It is nearly the only skill that grants a defensive bonus to the wielder, and it is certainly the most effective. The greatest strength of Adrenal Defense is the fact that its bonus can apply to all attacks that the user perceives. Unlike parrying, which can only increase your DB against one opponent, Adrenal Defense can increase your DB against many opponents and if the user is also attacking, he may also parry against his opponent as well! This advantage really comes into play is in a combat situation against multiple foes, because his Adrenal Defense bonus will apply against all attackers (as long as he is aware of them).

However, the great strengths of Adrenal Defense are balanced by some fairly serious restrictions. To use Adrenal Defense a character must obey the following restrictions.

• Not wear any armor (i.e., AT 5 or higher)

• Not be encumbered (i.e., no MMPs from weight penalties)

• If the Special Attacks skill bonus is lower than the weapon OB used to deliver the special attack, there is no modifier to the Special Attacks skill bonus.

• The character may sacrifice some of his weapon OB (up to his Special Attacks skill bonus) to increase his chances of the success of his special attack. This is added to the roll for the success of the special attack maneuver. If the character has any remaining bonus left, he may allocate it between attacking and parrying as normal.

Example: *The Laughing Swordsman, a notorious bandit, has a weapon OB of +65 with a broadsword and a +80 bonus for the Disarm Foe skill. The character decides to disarm his opponent. Since his Disarm Foe skill bonus is higher than his applicable weapon OB, his Disarm Foe skill bonus is reduced to +65. The player decides to apply 30 points of his Disarm Foe skill bonus to his roll to disarm his opponent. The other 35 points are allocated to his weapon attack OB. The player splits his OB into a +25 bonus for attack and a +10 bonus to defense (e.g., a parry).*

The opponent of the Laughing Swordsman is actually Hsio Tung, an experienced arms instructor. Hsio's Feint skill bonus is +80, but his broadsword OB is +120. Knowing the large reward on the Laughing Bandit if he is captured, Hsio decides to attempt a quick Feint to penetrate his defenses. Since Hsio's Feint skill bonus is less than his weapon OB,

• Not have a large object in his hands (i.e., hands must be free)

• Be aware of the attacks directed against him (note that this does not necessarily mean "see the attacks")

• Take a 40% activity action (as one of the three allowable actions in a round)

There are some further modifications and limitations that apply to Adrenal Defense.

• Adrenal Defense is less effective against missile and thrown attacks. For purposes of defending against missile and thrown attacks, the total Adrenal Defense bonus is halved.

• Adrenal Defense cannot be used against directed spell attacks.

The reasoning behind these restrictions on the character using Adrenal Defense are shown below.

No Armor—This is an ironclad restriction and should be strictly observed by both the players and the Gamemaster. As a corollary to this restriction, the Gamemaster should not create spells or non-encumbering items that allow the user to gain the benefits of any armor type greater than AT 4. Failure to follow this guideline will lead to imbalance in the game.

Not Encumbered—This is another ironclad restriction. This restriction makes common sense, a martial artist cannot effortlessly dodge attacks from all sides when he is carrying a large iron chest or weighed down with many items.

Free Hands—This restriction can be bypassed with some weapon styles or martial arts styles that allow the user to wield certain weapons with Adrenal Defense at no penalty.

Attack Awareness—This is another important restriction that should be strictly observed. This restriction means that Adrenal Defense does not apply to surprise attacks and ambushes, it does not apply to attacks delivered by unseen opponents, and it does not apply if the senses of the user are obscured.

Optional Rule [Heroic]—The defender can be "aware" of his opponents through other senses than sight if the Gamemaster considers it appropriate.

Percentage Activity—The last restriction is that the user must take a 40% activity action to use his Adrenal Defense skill. This restriction can be bypassed in certain situations if the user has the appropriate Lesser or Greater Adrenal Defense option in a weapon style or martial arts style. To qualify for the reduced activity for Adrenal Defense, the user must be using the style to attack during the round.

ADRENAL RESISTANCE

Adrenal Resistance can be a very powerful skill if the combatant is suffering from high negative modifiers due to wounds or criticals. The disadvantage of this skill is that injuries can become aggravated due to the lack of ability to discern pain from wounds while this skill is active. In general, if the character engages in vigorous activity (e.g., combat, climbing a cliff face, etc.) while using this skill to avoid the penalties from his wounds, he will run a risk of doing further injury to himself. The higher the negative modifier of the wound, the greater the chance of aggravating an injury. The results of aggravating the injury should generally be either longer recovery time or a greater penalty once this skill ceases to be active.

14.3.8 · CHI POWERS SKILLS

There is no penalty for attempting back-to-back Chi Powers skills. As long as the player allocates the appropriate preparation action during the round, he may attempt the skill during the following round (or during the same round if allowed in the skill description). If the skill is being prepared for the following round, the static maneuver for the Chi Powers skill comes at the end of the Deliberate Phase of the current preparation round. Remember that a character is limited to one preparation action per round.

Optional Rule [Core]—Gamemasters may wish to add additional restrictions on attempting the Chi Powers skills back-to-back (i.e., round-to-round). This restriction may be justified by stating that these types of skills require a good deal of internal energy to be expended that exerts a considerable strain upon the user if he does not get a chance to "rest". This can be modeled in game terms by adding an additional -20 modifier to the static maneuver for each consecutive round that these types of skills are being used.

Optional Rule [Heroic]—The Gamemaster may wish to reduce the penalty to an additional -10 modifier for the static maneuver for each consecutive round that a Chi Powers skill is used.

Optional Rule [Heroic]—Gamemasters may wish to allow characters to carry the effects from an Adrenal maneuver to carry over from round to round. If the Gamemaster allows this, the character should make a new static maneuver every round (using the Adrenal skill). This skill roll suffers from a special penalty of -10 per round beyond the first round (this is cumulative; so carrying Adrenal Speed to a second round is a -10; a third round will be -20; a fourth round will be -30; etc.).

◆ 14.4 ◆
STYLE VERSUS STYLE

If desired, the Gamemaster can introduce another element into the combat equation that adds extra depth when using martial arts styles or weapon styles.

14.4.1 SAME STYLES [HEROIC]

One of the great benefits of learning a martial arts style or weapon style is that the attacking and defensive techniques are taught through formalized exercises and training. If opponents are fighting using the same martial arts style or weapon style during combat, the person with the higher style bonus should receive some additional benefits due to his greater knowledge of the style

• The person with the higher style skill bonus receives a special initiative modifier of +1 per full 10 points of skill difference.

14.4.2 OPPOSING STYLES [HEROIC]

If opponents are fighting using different styles and one of the styles is considered an opposing style of the other, the practitioner should receive some special benefits. An opposing style is structured to be as effective as possible against the another style's principal attacks and counters. A martial arts style or weapon style is only considered an opposing style if the Gamemaster has designated it as such. The practitioner of the opposing style gains the following benefits:

• Attacks during the snap action phase, only suffer a –10 modification for the practitioner;

• The opponent suffers a –20 modifier to his style skill.

14.4.3 KNOWN STYLES [HEROIC]

The benefit of formalized training in weapon or martial arts styles can also become a drawback if your opponent is familiar with your style. A person who is knowledgeable about a particular style can easily anticipate the actions of an opponent using that style. If the combatant makes a successful Martial Arts Style Lore or Weapon Style Lore static maneuver, he gains a special +2 bonus to his initiative for the duration of the combat (as long as his opponent is using the known style).

14.4.4 UNKNOWN STYLES [HEROIC]

If a combatant is using a martial arts style or weapon style that in the Gamemaster's view is completely unfamiliar to his opponent (e.g., the style is foreign or highly secret), the combatant should get some special benefits. The possessor of the "secret" style gets a special bonus of +5 to his initiative for the first round of combat. This bonus decreases by 1 per round (until the bonus reaches zero).

◆ 14.5 ◆
NON-LETHAL COMBAT

Non-lethal combat can play an important role in martial arts campaigns. The ideas in this section can be used to run challenges between martial artists and simulate sparring practices.

14.5.1 · CHALLENGES AND SPARRING

An important part of a martial arts campaign is challenges and sparring between martial artists. The terms of the contest can vary from first blood to death. This section is meant to help Gamemasters resolve these types of contests during game sessions. In the case of non-lethal combat, both opponents attempt to regulate their attacks to not seriously injure their opponent. The terms and conventions of the contest allow both opponents to safely hold back their attacks in order to avoid seriously harming one another. In game terms, this is modeled by using Subduing criticals instead of the normal critical type indicated by the attack table.

QUICK RESOLUTION METHOD

Some challenges end at the first blow or first touch. When the challenge is only to a first blow, consider the first truly damaging blow is to determine the match. Before the challenge, the Gamemaster should determine what level of critical severity would end the match. For the typical challenge, a good choice would be the first 'A' or 'B' critical inflicted on a combatant. Of course, higher level criticals could also be used to determine the winner of the challenge, but the degree of potential damage inflicted by these criticals is more in line with a much more serious duel and thus should be modeled with the detailed challenge resolution method in the next section. When determining the result of a critical delivered in a first blow competition, roll all criticals on the Subduing Critical Strike Table. Comparing the severity of the blow actually delivered against the required level of severity for the challenge can help the Gamemaster describe the results of a challenge.

Example: *Li Chung has accepted a challenge from his rival Sun Wei. The Gamemaster rules that the rivals have a high degree of animosity towards each other so that the challenge will be to the first really punishing blow, a 'C' critical. The first round of combat ends uneventfully, but the second round of combat, Sun Wei open-ends his attack roll and overwhelms Li Chung's defenses, landing an 'E' critical. The challenge is over. The Gamemaster decides that this was an impressive victory, since the severity of the critical was much higher than the challenge conditions. The Gamemaster describes the scene as follows to Li Chung's player:*

"Sun Wei stands in the challenge ring, his hands are loose at his sides. He slowly moves into a sloppy defensive position and awaits your first action. Eager to wipe the arrogant look off his face, you move forward to execute an intricate hand strike against him. Suddenly he crouches low, avoiding your strike and executes a twisting leg strike that catches you underneath your chin. Before your body can even hit the ground, two lightning-fast punches strike your chest. You lay on the ground gasping for air. You do not think your ribs are broken. Sun Wei's laughter as he exits the challenge ring echoes in your ears." The Gamemaster then tells the player that his character has suffered 23 hits and an 'E' critical. When rolling for the critical result, the Gamemaster uses the Subduing Critical Attack Table.

DETAILED RESOLUTION METHOD

Not all challenges or sparring matches end at the first truly damaging blow. In some cases, the opponents wish to fight until one soundly defeats the other. This type of contest is using "challenge points" to track the progression of the contest. A "challenge point" is an abstract method to keep track of the amount of damage inflicted on an opponent. The number of challenge points inflicted on an opponent are computed as shown below.

• Each point of damage is considered to be equal to a challenge point.

• Each 'A' critical delivered is worth 5 challenge points.

• Each 'B' critical delivered is worth 10 challenge points.

• Each 'C' critical delivered is worth 25 challenge points.

• Each 'D' critical delivered is worth 40 challenge points.

• Each 'E' critical delivered is worth 60 challenge points.

The first combatant to inflict the agreed amount of challenge points on his opponent is considered to win the contest. The number of challenge points required to win a match also serves a gauge of the intensity of the contest. Once again, all criticals inflicted during non-lethal combat are resolved on the Subduing Critical Strike Table (instead of the normally indicated critical strike table).

CHALLENGE POINTS	
Type of Match	**Challenge Points**
Light sparring; first heavy blow	25
Normal sparring	50
Intense sparring; three heavy blows	75
Tournament match; knockdown	100
Championship match	150
Fight to near death	250

Depending on how closely the challenge point totals between the contestants are when the match is declared over, the Gamemaster can decide how closely matched the opponents were. For example, if a challenge match is declared to be a 100 point match and the final challenge point totals were 110 and 61 for the contestants, it could be said that the winner was clearly superior to his opponent. If on the other hand, the challenge point totals were much closer, the contestants would appear evenly matched.

This abstract method can be applied to other types of situations. For example, in the case of ring matches where the first to exit the ring loses, a total of 50 challenge points delivered in a single round could be required to force your opponent outside of the ring.

◆ 14.6 ◆
UNUSUAL
ENVIRONMENTS

In martial arts movies, the hero and villain usually fight in an unusual environment. Fights can take place on slippery rooftops, as the martial artists exchange blows and then make daring leaps across the void to the next rooftop or they can take place with the martial artists running on the heads of spectators, using each head as a stepping place as they move. Fights can also occur in the closed confines of a closet. An elaborate fight could take place in high wooden scaffolding, as the combatants strike at each other and leap to the next level of scaffolding, or more prosaically, a fight can occur on muddy, slippery ground. The possibilities are as endless as the Gamemaster's imagination. The best way to resolve these situations is to plan in advance what game modifications an environment will cause. The following discussions and tables of modifiers are meant to spark the Gamemaster's imagination. Critical results should be modified as appropriate to the environment. Depending on the

type of game that the Gamemaster wishes to present, he may adjust these modifications to reflect a more realistic style of combat or he may adjust them to allow for a more heroic style of combat.

FIGHTING IN RESTRICTED QUARTERS

Attempting to fight in a confined or constrained environment is difficult. Imagine trying to fight in a narrow alley or a cramped tunnel with a two-handed sword. This chart gives the Gamemaster some guidelines for modeling these types of situations (the modifiers shown are modifiers to OB). This table purposely does not give fine-grained detail by breaking out all the possible modifiers due to restricted environments. Ideally this table will be used as a guidepost for the Gamemaster to base his own decisions.

Constrained—This is meant to model the less than optimal situations for fighting. A constrained environment is an environment where the combatant does not have his normal range of movement necessary for the use of his weapon. As a rough rule of thumb, a combatant needs an open area of space around his body with a radius approximately equal to his height to use his weapon without restriction. In the constrained environment, the combatant is limited to one-half to three-quarters of his normal range of movement. Some examples could be attempting to fight in an outdoor setting that has a moderate number of trees and bushes. In urban environments this might represent a room filled with a lot of furniture. Another example could be attempting to fight while knee high in water.

Cramped—This is meant to model adverse conditions for fighting. In the cramped environment, the combatant is limited to under half of his normal range of movement. Some examples could be attempting to fight in a small tunnel that does not allow the combatant to stand upright, or attempting to fight while chest high in water. In an urban environment this might represent fighting in a very small room.

Nearly Immobilized—This is meant to model nearly impossible conditions for fighting. In the nearly immobilized environment, a combatant has almost no ability to move. An example could be attempting to fight while wedged in a very narrow alley that is barely wide enough for a person to pass through sideways. Another example could be attempting to fight in a very low tunnel that forces the combatant to crawl forward.

FIGHTING ON UNSTABLE OR SLIPPERY FOOTING

This section meant to model fighting on uncertain ground. In all of these cases, the melee combatant will suffer the greatest disadvantage because he needs to shift his weight to make melee attacks. Combatants that use thrown weapons or missile weapons will be affected to a much lesser extent because they will not have to adjust their footing as often. Any criticals delivered to a combatant who is fight-

RESTRICTED QUARTERS MODIFIERS						
	Unarmed	**1H Weapon**	**2H Weapon**	**Pole Arm**	**Thrown**	**Missile**
Constrained	-10	-20	-20	-30	-10	-10
Cramped	-30	-40	-60	-80	-30	-50
Nearly Immobilized	-80	-100	-120	-150	-80	-100

ing on slippery or unstable footing will also do an additional Unbalancing critical. Note that the modifiers shown below are all modifiers to OB.

Optional Rule [Heroic]: The Gamemaster may allow characters with the Acrobatics or Tumbling skill to reduce the result of any Unbalancing critical by the number of skill ranks they have developed in that skill. If a character possess both skills, he may decide which skill to use.

MODIFIERS FOR SLIPPERY SURFACES

	Melee	Thrown	Missile
Unstable	-20	-10	N/A
Slippery but Stable	-40	-20	-10
Slippery and Unstable	-60	-30	-20

Unstable Footing—This is meant to model fighting on teetering structures such as loose scaffolding or fighting in loose sand. Any critical delivered also delivers an Unbalancing critical (same roll) of two levels less severity. In the case of 'A' criticals, an 'A' Unbalancing critical is given with a -40 modifier to the roll. In the case of 'B' criticals, an 'A' Unbalancing critical is given with a -20 modifier to the roll. If a critical result says that a character is knocked down or falls down, this should be modified as appropriate to the environment. In the case of unstable wooden scaffolding, the character may fall from the structure. All moving maneuvers have their difficulty increased by one column (i.e., Medium maneuvers become Hard maneuvers, etc.).

Slippery but Stable Footing—This is meant to model fighting on slick floors. Any critical delivered also delivers an Unbalancing critical (same roll) of one level less severity. In the case of 'A' criticals, an 'A' Unbalancing critical is given with a -20 modifier to the roll. All moving maneuvers have their difficulty increased by one column (i.e., Medium maneuvers become Hard maneuvers, etc.).

Slippery and Unstable Footing—This is meant to model fighting on a slippery unstable structure or perhaps fighting in very slippery mud. Any critical delivered also delivers an Unbalancing critical (same roll). If a critical result says that a character is knocked down or falls down, this should be modified as appropriate to the environment. In the case of an unstable structure, the character may slip and fall. All moving maneuvers have their difficulty increased by two columns (i.e., Medium maneuvers become Very Hard maneuvers, etc.).

FIGHTING ON RESTRICTED FOOTING

Attempting to fight in an environment where footing and space is limited is very difficult. This case is meant to represent combat that takes place along narrow ledges and small rooftops. This is differentiated from the Restricted Quarters case because the combatants have the room necessary for motion but they do not have the ability to move freely due to lack of available footing. In this case, the Gamemaster can decide some skills cannot be attempted (Adrenal or Tumbling Evasion for example) and other skills may be at reduced effectiveness. In situations where the combatants are almost forced to stand in the same place because of the environment, any DB due to Adrenal Defense or Quickness could be halved. Any critical delivered also delivers an Unbalancing critical (same roll) of one

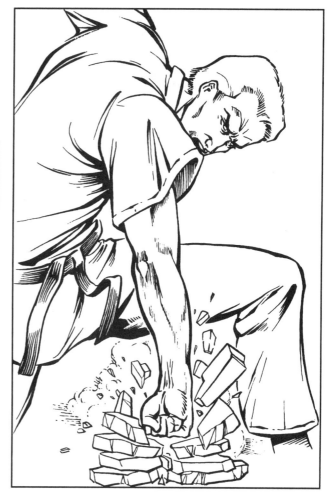

level less severity. In the case of 'A' criticals, an 'A' Unbalancing critical is given with a -20 modifier to the roll. If a critical result says that a character is knocked down or falls down, this should be modified as appropriate to the environment. In the case of an unstable structure, the character may slip and fall. All moving maneuvers have their difficulty increased by two columns (i.e., Medium maneuvers become Very Hard maneuvers, etc.).

Optional Rule [Heroic]: The Gamemaster may allow characters with the Acrobatics or Tumbling skill to reduce the result of any Unbalancing critical by the number of skill ranks they have developed in that skill. If a character possess both skills, he may decide which skill to use.

◆ 14.7 ◆
CINEMATIC COMBAT

Martial arts combat as seen in movies can be a large motivating factor for players deciding to play martial artists in a campaign. The players often create their character with a desire to emulate what they have seen in other mediums. Unfortunately, this natural desire can put the Gamemaster in a slight bind. One of the foundations of the *Rolemaster* system is realistic and potentially deadly combat. It is difficult to satisfy players' wishes to fight a large number of combatants when the Gamemaster knows that he may end up accidentally killing the player's character through an ill-timed critical roll. This section deals with ways to minimize this problem and ways to run cinematic combat within the *Rolemaster* system.

MARTIAL ARTS COMPANION

Part II

Section 14.8

Using Martial
Arts in
Modern
Settings

MOVING MANEUVER ATTACKS

In the movies, martial artists seem to be able to make incredible attacks as they are moving through the air or tumbling towards their foes. Realistically, these attacks are not too probable, but they are fun to try and emulate in a role playing game.

If a martial artist is making a moving maneuver that takes him near an opponent (e.g., a leaping maneuver or a tumbling maneuver), he may make a moving maneuver attack. The martial artist takes a modifier to his normal attack roll depending on the difficulty of the maneuver (see chart below). Unless the opponent can make an orientation roll, he may not return the attack against the martial artist that round. The orientation roll is modified by one degree of difficulty less than that of the maneuver made by the attacking martial artist.

MOVING MANEUVER ATTACK MOD	
Routine	-10
Easy	-20
Light	-40
Medium	-60
Hard	-70
Very Hard	-80
Extremely Hard	-90
Sheer Folly	-100
Absurd	-120

FIGHTING LARGE GROUPS

Typically in the movies, a martial artist will take on a large number of opponents and win! This type of action is difficult to model impartially in the *RMSS*, because one of its hallmarks is combat realism. What is necessary for this type of situation to work is that the Gamemaster must make a determination of the level of skill of the large group of opponents. If the opponents are all relatively unskilled compared to the martial artist (as a measure, if the average OB/DB combination of an individual attacker is less than half that of the martial artist), the Gamemaster can modify the normal combat sequence. If the opponents are all relatively skilled compared to the martial artist, the combat should proceed according to the normal *RMSS*.

When fighting a large number of unskilled opponents, a martial artist may do one (and only one) of the following each round.

- Each strike in melee combat may be considered as being able to attack to up to three unskilled opponents (none of the unskilled opponents may have a rear positional bonus against the martial artist unless the martial artist's current style possesses the All-Around Attack option).

- Any criticals delivered are modified by +1 per rank of attack skill used on the critical roll. A result of 100 or 66 cannot be attained this way (treat a 66 as a 65 and a 100 or higher as a 99).

These are powerful options that will allow martial artists to defeat large number of foes with relative ease and should be considered carefully before being allowed into the campaign.

FIGHTING WITH MAKESHIFT WEAPONS

Martial artists can attack with makeshift weapons with their martial arts skills. A martial artist may turn a piece of furniture or a ribbon or scarf into a dangerous weapon in cinematic combat.

In game terms, the use of the makeshift weapon can result in a special modifier to the martial artist's attack OB (+5 to +25) with a negative modifier to initiative (-1 to –5) due to the unfamiliarity of the makeshift weapon.

◆ 14.8 ◆
USING MARTIAL ARTS IN MODERN SETTINGS

When using this companion in modern settings, it is recommended to only use the Core rules. In addition, none of the Chi Powers skills or spell lists should be allowed. It is strongly recommended that Weapon Style skills not be applied to firearms.

Many of the martial arts styles and weapon styles already described in Sections 8.3 and 9.3 can be used in the modern setting with a few minor modifications. It is probably best to not allow any special maneuvers or techniques with any martial arts styles. Some more martial arts taught in the modern era are briefly listed in abbreviated form.

Akido—Akido is a Japanese martial art that stresses the use of pressure points to subdue an enemy. Akido specializes in Degree 3 Nerve Strikes and Degree 2 Locking Holds.

General Military Training—Military training offers a very basic introduction to martial arts, usually no unarmed attacking forms are higher than Degree 2

Special Forces Training—Special forces training offers some more advanced techniques in martial arts. Usually a striking attack form is known to Degree 3 and in some rare cases Lesser Adrenal Defense might be known as well.

15.0
CREATING STYLES

Part II

Sections
15.0, 15.1

Creating
Styles

Cultures and
Martial Arts

The first thing to do when starting to create a new martial arts style or weapon style is to try to develop a mental picture of style. Try to imagine how a skilled practitioner of this style would fight. After the concept of the style has been determined, it is time to turn to the mechanics of actually figuring out the point cost of the style. If the style is primarily weapon based, it should be a weapon style. If the style is primarily unarmed combat based, it should be a martial arts style.

The next decisions revolve around the characteristics of the style. If the style is very aggressive, it should include initiative bonuses and in the case of unarmed combat, high damage threshold martial arts attacks. If the style is very defensive, it should include Lesser or Greater Adrenal Defense and other combat options that do not directly relate to attacks. If the style promotes mobility, it should have bonuses for movement-related skills in combat.

If the Gamemaster allows special maneuvers or techniques with a martial arts style, he should follow these general guidelines. Basic martial arts styles should not have more than two special maneuvers. Advanced martial arts styles should not have more than four special maneuvers. When designing a special maneuver or technique keep in mind several points. Special maneuvers or techniques should have some relevance to the overall style and not be included to prop up some shortcoming of the style. If a special maneuver has effects that can substantially affect game play, it must rely on a static maneuver to see if it was performed successfully. If a special maneuver or technique duplicates or improves the effects of an existing skill, it should rely on that skill bonus to determine the success of the static maneuver. Special maneuvers and techniques are meant to help flesh out a particular style, and should be secondary to the actual style skills chosen with the style point system as outlined in Section 9.1.

It is important that the Gamemaster carefully consider the total style point cost of the newly created style. The total style point cost will determine whether the style is considered an Advanced or Basic style, which will have an effect on how easy it is to learn the new style. The total style point cost becomes more important if the Gamemaster is using the optional cultural modifications to martial arts styles and weapon styles as shown in this section.

CHARACTER-CREATED STYLES

If the Gamemaster allows, players can have their characters create their own martial arts style or weapon style. The creation process follows all of the above guidelines with the Gamemaster acting as the final arbitrator for what is allowed in the style. The mechanics for character-created styles are as follows.

• The character must know all the skills that the style will incorporate (e.g., if the style incorporates Adrenal Defense, the character must know Adrenal Defense);

• The character must develop 10 ranks in the style before he can use the style. This represents the research and training that he must undergo when creating the style;

• When the character has developed 20 ranks in the style, it can be taught to others and is considered a real style.

◆ 15.1 ◆
CULTURES AND MARTIAL ARTS

This section presents some additional examples of applying this companion to historical cultures. We have made a point of including a non-Eastern culture in this book to emphasize the point that the martial arts style and weapon style system can be applied to any culture or society.

As a quick review, the style point ranges that determine Basic or Advanced status of a martial arts style or weapon styles as follows.

STYLE POINT COSTS	
Basic Weapon Style	0 to 30 style points
Advanced Weapon Style	31 to 60 style points
Basic Martial Arts Style	0 to 30 style points
Advanced Martial Arts Style	31 to 60 style points

Optional Rule [Core]: The Gamemaster may decide to modify these style point ranges for different cultures. It is not recommended that the Gamemaster change any of the point ranges by greater than +/- 10 style points. See the examples in Sections 8.3 and 9.3 for variable point ranges due to culture.

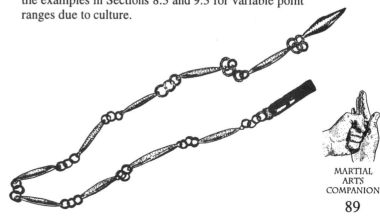

MARTIAL
ARTS
COMPANION

MORE OBSERVATIONS ON MARTIAL ARTS

Part II

Sections
16.0, 16.1

More
Observations
on Martial
Arts

Original
Argument

In *Gamemaster Law*, Section 19.1, there is a discussion regarding whether martial arts are unbalanced in comparison to other forms of attacks. This discussion illuminates many of the design decisions made by the authors of Rolemaster and deserves close attention by Gamemasters who wish to think further about the role of martial arts in the campaign. This section will briefly summarize the main points of that argument and then re-examine the argument in light of the changes in martial arts contained within this companion.

◆ 16.1 ◆
ORIGINAL ARGUMENT

The original argument looked at the offensive capabilities of the Warrior monk and fighter and compared them at several different levels of development. Examining the Master Character Table (T-5.8, page 334 in *RMSR*), we look at the Warrior monk and fighter professions at several levels. The Master Character Table entries were created with the intent of maximizing offense and defense at each level (training packages and hobbies were not used but Adolescent skill ranks were used).

THE MASTER CHARACTER TABLE

At the first level, the Fighter has an OB of 50 and the Warrior monk an OB of 30. The Fighter has a DB of 30 (shield) and the Warrior monk has a DB of 25 (Quickness and Adrenal Defense). It seems the Fighter has the advantage at the first level with a combined OB/DB of 80 compared to the Warrior monk's combined OB/DB of 55.

At the fifth level, the Fighter has an OB of 95 and the Warrior monk an OB of 70. The Fighter has a DB of 30 (shield) and the Warrior monk has a DB of 74 (Adrenal Defense is really starting to kick in). The Warrior monk has the advantage here with a combined OB/DB of 144 compared to the Fighter's combined OB/DB of 125.

At the tenth level, the Fighter has a combined OB/DB of 152 while the Warrior monk has a combined OB/DB of 202! The Warrior monk continues to pull away from the Fighter as they both go higher in levels. From this analysis, it does appear that the Warrior monk is unbalanced in regard to the Fighter.

DEVELOPMENT POINTS

What offsets the Warrior monk's superiority in combined OB/DB? The Warrior monk does not have the advantage of gaining martial arts skill ranks during Adolescent development. In addition the Warrior monk's Martial Arts Group bonus is lower than the Fighter's Weapon Group bonus. This means is that the Warrior monk is spending much more DP in order to offset this advantage. On average the Warrior monk will spend two to five times the DP compared to the Fighter to gain his combat skills.

INTO THE FRAY

Ignoring the issue of DPs for now, let us look at a tenth level Fighter and Warrior monk squaring off for combat. If the combatants start out at the distance, the Fighter because of his overall lesser expenditure in DPs for his combat abilities will have skills in a missile or thrown weapon attack. The Warrior monk will suffer a penalty to his Adrenal Defense trying to defend against these attacks. In this case, the Fighter manages to inflict some preliminary damage before the melee combat begins.

Let us assume however that the combatants start nose to nose. Who will win this battle? The Fighter has the edge in concussion damage, as nearly all weapons can inflict 30 points of damage against an unarmored foe. The average martial arts attack will inflict 10 concussion points of damage against an armored foe. (Assuming of course that the Warrior monk is unarmored in order to take advantage of his superior Adrenal Defense and the Fighter is armored because it would be foolish not to) The Fighter appears to be ahead here, as he can inflict enough damage on the Warrior monk to take him into penalties due to concussion points damage. Most weapons inflict their first critical against unarmored foes at 85 whereas most martial arts attacks inflict their first critical at 103 versus armored foes. But the Warrior monk's combined OB/DB total is on average 50 points higher than the Fighter's, this means that the Warrior monk will on average inflict more criticals compared to the Fighter.

The Warrior monk appears as more effective in combat by a slim margin. If the combat can last for more than several rounds, the edge will start to go to the Fighter as the concussion damage mounts against the Warrior monk.

In the case of a battle with multiple foes, the Warrior monk is much more effective than the Fighter because his Adrenal Defense bonus can be used against multiple foes. The Fighter is limited to using his shield and parrying against the opponent he is attacking. A Warrior monk will suffer much less damage on average against multiple opponents than the Fighter because of the Adrenal Defense skill.

OTHER TYPES OF OPPONENTS

The Warrior monk has other weakness against other types of opponents and situations. If a Warrior monk is taken by surprise, his Adrenal Defense offers no protection and attacks against him if successful will be very deadly. Unlike the Fighter, the Warrior monk has no armor to protect him if his defense fails.

In addition, the Warrior monk is much more vulnerable to animal attacks which tend to attack the upper torso. Examination of the Animal Attack Tables will reveal that AT 1 is the worst armor type to have against animal attacks by a large margin.

When facing Undead, the Warrior monk has several problems. First his specialization in martial arts has probably left him without a serious long range attack, so he will have to close with the Undead creatures. In addition, most Undead require a magical weapon to strike them.

Bonus Items

The above point is important regarding magical bonus items and Warrior monks is important enough to be repeated. There are not very many magical items to improve a Warrior monk's combat abilities, unlike that of the Fighter.

◆ 16.2 ◆
CORE RULES

How do things change after the inclusion of the core rules from the *Martial Arts Companion*?

With the advent of the core rules, several things change drastically for the Warrior monk. The most important changes are the redefinition of both Adrenal Defense and martial arts attacks. Adrenal Defense is no longer a "free" skill in the sense that the Warrior monk must state that he is using Adrenal Defense which will take 40% of his available activity during the combat round. It is important to remember that if the Warrior monk decides to attack as well as use this skill, then his OB will be modified negatively by this division of concentration per the standard rules of *RMSR*. The unified martial arts attacks skills significantly reduce the overall development point cost for the martial artist who wishes to specialize in unarmed attacks.

The Master Character Table

Looking above at our previous discussion, at the first level the combination of OB/DB for the Fighter remains at 80 while the Warrior monk's drops to a meager 15 (it is 45 if the martial artist does not use Adrenal Defense!). At fifth level the Warrior monk begins to gain back some ground, the Fighter's total OB/DB combination is 125 and the Warrior monk's total OB/DB combination is 104. It is still not even, but it is beginning to approach parity. At tenth level, the Warrior monk again surpasses the Fighter's with a combined OB/DB total of 162 to the Fighter's combined OB/DB total of 152. At higher levels, the Warrior monk continues to pull away slowly from the Fighter though at a slower rate.

Development Points

This change would seem to make the Fighter ascendant over the Warrior monk except for another important change. Martial arts attacks have been changed and incorporated in one skill instead of four separate skills for each type of martial arts attack. The Warrior monk now has more development points available per level, but this is somewhat balanced by the need to develop a Martial Arts Style skill in order to become an effective unarmed combatant.

Into the Fray

Let us again examine the combat between the tenth level Warrior monk and Fighter. If the combatants again start off at a distance, the edge still goes to the Fighter but it is a smaller edge. The missile or thrown weapon attacks still greatly reduce the Warrior monk's Adrenal Defense bonus, but the Warrior monk has greater versatility due to his lessened expenditure of development points. The Warrior monk can respond with a missile or thrown weapon attack

of his own or he can utilize specialized defense maneuvers like Adrenal Deflections to increase his defense against the missile or thrown weapon attacks. While both of these options were available to a Warrior monk created with *RMSR*, they probably would not have been valid options due to the high development point expenditure required for the melee combat skills.

Let us again examine the two combatants once they arrive in melee combat. The Fighter still has the edge in armor protection. In addition, the reduction of the Warrior monk's combined OB/DB has put the two professions in relative parity. In this case, the Fighter seems to win out with the clear edge in concussion damage and at least parity in critical infliction with the Warrior monk.

What balances this seeming disparity is the inclusion of the Martial Arts Style skills. Certain Martial Arts Style skills can allow the Warrior monk to use his Adrenal Defense as a 10% activity rather than a 40% activity. This results in the Warrior monk gaining a additional 30 points in his OB/DB combination. In addition, a Martial Arts Style skill can allow the Warrior monk to gain special bonuses in combat such as an initiative bonus or bonus to certain combat-related skills while using his style. It is important to remember that the Fighter may also choose to specialize in Weapon Style skills that offer some of the same advantages if he desires.

The other points made in the original *Gamemaster Law* argument regarding other types of opponents and bonus items remain valid.

◆ 16.3 ◆
HEROIC RULES

If Heroic rules and options are used, how much does the play balance shift?

With the inclusion of the Heroic rules and options, the Warrior monk gains the benefit of specialized training packages and background options during character creation. Because the Fighter also gains these options, play balance remains unaltered. The Warrior monk also gains the benefit of special maneuvers with certain Martial Arts Style skills that allow him to gain short-term advantages in the combat round. In this case the Warrior monk becomes slightly more effective in the combat round.

◆ 16.4 ◆
FANTASTIC RULES

If the Fantastic rules and options are used, how much does the play balance shift?

If the Fantastic rules and options are used, the play balance does shift towards the Warrior monk. The Warrior monk now has access to Chi Powers skills and Cinematic combat options that he can use to his full advantage. The Fighter will also have access to these skills and options, but he will have to expend much more effort than the Warrior monk to be effective at them.

PART III
APPENDICES

PART III CONTENTS

17.0
THE TRAINING PACKAGES

Part III

Section 17.0

The Training
Packages

This section deals with the new training packages and new training package options that are available to characters. For the basic rules for training packages see the *RMSR*. Shown below are the new options available for training packages.

PROFESSIONAL QUALIFIERS

The idea behind this concept is that certain training packages should be easier to learn if the character meets certain qualifications. The result is a reduced cost (and sometimes time) for developing the training package. The professional qualifiers needed for each training package (if any) are listed in the description of the training package. If a character does not meet the standards for the professional qualifier, he may still learn the training package but he must pay the full price for it. When a professional qualifier is shown, the associated discount to the cost of the training package is also shown.

LIFESTYLE SKILLS

Lifestyle skills are a new concept introduced in this book. Lifestyle skills allow a character to develop certain specific skills to a higher level of expertise than normally possible with training packages. Only certain lifestyle training packages can offer this benefit. Examples of training packages using lifestyle skills in this companion are the Chi Master, Weapon Master, and Temple Monk lifestyle training packages. When a skill is designated as being a "lifestyle" skill in a training package, that skill may be taken as high as 15 ranks by the training package (rather than the normal limit of 10 ranks).

NOTES FOR MODERN OR PULP GENRE

If the Gamemaster is running a Modern or Pulp era, only certain things from each of the training packages are applicable. The Gamemaster should examine each training package and decide upon its appropriateness to the genre he is running. For example, if running in a modern game, all references to ma# 37gical skills should be ignored. In certain cases, a training package may award ranks in a skill that the Gamemaster is not using in his game. If this is the case, the Gamemaster should feel free to adjust the cost of the TP down by approximately 1 point per skill rank that is not awarded.

Part III

Section 17.0

The Training
Packages

New Training
Package Cost
Table T–2.7

NEW TRAINING PACKAGE COST TABLE T-2.7 (MARTIAL ARTS)

	Arms Instructor (L)	Bodyguard (V)	Caravan Guard (V)	Chi Master (L)	Martial Artist (L)	Martial Arts Challenger (L)	Martial Arts Champion (V)	Martial Arts Opera Performer (V)	Ninja (L)	School Master (V)	Secret Society Member (V)	Martial Arts Street Performer (V)	Temple Monk (L)	Wandering Monk (V)	Warrior-Priest (L)	Weapon Master (L)
Time	106	30	46	81	143	110	31	187	170	39	22	37	169	78	107	116
Rolemaster Standard Rules																
Fighter	26	20	27	70	49	42	25	41	54	31	17	25	68	55	32	44
Thief	31	23	30	70	51	45	29	39	48	33	13	19	69	56	34	51
Rogue	29	20	28	70	50	43	27	39	48	32	13	19	68	55	33	50
Warrior Monk	43	32	38	30	38	34	33	33	49	25	16	26	39	40	26	50
Layman	35	26	30	63	51	47	30	41	60	36	17	25	68	51	35	58
Magician	93	49	47	105	105	110	70	62	130	84	28	31	135	88	76	145
Illusionist	93	47	44	105	105	110	70	58	122	84	26	27	135	85	76	145
Cleric	58	36	37	94	80	80	47	54	104	62	26	31	109	74	57	100
Animist	57	35	34	94	78	78	46	54	96	61	24	31	108	74	56	98
Mentalist	66	39	40	62	59	69	44	46	97	46	24	31	75	56	42	95
Lay Healer	65	38	38	62	59	69	42	46	101	46	26	32	75	56	42	95
Healer	78	40	39	70	69	79	54	48	113	58	28	32	88	59	54	120
Sorcerer	93	49	47	103	103	109	70	59	132	82	30	32	132	86	76	145
Mystic	87	40	39	74	84	94	58	49	106	68	19	22	103	68	61	130
Ranger	36	26	30	82	58	51	33	45	62	40	17	26	81	62	40	62
Paladin	31	26	32	89	70	58	34	46	83	48	26	32	94	68	49	66
Monk	51	35	40	38	46	45	38	37	58	33	17	26	51	46	33	62
Dabbler	43	30	32	82	59	56	37	42	62	42	14	20	83	59	41	68
Bard	41	27	28	54	51	50	31	35	63	37	16	22	65	45	36	63
Magent	37	25	28	55	53	49	31	39	57	36	12	18	64	47	36	62
Arcane Companion																
Arcanist	97	48	47	103	104	112	70	59	132	84	29	33	134	86	76	148
Wizard	97	48	47	103	104	112	70	59	132	84	29	33	134	86	76	148
Chaotic	46	31	36	83	70	66	40	53	77	53	20	27	97	72	48	73
Magehunter	39	28	34	63	53	48	34	39	57	36	17	24	68	55	36	58
Treasure Companion																
Channeling Alchemist	58	36	37	94	80	80	47	62	114	62	26	33	109	74	57	100
Essence Alchemist	70	40	38	105	105	110	56	68	136	80	28	33	135	86	72	129
Mentalism Alchemist	62	37	38	62	59	69	41	46	96	45	24	31	75	56	41	92
Martial Arts Companion																
Taoist Monk	50	35	40	38	45	43	37	37	58	32	18	28	50	46	32	61
Zen Monk	51	35	40	38	45	43	39	37	58	33	17	26	50	46	33	64
Black Ops																
Academic	46	31	32	77	63	62	37	49	84	46	23	30	86	59	44	74
Fighter	26	20	25	69	47	40	24	41	52	30	17	25	65	50	30	41
Layman	35	26	28	61	49	45	29	41	58	31	17	25	63	46	33	46
Rogue	29	20	25	69	48	42	26	39	46	31	13	19	65	50	32	46
Scientist	58	34	36	86	79	74	48	52	95	61	25	30	104	68	57	93
Technician	40	28	29	74	58	54	34	42	65	41	18	25	77	52	40	66
Thief	31	23	28	69	50	43	28	39	47	32	13	19	66	51	32	48
Warrior Monk	43	32	36	29	36	33	32	33	47	23	16	26	36	35	25	47
Pulp Adventures																
Academic	46	31	32	77	63	62	37	49	84	46	23	30	86	59	44	74
Fighter	26	20	25	70	49	42	25	41	54	31	17	25	68	52	32	44
Layman	35	26	28	62	51	47	30	41	60	36	17	25	68	48	35	58
Noble Savage	50	38	43	63	54	49	30	46	69	34	31	64	70	57	36	54
Rogue	29	20	25	70	50	43	27	39	48	32	13	19	68	52	33	50
Technician	40	28	31	74	58	54	34	42	65	41	18	25	77	55	40	66
Thief	31	23	28	70	51	45	29	39	48	33	13	19	69	53	34	51
Warrior Monk	43	32	36	30	38	34	33	33	49	25	16	26	39	37	26	50
Healer	78	40	39	70	69	79	54	48	113	58	28	32	88	59	54	120
Mystic	87	40	39	74	84	94	58	49	106	68	19	22	103	68	61	130
Sorcerer	93	49	47	103	103	109	70	59	132	82	30	32	132	86	76	145
Ranger	36	26	28	82	58	51	33	45	62	40	17	26	81	58	40	62
Monk	51	35	38	38	46	45	38	37	58	33	17	26	51	43	33	62
Bard	41	27	28	54	51	50	31	35	63	37	16	22	65	45	36	63

Part III

Sections 17.1,
17.2

Arms
Instructor (L)

Bodyguard
(V)

◆ 17.1 ◆
ARMS INSTRUCTOR (L)

The arms instructor is a character who makes his living by teaching his skill at arms to wealthy students. Successful arms instructors need not only skill in combat, but also skill in diplomacy in order to keep their students coming back for more training.

"Focus on your target when you strike. Better, much better. A few more weeks and you might be able to at least look like you knew what you were doing when some young bravo slices you open in the dueling ring. "

Time to Acquire: 106 months

Starting Money: normal + 1d10 (open-ended)

Special:

Impressive scar	50
Wealthy student (1d2 silver/month)	30
Weapon, +10 non-magical	60
Extra d10 (open-ended) in money	20
Monthly income (1d10 students, 1d2 bp each)	30
Training hall in the city	30
Friendly patron	20
Certificates of mastery	0

Category or Skill	# of ranks
Armor Light skill category	1
Choice of one skill	1
Body Development skill category	n/a
Body Development	2
Combat Maneuvers skill category	n/a
choice of up to two skills	2 (total)
Influence skill category	1
Leadership	1
Lore General skill category	1
Weapon Styles Lore	1
Special Attack skill category	n/a
choice of up to two non-restricted skills	2 (total)
Urban skill category	1
Contacting	1
Weapon skill category A (choice)	2
choice of up to two skills	2 (total)
Weapon skill category B (choice)	1
choice of up to two skills	1 (total)

Professional Qualifier: A total of 10 ranks in skills from any of the following groups: Combat Maneuvers or Weapon Group. [-3 points]

Stat Gains: none

◆ 17.2 ◆
BODYGUARD (V)

The bodyguard specializes in protecting the life of a patron from attackers. The bodyguard learns how to anticipate and counter attacks as well as advising his client on the best course for his own personal safety.

"I would not recommend that course of action. So far I have managed to keep all of my clients alive, but if you insist on going to inspect the outlying estates with only a few men to protect you, I am afraid you will not survive the first week."

Time to Acquire: 30 months

Starting Money: normal

Special:

Current contract (2d10 bronze/month)	50
Weapon, +5 non-magical	40
Armor, +5 non-magical	30
Useful contacts in the city guard	40
Useful contacts in the underworld	20
Friendly wealthy patron	60
Common healing herbs (1d5)	40
Friendly tavern owner	0

Category or Skill	# of ranks
Armor Light skill category	1
choice of one skill	1
Awareness Perceptions skill category	n/a
Sense Ambush	2
Awareness Searching skill category	1
choice of one skill	1
Body Development skill category	n/a
Body Development	1
Combat Maneuvers skill category	n/a
choice of one non-Restricted skill	1
Influence skill category	1
choice of one skill	1
Urban skill category	1
Streetwise	1
Weapon skill category (choice)	1
choice of one skill	1

Stat Gains: none

Category or Skill	# of ranks
Armor Light skill category	1
choice of one skill	1
Awareness Perception skill category	n/a
choice of one skill	1
Body Development skill category	n/a
Body Development	1
Communication skill category	2
choice of up to four languages	4 (total)
Lore General skill category	2
choice of up to two skills	2 (total)
Outdoor Animal skill category	2
choice of up to two skills	2 (total)
Outdoor Environmental skill category	1
choice of one skill	1
Urban skill category	1
choice of one skill	1
Weapon skill category (choice)	1
choice of one skill	1

Stat Gains: none

◆ 17.3 ◆
CARAVAN GUARD (V)

The caravan guard is a character who escorts merchant caravans from city to city and protects them from bandit attacks. The caravan guard learns to be a shrewd judge of character, as well as a fierce combatant. Because the caravan guard is frequently outnumbered by less-experienced foes, he has learned to use strike quickly and decisively to protect himself. In the course of his journeys, a caravan guard will encounter many different cultures and customs.

"Let me tell you of the time I escorted the silk caravans from the free city of Morica. We were caught in a great storm deep in the burning wastes. Entire villages disappeared that year, victim to the engulfing sand. But we survived, through the grace of the gods and delivered the silk on time for our contract. The merchants had thought we must have died in the desert and when we arrived at our destination, each man that survived received a rich reward. I did not need to work for the rest of that year."

Time to Acquire: 46 months

Starting Money: normal

Special:

Friends with a wealthy merchant	50
Useful contact in foreign sector	50
Foreign merchandise (art, clothing)	40
Maps of foreign lands	20
Extra d10 (open-ended) in money	30
Useful contacts in the city guard	20
Horse	20
Friends with tavern owner	0

◆ 17.4 ◆
CHI MASTER (L)

The Chi Master has dedicated himself to leaning how to focus the energy of his mind and body to perform supernatural feats. The years of dedication and training required to reach the levels of mastery and control necessary have imbued the him with a strong will and tireless energy.

"Through inner stillness we gain self-enlightenment; a calm pond will reflect the moon. Anger and violence block our awareness; turbulent waters reveal nothing."

Time to Acquire: 81 months

Starting Money: normal

Special:

Scrolls (+10 to a general lore skill)	40
Apprentice student	20
Small training area in the outdoors	30
Common medicinal herbs (1d5)	20
Reputation as a master of the esoteric martial arts	0

Category or Skill	# of ranks
Chi Powers skills	
One Chi Powers Lifestyle skill	2
One other Chi Powers Lifestyle skill	2
Lore Obscure	0
Chi Powers Lore	2
Martial Arts Combat Maneuvers skill category	n/a
choice of up to two non-Restricted skills	2 (total)
Martial Arts Strikes skill category	1
Martial Arts Striking	1
Martial Arts Sweeps skill category	1
Martial Arts Sweeping	1
Self Control skill category	2
Meditation	2

Professional Qualifier: A total of 10 skill ranks in the Self Control skill category. [-3 points]

Lifestyle Skills: Two Chi Powers skills may be chosen as Lifestyle skills.

Stat Gains: Self Discipline

◆ 17.5 ◆
MARTIAL ARTIST (L)

A martial artist is a warrior trained in the ways of unarmed combat and maneuvering. However, a martial artist is also schooled in the areas of knowledge and the arts, especially in the care of the body. This is the generic package for those players not interested in the more specific training packages detailed in this section.

Note: This is revised from the *RMSR* version

"I have the honor to be a most humble student of Master Lee of the Central Disctrict. I hope that I do not disgrace my teacher in this competition. You may strike first worthy opponent."

Time to Acquire: 143 months

Starting Money: normal

Special:

Victory at local tournament	50
Scrolls (+10 non-magic to a specific lore)	40
Scrolls (+5 non-magic to a lore category)	30
Common herbs (1d5)	50
Bracers (+5 Martial Arts Striking)	30
Book (+5 non-magic to a specific lore)	30
Reputation as a skilled fighter	0

Category or Skill	# of ranks
Artistic Passive	2
choice of up to two skills	2 (total)
Body Development skill category	n/a
Body Development	2
Lore General skill category	2
Martial Arts Styles Lore	2
choice of up to two skills	2 (total)
Martial Arts Combat Maneuvers skill category	n/a
choice of one non-Restricted skill	2
Martial Arts Strikes skill category	3
Martial Arts Striking	2
Nerve Strikes	1
Martial Arts Sweeps skill category	3
Martial Arts Sweeping	2
Locking Holds	1
Self Control skill category	2
choice of up to two skills	2 (total)

Stat Gains: Strength, Agility

◆ 17.6 ◆
MARTIAL ARTS CHALLENGER (L)

The martial arts challenger is a character who lives and breathes in the martial arts world. He strives to prove himself the most skilled and powerful practitioner of his style of martial arts. By defeating all of the other martial artists in the area, he seeks to improve his reputation and the reputation of his chosen martial arts. Often the martial arts challenger seeks to build his reputation in order to open his own martial arts school.

"I am known as the outstanding youth in this district. I desire to test your knowledge of kung fu. Would you oblige me with a test of skill?"

Time to Acquire: 110 months

Starting Money: normal

Special:

Victory at local tournament	60
Victory at regional tournament	30
Weapon, +10 non -magical	25
Scrolls (+10 to Martial Arts Style Lore)	60
Rival martial arts school	40
Friendly martial arts teacher	50
Rival martial artist	20
Reputation as a good fighter	0

Category or Skill	# of ranks
Body Development skill category	n/a
Body Development	2
Combat Maneuvers skill category	n/a
choice of one skill	2
Influence skill category	1
choice of one skill	1
Lore General skill category	2
Martial Arts Style Lore	1
Weapon Style Lore	1
Martial Arts Combat Maneuvers skill category	n/a
choice of one skill	2
Martial Arts Strikes skill category	2
Martial Arts Striking	2
Martial Arts Sweeps skill category	2
Martial Arts Sweeping	2
Self Control skill category	2
choice of up to two non-Restricted skills	2 (total)
Special Attacks skill category	n/a
choice of up to two non-Restricted skills	2 (total)

Stat Gains: Strength

Professional Qualifier: Any training package that gives Martial Arts attacks skill ranks. [-3 points]

Part III

Sections
17.3, 17.4

Caravan
Guard (V)

Chi Master
(L)

MARTIAL
ARTS
COMPANION

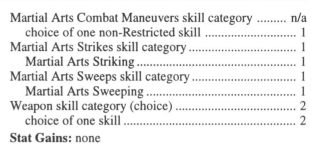

Part III

Sections
17.7, 17.8

Martial Arts
Champion (V)

Martial Arts
Performer (L)

◆ 17.7 ◆
MARTIAL ARTS CHAMPION (V)

The martial arts champion is a character who specializes in fighting for the causes of others. The he answers challenges posed to his family or employer. Not all martial arts champions fight for money, some are affiliated with a house or cause they serve by ties of blood or honor. Those martial arts champions that fight for money receive much less respect from their peers.

"I represent the honor of the House Fushan in this matter. I demand an apology in order to repair your slight against House Fushan's honor. I await your answer. If you do not wish to retract your words now, I will meet you tomorrow morning in the central square and restore House Fushan's honor over your unconscious body."

Time to Acquire: 31 months

Starting Money: normal

Special:

Upcoming match	40
Weapon, +10 non-magical	10
Ceremonial garb for challenges	60
Rival martial artist	40
Ornate weapon	30
Ornate armor	30
Favor from powerful organization	50
Reputation as a good fighter	0

Category or Skill	# of ranks
Armor Light skill category	1
choice of one skill	1
Body Development skill category	n/a
Body Development	1
Combat Maneuvers skill category	n/a
choice of one non-Restricted skill	1
Influence skill category	1
Public Speaking	1

Category or Skill	# of ranks
Martial Arts Combat Maneuvers skill category	n/a
choice of one non-Restricted skill	1
Martial Arts Strikes skill category	1
Martial Arts Striking	1
Martial Arts Sweeps skill category	1
Martial Arts Sweeping	1
Weapon skill category (choice)	2
choice of one skill	2

Stat Gains: none

◆ 17.8 ◆
MARTIAL ARTS OPERA PERFORMER (L)

The martial arts opera performer is a character who has been trained at a very early age to participate in a type of acrobatic opera company. The character has been trained to be flexible and acrobatic in order to accomplish the graceful but physically demanding traditional forms of the opera. To mimic the great warriors and heroes of the past, the performer has studied martial arts from a very young age. Most martial arts opera performers begin their apprenticeship at the age of six and continue in their profession the rest of their lives.

"I am the greatest performer of my time. My voice is without parallel, my movements are as graceful as the crane, and my skill is equal to that of the heroes of old."

Time to Acquire: 187 months

Starting Money: normal

Special:

Close friends with a famous performer	40
Extra d10 (open-ended) in money	50
Small gifts from patrons	20
Currently performing in a play	30
Instrument (+5 non-magical)	40
Friendly contacts with former troupe	60
Contacts in the arts world	40
Rich clothing	20
Reputation as a skilled performer	0

Category or Skill	# of ranks
Artistic Active skill category	5
Acting	2
choice of up to two skills	3 (total)
Athletic Gymnastics skill category	3
Tumbling	2
choice of one skill	1 (total)
Communications skill category	5
choice of up to three languages	5 (total)
Influence skill category	3
choice of up to two skills	2 (total)
Martial Arts Strikes skill category	1
Martial Arts Striking	1
Martial Arts Sweeps skill category	1
Martial Arts Sweeping	1
Self Control skill category	3
choice of up to two skills	3 (total)

Stat Gains: Agility

◆ 17.9 ◆
NINJA (L) ◆

The ninja is a character who has been raised by a secret clan of spies and assassins. Most of the character's life has been training for the jobs that he is going to do for his clan. In return for his training, the clan expects absolute loyalty – treachery is repaid in death for the offender. The clan teaches many types of skills including disguise, assassination, stealth, and endurance along with its weapon skills.

"I can scale sheer walls and enter through the smallest opening. I am a shadow. Your enemy will not see me until it is too late."

Time to Acquire: 170 months

Starting Money: normal

Special:

Disguise kit (+10 to Disguise skill)	40
Disguised weapon (staff/spear)	60
Current contract	20
Secret identity (merchant)	50
Common poison (1d2 doses)	30
Secret identity (pilgrim)	40
Secret identity (beggar)	40
Useful underworld contact	80
Traditional black spying outfit	0

Category or Skill	# of ranks
Athletic Gymnastic skill category	4
choice of up to two skills	4 (total)
Body Development skill category	n/a
Body Development	1
Combat Maneuvers skill category	n/a
choice of up to two skills	2 (total)
Martial Arts Combat Maneuvers skill category	n/a
choice of one non-Restricted skill	2
Martial Arts Strikes skill category	1
Martial Arts Striking	1
Martial Arts Sweeps skill category	1
Martial Arts Sweeping	1
Self Control skill category	2
choice of up to two skills	2 (total)
Subterfuge Attack skill category	n/a
choice of up to two skills	2 (total)
Subterfuge Stealth skill category	5
choice of up to four skills	5 (total)
Urban skill category	1
choice of one skill	1
Weapon skill category (choice)	1
choice of one skill	1

Stat Gains: Agility, Constitution

◆ 17.10 ◆
SCHOOL MASTER (V)

The school master is a character who has spent many years learning a specific martial arts style. His training involved long hours of practice and conditioning, but now the character is an acknowledged master of his given martial arts style.

"I am Master Kim of the Water Flowing School. My school teaches its students to use the energy of their attackers against them. Our teachings allow our students to gain inner calm and tranquility."

Time to Acquire: 39 months

Starting Money: normal

Special:

Friendly contact with another school	50
Students (1d10, income 1d2 bp)	60
Rival competing school in same area	40
Scrolls (+5 to a general lore skill)	30
Training hall in city	35
Weapon, +5 non-magical	20
Rival master of opposing style	20
Certificate in his martial arts style	0

Category or Skill	# of ranks
Body Development skill category	n/a
Body Development	1
Martial Arts Combat Maneuvers skill category	n/a
choice of up to two skills	2 (total)
Martial Arts Strikes skill category	2
Martial Arts Striking	2
Martial Arts Sweeps skill category	2
Martial Arts Sweeping	2
Self Control skill category	2
choice of up to two skills	2 (total)
Special Attacks skill category	n/a
choice of one non-Restricted skill	1
Weapon skill category (choice)	1
choice of one skill	1

Stat Gains: none

Part III

Sections
17.11, 17.12

Secret Society
Member (V)

Martial Arts
Street
Performer (V)

◆ 17.11 ◆
SECRET SOCIETY MEMBER (V)

The secret society member is a character who has been pulled from other walks of life and introduced to a secret movement. The current government does not support the movement's goals and thus the movement must keep a low profile. Members are taught how to fight and defend themselves for the time when the movement will come out of hiding and accomplish its goals.

"The Red Flag Society is dedicated to freeing the oppressed and overthrowing this corrupt regime. Join with us, I know you are a true patriot."

Time to Acquire: 22 months

Starting Money: normal

Special:

Friendly contact in the government	40
Friendly contact in the military forces	20
Knowledge of members in another city	40
Friendly low-ranking underworld contact	60
Wealth, 1d10 (open-ended)	30
Symbol of secret society	0

Category or Skill	# of ranks
Influence skill category	1
choice of one skill	1
Martial Arts Strikes or Sweeps skill categories	1
choice of one non-Restricted skill	1
Subterfuge Stealth skill category	2
choice of up to two skills	2 (total)
Urban skill category	1
choice of one skill	1

Stat Gains: none

◆ 17.12 ◆
MARTIAL ARTS STREET PERFORMER (V)

The martial arts street performer is a character who uses his martial arts skills to gain money from spectators. He has a glib and agile tongue that often appears more skillful than his martial arts skills. The martial arts street performer is also looked down upon by "more serious" (and wealthier) practitioners of the martial arts world. Yet one must eat, and it is honest work. Sometimes the performer is a martial artist who has fallen on hard times and is without patronage. Thus it can be very dangerous to bait inept street performers, as they may be skilled martial arts students new to their trade who will bitterly resent any slur on themselves and their newfound situation in life.

'Watch now as I perform this maneuver for your pleasure, risking my life and limbs in this dangerous feat. No performer in this province has attempted this feat since the unfortunate and horrific death of Master Lo some thirty years ago...'

Time to Acquire: 37 months

Starting Money: normal

Special:

Friends on the street	70
Scrolls (+5 to specific lore skill)	30
Props (+10 to performances)	50
Member of performing troupe	40
Small-time underworld contact	30
Extra money, 1d10 (open-ended)	40
Friendly tavern owner	0

Category or Skill	# of ranks
Artistic Active skill category	2
choice of two skills	2 (total)
Artistic Gymnastic skill category	1
choice of one skill	1
Influence skill category	2
Public Speaking	1
choice of one skill	1
Subterfuge Stealth skill category	2
choice of one skill	2
Urban skill category	3
choice of up to two skills	4 (total)

Stat Gains: none

Part III

Sections
17.13, 17.14

Temple Monk
(L)

Wandering
Monk (V)

◆ 17.13 ◆
TEMPLE MONK (L)

The temple monk is a character who has spent most of his life in the sheltered walls of a temple learning both his religious doctrines and his martial arts skills. The temple monk is often surprised by the corruption in the material world, but he is not defenseless thanks to his extensive training. A temple monk strives to renounce the material world and pursue only his spiritual development.

"Through strife and struggle, we gain knowledge and wisdom. I would be honored to test my skills against you. May my brothers give me guidance and strength."

Time to Acquire: 169 months

Starting Money: normal

Special:

Scroll (+10 to a general lore skill)	40
Healing Herbs, 1d5 of uncommon potency	50
Healing Herbs, 1d10 of common potency	30
Scroll (+10 to Martial Arts Style Lore)	40
Prayer beads (+10 to Meditation skill)	0

Category or Skill	# of ranks
Body Development skill category	n/a
Body Development	1
Lore General skill category	3
choice of up to three skills	5 (total)
Lore Technical skill category	2
choice of one skill	2
Martial Arts Combat Maneuvers skill category	n/a
One Lifestyle skill	4
Martial Arts Strikes skill category	2
Martial Arts Striking	1
Nerve Strikes	1
Martial Arts Sweeps skill category	2
Martial Arts Sweeping	1
Locking Holds	1
Self Control skill category	4
choice of up to two skills	4 (total)
Special Attacks skill category	n/a
choice of one skill	1
Special Defenses skill category	n/a
choice of up to two skills	2 (total)

Stat Gains: Self Discipline

Lifestyle Skills: Two Martial Arts Styles skills from the Martial Arts Combat Maneuvers skill category may be chosen as Lifestyle skills.

◆ 17.14 ◆
WANDERING MONK (V)

The wandering monk is a character who has spent some time in training at the temples of the region, but later decided that true wisdom is to be found by interacting with the people. In the course of his travels, the wandering monk learns the need for a strong defense and gains a better understanding of human nature.

"True knowledge is gained through experience in the outer world and not through solitude and meditation."

Time to Acquire: 78 months

Starting Money: normal

Special:

Prayer beads (+10 to Meditation)	50
Weapon, +5 non-magical	30
Book (+10 to a specific lore skill)	30
Book (+5 to a lore category)	20
Reputation as a holy hermit	0

Category or Skill	# of ranks
Artistic Passive skill category	2
choice of one skill	2
Body Development skill category	n/a
Body Development	1
Communication skill category	4
choice of up to two languages	4 (total)
Lore General skill category	2
choice of up to two skills	4 (total)
Lore Technical skill category	2
choice of one skill	2
Martial Arts Combat Maneuvers skill category	n/a
choice of one non-Restricted skill	2
Martial Arts Strikes skill category	1
Martial Arts Striking	1
Martial Arts Sweeps skill category	1
Martial Arts Sweeping	1
Self Control skill category	3
choice of up to three skills	3 (total)
Special Defenses skill category	n/a
choice of one skill	1

Stat Gains: none

MARTIAL
ARTS
COMPANION

Part III

**Sections
17.15, 17.16**

Warrior-priest
(L)

Weapon
Master (L)

◆ 17.15 ◆
WARRIOR-PRIEST (L)

The warrior-priest is a character who has studied at a militant temple to serve in the enforcement arm of the temple. The warrior-priest believes that he has been called to defend his religion and the goals it professes.

"The prophet said to lead a man to enlightenment; a teacher needs the classic works, the writings of the scholars, and a strong arm. I am the arm that leads souls to enlightenment."

Time to Acquire: 107 months

Starting Money: normal

Special:

Recent advancement in order	40
Prayer beads (+10 to Meditation)	70
Prayer scrolls (+10 to one general lore skill)	60
Weapon, +5 non-magical	30
Herbs, 1d10 common healing herbs	20
Reputation as a holy warrior	0

Category or Skill	# of ranks
Body Development skill category	n/a
Body Development	1
Lore General skill category	2
choice of up to two skills	2 (total)
Lore Technical skill category	1
choice of one skill	1
Martial Arts Combat Maneuvers skill category	n/a
choice of one skill	2
Martial Arts Strikes skill category	2
Martial Arts Striking	2
Martial Arts Sweeps skill category	2
Martial Arts Sweeping	2
Self Control skill category	2
choice of up to two skills	2 (total)
Weapon skill category (choice)	1
choice of one skill	1

Stat Gains: none

◆ 17.16 ◆
WEAPON MASTER (L)

The weapon master is a character who has dedicated his life to mastering the use of his weapon. He desires to be the most skilled practitioner of his chosen weapon in the world.

Note: This is revised from the *RMSR* version.

"I have studied the art of the sword for 30 years. My swordplay is without comparison. I will not accept your challenge because I will not fight a boy who only thinks he is a man."

Time to Acquire: 116 months

Starting Money: normal

Special:

Weapon, +10 non-magical	50
Victory in regional tournament	40
Weapon, +5 non-magical	30
Rival martial artist	40
Scrolls (+10 Weapon Style Lore)	50
Books (+10 to a General Lore skill)	30
Reputation as a very skilled fighter	0

Category or Skill	# of ranks
Body Development skill category	n/a
Body Development	2
Combat Maneuvers skill category	n/a
Weapon Style Lifestyle skill	4
Martial Arts Combat Maneuvers skill category	n/a
choice of one non-Restricted skill	2
choice of one other non-Restricted skill	2
Martial Arts Strikes skill category	1
Martial Arts Striking	1
Martial Arts Sweeps skill category	1
Martial Arts Sweeping	1
Special Attacks skill category	n/a
choice of up to two non-Restricted skills	2 (total)
Weapon skill category (choice)	4
choice of one skill	4

Stat Gains: Strength, Agility

Lifestyle Skills: One Weapon Style skill from the Combat Maneuvers skill category may be selected as a Lifestyle skill.

Length: 5 – 7 feet
Weight: 6 – 8 pounds
Fumble Range: 01 – 08 UM
Breakage #s: 1, 2, 3, 4, 5, 6, 7
Strength: 65 – 75 w

Range Modifiers: —

ATTACK TABLE 18.1

CHIGIRIKI

POLE ARM

	20	19	18	17	16	15	14	13	12	11	10	9	8	7	6	5	4	3	2	1	
150	16EK	18EK	20EK	22EK	22EK	22EK	26EK	26EK	21EK	22EK	27EK	27EK	25EK	25EK	30EK	33EK	26EK	29EK	32EK	34EK	150
149	16EK	18EK	20EK	22EG	22EG	22EG	26EG	26EG	21EG	22EG	27EG	27EG	25EG	25EG	30EG	33EG	26EG	29EG	32EG	34EG	149
148	16EK	18EK	20EK	22EK	22EK	22EK	26EK	26EK	21EK	22EK	27EK	27EK	25EK	25EK	30EK	33EK	26EK	29EK	32EK	34EK	148
147	16EK	18EK	20EK	22EG	22EG	22EG	26EG	26EG	21EG	22EG	27EG	27EG	25EG	25EG	30EG	33EG	26EG	29EG	32EG	34EG	147
146	16EK	18EK	20EG	22EK	22EK	22EK	26EK	26EK	21EK	22EK	27EK	27EK	25EK	25EK	30EK	33EK	26EK	29EK	32EK	34EK	146
145	16EK	18EK	20EK	22EG	22EG	22EG	26EG	26EG	21EG	22EG	27EG	27EG	25EG	25EG	30EG	33EG	26EG	29EG	32EG	34EG	145
144	16EK	18EK	20EG	22EK	22EK	22EK	26EK	26EK	21EK	22EK	27EK	27EK	25EK	25EK	30EK	33EK	26EK	29EK	32EK	34EK	144
143	16EG	18EK	20EK	22EG	22EG	22EG	26EG	26EG	21EG	22EG	27EG	27EG	25EG	25EG	30EG	33EG	26EG	29EG	32EG	34EG	143
142	16DK	18EG	20EG	22EK	22EK	22EK	26EK	26EK	21EK	22EK	27EK	27EK	25EK	25EK	30EK	33EK	26EK	29EK	32EK	34EK	142
141	16DK	18DK	20EK	22EG	22EG	22EG	26EG	26EG	21EG	22EG	27EG	27EG	25EG	25EG	30EG	33EG	26EG	29EG	32EG	34EG	141
140	16DK	18DK	20EG	22EK	22EK	22EK	26EK	26EK	21EK	22EK	27EK	27EK	25EK	25EK	30EK	33EK	26DK	29EK	32EK	34EK	140
139	16DK	18DK	20DK	22EG	22DG	22EG	26EG	26EG	21EG	22EG	27EG	27EG	25EG	25EG	30EG	33EG	26DG	29EG	32EG	34EG	139
138	16DK	18DK	20DK	22EK	22DK	22DK	26EK	26EK	21DK	22EK	27EK	27EK	25EK	25EK	30EK	33EK	26DK	29EK	32EK	34DK	138
137	16DK	18DG	20DK	22DG	22DG	22DG	26DG	26EG	21DG	22DG	27EG	27EG	25DG	25EG	30EG	33EG	26DG	29DG	32EG	34DG	137
136	16DK	18DK	20DK	22DK	22DK	22DK	26DK	26EK	21DK	22DK	27DK	27EK	25DK	25DK	30EK	33EK	26DK	29DK	32DK	34DK	136
135	16DG	18DG	20DG	22DG	22DG	22DG	26DG	26DG	21DG	22DG	27DG	27EG	25DG	25DG	30DG	33EG	26DG	29DG	32DG	34DG	135
134	16CK	18DK	20DK	22DK	22DK	22DK	26DK	26DK	21DK	22DK	27DK	27DK	25DK	25DK	30DK	33DK	26DK	29DK	32DK	34DK	134
133	16CK	18DG	20DG	22DG	22DG	22DG	26DG	26DG	21DG	22DG	27DG	27DG	25DG	25DG	30DG	33DG	26DG	29DG	32DG	34DG	133
132	16CK	18CK	20DK	22DK	22DK	22DK	26DK	26DK	21DK	22DK	27DK	27DK	25DK	25DK	30DK	33DK	26DK	29DK	32DK	34DK	132
131	16CK	18CK	20DG	22DG	22DG	22DG	26DG	26DG	21DG	22DG	27DG	27DG	25DG	25DG	30DG	33DG	26DG	27DG	32DG	32DG	131
130	16CK	18CK	20DK	22DK	22DK	22DK	26DK	26DK	21DK	22DK	27DK	27DK	25DK	25DK	30DK	33DK	26CK	27DK	32DK	32DK	130
129	16CG	18CK	20DG	22DG	22DG	22DG	26DG	26DG	21DG	22DG	27DG	27DG	25DG	25DG	30DG	33DG	26CG	25DG	32DG	30DG	129
128	16CK	18CG	20CK	22DK	22CK	22DK	26DK	26DK	21DK	22DK	27DK	27DK	25DK	25DK	30DK	33DK	26CK	25DK	32DK	30DK	128
127	16CG	18CK	20CK	22DG	22CG	22DG	26DG	26DG	21DG	22DG	27DG	27DG	25DG	25DG	30DG	33DG	26CG	25DG	32DG	30DG	127
126	16BK	18CG	20CK	22DK	22CK	22CK	26DK	26DK	21CK	22DK	27DK	27DK	25DK	25DK	30DK	33DK	24CK	25DK	32DK	30CK	126
125	16BK	18CK	20CK	22DG	22CG	22CG	26DG	26DG	21CG	22DG	27DG	27DG	25DG	25DG	30DG	33DG	24CG	25DG	32DG	30CG	125
124	16BK	18CG	20CG	22CK	22CK	22CK	26CK	26DK	21CK	22CK	27DK	27DK	25CK	25DK	30DK	33DK	22CK	25CK	32DK	30CK	124
123	16BK	18BK	20CK	22CG	22CG	22CG	26CG	26DG	21CG	22CG	27DG	27DG	25CG	25DG	30DG	33DG	22CG	25CG	32DG	30CG	123
122	16BK	18BK	20CG	22CK	22CK	22CK	26CK	26DK	21CK	22CK	27CK	27DK	25CK	25CK	30DK	33DK	22CK	25CK	32CK	30CK	122
121	16BG	18BK	20CK	22CG	22CG	22CG	26CG	26DG	21CG	22CG	27CG	27DG	25CG	25CG	30DG	33DG	22CG	23CG	30CG	27CG	121
120	16BK	18BK	20CG	22CK	22CK	22CK	26CK	26CK	21CK	22CK	27CK	27DK	25CK	25CK	30CK	33DK	22BK	23CK	30CK	27CK	120
119	16BG	18BG	20CK	22CG	22CG	22CG	26CG	26CG	21CG	22CG	27CG	27DG	25CG	25CG	30CG	33DG	22BG	21CG	28CG	25CG	119
118	16AK	18BK	20CG	22CK	22CK	22CK	26CK	26CK	21CK	22CK	27CK	27CK	25CK	25CK	30CK	33CK	22BK	21CK	28CK	25CK	118
117	16AK	18BG	20BK	22CG	22BG	22CG	26CG	26CG	21CG	22CG	27CG	27CG	25CG	25CG	30CG	33CG	22BG	21CG	28CG	25CG	117
116	16AK	18BK	20BK	22CK	22BK	22CK	26CK	26CK	21CK	20CK	27CK	25CK	25CK	25CK	30CK	31CK	21BK	21CK	28CK	25CK	116
115	16AK	18BG	20BG	22CG	22BG	22CG	26CG	26CG	21CG	20CG	27CG	25CG	25CG	25CG	30CG	31CG	21BG	21CG	28CG	25CG	115
114	16AK	18AK	20BK	22CK	22BK	22BK	26CK	26CK	21BK	19CK	27CK	23CK	25CK	25CK	30CK	29CK	19BK	21CK	28CK	25BK	114
113	16AK	18AK	20BG	22CG	22BG	22BG	26CG	26CG	21BG	19CG	27CG	23CG	25CG	25CG	30CG	29CG	19BG	21CG	28CG	25BG	113
112	16AG	18AK	20BK	22CK	22BK	22BK	26CK	26CK	21BK	19CK	27CK	23CK	25CK	25CK	30CK	29CK	19BK	21CK	28CK	25BK	112
111	16AK	18AK	20BG	22BG	22BG	22BG	26BG	26CG	21BG	19BG	25CG	23CG	25BG	25CG	28CG	29CG	19BG	20BG	26CG	23BG	111
110	16AG	18AK	20BK	22BK	22BK	22BK	26BK	26CK	21BK	19BK	25CK	23CK	25BK	25CK	28CK	29CK	19AK	20BK	26CK	23BK	110
109	16	18AG	20BG	22BG	22BG	22BG	26BG	26CG	21BG	19BG	23CG	23CG	25BG	25CG	26CG	29CG	19AG	18BG	24CG	21BG	109
108	16	18AK	20BK	22BK	22BK	22BK	26BK	26CK	21BK	19BK	23BK	23CK	25BK	25BK	26CK	29CK	19AK	18BK	24BK	21BK	108
107	16	18AG	20BG	22BG	22BG	22BG	26BG	26CG	21BG	19BG	23BG	23CG	25BG	25BG	26CG	29CG	19AG	18BG	24BG	21BG	107
106	16	18AK	20AK	22BK	22AK	22BK	26BK	26CK	21BK	17BK	23BK	22CK	25BK	25BK	26CK	27CK	17AK	18BK	24BK	21BK	106
105	16	18AG	20AK	22BG	22AG	22BG	26BG	24BG	19BG	17BG	23BG	22CG	25BG	23BG	26BG	27CG	17AG	18BG	24BG	21BG	105
104	16	18	20AK	22BK	22AK	22BK	26BK	24BK	19BK	16BK	23BK	20CK	25BK	23BK	26BK	25CK	16AK	18BK	24BK	21BK	104
103	16	18	20AG	22BG	22AG	22BG	26BG	22BG	18BG	16BG	23BG	20CG	25BG	22BG	26BG	25CG	16AG	18BG	24BG	21BG	103
102	16	18	20AK	22BK	22AK	22AK	26BK	22BK	18AK	16BK	23BK	20BK	25BK	22BK	26BK	25BK	16AK	18BK	24BK	21AK	102
101	16	18	20AG	20BG	22AG	22AG	24BG	22BG	18AG	16BG	22BG	20BG	23BG	22BG	24BG	25BG	16AG	16BG	22BG	19AG	101
100	16	18	20AK	20BK	22AK	22AK	24BK	22BK	18AK	16BK	22BK	20BK	23BK	22BK	24BK	25BK	16AK	16BK	22BK	19AK	100
99	16	18	20AG	19BG	22AG	22AG	22BG	22BG	18AG	16BG	20BG	20BG	22BG	22BG	22BG	25BG	16	14BG	20BG	17AG	99
98	16	18	20AK	19AK	22AK	22AK	22AK	22BK	18AK	16AK	20BK	20BK	22AK	22BK	22BK	25BK	16	14AK	20BK	17AK	98
97	16	18	20AG	19AG	22AG	22AG	22AG	22BG	18AG	16AG	20BG	20BG	22AG	22BG	22BG	25BG	16	14AG	20BG	17AG	97
96	16	18	20AK	19AK	22AK	22AK	22AK	22BK	18AK	15AK	20BK	18BK	22AK	22BK	22BK	22BK	14	14AK	20BK	17AK	96
95	16	18	20AG	19AG	22AG	22AG	22AG	21BG	17AG	15AG	20BG	18BG	22AG	20BG	22BG	22BG	14	14AG	20BG	17AG	95
94	16	18	20	19AK	22	22AK	22AK	21BK	17AK	13AK	20AK	16BK	22AK	20AK	22BK	20BK	13	14AK	20AK	17AK	94
93	16	18	20	19AG	22	22AG	22AG	19BG	15AG	13AG	20AG	16BG	22AG	19AG	22BG	20BG	13	14AG	20AG	17AG	93
92	16	18	20	19AK	22	22AK	22AK	19BK	15AK	13AK	20AK	16BK	22AK	19AK	22BK	20BK	13	14AK	20AK	17AK	92
91	16	18	20	18AG	22	22AG	21AG	19BG	15AG	13AG	18AG	16BG	20AG	19AG	20BG	20BG	13	12AG	18AG	15AG	91
90	16	18	20	18AK	22	22AK	21AK	19AK	15AK	13AK	18AK	16BK	20AK	19AK	20AK	20BK	13	12AK	18AK	15AK	90
89	16	18	20	16AG	22	22	19AG	19AG	15	13AG	16AG	16BG	19AG	19AG	18AG	20BG	13	10AG	16AG	12	89
88	16	18	20	16AK	22	22	19AK	19AK	15	13AK	16AK	16BK	19AK	19AK	18AK	20BK	13	10AK	16AK	12	88
87	16	18	20	16AG	22	22	19AG	19AG	15	13AG	16AG	16BG	19AG	19AG	18AG	20BG	13	10AG	16AG	12	87
86	16	18	20	16AK	22	22	19AK	19AK	15	12AK	16AK	15AK	19AK	19AK	18AK	18AK	11	10AK	16AK	12	86
85	16	18	20	16AG	22	22	19AG	17AG	14	12AG	16AG	15AG	19AG	17AG	18AG	18AG	11	10AG	16AG	12	85
84	16	17	19	16	20	20	19	17AK	14	11	16AK	13AK	19	17AK	18AK	16AK	9	10	16AK	12	84
83	16	17	19	16	20	20	19	16AG	13	11	16AG	13AG	19	15AG	18AG	16AG	9	10	16AG	12	83
82	16	15	17	16	19	19	19	16AK	13	11	16AK	13AK	19	15AK	18AK	16AK	9	10	16AK	12	82
81	16	15	17	15	19	19	17	16AG	13	11	15AG	13AG	17	15AG	17AG	16AG	9	9	14AG	10	81
80	16	15	17	15	19	19	17	16AK	13	11	15AK	13AK	17	15AK	17AK	16AK	9	9	14AK	10	80
79	16	15	17	13	19	19	16	16AG	13	11	13	13AG	15	15	15AG	16AG	9	7	12	8	79
78	16	15	17	13	19	19	16	16AK	13	11	13	13AK	15	15	15AK	16AK	9	7	12	8	78
77	16	15	17	13	19	19	16	16AG	13	11	13	13AG	15	15	15AG	16AG	9	7	12	8	77
76	16	15	17	13	19	19	16	16AK	13	9	13	11AK	15	15	15AK	14AK	8	7	12	8	76
75	16	15	17	13	19	19	16	14AG	11	9	13	11AG	15	14	15AG	14AG	8	7	12	8	75
74	15	14	16	13	17	17	16	14	11	8	13	10AK	15	14	15	12AK	6	–	12	–	74
73	15	14	16	13	17	17	16	13	10	8	13	10AG	15	12	15	12AG	6	–	12	–	73
72	14	13	15	13	16	16	16	13	10	8	13	10AK	15	12	15	12AK	6	–	12	–	72
71	14	13	15	12	16	16	14	13	10	8	11	10AG	14	12	13	12AG	6	–	10	–	71
70	14	13	15	12	16	16	14	13	10	8	11	10AK	14	12	13	12AK	6	–	10	–	70
69	14	13	15	11	16	16	13	13	10	8	10	10	12	12	11	12	–	–	8	–	69
68	14	13	15	11	16	16	13	13	10	8	10	10	12	12	11	12	–	–	8	–	68
67	14	13	15	11	16	16	13	13	10	8	10	10	12	12	11	12	–	–	8	–	67
66	14	13	15	11	16	16	13	13	10	6	10	8	12	12	11	10	–	–	8	–	66
65	14	13	15	11	16	16	13	11	9	6	10	8	12	11	11	10	–	–	8	–	65
64	13	12	13	11	15	15	13	11	9	5	10	6	12	11	11	8	–	–	–	–	64
63	13	12	13	11	15	15	13	9	7	5	10	6	12	9	11	8	–	–	–	–	63
62	12	11	12	11	13	13	13	9	7	5	10	6	12	9	11	8	–	–	–	–	62
61	12	11	12	9	13	13	11	9	7	5	8	6	11	9	9	8	–	–	–	–	61
60	12	11	12	9	13	13	11	9	7	5	8	6	11	9	9	8	–	–	–	–	60
55-59	12	11	12	8	13	13	9	9	7	–	6	–	9	9	7	–	–	–	–	–	55-59
50-54	10	9	10	7	11	11	9	6	5	–	–	–	8	6	–	–	–	–	–	–	50-54
45-49	10	9	10	5	11	11	6	6	5	–	–	–	6	6	–	–	–	–	–	–	45-49
43-44	9	7	8	–	9	9	–	–	–	–	–	–	–	–	–	–	–	–	–	–	43-44
38-42	8	6	7	–	8	8	–	–	–	–	–	–	–	–	–	–	–	–	–	–	38-42
33-37	8	6	7	–	7	7	–	–	–	–	–	–	–	–	–	–	–	–	–	–	33-37
28-32	6	4	5	–	5	5	–	–	–	–	–	–	–	–	–	–	–	–	–	–	28-32
18-27	5	–	–	–	–	–	–	–	–	–	–	–	–	–	–	–	–	–	–	–	18-27

ATTACK TABLE 18.2
KAMA
ONE-HANDED EDGED

Length: 1 – 2 feet
Weight: 3 – 5 pounds
Fumble Range: 01 – 05 UM
Breakage #s: 1, 2, 3, 4, 5, 6, 7
Strength: 65 – 75 w
Range Modifiers: —

	20	19	18	17	16	15	14	13	12	11	10	9	8	7	6	5	4	3	2	1	
150	11DK	13DK	15EK	17EK	18EK	18EK	20EK	20EK	18EK	19EK	23EK	23EK	18ES	18ES	23ES	26ES	20ES	23ES	26ES	28ES	150
149	11DK	13DK	15EK	17EK	18EK	18EK	20EK	20EK	18ES	19ES	23EK	23EK	18ES	18ES	23ES	26ES	20ES	23ES	26ES	28ES	149
148	11DK	13DK	15EK	17EK	18EK	18EK	20EK	20EK	18EK	19EK	23ES	23EK	18EK	18ES	23EK	26ES	20ES	23EK	26EK	28EK	148
147	11DK	13DK	15EK	17EK	18EK	18EK	20EK	20EK	18ES	19ES	23EK	23ES	18ES	18EK	23ES	26EK	20EK	23ES	26ES	28ES	147
146	11DK	13DK	15EK	17EK	18EK	18EK	20EK	20EK	18EK	19EK	23ES	23EK	18EK	18ES	23EK	26ES	20ES	23ES	26ES	28EK	146
145	11DK	13DK	15EK	17EK	18EK	18EK	20EK	20EK	18ES	19ES	23EK	23ES	18ES	18EK	23ES	26EK	20ES	23EK	26EK	28ES	145
144	11CK	13DK	15EK	17EK	18EK	18EK	20EK	20EK	18EK	19EK	23ES	23EK	18EK	18ES	23EK	26ES	20ES	23ES	26ES	28EP	144
143	11CK	13CK	15EK	17EK	18EK	18EK	20EK	20EK	18ES	19ES	23EK	23ES	18ES	18EK	23ES	26EK	20EK	23ES	26EP	28ES	143
142	11CK	13CK	15DK	17EK	18DK	18ES	20EK	20EK	18EK	19EK	23ES	23EK	18EK	18ES	23EK	26ES	20ES	23EK	26ES	28ES	142
141	11CK	13CK	15DK	17EK	18DK	18DK	20ES	20EK	18EK	19EK	23EK	23ES	18ES	18EK	23ES	26EK	20ES	23ES	26ES	28EK	141
140	11CK	13CK	15DK	17DK	18DK	18DK	20DK	20EK	18DK	19EP	23EK	23EK	18ES	18ES	23EK	26ES	20EP	23ES	26ES	28ES	140
139	11CK	13CK	15DK	17DK	18DK	18DK	20DK	20ES	18DK	19DK	23EP	23ES	18EP	18ES	23ES	26EK	20DS	23EP	26EK	28ES	139
138	11CK	13CK	15DK	17DK	18DK	18DK	20DK	20DK	18DS	19DK	23DK	23EK	18DS	18EP	23ES	26ES	20DK	23DS	26ES	28EP	138
137	11BK	13CK	15DK	17DK	18DK	18DK	20DK	20DK	18DK	19DS	23DK	23EK	18DS	18DS	23EP	26ES	20DS	23DS	26ES	28DS	137
136	11BK	13CK	15DK	17DK	18DK	18DK	20DK	20DK	18DS	19DK	23DS	23EP	18DK	18DS	23DS	26EP	20DS	23DK	26EP	28DS	136
135	11BK	13BK	15DK	17DK	18DS	18DK	20DK	20DK	18DK	19DS	23DK	23DK	18DS	18DS	23DS	26DS	20DK	23DS	26DS	28DK	135
134	11BK	13BK	15CK	17DK	18CK	18DK	20DK	20DK	18DS	19DK	23DS	23DK	18DK	18DK	23DK	26DS	20DS	23DS	26DS	28DS	134
133	11BK	13BK	15CK	17DK	18CK	18DS	20DK	20DK	18DK	19DS	23DK	23DK	18DS	18DS	23DS	26DS	20DS	23DP	26DK	28DK	133
132	11BK	13BK	15CK	17DK	18CK	18CK	20DK	20DK	18DS	19DK	23DS	23DS	18DK	18DK	23DK	26DK	20DK	23DS	26DS	28DS	132
131	11AK	13BK	15CK	17DK	18CK	18CK	20DS	20DK	18DK	19DS	23DK	23DK	18DS	18DS	23DS	26DS	20DS	22DK	26DK	26DP	131
130	11AK	13BK	15CK	17CK	18CK	18CK	20CK	20DK	18DP	19DK	23DS	23DS	18DK	18DK	23DK	26DK	20DS	22DS	26DS	26DS	130
129	11AK	13BK	15CK	17CK	18CK	18CK	20CK	20DK	18CK	19DK	23DK	23DK	18DS	18DS	23DS	26DS	20DP	20DK	26DS	25DS	129
128	11AP	13BK	15CK	17CK	18CK	18CK	20CK	20DK	18CK	18DP	23DS	22DS	18DS	18DK	23DK	26DK	20CS	20DS	26DP	25DK	128
127	11AK	13AK	15CK	17CK	18CS	18CK	20CK	20DS	18CS	18CK	23DK	22DK	18DP	18DS	23DS	26DS	20CS	20DP	26DS	25DS	127
126	11AK	13AK	15BK	17CK	18BK	18CK	20CK	20CK	18CK	17CK	23DP	20DS	18CS	18DS	23DK	26DK	19CK	20CS	26DK	25DS	126
125	11AS	13AK	15BK	17CK	18BK	18CK	20CK	20CK	18CS	17CS	23CK	20DK	18CS	18DP	23DS	26DS	19CS	20CS	26DS	25DP	125
124	11	13AK	15BK	17CK	18BK	18CS	20CS	20CK	18CK	17CK	23CK	20DS	18CS	18CS	23DS	26DK	17CS	20CK	26DK	25CS	124
123	11	13AP	15BK	17CK	18BK	18BK	20CK	20CK	18CS	17CS	22CS	20DK	18CK	18CK	23DP	25DS	17CP	20CS	26DS	25CK	123
122	11	13AK	15BK	17CK	18BS	18BK	20CK	20CK	18CK	17CK	22CK	20DK	18CS	18CS	23CS	25DS	17CK	20CS	26DS	25CS	122
121	11	13AK	15BK	17CK	18BK	18BK	20CP	20CK	18CS	17CS	20CS	20DP	18CK	18CK	23CS	23DP	17CS	19CP	25DP	23CS	121
120	11	13AS	15BK	17BK	18BK	18BK	20BK	20CK	18CK	17CK	20CK	20CK	18CS	18CS	23CK	23CS	17CK	19CS	25CS	23CK	120
119	11	13	15BK	17BK	18BP	18BK	20BK	20CK	17CP	17CS	20CS	20CK	18CK	18CK	22CS	23CS	17CS	17CK	23CS	21CS	119
118	11	13	15AK	17BK	18AK	18BS	20BK	20CS	17BK	16CK	20CK	19CS	18CS	18CS	22CK	23CK	17CP	17CS	23CK	21CP	118
117	11	13	15AK	17BK	18AK	18BK	20BK	20CK	16BK	16CK	20CS	19CK	18CK	18CK	20CS	23CS	17BS	17CK	23CS	21CS	117
116	11	13	15AK	17BK	18AK	18BK	20BK	20CK	16BS	14CP	20CK	17CS	18CS	18CS	20CK	23CK	16BS	17CS	23CK	21CS	116
115	11	13	15AK	17BK	18AK	18BP	20BK	20CP	16BK	14BK	20CS	17CK	18CP	18CK	20CS	23CS	16BK	17CP	23CS	21CK	115
114	11	13	15AK	17BK	18AK	18AK	20BS	20BK	16BS	14BK	20CK	17CS	18BS	17CS	20CK	23CP	15BS	17BS	23CS	21CS	114
113	11	13	15AS	17BK	18AS	18AK	20BK	20BK	16BK	14BS	19CP	17CK	18BS	17CS	20CS	21CS	15BS	17BS	23CP	21CS	113
112	11	13	15AK	17BK	18AK	18AK	20BK	19BK	16BS	14BK	19BK	17CS	18BS	16CP	20CK	21CK	15BP	17BK	23CS	21CP	112
111	11	13	15AK	17BS	18AK	18AK	20BP	19BK	16BK	14BS	17BK	17CK	18BK	16BS	20CS	20CS	15BK	16BS	21CK	19BS	111
110	11	13	15AP	17AK	18AP	18AK	20AK	17BK	16BS	14BK	17BS	17CS	18BS	16BK	20CS	20CK	15BS	16BS	21CS	19BS	110
109	11	13	15	17AK	18	18AK	20AK	17BK	14BK	14BS	17BK	17CK	17BK	16BS	19CP	20CS	15BK	14BP	20CK	17BK	109
108	11	13	15	16AK	18	18AS	19AK	17BK	14BP	13BK	17BS	16CS	17BS	16BK	19BK	20CK	15BS	14BS	20CS	17BS	108
107	11	13	15	16AK	18	18AK	19AK	17BK	13AK	13BS	17BK	16CK	16BK	16BS	17BS	20CS	15BP	14BK	20CS	17BK	107
106	11	13	15	15AK	18	18AK	17AK	17BS	13AK	12BK	17BS	14CK	16BS	16BP	17BK	20CP	14AS	14BS	20CP	17BS	106
105	11	13	15	15AK	18	18AP	17AK	17BK	13AS	12BK	17BK	14CP	16BK	16BK	17BS	20BS	14AK	14BK	20BS	17BP	105
104	11	13	15	15AK	18	18	17AK	17BK	13AK	12BP	17BS	14BK	16BS	14BS	17BK	20BS	12AS	14BS	20BS	17BS	104
103	11	13	14	15AS	18	17	17AS	17BP	13AS	12AK	16BK	14BS	16BP	14BK	17BS	18BK	12AK	14BP	20BK	17BS	103
102	11	13	14	15AK	18	17	17AK	16AK	13AK	12AS	16BS	14BK	16AS	13BS	17BP	18BS	12AS	14AS	20BS	17BK	102
101	11	13	13	15AK	18	16	17AK	16AK	13AS	12AK	14BK	14BS	16AK	13BK	17BS	16BK	12AS	13AS	18BK	16BS	101
100	11	13	13	15AP	18	16	17AP	15AK	13AK	12AS	14BP	14BK	16AS	13BS	17BK	16BS	12AP	13AS	18BS	16BS	100
99	11	13	13	15	18	16	17	15AK	12AS	12AK	14AK	14BS	14AK	13BP	16BS	16BP	12AS	11AK	16BS	14BP	99
98	11	13	13	14	18	16	16	15AK	12AK	11AS	14AK	13BK	14AS	13AS	16BK	16BS	12AS	11AS	16BP	14AS	98
97	11	13	13	14	18	16	16	15AK	11AP	11AK	14AS	13BS	13AP	13AS	14BS	16BK	12AK	11AS	16BS	14AS	97
96	11	13	13	13	18	16	15	15AS	11	9AS	14AK	11BK	13AK	13AK	14BS	16BS	11AS	11AP	16BK	14AK	96
95	11	13	13	13	18	16	15	15AK	11	9AK	14AS	11BS	13AS	13AS	14BP	16BK	11AP	11AS	16BS	14AS	95
94	11	13	13	13	18	16	15	15AK	11	9AS	14AK	11BK	13AK	12AK	14AS	16BS	10	11AK	16BK	14AS	94
93	11	12	12	13	17	14	15	15AS	11	9AK	13AS	11BS	13AS	12AS	14AS	15BK	10	11AS	16BS	14AK	93
92	11	12	12	13	17	14	15	14AK	11	9AP	13AK	11BK	13AK	11AP	14AS	15BS	10	11AK	16BS	14AS	92
91	11	11	11	13	16	13	15	14AK	11	9	11AS	11BK	13AS	11AK	14AK	13BP	10	10AS	15BP	12AP	91
90	11	11	11	13	16	13	15	12AP	11	9	11AK	11BP	13AP	11AS	14AS	13AS	10	10AP	15AS	12AS	90
89	11	11	11	13	16	13	15	12	10	9	11AS	11AK	12	11AK	13AK	13AK	10	8	13AK	10AK	89
88	11	11	11	12	16	13	14	12	10	8	11AK	10AK	12	11AS	13AS	13AS	10	8	13AS	10AS	88
87	11	11	11	12	16	13	14	12	9	8	11AP	10AS	11	11AK	11AP	13AK	10	8	13AK	10AK	87
86	11	11	11	10	16	13	12	12	9	7	11	8AK	11	11AS	11AK	13AS	8	8	13AS	10AS	86
85	11	11	11	10	16	13	12	12	9	7	11	8AS	11	11AP	11AS	13AK	8	8	13AP	10AP	85
84	11	11	11	10	16	13	12	12	9	7	11	8AK	11	10	11AK	13AS	7	8	13AS	10	84
83	10	10	10	10	14	12	12	12	9	7	10	8AS	11	10	11AS	11AP	7	8	13AS	10	83
82	10	10	10	10	14	12	12	11	9	7	10	8AK	11	9	11AK	11AS	7	8	13AK	10	82
81	9	9	9	10	13	11	12	11	9	7	8	8AP	11	9	11AS	10AK	7	7	11AS	8	81
80	9	9	9	10	13	11	12	10	9	7	8	8AK	11	9	11AP	10AS	7	7	11AP	8	80
79	9	9	9	10	13	11	12	10	8	7	8	8AS	10	9	10	10AK	7	5	10AS	7	79
78	9	9	9	9	13	11	11	10	8	6	8	7AK	10	9	10	10AS	7	5	10AK	7	78
77	9	9	9	9	13	11	11	10	6	6	8	7AS	9	9	8	10AK	7	5	10AS	7	77
76	9	9	9	8	13	11	10	10	6	4	8	5AK	9	9	8	10AS	6	5	10AS	7	76
75	9	9	9	8	13	11	10	10	6	4	8	5AS	9	9	8	10AP	6	5	10AP	7	75
74	9	9	9	8	13	11	10	10	6	4	8	5AP	9	8	8	10	5	–	10	–	74
73	9	9	8	8	12	10	10	10	6	4	7	5	9	8	8	8	5	–	10	–	73
72	9	9	8	8	12	10	10	8	6	4	7	5	9	6	8	8	5	–	10	–	72
71	8	8	7	8	11	9	10	8	6	–	5	–	9	6	8	6	5	–	8	–	71
70	8	8	7	8	11	9	10	7	6	–	5	–	9	6	8	6	5	–	8	–	70
69	8	8	7	8	11	9	10	7	5	–	5	–	8	6	7	6	–	–	6	–	69
68	8	8	7	7	11	9	8	7	5	–	5	–	8	6	7	6	–	–	6	–	68
67	8	8	7	7	11	9	8	7	4	–	5	–	6	6	5	6	–	–	6	–	67
66	8	8	7	6	11	9	7	7	4	–	–	–	6	6	5	–	–	–	6	–	66
65	8	8	7	6	11	9	7	7	4	–	–	–	6	6	5	–	–	–	6	–	65
64	8	8	7	6	11	9	7	7	4	–	–	–	6	5	5	–	–	–	–	–	64
63	7	7	6	6	10	8	7	7	4	–	–	–	6	5	5	–	–	–	–	–	63
62	7	7	6	6	10	8	7	6	–	–	–	–	6	4	–	–	–	–	–	–	62
61	7	6	5	6	9	6	7	6	–	–	–	–	6	4	–	–	–	–	–	–	61
58-60	7	6	5	6	9	6	7	5	–	–	–	–	6	4	–	–	–	–	–	–	58-60
54-57	7	6	5	5	9	6	6	5	–	–	–	–	4	–	–	–	–	–	–	–	54-57
52-53	6	5	4	4	8	5	5	–	–	–	–	–	4	–	–	–	–	–	–	–	52-53
47-51	5	4	3	–	6	4	–	–	–	–	–	–	–	–	–	–	–	–	–	–	47-51
44-46	5	4	–	–	6	–	–	–	–	–	–	–	–	–	–	–	–	–	–	–	44-46
42-43	4	4	–	–	5	–	–	–	–	–	–	–	–	–	–	–	–	–	–	–	42-43
37-41	4	3	–	–	4	–	–	–	–	–	–	–	–	–	–	–	–	–	–	–	37-41
34-36	4	–	–	–	–	–	–	–	–	–	–	–	–	–	–	–	–	–	–	–	34-36
27-33	2	–	–	–	–	–	–	–	–	–	–	–	–	–	–	–	–	–	–	–	27-33

ATTACK TABLE 18.3
KATANA
TWO-HANDED

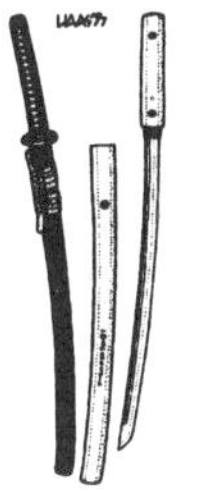

Length: 4 – 6 feet
Weight: 5 – 8 pounds
Fumble Range: 01 – 05 UM
Breakage #s: 1, 2, 3, 4, 5, 6, 7
Strength: 80 – 90
Range Modifiers: —

	20	19	18	17	16	15	14	13	12	11	10	9	8	7	6	5	4	3	2	1	
150	8EK	9EK	12EK	14EK	15EK	15EK	17EK	17EK	16EK	20EK	24EK	24EK	21ES	21ES	25ES	29ES	24ES	26ES	30ES	32ES	150
149	8EK	9EK	12EK	14EK	15EK	15EK	17EK	17EK	16EK	20EK	24EK	24EK	21ES	21ES	25ES	29ES	24EP	26ES	30ES	32ES	149
148	8EK	9EK	12EK	14EK	15EK	15EK	17EK	17EK	16EK	20ES	24ES	24EK	21ES	21EK	25ES	29ES	24ES	26ES	30ES	32ES	148
147	8EK	9EK	12EK	14EK	15EK	15ES	17EK	17EK	16EK	20EK	24EK	24EP	21EK	21EP	25ES	29EP	24ES	26EP	30ES	32ES	147
146	8EK	9EK	12EK	14EK	15EK	15EK	17ES	17EK	16EK	20EK	24EK	24ES	21EP	21ES	25EP	29EK	24EP	26ES	30ES	32EP	146
145	8DK	9EK	12EK	14EK	15EK	15EK	17EK	17ES	16ES	20EP	24ES	24EK	21ES	21ES	25EK	29ES	24ES	26EP	30ES	32ES	145
144	8DK	9DK	12EK	14EK	15EK	15EK	17EK	17EK	16EK	20EK	24EK	24ES	21EK	21EK	25ES	29EP	24ES	26ES	30EP	32EP	144
143	8DK	9DK	12EK	14EK	15ES	15EK	17EK	17EK	16EK	20EK	24EK	24EP	21EP	21EP	25EP	29EK	24EP	26EP	30ES	32ES	143
142	8DK	9DK	12DK	14EK	15DK	15EP	17EK	17EK	16EK	20ES	24ES	24EK	21ES	21ES	25EK	29ES	24ES	26ES	30EP	32EP	142
141	8DK	9DK	12DK	14EK	15DK	15DK	17EP	17EK	16EK	20EK	24EK	24ES	21EK	21EK	25ES	29EP	24ES	26EP	30ES	32ES	141
140	8CK	9DK	12DK	14DK	15DK	15DK	17DK	17EK	16EK	20ES	24EK	24EK	21EP	21EP	25EP	29EK	24EP	26ES	30EP	32EP	140
139	8CK	9DK	12DK	14DK	15DS	15DK	17DK	17EP	16EP	20EK	24ES	24EP	21ES	21ES	25EK	29ES	24ES	26EP	30ES	32ES	139
138	8CK	9CK	12DK	14DK	15DK	15DS	17DK	17DK	16DK	20EP	24EK	24ES	21EK	21ES	25ES	29EP	24EK	26ES	30EP	32EP	138
137	8CK	9CK	12DK	14DK	15DK	15DK	17DK	17DK	16DK	20DK	24EP	24EK	21EP	21EK	25ES	29EK	24DS	26EK	30ES	32ES	137
136	8CK	9CK	12DK	14DK	15DK	15DK	17DS	17DK	16DK	20DK	24DK	24ES	21DS	21EP	25EP	29ES	24DP	25DS	30EP	30EK	136
135	8BK	9CK	12DK	14DK	15DP	15DK	17DK	17DS	16DS	20DS	24DS	24EP	21DS	21DS	25EK	29EP	24DS	25DS	30ES	30DS	135
134	8BK	9CK	12CK	14DK	15CK	15DK	17DK	17DK	16DK	20DK	24DK	24DK	21DS	21DS	25DS	29EK	24DS	23DS	30EK	28DS	134
133	8BK	9CK	12CK	14DK	15CK	15DP	17DK	17DK	16DK	20DK	24DS	24DK	21DK	21DS	25DP	29DS	24DP	23DP	30DS	28DS	133
132	8BK	9BK	12CK	14DK	15CK	15CK	17DK	17DK	16DK	20DP	24DK	24DK	21DP	21DK	25DK	29DS	24DS	23DS	30DS	28DS	132
131	8BK	9BK	12CK	14DK	15CS	15CK	17DP	17DS	16DS	20DK	24DK	24DP	21DS	21DP	25DS	29DS	22DS	23DP	30DS	28DP	131
130	8AK	9BK	12CK	14CK	15CK	15CK	17CK	17DK	16DK	20DK	24DP	24DK	21DK	21DS	25DP	29DP	22DP	23DS	30DS	28DS	130
129	8AK	9BK	12CK	14CK	15CK	15CS	17CK	17DK	16DK	20DS	24DK	24DK	21DP	21DK	25DK	29DK	21DS	23DP	30DS	28DP	129
128	8AS	9BK	12CK	14CK	15CK	15CK	17CK	17DK	16DK	20DK	24DK	24DK	21DS	21DP	25DS	29DS	21DS	23DS	30DS	28DS	128
127	8AK	9BK	12CK	14CK	15CP	15CK	17CS	17DP	16DP	20DS	24DK	24DP	21DK	21DS	25DP	29DP	21DP	23DP	30DP	28DP	127
126	8AK	9AK	12BK	14CK	15BK	15CK	17CK	17CK	16CK	18DK	24DK	22DK	21DP	21DK	25DK	29DK	21DS	21DS	28DS	26DS	126
125	8AP	9AK	12BK	14CK	15BK	15CK	17CK	17CK	16CK	18DP	24DS	22DK	21DS	21DP	25DS	29DS	21DK	21DP	28DP	26DP	125
124	8	9AK	12BK	14CK	15BK	15CP	17CS	17CK	16CK	17CK	24DK	21DK	21DK	21DS	25DP	29DP	21CS	20DS	26DS	24DS	124
123	8	9AS	12BK	14CK	15BS	15BK	17CK	17CS	16CS	17CK	24DP	21DP	21DP	21DS	25DK	29DK	21CS	20DK	26DP	24DP	123
122	8	9AK	12BK	14CK	15BK	15BK	17CK	17CK	16CK	17CS	24CK	21DK	21CS	21DK	25DS	29DS	21CP	20CS	26DS	24DS	122
121	8	9AK	12BK	14CK	15BK	15BS	17CP	17CK	16CK	17CK	22CS	21DK	21CS	21DP	25DS	27DP	19CS	20CS	26DP	24DK	121
120	8	9AP	12BK	14BK	15BK	15BK	17BK	17CK	16CK	17CK	22CK	21DK	21CK	21CS	25DP	27DK	19CP	20CS	26DS	24CS	120
119	8	9	12BK	14BK	15BP	15BK	17BK	17CS	16CS	17CP	21CS	21DP	21CP	21CK	25DK	25DS	18CS	20CP	26DP	24CS	119
118	8	9	12AK	14BK	15AK	15BS	17BK	17CK	16CK	17CK	21CK	21CK	21CS	21CP	25CS	25DP	18CP	20CS	26DS	24CS	118
117	8	9	12AK	14BK	15AK	15BK	17BS	17CK	16CK	17CK	21CK	21CK	21CK	21CS	25CP	25DK	18CS	20CP	26DK	24CS	117
116	8	9	12AK	14BK	15AS	15BK	17BK	16CK	15CK	16CS	21CP	19CK	21CP	21CK	24CK	25CS	18CP	18CS	24CS	22CP	116
115	8	9	12AS	14BK	15AK	15BP	17BK	16CP	15CP	16CK	21CK	19CP	21CS	21CP	24CS	25CS	18CS	18CP	24CS	22CS	115
114	8	9	12AK	14BK	15AK	15AK	17BS	15BK	14BK	15CS	21CK	18CK	21CK	21CS	22CP	25CS	18CP	16CS	22CP	20CP	114
113	8	9	12AK	14BK	15AS	15AK	17BK	15BK	14BK	15CK	21CS	18CK	21CP	21CK	22CK	25CP	18CS	16CP	22CS	20CS	113
112	8	9	12AK	14BK	15AK	15AK	17BK	15BK	14BK	15CP	21CK	18CK	21CS	21CP	22CS	25CK	18CK	16CS	22CP	20CP	112
111	8	9	12AK	14BS	15AK	15AS	17BP	15BS	14BS	15BK	19CS	18CP	21CS	21CS	22CP	23CS	16BS	16CP	22CS	20CS	111
110	8	9	12AP	14AK	15AP	15AK	17AK	15BK	14BK	15BK	19CK	18CK	21CK	21CK	22CK	23CP	16BP	16CS	22CP	20CP	110
109	8	9	12	13AK	15	15AK	16AK	15BK	14BK	15BS	18CP	18CK	21CP	20CP	22CS	21CK	15BS	16CK	22CS	20CS	109
108	8	9	12	13AK	15	15AS	16AK	15BK	14BK	15BK	18BK	18CK	21BS	20CS	22CP	21CS	15BP	16BS	22CP	20CP	108
107	8	9	12	12AK	15	15AK	15AK	15BS	14BS	15BK	18BS	18CP	21BS	18CK	22CK	21CP	15BS	16BS	22CS	20CS	107
106	8	9	11	12AK	15	14AK	15AS	14BK	13BK	13BP	18BK	16CK	20BS	18CP	21CS	21CK	15BP	15BP	20CK	18CK	106
105	8	9	11	12AS	15	14AP	15AK	14BK	13BK	13BK	18BS	16CK	20BK	18BS	21CS	21CS	15BK	15BS	20CS	18BS	105
104	8	9	10	12AK	15	13	15AK	13BK	12BK	12BK	18BK	15CK	18BP	18BK	19CP	21CP	15BS	13BP	18CP	16BS	104
103	8	9	10	12AK	15	13	15AS	13BP	12BP	12BS	18BK	15CP	18BS	18BP	19CK	21CK	15BP	13BS	18CS	16BP	103
102	8	9	10	12AK	15	13	15AK	13AK	12AK	12BK	18BP	15BK	18BK	18BS	19BS	21CS	15BS	13BK	18CP	16BS	102
101	8	9	10	12AK	14	13	15AK	13AK	12AK	12BS	16BK	15BK	18BP	18BK	19BP	20CP	13BP	13BP	18CS	16BP	101
100	8	9	10	12AP	14	13	15AP	13AK	12AK	12BK	16BK	15BK	18BS	18BP	19BK	20CK	13BS	13BS	18CK	16BS	100
99	8	9	10	11	13	13	14	13AS	12AS	12BP	15BS	15BP	18BK	17BS	19BS	18BS	12BK	13BP	18BS	16BP	99
98	8	9	10	11	13	13	14	13AK	12AK	12AK	15BK	15BK	18BP	17BK	19BP	18BS	12AS	13BS	18BS	16BS	98
97	8	9	10	10	13	13	13	13AK	12AK	12AS	15BS	15BK	18BS	16BP	19BK	18BS	12AS	13BP	18BP	16BS	97
96	8	9	9	10	13	12	13	12AP	11AP	11AK	15BK	13BK	17BK	16BS	17BS	18BP	12AS	11BS	16BS	14BK	96
95	8	9	9	10	13	12	13	12AK	11AK	11AS	15BP	13BP	17BP	16BK	17BP	18BK	12AP	11BK	16BP	14BP	95
94	8	8	9	10	13	11	13	11AK	10AK	10AK	15AK	12BK	16AS	16BP	16BK	18BS	12AS	10AS	15BS	12BS	94
93	8	8	9	10	13	11	13	11AS	10AS	10AK	15AS	12BK	16AK	16BS	16BS	18BP	12AP	10AS	15BP	12BP	93
92	8	8	9	10	13	11	13	11AK	10AK	10AP	15AK	12BK	16AP	16BK	16BP	18BK	12AS	10AS	15BS	12BS	92
91	8	8	9	10	12	11	13	11AK	10AK	10AK	13AS	12BP	16AS	16BP	16BK	16BS	10AK	10AP	15BP	12BK	91
90	8	8	9	10	12	11	13	11AP	10AP	10AK	13AK	12BK	16AK	16AS	16BS	16BP	10AP	10AS	15BS	12AP	90
89	8	8	9	9	11	11	12	11	10	10AS	12AS	12BK	16AP	14AS	16BS	14BK	9AS	10AP	15BK	12AS	89
88	8	8	9	9	11	11	12	11	10	10AK	12AK	12BK	16AS	14AK	16BP	14BS	9AP	10AS	15BS	12AP	88
87	8	8	9	8	11	11	11	11	10	10AS	12AP	12BP	16AK	13AP	16BK	14BP	9AS	10AK	15BP	12AS	87
86	7	8	8	8	11	10	11	10	9	8AK	12AK	10AK	14AP	13AS	14AS	14BK	9AP	8AP	13BS	10AP	86
85	7	8	8	8	11	10	11	10	9	8AP	12AK	10AK	14AS	13AK	14AS	14BS	9AK	8AS	13BP	10AK	85
84	7	7	7	8	11	9	11	8	8	7	12AS	9AK	13AK	13AP	12AP	14BP	9	6AP	11BS	8AP	84
83	7	7	7	8	11	9	11	8	8	7	12AK	9AK	13AP	13AS	12AK	14BK	9	6AS	11BK	8AS	83
82	7	7	7	8	11	9	11	8	8	7	12AS	9AP	13AS	13AK	12AS	14AS	9	6AP	11AP	8AP	82
81	7	7	7	8	10	9	11	8	8	7	10AK	9AK	13AK	13AP	12AP	12AP	7	6AS	11AS	8AS	81
80	7	7	7	8	10	9	11	8	8	7	10AP	9AK	13AP	13AS	12AK	12AK	7	6AK	11AP	8AK	80
79	7	7	7	7	9	9	10	8	8	7	9	9AK	13	12AK	12AS	10AS	6	–	11AS	–	79
78	7	7	7	7	9	9	10	8	8	7	9	9AP	13	12AP	12AP	10AP	6	–	11AP	–	78
77	7	7	7	7	9	9	8	8	8	7	9	9AK	13	10AS	12AK	10AK	6	–	11AS	–	77
76	6	6	6	7	9	8	8	7	7	6	9	7AK	12	10AK	11AS	10AS	6	–	9AK	–	76
75	6	6	6	7	9	8	8	7	7	6	9	7AK	12	10AP	11AP	10AP	6	–	9AP	–	75
74	6	6	6	7	9	7	8	6	6	5	9	6AP	10	10	9AK	10AK	–	–	7AS	–	74
73	6	6	6	7	9	7	8	6	6	5	9	6AK	10	10	9AS	10AS	–	–	7AP	–	73
72	6	6	6	7	9	7	8	6	6	5	9	6AK	10	10	9AS	10AP	–	–	7AS	–	72
71	6	6	6	7	8	7	8	6	6	5	7	6AK	10	10	9AP	9AK	–	–	7AP	–	71
70	6	6	6	7	8	7	8	6	6	5	7	6AP	10	10	9AK	9AS	–	–	7AK	–	70
69	6	6	6	6	7	7	7	6	6	–	6	–	10	9	9	7AP	–	–	–	–	69
68	6	6	6	6	7	7	7	6	6	–	6	–	10	9	9	7AK	–	–	–	–	68
67	6	6	6	5	7	7	6	6	6	–	6	–	10	8	9	7AS	–	–	–	–	67
66	5	5	5	5	7	6	6	5	5	–	6	–	9	8	8	7AP	–	–	–	–	66
65	5	5	5	5	7	6	6	5	5	–	6	–	9	8	8	7AK	–	–	–	–	65
64	5	4	4	5	7	5	6	4	4	–	–	–	8	8	6	–	–	–	–	–	64
63	5	4	4	5	7	5	6	4	4	–	–	–	8	8	6	–	–	–	–	–	63
62	5	4	4	5	7	5	6	4	4	–	–	–	8	8	6	–	–	–	–	–	62
61	5	4	4	5	6	5	6	4	4	–	–	–	8	8	6	–	–	–	–	–	61
60	5	4	4	5	6	5	6	4	4	–	–	–	8	8	6	–	–	–	–	–	60
57-59	5	4	4	4	5	5	5	–	–	–	–	–	8	6	–	–	–	–	–	–	57-59
55-56	4	4	3	3	5	4	4	–	–	–	–	–	6	5	–	–	–	–	–	–	55-56
53-54	4	3	3	3	5	3	4	–	–	–	–	–	5	5	–	–	–	–	–	–	53-54
50-52	4	3	3	–	5	3	–	–	–	–	–	–	5	–	–	–	–	–	–	–	50-52
47-49	4	3	–	–	3	–	–	–	–	–	–	–	–	–	–	–	–	–	–	–	47-49
45-46	3	3	–	–	3	–	–	–	–	–	–	–	–	–	–	–	–	–	–	–	45-46
40-44	3	2	–	–	–	–	–	–	–	–	–	–	–	–	–	–	–	–	–	–	40-44
30-39	2	–	–	–	–	–	–	–	–	–	–	–	–	–	–	–	–	–	–	–	30-39

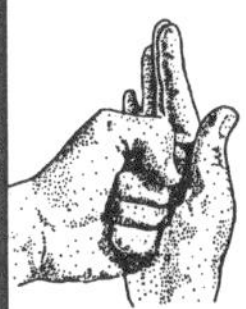

ATTACK TABLE 18.4
METAL WHIP
ONE-HANDED CONCUSSION

Length: 5 – 8 feet
Weight: 3 – 7 pounds
Fumble Range: 01 – 06 UM
Breakage #s: 1, 2, 3, 4, 5, 6
Strength: 75 – 86
Range Modifiers: —

	20	19	18	17	16	15	14	13	12	11	10	9	8	7	6	5	4	3	2	1	
150	12CK	14DK	16EK	18EK	18EK	18EK	20EK	20EK	19EK	18EK	22EK	22EK	20EK	20EK	22EK	26EK	20EK	22EK	25EK	28EK	150
149	12CK	14DK	16EK	18EK	18EK	18EK	20EK	20EK	19EK	18EK	22EK	22EK	20EK	20EK	22EK	26EK	20EK	22EK	25EK	28EK	149
148	12CK	14DK	16EK	18EK	18EK	18EK	20EK	20EK	19EK	18EK	22EK	22EK	20EK	20EK	22EK	26EK	20EK	22EK	25EK	28EK	148
147	12CK	14DK	16EK	18EK	18EK	18EK	20EK	20EK	19EK	18EK	22EK	22EK	20EK	20EK	22EK	26EK	20EK	22EK	25EK	28EK	147
146	12BK	14CK	16DK	18EK	18DK	18EK	20EK	20EK	19EK	18EK	22EK	22EK	20EK	20EK	22EK	26EK	20EK	22EK	25EK	28EK	146
145	12BK	14CK	16DK	18EK	18DK	18DK	20EK	20EK	19EK	18EK	22EK	22EK	20EK	20EK	22EK	26EK	20EK	22EK	25EK	28EK	145
144	12BK	14CK	16DK	18DK	18DK	18DK	20DK	20EK	19EK	18EK	22EK	22EK	20EK	20EK	22EK	26EK	20EK	22EK	25EK	28EK	144
143	12BK	14CK	16DK	18DK	18DK	18DK	20DK	20EK	19EK	18EK	22EK	22EK	20EK	20EK	22EK	26EK	20EG	22EK	25EK	28EK	143
142	12AK	14BK	16CK	18DK	18CK	18DK	20DK	20DK	19EK	18EK	22EK	22EK	20EK	20EK	22EK	26EK	20EK	22EG	25EK	28EK	142
141	12AK	14BK	16CK	18DK	18CK	18DK	20DK	20DK	19DK	18EK	22EK	22EK	20EK	20EK	22EK	26EK	20EP	22EK	25EK	28EP	141
140	12AK	14BK	16CK	18DK	18CK	18CK	20DK	20DK	19DK	18DK	22EK	22EK	20EK	20EK	22EK	26EK	20DK	22EP	25EK	28EK	140
139	12	14BK	16CK	18DK	18CK	18CK	20DK	20DK	19DK	18DK	22DK	22EK	20EK	20EK	22EK	26EK	20DK	22DK	25EP	28EG	139
138	12	14AK	16BK	18CK	18BK	18CK	20CK	20DK	19DK	18DK	22DK	22EK	20DK	20EK	22EK	26EK	20DK	22DK	25EK	28DK	138
137	12	14AK	16BK	18CK	18BK	18CK	20CK	20DK	19DK	18DK	22DK	22DK	20DK	20EK	22EK	26EK	20DK	22DK	25EG	28DK	137
136	12	14AK	16BK	18CK	18BK	18CK	20CK	20DK	19DK	18DK	22DK	22DK	20DK	20DK	22EK	26EK	20DK	22DK	25DK	28DK	136
135	12	14AK	16BK	18CK	18BK	18BK	20CK	20DK	19DK	18DK	22DK	22DK	20DK	20DK	22DK	26EK	20DK	22DK	25DK	28DK	135
134	12	14	16AK	18CK	18AK	18BK	20CK	20CK	19DK	18DK	22DK	22DK	20DK	20DK	22DK	26DK	20DK	22DK	25DK	28DK	134
133	12	14	16AK	18CK	18AK	18BK	20CK	20CK	19DK	18DK	22DK	22DK	20DK	20DK	22DK	26DK	20DG	22DK	25DK	28DK	133
132	12	14	16AK	18BK	18AK	18BK	20BK	20CK	19CK	18DK	22DK	22DK	20DK	20DK	22DK	26DK	20DK	22DK	25DK	28DK	132
131	12	14	16AK	18BK	18AK	18BK	20BK	20CK	19CK	18DK	22DK	22DK	20DK	20DK	22DK	26DK	20DP	22DG	25DK	28DK	131
130	12	14	16AK	18BK	18AG	18AK	20BK	20CK	19CK	18CK	22DK	22DK	20DK	20DK	22DK	26DK	20CK	22DK	25DK	28DK	130
129	12	14	16	18BK	18	18AK	20BK	20CK	19CK	18CK	22DK	22DK	20DK	20DK	22DK	26DK	20CK	22DP	25DK	28DP	129
128	12	14	16	18BK	18	18AK	20BK	20CK	19CK	18CK	22CK	22DK	20DK	20DK	22DK	26DK	20CK	22CK	25DK	28DK	128
127	12	14	16	18BK	18	18AK	20BG	20CK	19CK	18CK	22CK	22DK	20DK	20DK	22DK	26DK	20CK	22CK	25DK	28DG	127
126	12	14	16	18AK	18	18AK	20AK	20BK	19CK	18CK	22CK	22DK	20CK	20DK	22DK	26DK	20CK	22CK	25DK	28CK	126
125	12	14	16	18AK	18	18AG	20AK	20BK	19CK	18CK	22CK	22DK	20CK	20DK	22DP	26DK	20CK	22CK	25DP	28CK	125
124	12	14	16	18AK	18	18	20AK	20BK	19CK	18CK	22CK	22CK	20CK	20CK	22DK	26DK	20CK	22CK	25DK	28CK	124
123	12	14	16	18AK	18	18	20AK	20BK	19BK	18CG	22CK	22CK	20CK	20CK	22DG	26DP	20CK	22CK	25DG	28CK	123
122	12	14	16	18AK	18	18	20AK	20BK	19BK	18CK	22CK	22CK	20CK	20CK	22CK	26DK	20CG	22CK	25CK	28CK	122
121	12	14	16	18AK	18	18	20AK	20BK	19BK	18CP	22CK	22CK	20CK	20CK	22CK	26DG	20CK	21CK	25CK	26CK	121
120	12	14	16	18AK	18	18	20AG	20BK	19BK	18BK	22CG	22CK	20CK	20CK	22CK	26CK	20CP	21CK	25CK	26CK	120
119	12	14	16	18	18	18	20	20BG	19BK	18BK	22CK	22CK	20CK	20CK	22CK	26CK	20BK	19CG	25CK	25CK	119
118	12	14	16	18	18	18	20	20AK	19BK	18BK	22CP	22CK	20CK	20CK	22CK	26CK	20BK	19CK	25CK	25CK	118
117	12	14	16	18	18	18	20	20AK	19BG	18BK	22BK	22CK	20CP	20CK	22CK	26CK	19BK	19CP	25CK	25CK	117
116	12	14	16	18	18	18	20	20AK	19BK	18BK	22BK	22CK	20CK	20CK	22CK	26CK	19BK	19BK	25CK	25CP	116
115	12	14	16	18	18	18	20	20AK	19BP	18BK	22BK	22CK	20CG	20CK	22CK	26CK	17BK	19BK	25CK	25CK	115
114	12	14	16	18	18	18	20	20AK	19AK	18BK	22BK	22CG	20BK	20CK	22CK	26CK	17BK	19BK	25CK	25CG	114
113	12	14	16	18	18	18	20	20AK	19AK	18BG	22BK	22CK	20BK	20CK	22CK	26CK	17BK	19BK	25CK	25BK	113
112	12	14	16	18	18	18	20	20AK	19AK	18BK	22BK	22CP	20BK	20CK	22CK	26CK	17BG	19BK	25CK	25BK	112
111	12	14	16	18	18	18	20	20AK	19AK	17BP	22BK	21BK	20BK	20BK	22CP	26CK	17BK	18BK	24CK	23BK	111
110	12	14	16	18	18	18	20	20AG	19AK	17AK	22BK	21BK	20BK	20BK	22CK	26CK	17BP	18BK	24CP	23BK	110
109	12	14	16	18	18	18	20	20	19AK	16AK	22BG	19BK	20BK	20BK	22CG	26CK	17AK	17BK	22CK	21BK	109
108	12	14	16	18	18	18	20	20	19AK	16AK	22BK	19BK	20BK	20BK	22BK	26CP	17AK	17BG	22CG	21BK	108
107	12	14	16	18	18	18	20	20	19AG	16AK	22BP	19BK	20BK	20BK	22BK	26CK	16AK	17BK	22BK	21BK	107
106	12	14	16	18	18	18	20	20	19AK	16AK	21AK	19BK	20BK	20BK	22BK	26CG	16AK	17BP	22BK	21BK	106
105	12	14	16	18	18	18	20	20	19AP	16AK	21AK	19BK	20BP	20BK	22BK	25BK	15AK	17AK	22BK	21BK	105
104	12	14	16	18	18	18	20	20	19	16AK	19AK	19BK	20BK	20BK	22BK	25BK	15AK	17AK	22BK	21BP	104
103	12	14	16	18	18	18	20	20	19	16AK	19AK	19BK	20BG	20BK	22BK	23BK	15AK	17AK	22BK	21BK	103
102	12	14	16	18	18	18	20	20	19	16AG	19AK	19BK	20AK	20BK	22BK	23BK	15AK	17AK	22BK	21BG	102
101	12	14	16	18	18	18	20	19	18	14AK	19AK	18BG	20AK	20BP	21BK	23BK	15AG	15AK	20BK	19AK	101
100	12	14	16	18	18	18	20	19	18	14AP	19AK	18BK	20AK	20BK	21BK	23BK	15AK	15AG	20BP	19AK	100
99	12	14	16	18	18	18	20	17	17	13	19AK	17BP	20AK	20BG	19BK	23BK	15AP	14AK	19BK	17AK	99
98	12	14	16	18	18	18	20	17	17	13	19AK	17AK	20AK	20AK	19BK	23BK	15	14AP	19BG	17AK	98
97	12	14	16	18	18	18	20	17	17	13	19AG	17AK	20AK	20AK	19BP	23BK	14	14AK	19BK	17AK	97
96	12	14	16	17	18	18	19	17	17	13	18AK	17AK	20AK	19AK	19BK	23BK	14	14AG	19BP	17AK	96
95	12	14	16	17	18	18	19	17	17	13	18AP	17AK	20AK	19AK	19BG	21BK	12	14AK	19BK	17AP	95
94	12	14	16	16	18	18	17	17	17	13	17	17AK	20AK	17AK	19AK	21BK	12	14AP	19BG	17AK	94
93	12	14	16	16	18	18	17	17	17	13	17	17AK	20AK	17AK	19AK	20BP	12	14	19AK	17AG	93
92	12	14	16	16	18	18	17	17	17	13	17	17AK	20AP	17AK	19AK	20BK	12	14	19AK	17AK	92
91	12	14	15	16	17	17	17	16	15	12	17	15AK	19AK	17AK	18AK	20BG	12	12	17AK	16AP	91
90	12	14	15	16	17	17	17	16	15	12	17	15AK	19AG	17AK	18AK	20AK	12	12	17AK	16AK	90
89	12	14	14	16	16	16	17	15	14	11	17	14AK	17	17AK	17AK	20AK	12	11	16AK	14AG	89
88	12	14	14	16	16	16	17	15	14	11	17	14AK	17	17AK	17AK	20AK	12	11	16AK	14	88
87	12	14	14	16	16	16	17	15	14	11	17	14AG	17	17AP	17AK	20AK	11	11	16AK	14	87
86	12	14	14	14	16	16	16	15	14	11	15	14AK	17	16AK	17AK	20AK	11	11	16AK	14	86
85	12	14	14	14	16	16	16	15	14	11	15	14AP	17	16AG	17AK	18AK	10	11	16AP	14	85
84	12	14	14	13	16	16	15	15	14	11	14	14	17	15	17AK	18AK	10	11	16AK	14	84
83	12	14	14	13	16	16	15	15	14	11	14	14	17	15	17AK	16AK	10	11	16AG	14	83
82	12	14	14	13	16	16	15	15	14	11	14	14	17	15	17AP	16AK	10	11	16AK	14	82
81	12	13	13	13	14	14	15	14	13	10	14	12	16	15	15AK	16AK	10	9	14AP	12	81
80	12	13	13	13	14	14	15	14	13	10	14	12	16	15	15AG	16AK	10	9	14AK	12	80
79	12	12	12	13	13	13	15	12	12	9	14	11	15	15	14	16AK	10	8	12AG	10	79
78	12	12	12	13	13	13	15	12	12	9	14	11	15	15	14	16AK	10	8	12	10	78
77	12	12	12	13	13	13	15	12	12	9	14	11	15	15	14	16AP	8	8	12	10	77
76	12	12	12	12	13	13	14	12	12	9	12	11	15	14	14	16AK	8	8	12	10	76
75	12	12	12	12	13	13	14	12	12	9	12	11	15	14	14	15AG	7	8	12	10	75
74	12	12	12	11	13	13	12	12	12	9	11	11	15	12	14	15	7	8	12	10	74
73	12	12	12	11	13	13	12	12	12	9	11	11	15	12	14	13	7	8	12	10	73
72	12	12	12	11	13	13	12	12	12	9	11	11	15	12	14	13	7	8	12	10	72
71	11	11	11	11	12	12	12	11	11	8	11	9	14	12	12	13	7	7	11	8	71
70	11	11	11	11	12	12	12	11	11	8	11	9	14	12	12	13	7	7	11	8	70
69	10	10	10	11	11	11	12	10	9	6	11	8	12	12	11	13	7	5	9	7	69
68	10	10	10	11	11	11	12	10	9	6	11	8	12	12	11	13	7	5	9	7	68
67	10	10	10	11	11	11	12	10	9	6	11	8	12	12	11	13	6	5	9	7	67
66	10	10	10	10	11	11	11	10	9	6	9	8	12	11	11	13	6	5	9	7	66
65	10	10	10	10	11	11	11	10	9	6	9	8	12	11	11	11	5	5	9	7	65
64	10	10	10	9	11	11	10	10	9	6	8	8	12	10	11	11	5	–	9	–	64
63	10	10	10	9	11	11	10	10	9	6	8	8	12	10	11	10	5	–	9	–	63
62	10	10	10	9	11	11	10	10	9	6	8	8	12	10	11	10	5	–	9	–	62
61	10	9	9	9	10	10	10	8	8	5	8	7	11	10	9	10	5	–	8	–	61
60	10	9	9	9	10	10	10	8	8	5	8	7	11	10	9	10	–	–	8	–	60
59	9	8	8	9	9	9	10	7	7	4	8	5	10	10	8	10	–	–	6	–	59
55-58	9	8	8	9	9	9	9	7	7	4	8	5	10	9	8	9	–	–	6	–	55-58
50-54	9	8	8	6	9	9	7	7	7	–	5	–	9	7	8	6	–	–	–	–	50-54
45-49	7	7	6	6	6	6	7	5	4	–	–	–	7	7	5	6	–	–	–	–	45-49
40-44	7	7	6	4	6	6	5	–	–	–	–	–	7	5	–	–	–	–	–	–	40-44
35-39	6	5	4	–	4	4	–	–	–	–	–	–	5	–	–	–	–	–	–	–	35-39
25-34	5	4	–	–	–	–	–	–	–	–	–	–	–	–	–	–	–	–	–	–	25-34
15-24	3	–	–	–	–	–	–	–	–	–	–	–	–	–	–	–	–	–	–	–	15-24

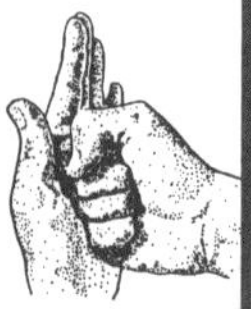

ATTACK TABLE 18.5
NUNCHAKU
TWO-HANDED

Length: 2 – 3 feet
Weight: 2 – 3 pounds
Fumble Range: 01 – 07 UM
Breakage #s: 1, 2, 3, 4, 5, 6, 7
Strength: 65 – 75 w

Range Modifiers: —

	20	19	18	17	16	15	14	13	12	11	10	9	8	7	6	5	4	3	2	1	
150	19DK	22DK	24EK	25EK	27EK	27EK	30EK	30EK	28EK	30EK	34EK	34EK	33EK	33EK	37EK	40EK	34EK	37EK	40EK	42EK	150
149	19DK	22DK	24EK	25EK	27EK	27EK	30EK	30EK	28EK	30EK	34EK	34EK	33EK	33EK	37EK	40EK	34EK	37EK	40EK	42EK	149
148	19DK	22DK	24EK	25EK	27EK	27EK	30EK	30EK	28EK	30EK	34EK	34EK	33EK	33EK	37EK	40EK	34EK	37EK	40EK	42EK	148
147	19DK	22DK	24EK	25EK	27EK	27EK	30EK	30EK	28EK	30EK	34EK	34EK	33EK	33EK	37EK	40EK	34EK	37EK	40EK	42EK	147
146	19DK	22DK	24EK	25EK	27EK	27EK	30EK	30EK	28EK	30EK	34EK	34EK	33EK	33EK	37EK	40EK	34EK	37EK	40EK	42EK	146
145	19DK	22DK	24EK	25EK	27EK	27EK	30EK	30EK	28EK	30EK	34EK	34EK	33EK	33EK	37EK	40EK	34EK	37EK	40EK	42EK	145
144	19DK	22DK	24EK	25EK	27EK	27EK	30EK	30EK	28EK	30EK	34EK	34EK	33EK	33EK	37EK	40EK	34EK	37EK	40EK	42EK	144
143	19DK	22DK	24EK	25EK	27EK	27EK	30EK	30EK	28EK	30EK	34EK	34EK	33EK	33EK	37EK	40EK	32EK	34EK	40EK	39EK	143
142	19CK	22DK	24DK	25EK	27EK	27EK	30EK	30EK	28EK	30EK	34EK	34EK	33EK	33EK	37EK	40EK	32EK	34EK	40EK	39EK	142
141	19CK	22CK	24DK	25EK	27DK	27EK	30EK	30EK	28EK	30EK	34EK	34EK	33EK	33EK	37EK	40EK	30EK	32EK	40EK	37EK	141
140	19CK	22CK	24DK	25DK	27DK	27DK	30EK	30EK	28EK	30EK	34EK	34EK	33EK	33EK	37EK	40EK	30EK	32EK	40EK	37EK	140
139	19CK	22CK	24DK	25DK	27DK	27DK	30DK	30EK	28EK	30EK	34EK	34EK	33EK	33EK	37EK	40EK	30DK	32EK	40EK	37EK	139
138	19CK	22CK	24DK	25DK	27DK	27DK	30DK	30DK	28DK	30EK	34EK	34EK	33EK	33EK	37EK	40EK	30DK	32DK	40EK	37EK	138
137	19CK	22CK	24DK	25DK	27DK	27DK	30DK	30DK	28DK	30DK	34EK	34EK	33DK	33EK	37EK	40EK	30DK	32DK	40EK	37DK	137
136	19CK	22CK	24DK	25DK	27DK	27DK	30DK	30DK	28DK	30DK	34DK	34EK	33DK	33DK	37EK	40EK	30DK	32DK	40EK	37DK	136
135	19CK	22CK	24DK	25DK	27DK	27DK	30DK	30DK	28DK	30DK	34DK	34DK	33DK	33DK	37EK	40EK	30DK	32DK	40DK	37DK	135
134	19BK	22CK	24DK	25DK	27DK	27DK	30DK	30DK	28DK	30DK	34DK	34DK	33DK	33DK	37DK	40DK	30DK	32DK	40DK	37DK	134
133	19BK	22CK	24CK	25DK	27DK	27DK	30DK	30DK	28DK	30DK	34DK	34DK	33DK	33DK	37DK	40DK	27DK	30DK	40DK	34DK	133
132	19BK	22BK	24CK	25DK	27DK	27DK	30DK	30DK	28DK	30DK	34DK	34DK	33DK	33DK	37DK	40DK	27DK	30DK	40DK	34DK	132
131	19BK	22BK	24CK	25DK	27CK	27DK	30DK	30DK	28DK	28DK	34DK	34DK	33DK	33DK	37DK	40DK	25DK	27DK	37DK	31DK	131
130	19BK	22BK	24CK	25DK	27CK	27DK	30DK	30DK	28DK	28DK	34DK	34DK	33DK	33DK	37DK	40DK	25DK	27DK	37DK	31DK	130
129	19BK	22BK	24CK	25CK	27CK	27CK	30DK	30DK	28DK	26DK	34DK	34DK	33DK	33DK	37DK	40DK	25DK	27DK	35DK	31DK	129
128	19BK	22BK	24CK	25CK	27CK	27CK	30DK	30DK	28DK	26DK	34DK	32DK	33DK	33DK	37DK	40DK	25DK	27DK	35DK	31DK	128
127	19BK	22BK	24CK	25CK	27CK	27CK	30CK	30DK	28DK	26DK	34DK	32DK	33DK	33DK	34DK	40DK	25CK	27DK	35DK	31DK	127
126	19AK	22BK	24CK	25CK	27CK	27CK	30CK	30CK	28CK	26DK	32DK	30DK	33DK	33DK	34DK	40DK	25CK	27DK	35DK	31DK	126
125	19AK	22BK	24CK	25CK	27CK	27CK	30CK	30CK	28CK	26DK	32DK	30DK	33DK	33DK	32DK	40DK	25CK	27CK	35DK	31DK	125
124	19AK	22BK	24BK	25CK	27CK	27CK	30CK	30CK	28CK	26CK	30DK	30DK	33DK	33DK	32DK	40DK	25CK	27CK	35DK	31CK	124
123	19AK	22AK	24BK	25CK	27CK	27CK	30CK	30CK	28CK	26CK	30DK	30DK	33CK	33DK	32DK	40DK	23CK	25CK	35DK	29CK	123
122	19AK	22AK	24BK	25CK	27CK	27CK	30CK	30CK	28CK	26CK	30CK	30DK	33CK	33DK	32DK	40DK	23CK	25CK	35DK	29CK	122
121	19AK	22AK	24BK	25CK	27BK	27CK	30CK	30CK	26CK	24CK	30CK	30DK	33CK	31CK	32DK	37DK	21CK	23CK	32DK	26CK	121
120	19AK	22AK	24BK	23CK	27BK	27CK	30CK	28CK	26CK	24CK	30CK	30DK	33CK	31CK	32DK	37DK	21CK	23CK	32CK	26CK	120
119	19AK	22AK	24BK	23CK	27BK	27CK	30CK	28CK	24CK	22CK	30CK	30CK	33CK	29CK	32DK	35DK	21CK	23CK	30CK	26CK	119
118	19	22AK	24BK	21BK	27BK	27BK	30CK	26CK	24CK	22CK	30CK	27CK	33CK	29CK	32CK	35CK	21CK	23CK	30CK	26CK	118
117	19	22AK	23BK	21BK	27BK	27BK	30CK	26CK	24CK	22CK	30CK	27CK	33CK	29CK	30CK	35CK	21CK	23CK	30CK	26CK	117
116	19	22AK	23BK	21BK	27BK	27BK	30CK	26CK	24CK	22CK	27CK	25CK	33CK	29CK	30CK	35CK	21CK	23CK	30CK	26CK	116
115	19	22AK	21AK	21BK	27BK	27BK	28BK	26CK	24CK	22CK	27CK	25CK	33CK	29CK	27CK	35CK	21BK	23CK	30CK	26CK	115
114	19	22	21AK	21BK	27BK	27BK	28BK	26CK	24CK	22CK	25CK	25CK	33CK	29CK	27CK	35CK	21BK	23CK	30CK	26CK	114
113	19	22	21AK	21BK	27BK	27BK	26BK	26BK	24BK	22CK	25CK	25CK	33CK	29CK	27CK	35CK	19BK	20BK	30CK	23CK	113
112	19	22	21AK	21BK	27BK	25BK	26BK	26BK	24BK	22CK	25CK	25CK	31CK	29CK	27CK	35CK	19BK	20BK	30CK	23CK	112
111	19	22	21AK	21BK	27AK	25BK	26BK	26BK	23BK	20CK	25CK	25CK	31CK	27CK	27CK	32CK	17BK	18BK	27CK	21BK	111
110	19	22	21AK	20BK	27AK	23BK	26BK	24BK	23BK	20BK	25CK	25CK	29CK	27CK	27CK	32CK	17BK	18BK	27CK	21BK	110
109	19	22	21AK	20BK	27AK	23BK	26BK	24BK	21BK	18BK	25CK	25CK	29BK	25CK	27CK	30CK	17BK	18BK	25CK	21BK	109
108	19	22	21AK	18BK	27AK	23BK	26BK	22BK	21BK	18BK	25CK	23CK	29BK	25CK	27CK	30CK	17BK	18BK	25CK	21BK	108
107	19	22	19AK	18AK	27AK	23AK	26BK	22BK	21BK	18BK	25BK	23CK	29BK	25CK	25CK	30CK	17BK	18BK	25CK	21BK	107
106	19	20	19	18AK	25AK	23AK	26BK	22BK	21BK	18BK	23BK	21CK	29BK	25BK	25CK	30CK	17BK	18BK	25CK	21BK	106
105	19	20	18	18AK	25AK	23AK	24BK	22BK	21BK	18BK	23BK	21CK	29BK	25BK	23CK	30CK	17BK	18BK	25BK	21BK	105
104	19	19	18	18AK	23AK	23AK	24BK	22BK	21BK	18BK	21BK	21CK	29BK	25BK	23CK	30CK	17BK	18BK	25BK	21BK	104
103	19	19	18	18AK	23AK	23AK	22AK	22BK	21BK	18BK	21BK	21BK	29BK	25BK	23CK	30CK	15AK	16BK	25BK	18BK	103
102	19	19	18	18AK	23AK	22AK	22AK	22BK	21BK	18BK	21BK	21BK	27BK	25BK	23BK	30BK	15AK	16BK	25BK	18BK	102
101	19	19	18	18AK	23	22AK	22AK	22AK	19AK	16BK	21BK	21BK	27BK	23BK	23BK	27BK	12AK	13BK	22BK	15BK	101
100	19	19	18	17AK	23	20AK	22AK	20AK	19AK	16BK	21BK	21BK	25BK	23BK	23BK	27BK	12AK	13AK	22BK	15BK	100
99	19	19	18	17AK	23	20AK	22AK	20AK	17AK	15BK	21BK	21BK	25BK	20BK	23BK	25BK	12AK	13AK	20BK	15BK	99
98	19	19	18	15AK	23	20AK	22AK	18AK	17AK	15BK	21BK	19BK	25BK	20BK	23BK	25BK	12AK	13AK	20BK	15AK	98
97	19	19	16	15AK	23	20AK	22AK	18AK	17AK	15AK	21BK	19BK	25BK	20BK	20BK	25BK	12AK	13AK	20BK	15AK	97
96	18	17	16	15	22	20	22AK	18AK	17AK	15AK	19BK	17BK	25BK	20BK	20BK	25BK	12AK	13AK	20BK	15AK	96
95	18	17	15	15	22	20	20AK	18AK	17AK	15AK	19BK	17BK	25AK	20BK	18BK	25BK	12AK	13AK	20BK	15AK	95
94	17	16	15	15	20	20	20AK	18AK	17AK	15AK	17BK	17BK	25AK	20BK	18BK	25BK	12AK	13AK	20BK	15AK	94
93	17	16	15	15	20	20	18AK	18AK	17AK	15AK	17AK	17BK	25AK	20BK	18BK	25BK	10AK	11AK	20BK	13AK	93
92	17	16	15	15	20	18	18AK	18AK	17AK	15AK	17AK	17BK	23AK	20BK	18BK	25BK	10AK	11AK	20BK	13AK	92
91	17	16	15	15	20	18	18	18AK	15AK	13AK	17AK	17BK	23AK	18AK	18BK	22BK	8	9AK	17BK	10AK	91
90	17	16	15	14	20	16	18	16AK	15AK	13AK	17AK	17BK	20AK	18AK	18BK	22BK	8	9AK	17AK	10AK	90
89	17	16	15	14	20	16	18	16AK	14AK	11AK	17AK	17BK	20AK	16AK	18BK	20BK	8	9AK	15AK	10AK	89
88	17	16	15	12	20	16	18	15	14	11AK	17AK	15BK	20AK	16AK	18BK	20BK	8	9AK	15AK	10AK	88
87	17	16	13	12	20	16	18	15	14	11AK	17AK	15AK	20AK	16AK	16BK	20BK	8	9	15AK	10AK	87
86	16	15	13	12	18	16	18	15	14	11AK	15AK	12AK	20AK	16AK	16AK	20AK	–	–	15AK	10AK	86
85	16	15	12	12	18	16	16	15	14	11AK	15AK	12AK	20AK	16AK	13AK	20AK	–	–	15AK	–	85
84	14	13	12	12	16	16	16	15	14	11AK	12AK	12AK	20AK	16AK	13AK	20AK	–	–	15AK	–	84
83	14	13	12	12	16	16	15	15	14	11	12AK	12AK	20AK	16AK	13AK	20AK	–	–	15AK	–	83
82	14	13	12	12	16	15	15	15	14	11	12AK	12AK	18AK	16AK	13AK	20AK	–	–	15AK	–	82
81	14	13	12	12	16	15	15	15	12	9	12AK	12AK	18	14AK	13AK	17AK	–	–	12AK	–	81
80	14	13	12	10	16	13	15	13	12	9	12AK	12AK	16	14AK	13AK	17AK	–	–	12AK	–	80
79	14	13	12	10	16	13	15	13	10	7	12AK	12AK	16	12AK	13AK	15AK	–	–	10AK	–	79
78	14	13	12	9	16	13	15	11	10	7	12	10AK	16	12AK	13AK	15AK	–	–	10AK	–	78
77	14	13	10	9	16	13	15	11	10	7	12	10AK	16	12AK	11AK	15AK	–	–	10AK	–	77
76	13	12	10	9	15	13	15	11	10	7	10	8AK	16	12	11AK	15AK	–	–	10AK	–	76
75	13	12	9	9	15	13	13	11	10	7	10	8AK	16	12	9AK	15AK	–	–	10	–	75
74	12	11	9	9	13	13	13	11	10	–	8	8AK	16	12	9AK	15AK	–	–	–	–	74
73	12	11	9	9	13	13	11	11	10	–	8	8AK	16	12	9AK	15AK	–	–	–	–	73
72	12	11	9	9	13	11	11	11	10	–	8	8AK	14	12	9AK	15AK	–	–	–	–	72
71	12	11	9	9	13	11	11	11	8	–	8	–	14	10	9AK	12AK	–	–	–	–	71
70	12	11	9	7	13	10	11	9	8	–	8	–	12	10	–	12AK	–	–	–	–	70
69	12	11	9	7	13	10	11	9	7	–	–	–	12	8	–	10	–	–	–	–	69
68	12	11	9	6	13	10	11	7	7	–	–	–	12	8	–	10	–	–	–	–	68
67	12	11	7	6	13	10	11	7	7	–	–	–	12	8	–	10	–	–	–	–	67
66	11	9	7	6	11	10	11	7	7	–	–	–	12	8	–	10	–	–	–	–	66
65	11	9	6	6	11	10	9	7	7	–	–	–	12	8	–	10	–	–	–	–	65
64	9	8	6	6	10	10	9	7	–	–	–	–	12	–	–	–	–	–	–	–	64
63	9	8	6	–	10	10	7	–	–	–	–	–	12	–	–	–	–	–	–	–	63
62	9	8	6	–	10	8	7	–	–	–	–	–	10	–	–	–	–	–	–	–	62
61	9	8	6	–	10	8	7	–	–	–	–	–	10	–	–	–	–	–	–	–	61
60	9	8	–	–	10	6	7	–	–	–	–	–	8	–	–	–	–	–	–	–	60
59	9	8	–	–	10	6	7	–	–	–	–	–	8	–	–	–	–	–	–	–	59
57-58	9	8	–	–	10	6	–	–	–	–	–	–	8	–	–	–	–	–	–	–	57-58
56	8	6	–	–	8	6	–	–	–	–	–	–	8	–	–	–	–	–	–	–	56
55	8	6	–	–	8	–	–	–	–	–	–	–	–	–	–	–	–	–	–	–	55
50-54	7	5	–	–	6	–	–	–	–	–	–	–	–	–	–	–	–	–	–	–	50-54
47-49	7	–	–	–	–	–	–	–	–	–	–	–	–	–	–	–	–	–	–	–	47-49
45-46	6	–	–	–	–	–	–	–	–	–	–	–	–	–	–	–	–	–	–	–	45-46
40-44	4	–	–	–	–	–	–	–	–	–	–	–	–	–	–	–	–	–	–	–	40-44

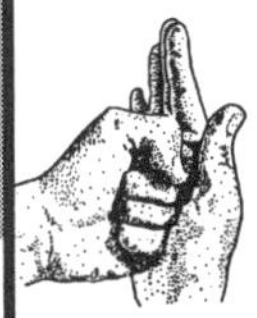

ATTACK TABLE 18.6
TETSUBO
TWO-HANDED

Length: 5 – 7 feet
Weight: 10 – 18 pounds
Fumble Range: 01 – 09 UM
Breakage #s: 1, 2, 3, 4, 5, 6, 7
Strength: 76 – 85
Range Modifiers: —

	20	19	18	17	16	15	14	13	12	11	10	9	8	7	6	5	4	3	2	1	
150	22EK	25EK	27EK	29EK	29EK	29EK	31EK	31EK	29EK	30EK	33EK	33EK	31EK	31EK	36EK	40EK	36EK	39EK	41EK	44EK	150
149	22EK	25EK	27EK	29EK	29EK	29EK	31EK	31EK	29EK	30EK	33EK	33EK	31EK	31EK	36EK	40EK	36EK	39EK	41EK	44EK	149
148	22EK	25EK	27EK	29EK	29EK	29EK	31EK	31EK	29EK	30EK	33EK	33EK	31EK	31EK	36EK	40EK	36EK	39EK	41EK	44EK	148
147	22EK	25EK	27EK	29EK	29EK	29EK	31EK	31EK	29EK	30EK	33EK	33EK	31EK	31EK	36EK	40EK	36EK	39EK	41EK	44EK	147
146	22EK	25EK	27EK	29EK	29EK	29EK	31EK	31EK	29EK	30EK	33EK	33EK	31EK	31EK	36EK	40EK	36EK	39EK	41EK	44EK	146
145	22EK	25EK	27EK	29EK	29EK	29EK	31EK	31EK	29EK	30EK	33EK	33EK	31EK	31EK	36EK	40EK	36EK	39EK	41EK	44EK	145
144	22EK	25EK	27EK	29EK	29EK	29EK	31EK	31EK	29EK	30EK	33EK	33EK	31EK	31EK	36EK	40EK	36EK	39EK	41EK	44EK	144
143	22EK	25EK	27EK	29EK	29EK	29EK	31EK	31EK	29EK	30EK	33EK	33EK	31EK	31EK	36EK	40EK	36EK	39EK	41EK	44EK	143
142	22DK	25EK	27EK	29EK	29EK	29EK	31EK	31EK	29EK	30EK	33EK	33EK	31EK	31EK	36EK	40EK	36EK	39EK	41EK	44EK	142
141	22DK	25DK	27EK	29EK	29EK	29EK	31EK	31EK	29EK	30EK	33EK	33EK	31EK	31EK	36EK	40EK	36EK	39EK	41EK	44EK	141
140	22DK	25DK	27EK	29EK	29EK	29EK	31EK	31EK	29EK	30EK	33EK	33EK	31EK	31EK	36EK	40EK	36EK	39EK	41EK	44EK	140
139	22DK	25DK	27DK	29EK	29DK	29EK	31EK	31EK	29EK	30EK	33EK	33EK	31EK	31EK	36EK	40EK	36EK	39EK	41EK	44EK	139
138	22DK	25DK	27DK	29EK	29DK	29DK	31EK	31EK	29EK	30EK	33EK	33EK	31EK	31EK	36EK	40EK	36DK	39EK	41EK	44EK	138
137	22DK	25DK	27DK	29DK	29DK	29DK	31DK	31EK	29EK	30EK	33EK	33EK	31EK	31EK	36EK	40EK	36DK	39DK	41EK	44EK	137
136	22DK	25DK	27DK	29DK	29DK	29DK	31DK	31EK	29DK	30DK	33EK	33EK	31DK	31EK	36EK	40EK	36DK	39DK	41EK	44DK	136
135	22DK	25DK	27DK	29DK	29DK	29DK	31DK	31DK	29DK	30DK	33DK	33EK	31DK	31DK	36EK	40EK	36DK	39DK	41EK	44DK	135
134	22DK	25DK	27DK	29DK	29DK	29DK	31DK	31DK	29DK	30DK	33DK	33DK	31DK	31DK	36DK	40EK	36DK	39DK	41DK	44DK	134
133	22CK	25DK	27DK	29DK	29DK	29DK	31DK	31DK	29DK	30DK	33DK	33DK	31DK	31DK	36DK	40DK	36DK	36DK	41DK	44DK	133
132	22CK	25DK	27DK	29DK	29DK	29DK	31DK	31DK	29DK	30DK	33DK	33DK	31DK	31DK	36DK	40DK	36DK	36DK	41DK	44DK	132
131	22CK	25CK	27DK	29DK	29DK	29DK	31DK	31DK	29DK	30DK	33DK	33DK	31DK	31DK	36DK	40DK	33DK	34DK	41DK	41DK	131
130	22CK	25CK	27DK	29DK	29DK	29DK	31DK	31DK	29DK	30DK	33DK	33DK	31DK	31DK	36DK	40DK	33DK	34DK	41DK	41DK	130
129	22CK	25CK	27DK	29DK	29DK	29DK	31DK	31DK	29DK	30DK	33DK	33DK	31DK	31DK	36DK	40DK	31DK	34DK	41DK	38DK	129
128	22CK	25CK	27DK	29DK	29CK	29DK	31DK	31DK	29DK	30DK	33DK	33DK	31DK	31DK	36DK	40DK	31DK	34DK	41DK	38DK	128
127	22CK	25CK	27CK	29DK	29CK	29DK	31DK	31DK	29DK	30DK	33DK	33DK	31DK	31DK	36DK	40DK	31DK	34DK	41DK	38DK	127
126	22CK	25CK	27CK	29DK	29CK	29CK	31DK	31DK	29DK	30DK	33DK	33DK	31DK	31DK	36DK	40DK	31DK	34DK	41DK	38DK	126
125	22CK	25CK	27CK	29DK	29CK	29CK	31DK	31DK	29DK	30DK	33DK	33DK	31DK	31DK	36DK	40DK	31CK	34DK	41DK	38DK	125
124	22BK	25CK	27CK	29DK	29CK	29CK	31CK	31DK	29DK	30DK	33DK	33DK	31DK	31DK	36DK	40DK	31CK	34DK	41DK	38DK	124
123	22BK	25CK	27CK	29CK	29CK	29CK	31CK	31DK	29DK	30DK	33DK	33DK	31DK	31DK	36DK	40DK	31CK	31CK	41DK	38DK	123
122	22BK	25CK	27CK	29CK	29CK	29CK	31CK	31DK	29CK	30DK	33DK	33DK	31DK	31DK	36DK	40DK	31CK	31CK	41DK	38CK	122
121	22BK	25BK	27CK	29CK	29CK	29CK	31CK	31DK	29CK	28CK	33DK	33DK	31CK	31DK	36DK	40DK	29CK	29CK	39DK	35CK	121
120	22BK	25BK	27CK	29CK	29CK	29CK	31CK	31CK	29CK	28CK	33DK	33DK	31CK	31DK	36DK	40DK	29CK	29CK	39DK	35CK	120
119	22BK	25BK	27CK	29CK	29CK	29CK	31CK	31CK	29CK	26CK	33CK	33DK	31CK	31CK	36DK	40DK	27CK	29CK	36DK	33CK	119
118	22BK	25BK	27CK	29CK	29CK	29CK	31CK	31CK	29CK	26CK	33CK	33DK	31CK	31CK	36DK	40DK	27CK	29CK	36CK	33CK	118
117	22BK	25BK	27CK	29CK	29CK	29CK	31CK	31CK	29CK	26CK	33CK	30CK	31CK	31CK	36CK	40DK	27CK	29CK	36CK	33CK	117
116	22BK	25BK	27CK	29CK	29BK	29CK	31CK	31CK	29CK	26CK	30CK	30CK	31CK	31CK	33CK	37CK	27CK	29CK	36CK	33CK	116
115	22AK	25BK	27BK	29CK	29BK	29CK	31CK	31CK	29CK	26CK	30CK	28CK	31CK	31CK	33CK	37CK	27CK	29CK	36CK	33CK	115
114	22AK	25BK	27BK	29CK	29BK	29CK	31CK	31CK	29CK	26CK	28CK	28CK	31CK	31CK	31CK	35CK	27CK	29CK	36CK	33CK	114
113	22AK	25BK	27BK	29CK	29BK	29BK	31CK	31CK	29CK	26CK	28CK	28CK	31CK	31CK	31CK	35CK	27CK	26CK	36CK	33CK	113
112	22AK	25BK	27BK	29CK	29BK	29BK	31CK	31CK	29CK	26CK	28CK	28CK	31CK	31CK	31CK	35CK	27BK	26CK	36CK	33CK	112
111	22AK	25AK	27BK	29CK	29BK	29BK	31BK	29CK	27CK	25CK	28CK	28CK	31CK	29CK	31CK	35CK	24BK	24CK	33CK	30CK	111
110	22AK	25AK	27BK	29CK	29BK	29BK	31BK	29CK	27CK	25CK	28CK	28CK	31CK	29CK	31CK	35CK	24BK	24BK	33CK	30CK	110
109	22AK	25AK	27BK	29BK	29BK	29BK	31BK	27CK	25CK	23CK	28CK	28CK	31CK	27CK	31CK	35CK	22BK	24BK	31CK	27CK	109
108	22AK	25AK	27BK	29BK	29BK	29BK	31BK	27CK	25BK	23CK	28CK	28CK	31CK	27CK	31CK	35CK	22BK	24BK	31CK	27BK	108
107	22AK	25AK	27BK	29BK	29BK	29BK	31BK	27CK	25BK	23CK	28CK	26CK	31CK	27CK	31CK	35CK	22BK	24BK	31CK	27BK	107
106	22	25AK	27BK	28BK	29BK	29BK	31BK	27CK	25BK	23BK	26CK	26CK	31BK	27CK	29CK	32CK	22BK	24BK	31CK	27BK	106
105	22	25AK	27BK	28BK	29AK	29BK	29BK	27BK	25BK	23BK	26CK	24CK	29BK	27CK	29CK	32CK	22BK	24BK	31CK	27BK	105
104	22	25AK	27BK	26BK	29AK	29BK	29BK	27BK	25BK	23BK	24BK	24CK	29BK	27CK	27CK	30CK	22BK	24BK	31CK	27BK	104
103	22	25AK	27AK	26BK	29AK	29BK	27BK	27BK	25BK	23BK	24BK	24CK	27BK	27BK	27CK	30CK	22BK	22BK	31CK	27BK	103
102	22	25AK	27AK	26BK	29AK	29BK	27BK	27BK	25BK	23BK	24BK	24CK	27BK	27BK	27CK	30CK	22BK	22BK	31BK	27BK	102
101	22	25	25AK	26BK	29AK	28AK	27BK	25BK	23BK	21BK	24BK	24CK	27BK	25BK	27CK	30CK	20BK	19BK	28BK	24BK	101
100	22	25	25AK	26BK	29AK	28AK	27BK	25BK	23BK	21BK	24BK	24BK	27BK	25BK	27BK	30CK	20BK	19BK	28BK	24BK	100
99	22	25	24AK	26BK	29AK	26AK	27BK	23BK	21BK	19BK	24BK	24BK	27BK	23BK	27BK	30BK	18AK	19BK	26BK	22BK	99
98	22	25	24AK	26BK	29AK	26AK	27AK	23BK	21BK	19BK	24BK	24BK	27BK	23BK	27BK	30BK	18AK	19BK	26BK	22BK	98
97	22	25	24AK	26BK	29AK	26AK	27AK	23BK	21BK	19BK	24BK	22BK	27BK	23BK	27BK	30BK	18AK	19BK	26BK	22BK	97
96	22	25	24AK	24BK	28AK	26AK	27AK	23BK	21BK	19BK	22BK	22BK	27BK	23BK	24BK	27BK	18AK	19AK	26BK	22BK	96
95	22	25	24AK	24AK	28AK	26AK	25AK	23BK	21BK	19BK	22BK	20BK	25BK	23BK	24BK	27BK	18AK	19AK	26BK	22BK	95
94	22	25	24AK	22AK	26AK	26AK	25AK	23BK	21AK	19BK	20BK	20BK	25BK	23BK	22BK	25BK	18AK	19AK	26BK	22AK	94
93	22	25	24AK	22AK	26	26AK	23AK	23BK	21AK	19BK	20BK	20BK	23BK	23BK	22BK	25BK	18AK	17AK	26BK	22AK	93
92	22	25	24AK	22AK	26	26AK	23AK	23BK	21AK	19BK	20BK	20BK	23BK	23BK	22BK	25BK	18AK	17AK	26BK	22AK	92
91	22	24	22	22AK	26	24AK	23AK	21BK	19AK	17AK	20BK	20BK	23AK	21BK	22BK	25BK	15AK	14AK	23BK	19AK	91
90	22	24	22	22AK	26	24AK	23AK	21AK	19AK	17AK	20BK	20BK	23AK	21BK	22BK	25BK	15AK	14AK	23BK	19AK	90
89	22	22	20	22AK	26	22AK	23AK	19AK	18AK	15AK	20BK	20BK	23AK	19BK	22BK	25BK	13AK	14AK	20BK	16AK	89
88	22	22	20	22AK	26	22	23AK	19AK	18AK	15AK	20AK	20BK	23AK	19BK	22BK	25BK	13AK	14AK	20BK	16AK	88
87	22	22	20	22AK	26	22	23AK	19AK	18AK	15AK	20AK	18BK	23AK	19AK	22BK	25BK	13AK	14AK	20BK	16AK	87
86	22	22	20	20AK	24	22	23AK	19AK	18AK	15AK	18AK	18BK	23AK	19AK	20BK	22BK	13	14AK	20AK	16AK	86
85	22	22	20	20AK	24	22	21AK	19AK	18AK	15AK	18AK	16BK	21AK	19AK	20BK	22BK	13	14AK	20AK	16AK	85
84	22	22	20	18AK	22	22	21	19AK	18AK	15AK	16AK	16BK	21AK	19AK	18BK	20BK	13	14AK	20AK	16AK	84
83	22	22	20	18AK	22	22	19	19AK	18AK	15AK	16AK	16AK	19AK	19AK	18AK	20BK	13	12AK	20AK	16AK	83
82	22	22	20	18AK	22	22	19	19AK	18AK	15AK	16AK	16AK	19AK	19AK	18AK	20AK	13	12	20AK	16AK	82
81	20	21	19	18	22	20	19	17AK	16AK	13AK	16AK	16AK	19AK	17AK	18AK	20AK	11	9	18AK	13AK	81
80	20	21	19	18	22	20	19	17AK	16	13AK	16AK	16AK	19AK	17AK	18AK	20AK	11	9	18AK	13	80
79	19	19	17	18	22	18	19	15AK	14	11AK	16AK	16AK	19AK	15AK	18AK	20AK	9	9	15AK	11	79
78	19	19	17	18	22	18	19	15AK	14	11AK	16AK	16AK	19AK	15AK	18AK	20AK	9	9	15AK	11	78
77	19	19	17	18	22	18	19	15AK	14	11AK	16AK	14AK	19AK	15AK	18AK	20AK	9	9	15AK	11	77
76	19	19	17	16	20	18	19	15AK	14	11	14AK	14AK	19	15AK	15AK	17AK	9	–	15AK	11	76
75	19	19	17	16	20	18	17	15AK	14	11	14AK	12AK	17	15AK	15AK	17AK	9	–	15AK	11	75
74	19	19	17	14	18	18	17	15	14	11	12AK	12AK	17	15AK	13AK	15AK	–	–	15AK	–	74
73	19	19	17	14	18	18	15	15	14	11	12AK	12AK	15	15AK	13AK	15AK	–	–	15AK	–	73
72	19	19	17	14	18	18	15	15	14	11	12	12AK	15	15AK	13AK	15AK	–	–	15AK	–	72
71	17	17	15	14	18	16	15	13	12	9	12	12AK	15	13	13AK	15AK	–	–	13AK	–	71
70	17	17	15	14	18	16	15	13	12	9	12	12AK	15	13	13AK	15AK	–	–	13	–	70
69	16	16	13	14	18	14	15	11	10	7	12	12AK	15	11	13AK	15AK	–	–	10	–	69
68	16	16	13	14	18	14	15	11	10	7	12	12AK	15	11	13AK	15AK	–	–	10	–	68
67	16	16	13	14	18	14	15	11	10	7	12	10AK	15	11	13AK	15AK	–	–	10	–	67
66	16	16	13	13	16	14	15	11	10	7	10	10	15	11	11	12AK	–	–	10	–	66
65	16	16	13	13	16	14	13	11	10	7	10	8	13	11	11	12	–	–	10	–	65
64	16	16	13	11	14	14	13	11	10	–	8	8	13	11	9	10	–	–	–	–	64
63	16	16	13	11	14	14	11	11	10	–	8	8	11	11	9	10	–	–	–	–	63
62	16	16	13	11	14	14	11	11	10	–	8	8	11	11	9	10	–	–	–	–	62
61	15	14	12	11	14	13	11	9	9	–	8	8	11	9	9	10	–	–	–	–	61
60	15	14	12	11	14	13	11	9	9	–	8	–	11	9	9	10	–	–	–	–	60
59	13	12	10	11	14	11	11	7	7	–	–	–	11	7	–	–	–	–	–	–	59
55-58	13	12	10	10	14	11	10	7	7	–	–	–	10	7	–	–	–	–	–	–	55-58
50-54	13	12	9	7	11	10	7	–	–	–	–	–	7	–	–	–	–	–	–	–	50-54
49	11	9	6	–	11	7	7	–	–	–	–	–	7	–	–	–	–	–	–	–	49
45-48	11	9	6	–	10	7	–	–	–	–	–	–	–	–	–	–	–	–	–	–	45-48
40-44	10	9	–	–	7	–	–	–	–	–	–	–	–	–	–	–	–	–	–	–	40-44
35-39	8	6	–	–	–	–	–	–	–	–	–	–	–	–	–	–	–	–	–	–	35-39
25-34	6	–	–	–	–	–	–	–	–	–	–	–	–	–	–	–	–	–	–	–	25-34

ATTACK TABLE 18.7

THREE-SECTION STAFF

TWO-HANDED

Length: 5 – 7 feet
Weight: 4 – 8 pounds
Fumble Range: 01 – 06 UM
Breakage #s: 1, 2, 3, 4, 5, 6, 7
Strength: 65 – 75 w

Range Modifiers: —

	20	19	18	17	16	15	14	13	12	11	10	9	8	7	6	5	4	3	2	1	
150	13CK	15CK	15EK	17EK	20EK	20EK	22EK	22EK	21EK	23EK	26EK	26EK	28EK	28EK	33EK	36EK	30EK	33EK	36EK	38EK	150
149	13CK	15CK	15EK	17EK	20EK	20EK	22EK	22EK	21EK	23EK	26EK	26EK	28EK	28EK	33EK	36EK	30EK	33EK	36EK	38EK	149
148	13CK	15CK	15EK	17EK	20EK	20EK	22EK	22EK	21EK	23EK	26EK	26EK	28EK	28EK	33EK	36EK	30EK	33EK	36EK	38EK	148
147	13CK	15CK	15EK	17EK	20EK	20EK	22EK	22EK	21EK	23EK	26EK	26EK	28EK	28EK	33EK	36EK	30EK	33EK	36EK	38EK	147
146	13CG	15CK	15EK	17EG	20EK	20EK	22EK	22EK	21EK	23EK	26EK	26EK	28EK	28EK	33EK	36EK	30EK	33EK	36EK	38EK	146
145	13BK	15CK	15EG	17EK	20EK	20EK	22EK	22EK	21EK	23EK	26EK	26EK	28EK	28EK	33EK	36EK	30EK	33EK	36EK	38EK	145
144	13BK	15CG	15DK	17EK	20DK	20EK	22EK	22EK	21EK	23EK	26EK	26EK	28EK	28EK	33EK	36EK	30EK	33EK	36EK	38EK	144
143	13BK	15BK	15DK	17EG	20DK	20DK	22EK	22EK	21EK	23EK	26EK	26EK	28EK	28EK	33EK	36EK	30EK	33EK	36EK	38EK	143
142	13BK	15BK	15DK	17DK	20DK	20DK	22DK	22EK	21EG	23EK	26EK	26EK	28EK	28EK	33EK	36EK	30DK	33EK	36EK	38EK	142
141	13BK	15BK	15DK	17DK	20DK	20DK	22DK	22EG	21DK	23EG	26EK	26EK	28EK	28EK	33EK	36EK	30DK	33DK	36EK	38EK	141
140	13BG	15BK	15DK	17DK	20DK	20DK	22DK	22DK	21DK	23DK	26EG	26EK	28EK	28EK	33EK	36EK	30DK	33DK	36EK	38DK	140
139	13AK	15BK	15DG	17DK	20DK	20DK	22DK	22DK	21DK	23DK	26DK	26EG	28DK	28EK	33EK	36EK	30DK	33DK	36EK	38DK	139
138	13AK	15BK	15CK	17DG	20DK	20DK	22DK	22DK	21DK	23DK	26DK	26DK	28DK	28DK	33EK	36EK	30DK	33DK	36DK	38DK	138
137	13AK	15BG	15CK	17DK	20CK	20DK	22DK	22DK	21DK	23DK	26DK	26DK	28DK	28DK	33DK	36EK	30DK	33DK	36DK	38DK	137
136	13AK	15AK	15CK	17DK	20CK	20DG	22DK	22DK	21DK	23DK	26DK	26DK	28DK	28DK	33DK	36DK	30DK	33DK	36DK	38DK	136
135	13AG	15AK	15CK	17DG	20CK	20CK	22DK	22DK	21DK	23DK	26DK	26DK	28DK	28DK	33DK	36DK	30DK	33DK	36DK	38DK	135
134	13	15AK	15CK	17CK	20CK	20CK	22DG	22DK	21DK	23DK	26DK	26DK	28DK	28DK	33DK	36DK	30DK	33DK	36DK	38DK	134
133	13	15AK	15CG	17CK	20CK	20CK	22CK	22DK	21DK	23DK	26DK	26DK	28DK	28DK	33DK	36DK	30CK	33DK	36DK	38DK	133
132	13	15AK	15BK	17CK	20CK	20CK	22CK	22DK	21DG	23DK	26DK	26DK	28DK	28DK	33DK	36DK	30CK	33DK	36DK	38DK	132
131	13	15AK	15BK	17CK	20CG	20CK	22CK	22DK	21CK	23DK	26DK	26DK	28DK	28DK	33DK	36DK	30CK	33CK	36DK	38DK	131
130	13	15AG	15BK	17CG	20BK	20CK	22CK	22DG	21CK	23DG	26DK	26DK	28DK	28DK	33DK	36DK	30CK	33CK	36DK	38DK	130
129	13	15	15BK	17CK	20BK	20CK	22CK	22CK	21CK	23CK	26DG	26DK	28DK	28DK	33DK	36DK	30CK	33CK	36DK	38CK	129
128	13	15	15BK	17CK	20BK	20CG	22CK	22CK	21CK	23CK	26CK	26DK	28CK	28DK	33DK	36DK	30CK	33CK	36DK	38CK	128
127	13	15	15BG	17CG	20BK	20BK	22CK	22CK	21CK	23CK	26CK	26DK	28CK	28DK	33DK	36DK	30CK	33CK	36DK	38CK	127
126	13	15	15AK	17BK	20BK	20BK	22CK	22CK	21CK	23CK	26CK	26DG	28CK	28CK	33DK	36DK	30CK	33CK	36DK	38CK	126
125	13	15	15AK	17BK	20BK	20BK	22CG	22CK	21CK	23CK	26CK	26CK	28CK	28CK	33DK	36DK	30BK	33CK	36CK	38CK	125
124	13	15	15AK	17BK	20BG	20BK	22BK	22CK	21CK	23CK	26CK	26CK	28CK	28CK	33CK	36DK	30BK	33CK	36CK	38CK	124
123	13	15	15AK	17BK	20AK	20BK	22BK	22CK	21CK	23CK	26CK	26CK	28CK	28CK	33CK	36DG	30BK	33CK	36CK	38CK	123
122	13	15	15AK	17BG	20AK	20BK	22BK	22CK	21CG	23CK	26CK	26CK	28CK	28CK	33CK	36CK	30BK	33BK	36CK	38CK	122
121	13	15	15AK	17BK	20AK	20BK	22BK	22CK	21BK	23CK	26CK	26CK	28CK	28CK	33CK	36CK	30BK	33BK	36CK	38CK	121
120	13	15	15AG	17BK	20AK	20BG	22BK	22CK	21BK	23CG	26CK	26CK	28CK	28CK	33CK	36CK	30BK	33BK	36CK	38CK	120
119	13	15	15	17BG	20AK	20AK	22BK	22CG	21BK	23BK	26CK	26CK	28CK	28CK	33CK	36CK	30BK	33BK	36CK	38CK	119
118	13	15	15	17AK	20AK	20AK	22BK	22BK	21BK	23BK	26CK	26CK	28CG	28CK	33CK	36CK	30BK	33BK	36CK	38BK	118
117	13	15	15	17AK	20AG	20AK	22BK	22BK	21BK	23BK	26CG	26CK	28BK	28CK	33CK	36CK	30BK	33BK	36CK	38BK	117
116	13	15	15	17AK	20	20AK	22BG	22BK	21BK	23BK	26BK	26CK	28BK	28CK	33CK	36CK	30AK	33BK	36CK	38BK	116
115	13	15	15	17AK	20	20AK	22AK	22BK	21BK	23BK	26BK	26CK	28BK	28CG	33CK	36CK	30AK	33BK	36CK	38BK	115
114	13	15	15	17AK	20	20AK	22AK	22BK	21BK	23BK	26BK	26CG	28BK	28BK	33CK	36CK	30AK	33BK	36CK	38BK	114
113	13	15	15	17AG	20	20AK	22AK	22BK	21BK	23BK	26BK	26BK	28BK	28BK	33CK	36CK	30AK	33BK	36BK	38BK	113
112	13	15	15	17AK	20	20AG	22AK	22BK	21BG	23BK	26BK	26BK	28BK	28BK	33CG	36CK	30AK	33AK	36BK	38BK	112
111	13	15	15	17AK	20	20	22AK	22BK	21AK	23BK	26BK	26BK	28BK	28BK	33BK	36CK	30AK	31AK	36BK	36BK	111
110	13	15	15	17AG	20	20	22AK	22BK	21AK	23BK	26BK	26BK	28BK	28BK	33BK	36CK	30AK	31AK	36BK	36BK	110
109	13	15	15	17	20	20	22AK	22BK	21AK	23BG	26BK	26BK	28BK	28BK	33BK	36CG	30AK	29AK	36BK	34BK	109
108	13	15	15	17	20	20	22AK	22BG	21AK	23AK	26BK	26BK	28BK	28BK	33BK	36BK	30AK	29AK	36BK	34BK	108
107	13	15	15	17	20	20	22AG	22AK	21AK	23AK	26BK	26BK	28BG	28BK	33BK	36BK	30	29AK	36BK	34AK	107
106	13	15	15	17	20	20	22	22AK	21AK	23AK	26BG	26BK	28AK	28BK	33BK	36BK	28	29AK	36BK	34AK	106
105	13	15	15	17	20	20	22	22AK	21AK	23AK	26AK	26BK	28AK	28BK	33BK	36BK	28	29AK	36BK	34AK	105
104	13	15	15	17	20	20	22	22AK	21AK	23AK	26AK	26BK	28AK	28BK	33BK	36BK	26	29AK	36BK	34AK	104
103	13	15	15	17	20	20	22	22AK	21AK	22AK	26AK	24BK	28AK	28BG	33BK	36BK	26	29AK	34BK	34AK	103
102	13	15	15	17	20	20	22	22AK	21AG	22AK	26AK	24BK	28AK	28AK	33BK	36BK	26	29	34BK	34AK	102
101	13	15	15	17	20	20	22	22AK	21	20AK	26AK	23BG	28AK	28AK	33BK	36BK	26	27	32BK	31AK	101
100	13	15	15	17	20	20	22	22AK	21	20AK	26AG	23AK	28AK	28AK	33BK	36BK	26	27	32AK	31AK	100
99	13	15	15	17	20	20	22	22AK	21	20AK	26AK	23AK	28AK	28AK	33BG	36BK	26	25	32AK	29AK	99
98	13	15	15	17	20	20	22	22AK	21	20AG	26AK	23AK	28AK	28AK	33AK	36BK	26	25	32AK	29AK	98
97	13	15	15	17	20	20	22	22AG	21	20	26AK	23AK	28AK	28AK	33AK	36BK	26	25	32AK	29AK	97
96	13	15	15	17	20	20	22	22	21	20	26AK	23AK	28AK	28AK	33AK	36BK	24	25	32AK	29	96
95	13	15	15	17	20	20	22	22	21	20	26AK	23AK	28AG	28AK	33AK	36BG	24	25	32AK	29	95
94	13	15	15	17	20	20	22	22	21	20	24AG	23AG	28	28AK	33AK	34AK	23	25	32AK	29	94
93	13	15	15	17	20	20	22	22	21	19	24	21AK	28	28AK	33AK	34AK	23	25	30AK	29	93
92	13	15	15	17	20	20	22	22	21	19	23	21AK	28	28AK	33AK	32AK	23	25	30AK	29	92
91	13	15	15	17	20	20	22	21	20	17	23	19AK	28	28AK	33AK	32AK	23	23	27AK	26	91
90	13	15	15	17	20	20	22	21	20	17	23	19AK	28	28AG	31AK	32AK	23	23	27AK	26	90
89	13	15	15	17	20	20	22	19	18	17	23	19AK	28	28	31AK	32AK	23	21	27AK	24	89
88	13	15	15	17	20	20	22	19	18	17	23	19AG	28	28	29AK	32AK	23	21	27AK	24	88
87	13	15	15	17	20	20	22	19	18	17	23	19	28	28	29AK	32AK	23	21	27	24	87
86	13	15	15	17	20	20	21	19	18	17	23	19	28	26	29AK	32AK	21	21	27	24	86
85	13	15	15	17	20	20	21	19	18	17	23	19	28	26	29AG	32AK	21	21	27	24	85
84	13	15	15	17	20	20	19	19	18	17	21	19	28	25	29	30AK	19	21	27	24	84
83	13	15	15	17	20	20	19	19	18	16	21	18	28	25	29	30AK	19	21	25	24	83
82	13	15	15	17	20	20	19	19	18	16	19	18	28	25	29	27AK	19	21	25	24	82
81	13	15	14	16	20	19	19	18	17	14	19	16	26	25	29	27AK	19	19	23	21	81
80	13	15	14	16	20	19	19	18	17	14	19	16	26	25	27	27AG	19	19	23	21	80
79	13	15	13	15	20	18	19	16	16	14	19	16	25	25	27	27	19	16	23	19	79
78	13	15	13	15	20	18	19	16	16	14	19	16	25	25	25	27	19	16	23	19	78
77	13	15	13	15	20	18	19	16	16	14	19	16	25	25	25	27	19	16	23	19	77
76	13	15	13	15	19	18	18	16	16	14	19	16	25	23	25	27	17	16	23	19	76
75	13	15	13	15	19	18	18	16	16	14	19	16	25	23	25	27	17	16	23	19	75
74	12	14	13	15	18	18	16	16	16	14	18	16	25	21	25	25	15	16	23	19	74
73	12	14	13	15	18	18	16	16	16	13	18	14	25	21	25	25	15	16	20	19	73
72	11	13	13	15	18	18	16	16	16	13	16	14	25	21	25	23	15	16	20	19	72
71	11	13	12	14	18	16	16	15	14	11	16	13	23	21	25	23	15	14	18	17	71
70	11	13	12	14	18	16	16	15	14	11	16	13	23	21	23	23	15	14	18	17	70
69	11	13	11	13	18	15	16	14	13	11	16	13	21	21	23	23	15	12	18	14	69
68	11	13	11	13	18	15	16	14	13	11	16	13	21	21	21	23	15	12	18	14	68
67	11	13	11	13	18	15	16	14	13	11	16	13	21	21	21	23	15	12	18	14	67
66	11	13	11	13	16	15	15	14	13	11	16	13	21	19	21	23	13	12	18	14	66
65	11	13	11	13	16	15	15	14	13	11	16	13	21	19	21	23	13	12	18	14	65
64	10	12	11	13	15	15	14	14	13	11	14	13	21	17	21	20	11	12	18	14	64
63	10	12	11	13	15	15	14	14	13	10	14	11	21	17	21	20	11	12	16	14	63
62	9	11	11	13	15	15	14	14	13	10	13	11	21	17	21	18	11	12	16	14	62
61	9	11	10	12	15	14	14	12	12	8	13	9	19	17	21	18	11	10	13	12	61
55-60	9	11	9	10	15	12	13	11	10	8	13	9	18	17	17	18	10	8	13	10	55-60
50-54	8	9	9	10	12	12	11	10	10	7	10	7	17	14	16	14	7	–	11	–	50-54
47-49	8	9	7	8	12	10	11	8	8	5	9	6	14	14	13	13	–	–	9	–	47-49
38-46	7	8	6	7	10	9	8	7	6	–	8	–	13	11	10	10	–	–	–	–	38-46
35-37	6	7	5	6	9	7	7	5	5	–	–	–	10	9	8	–	–	–	–	–	35-37
34	5	6	5	6	7	7	5	–	–	–	–	–	10	7	8	–	–	–	–	–	34
30-33	4	5	5	6	7	7	5	–	–	–	–	–	9	7	–	–	–	–	–	–	30-33
24-29	4	5	3	4	7	5	–	–	–	–	–	–	7	–	–	–	–	–	–	–	24-29
18-24	3	3	–	–	4	–	–	–	–	–	–	–	–	–	–	–	–	–	–	–	18-24

MARTIAL ARTS COMPANION
109

Attack Table 18.8
Wakizashi
One-Handed Edged

Length: 2 – 3 feet
Weight: 2 – 4 pounds
Fumble Range: 01 – 02 UM
Breakage #s: 1, 2, 3, 4, 5
Strength: 75 – 86
Range Modifiers: —

	20	19	18	17	16	15	14	13	12	11	10	9	8	7	6	5	4	3	2	1	
150	5CK	7DK	9EK	8EK	10EK	10EK	13EK	13EK	11EK	13EK	17EK	17EK	17ES	17ES	21ES	23ES	18ES	21ES	24ES	26ES	150
149	5CK	7DK	9EK	8EK	10EK	10EK	13EK	13EK	11EK	13EK	17EK	17ES	17EP	17ES	21EP	23ES	18ES	21ES	24ES	26ES	149
148	5CK	7DK	9EK	8EK	10EK	10EK	13EK	13EK	11EK	13EK	17EK	17EK	17ES	17EP	21ES	23ES	18ES	21ES	24ES	26ES	148
147	5CK	7DK	9EK	8EK	10EK	10EK	13EK	13EK	11EK	13EK	17ES	17ES	17EK	17ES	21EK	23EP	18ES	21EP	24ES	26ES	147
146	5CK	7DK	9EK	8EK	10EK	10EK	13EK	13EK	11EK	13EK	17EK	17EK	17ES	17EK	21ES	23EK	18EP	21ES	24EP	26EP	146
145	5BK	7CK	9EK	8EK	10ES	10EK	13EK	13EK	11EK	13EK	17ES	17EP	17EP	17ES	21EP	23ES	18ES	21EP	24ES	26ES	145
144	5BK	7CK	9DK	8EK	10DK	10ES	13EK	13EK	11EK	13ES	17EK	17EK	17ES	17EP	21ES	23EP	18EP	21ES	24EP	26EP	144
143	5BK	7CK	9DK	8EK	10DK	10DK	13ES	13ES	11ES	13EK	17EP	17ES	17EK	17ES	21EK	23EK	18ES	21EP	24ES	26ES	143
142	5BK	7CK	9DK	8DK	10DK	10DK	13DK	13EK	11EK	13ES	17EK	17EK	17ES	17EK	21ES	23ES	18EP	21ES	24EP	26EP	142
141	5BK	7CK	9DK	8DK	10DK	10DK	13DK	13EP	11EP	13EK	17ES	17EP	17EP	17ES	21EP	23EP	18ES	21EP	24ES	26ES	141
140	5BK	7BK	9DK	8DK	10DK	10DS	13DK	13DK	11DK	13EP	17EK	17ES	17EK	17EP	21ES	23EK	18EP	21ES	24EP	26EP	140
139	5AK	7BK	9DK	8DK	10DS	10DK	13DK	13DK	11DK	13DK	17EP	17EK	17ES	17EK	21EK	23ES	18ES	21EP	24ES	26ES	139
138	5AK	7BK	9CK	8DK	10CK	10DK	13DK	13DK	11DK	13DK	17DK	17ES	17EK	17ES	21ES	23EP	18EK	21ES	24EP	26EP	138
137	5AK	7BK	9CK	8DK	10CK	10DP	13DS	13DK	11DK	13DK	17DK	17EP	17EP	17EK	21EP	23EK	18DS	21EK	24ES	26ES	137
136	5AK	7BK	9CK	8DK	10CS	10CK	13DK	13DK	11DK	13DK	17DK	17DK	17DS	17EP	21ES	23ES	18DS	21DS	24EP	26EK	136
135	5AS	7AK	9CK	8DK	10CK	10CK	13DP	13DK	11DK	13DS	17DS	17DS	17DP	17DS	21EK	23EP	18DS	21DS	24ES	26DS	135
134	5	7AK	9CK	8CK	10CK	10CK	13CK	13DK	11DK	13DK	17DK	17DK	17DS	17DS	21DK	23EK	18DS	21DS	24EK	26DS	134
133	5	7AK	9CK	8CK	10CP	10CS	13CK	13DS	11DS	13DS	17DS	17DS	17DK	17DP	21DS	23DK	18DP	21DP	24DS	26DS	133
132	5	7AK	9BK	8CK	10BK	10CK	13CK	13DK	11DK	13DK	17DK	17DK	17DS	17DS	21DS	23DS	18DS	21DS	24DS	26DS	132
131	5	7AK	9BK	8CK	10BK	10CK	13CK	13DP	11DP	13DS	17DP	17DP	17DP	17DK	21DK	23DP	18DP	21DP	24DP	26DP	131
130	5	7AS	9BK	8CK	10BS	10CP	13CK	13CK	11CK	13DK	17DK	17DK	17DS	17DS	21DP	23DS	18DS	21DS	24DS	26DS	130
129	5	7	9BK	8CK	10BK	10BK	13CS	13CK	11CK	13DP	17DS	17DS	17DK	17DP	21DS	23DK	18DP	21DP	24DP	26DP	129
128	5	7	9BK	8CK	10BK	10BK	13CK	13CK	11CK	13CK	17DK	17DK	17DS	17DS	21DP	23DS	18DS	21DS	24DS	26DS	128
127	5	7	9BK	8CK	10BP	10BK	13CP	13CK	11CK	13CK	17DP	17DP	17DP	17DK	21DK	23DP	18DP	21DP	24DP	26DP	127
126	5	7	9AK	8BK	10AK	10BS	13BK	13CK	11CK	13CS	17CK	17DS	17DK	17DS	21DS	23DS	18DS	20DS	24DS	24DS	126
125	5	7	9AK	8BK	10AK	10BK	13BK	13CS	11CS	13CK	17CS	17DK	17DS	17DP	21DP	23DK	18DK	20DP	24DP	24DP	125
124	5	7	9AK	8BK	10AK	10BK	13BK	13CK	11CK	13CP	17CK	17DS	17DK	17DK	21DS	23DS	18CS	18DS	24DS	23DS	124
123	5	7	9AS	8BK	10AS	10BP	13BK	13CS	11CS	13CK	17CS	17DP	17DP	17DS	21DK	23DP	18CS	18DK	24DP	23DP	123
122	5	7	9AK	8BK	10AK	10AK	13BK	13CK	11CK	13CS	17CK	17CK	17CS	17DK	21DP	23DS	18CP	18CS	24DS	23DS	122
121	5	7	9AK	8BK	10AK	10AK	13BS	13CP	11CP	12CK	17CS	16CP	17CP	17DP	21DS	23DK	17CS	18CS	24DK	23DK	121
120	5	7	9AP	8BK	10AP	10AK	13BK	13BK	11BK	12CS	17CK	16CS	17CS	17CP	21DP	23DP	17CP	18CS	24DS	23CS	120
119	5	7	9	8BK	10	10AS	13BP	13BK	11BK	11CK	17CP	15CK	17CK	17CS	21DK	23DS	15CS	18CP	24DP	23CS	119
118	5	7	9	8AK	10	10AK	13AK	13BK	11BK	11CP	17CK	15CS	17CS	17CP	21CK	23DP	15CP	18CS	24DS	23CP	118
117	5	7	9	8AK	10	10AK	13AK	13BK	11BK	11BK	17CS	15CP	17CP	17CK	21CS	23DK	15CS	18CP	24DK	23CS	117
116	5	7	9	8AK	10	10AK	13AK	12BK	11BK	11BS	16CK	15CK	17CS	17CS	21CS	23CK	15CP	17CS	22CS	21CP	116
115	5	7	9	8AK	10	10AP	13AK	12BS	11BS	11BK	16CP	15CS	17CK	17CK	21CK	23CS	15CS	17CP	22CS	21CS	115
114	5	7	9	8AS	10	10	13AS	11BK	11BK	11BS	15BS	15CK	17CS	17CP	21CP	23CP	15CP	16CS	21CP	19CP	114
113	5	7	9	8AK	10	10	12AK	11BS	10BS	11BK	15BK	15CP	17CP	17CS	21CS	21CS	15CS	16CP	21CS	19CS	113
112	5	7	9	7AK	10	10	12AS	11BK	10BK	11BP	15BS	15CS	17CK	17CK	21CP	21CK	15CK	16CS	21CP	19CP	112
111	5	7	9	7AK	10	10	11AK	11BP	9BP	10BK	15BP	13CK	17CS	17CS	21CK	20CS	14BP	16CP	21CS	19CS	111
110	5	7	9	7AP	10	10	11AP	11AK	9AK	10BK	15BK	13CS	17CK	17CP	21CS	20CP	14BS	16CS	21CP	19CK	110
109	5	7	9	7	10	10	11	11AK	9AK	9BS	15BS	12CP	17CP	17CK	20CP	20CS	13BP	16CK	21CS	19CS	109
108	5	7	9	7	10	10	11	11AK	9AK	9BK	15BK	12BK	17BS	17CS	20CS	20CK	13BS	16BS	21CP	19CP	108
107	5	7	9	7	10	10	11	11AK	9AK	9BP	15BP	12BP	17BP	17CK	18CK	20CS	13BP	16BP	21CS	19CS	107
106	5	7	8	7	10	9	11	10AK	9AK	9AK	13BK	12BS	17BS	17CP	18CP	20CP	13BS	14BS	19CP	18CK	106
105	5	7	8	7	10	9	11	10AK	9AK	9AK	13BS	12BK	17BK	17BP	18CS	20CS	13BP	14BP	19CS	18BS	105
104	5	7	8	7	10	8	11	9AS	9AS	9AK	12BK	12BS	17BS	17BS	18CP	20CK	13BS	13BS	18CK	16BS	104
103	5	7	8	7	9	8	10	9AK	9AK	9AS	12BP	12BP	17BP	16BP	18CK	18CP	13BK	13BP	18CS	16BP	103
102	5	7	8	6	9	8	10	9AS	9AS	9AK	12AS	12BK	17BS	16BK	18BK	18CS	13BS	13BS	18CP	16BS	102
101	5	7	8	6	8	8	9	9AK	8AK	9AP	12AK	11BS	17BK	15BS	18BP	17CP	12BP	13BP	18CS	16BP	101
100	5	7	8	6	8	8	9	9AP	8AP	9AK	12AS	11BK	17BS	15BK	18BS	17CK	12BS	13BS	18CK	16BS	100
99	5	7	8	6	8	8	9	9	8	8AS	12AK	10BP	17BP	15BP	17BK	17BK	11BK	13BK	18BS	16BP	99
98	5	7	8	6	8	8	9	9	8	8AK	12AP	10BS	17BK	15BS	17BS	17BS	11AS	13BS	18BS	16BS	98
97	5	7	8	6	8	8	9	9	8	8AS	12AK	10BK	17BS	15BK	16BP	17BP	11AP	13BP	18BP	16BP	97
96	5	6	7	6	8	8	9	9	8	8AK	11AS	10BS	16BK	15BS	16BS	17BS	11AS	12BS	16BS	14BS	96
95	5	6	7	6	8	8	9	9	8	8AP	11AK	10BP	16BP	15BP	16BK	17BK	11AP	12BK	16BP	14BK	95
94	5	6	6	6	8	7	9	8	8	8	10AP	10AS	15AP	15BK	16BS	17BS	11AS	10AS	15BS	13BS	94
93	5	6	6	6	8	7	9	8	7	8	10AK	10AK	15AS	13BS	16BP	15BP	11AP	10AS	15BP	13BP	93
92	5	6	6	5	8	7	9	8	7	8	10AS	10AP	15AP	13BK	16BS	15BS	11AS	10AP	15BS	13BS	92
91	5	6	6	5	7	7	8	8	6	7	10AK	9AK	15AK	12BP	16BK	14BK	10AP	10AS	15BP	13BK	91
90	5	6	6	5	7	7	8	8	6	7	10AP	9AS	15AS	12AP	16BP	14BS	10AS	10AP	15BS	13AS	90
89	5	6	6	5	7	7	8	8	6	6	10	8AK	15AK	12AS	14BS	14BP	9AK	10AS	15BP	13AP	89
88	5	6	6	5	7	7	8	8	6	6	10	8AP	15AP	12AK	14BP	14BS	9AS	10AP	15BS	13AS	88
87	5	6	6	5	7	7	8	8	6	6	10	8AS	15AS	12AP	13BK	14BK	9AP	10AS	15BK	13AP	87
86	4	5	6	5	7	6	8	7	6	6	9	8AK	13AK	12AS	13AK	14BP	9AS	9AP	13BS	11AS	86
85	4	5	6	5	7	6	8	7	6	6	9	8AS	13AS	12AK	13AS	14BS	9AK	9AS	13BP	11AP	85
84	4	5	5	5	7	6	8	6	6	6	8	8AP	12AP	12AS	13AP	14BP	9	8AK	12BS	9AS	84
83	4	5	5	5	6	6	7	6	6	6	8	8AK	12AK	11AP	13AS	13BK	9	8AS	12BK	9AP	83
82	4	5	5	4	6	6	7	6	6	6	8	8AS	12AS	11AS	13AK	13AS	9	8AP	12AS	9AS	82
81	4	5	5	4	6	6	6	6	5	5	8	7AK	12AK	10AK	13AS	11AP	7	8AS	12AS	9AP	81
80	4	5	5	4	6	6	6	6	5	5	8	7AP	12AP	10AS	13AP	11AK	7	8AK	12AS	9AS	80
79	4	5	5	4	6	6	6	6	5	4	8	6	12	10AP	12AS	11AS	6	8	12AP	9AK	79
78	4	5	5	4	6	6	6	6	5	4	8	6	12	10AK	12AK	11AP	6	8	12AS	9AS	78
77	4	5	5	4	6	6	6	6	5	4	8	6	12	10AS	10AS	11AK	6	8	12AP	9AP	77
76	4	4	5	4	6	5	6	5	5	4	7	6	11	10AK	10AP	11AS	6	6	10AS	8AS	76
75	4	4	5	4	6	5	6	5	5	4	7	6	11	10AP	10AS	11AP	6	6	10AP	8AK	75
74	3	4	4	4	6	5	6	4	5	4	6	6	10	10	10AK	11AK	6	5	9AS	6	74
73	3	4	4	4	5	5	5	4	4	4	6	6	10	9	10AP	10AS	6	5	9AP	6	73
72	3	4	4	3	5	5	5	4	4	4	6	6	10	9	10AS	10AP	6	5	9AS	6	72
71	3	4	4	3	5	5	4	4	4	4	6	5	10	8	10AP	8AK	5	5	9AP	6	71
70	3	4	4	3	5	5	4	4	4	4	6	5	10	8	10AK	8AS	5	5	9AS	6	70
69	3	4	4	3	5	5	4	4	4	3	6	4	10	8	9	8AP	4	–	9AK	–	69
68	3	4	4	3	5	5	4	4	4	3	6	4	10	8	9	8AK	4	–	9AS	–	68
67	3	4	4	3	5	5	4	4	4	3	6	4	10	8	8	8AS	4	–	9AP	–	67
66	3	4	4	3	5	4	4	4	4	3	5	4	9	8	8	8AP	4	–	7AS	–	66
65	3	4	4	3	5	4	4	4	4	3	5	4	9	8	8	8AK	4	–	7AK	–	65
64	3	3	3	3	5	3	4	3	4	–	4	–	8	8	8	8	–	–	6	–	64
63	3	3	3	3	4	3	4	3	3	–	4	–	8	7	8	7	–	–	6	–	63
62	3	3	3	2	4	3	4	3	3	–	4	–	8	7	8	7	–	–	6	–	62
61	3	3	3	2	3	3	3	3	2	–	4	–	8	6	8	5	–	–	6	–	61
60	3	3	3	2	3	3	3	3	2	–	4	–	8	6	8	5	–	–	6	–	60
57-59	3	3	3	2	3	3	3	–	2	–	–	–	8	6	6	5	–	–	–	–	57-59
54-56	2	3	2	2	3	3	–	–	–	–	–	–	7	6	5	–	–	–	–	–	54-56
52-53	2	2	2	–	3	2	–	–	–	–	–	–	6	5	5	–	–	–	–	–	52-53
50-51	2	2	2	–	2	2	–	–	–	–	–	–	6	4	–	–	–	–	–	–	50-51
47-49	2	2	–	–	2	–	–	–	–	–	–	–	6	4	–	–	–	–	–	–	47-49
45-46	2	2	–	–	–	–	–	–	–	–	–	–	5	–	–	–	–	–	–	–	45-46
40-44	1	1	–	–	–	–	–	–	–	–	–	–	4	–	–	–	–	–	–	–	40-44
30-39	1	–	–	–	–	–	–	–	–	–	–	–	–	–	–	–	–	–	–	–	30-39

	A	B	C	D	E
01-05	Foe watches as you stumble over your own feet. He is not worried. +0H	Foe manages to slip out of your grasp. +0H	You do not move quickly enough to press your momentary advantage. +1H	Glancing strike causes foe some concern. +2H	At the critical moment you hesitate and foe slips away out of your grasp. +3H
06-10	You manage to inflict some minor damage to your foe. +1H	Mistimed attack is lucky to even strike the foe. Better luck next time. +2H	Foe breaks out of your grasp easily. +2H	You catch your foe in an arm lock but he manages to break your grasp. +3H	Arm lock sets foe up for a weak snap kick. Foe stumbles back a step. You have initiative next round. +4H
11-15	You maneuver your opponent into an awkward stance. You gain initiative next round. +2H	Foe barely escapes out of your grasp. You gain initiative next round. +3H	Your swift attack causes your foe to stumble backward and nearly fall. You have initiative next round. (+20)	You step past foe's strike and entangle his weapon arm. Foe must parry next round to reclaim his balance. +2H – (×-20)	Your deceptive attack catches foe on the side of the head. He is dazed by your blow. You move in to exploit the gap in his defenses. +2H – ✿ – (+10)
16-20	You catch foe in a painful wrist lock. He manages to break free but your have initiative next round. +3H – (+10)	Foe senses your intent and concentrates on defending himself. You have initiative next round. (×-10)	Your darting attacks have your foe growing worried. He starts to become more defensive. You have initiative for the next 2 rounds. +2H – (×-20)	You manage to tied foe up in an arm lock. He must parry next round and you have initiative for the next two rounds as he attempts to extract himself. (×-40)	You grab foe's hand and maneuver him into the path of your foot. Foe is doubled over by the force of the blow. +3H – ✿⊗
21-30	Clever wrist lock handicaps foe. You have initiative for the next 2 rounds. +2H – (+20)	You manage to pull foe's shirt over his head. +1H – (×-30) – (+10)	You sprain foe's weapon hand finger. +3H – (×-20) – (-10)	Jerking twist to foe's elbow nearly dislocates it. Foe drops his weapon. +4H – (-20)	You throw foe into the nearest hard object and he hits hard. His neck is sprained. +4H – 2✿ – (-20)
31-40	You twist foe's arm behind his back. He breaks free but strains his muscles. +5H – (×-20)	Brusing grip on his weapon arm causes foe to wince in pain. If foe is not wearing arm greaves, he drops his weapon. +4H – (×-25)	One-handed hold spins foe around and nearly dislocates his shoulder. +5H – ✿	Your encircling grip sets foe up for a brutal head butt. Foe's nose is broken. You have initiative next round. +6H – ✿ – (-20)	Your controlling hold spinds foe around in the direction you wish. You have initiative next round. ✿ – (+20)
41-50	Foe attacks too slowly. You grab his weapon and nearly disarm him. +2H – (×-25)	You catch foe in a painful armlock. +4H – ✿	You catch foe's leg as he makes an ill-advised attempt to kick you. You throw him off-balance to the ground. He twists his ankle. +5H – 2✿ – (-20)	You tie foe up in a painful hold. He struggles futilely against your grip. You have initiative for the next 3 rounds. 3✿ – (+10)	You grab foe's weapon arm as he attacks. You have initiative for the next three rounds. ✿ – (+30)
51-55	You grab foe and pull him off-balance. He falls hard to the ground. +5H – ✿	You manage to sprain foe's wrist with a final twist before he breaks free from your hold. +2H – ✿ – (-20)	Controlling hold drives foe to the ground. You may attack next round with positional modifiers. You have initiative next round. ✿ – (+20)	You leap over foe's strike and grab the back of his head. Throw foe 5' in the direction of your choice. You have initiative for the next 2 rounds. +6H – 2✿	Strong hold forces foe to fall to his knees. He then recieves your knee in his face. His nose is broken. +4H – 2✿⊗ – (-20)
56-60	Foe cleverly manages to avoid your attack by falling to the ground. +5H – ✿ – (+10)	You use foe's momentum against him. He stumbles to the ground. +3H – ✿ – (-20)	Foe is taken unawares by your hip throw. He falls and nearly impales himself on his weapon. Check for weapon breakage. +5H – ✿×	You catch foe's hand and use a wrist lock to disarm him. Foe struggles against you but you still have control. You have initiative for the next 2 rounds. 2✿- (+10)	Foe's ill-advised charge ends with him flying over your head. Foe impacts on the ground 5' behind you and loses his weapon. Check for weapon breakage. +5H – 3✿ – (-10)
61-65	Your controlling grip on foe's arm causes him to attempt to break free. Foe badly strains his shoulder muscle. +6H – 2✿ – (-10)	You grab foe's ear. He looks at you in amazement as you force him to dance around. You have the initiative for the next 6 rounds. (+20)	You grab foe's weapon hand and sprain his wrist with a twisting motion. Foe drops weapon and cradles his hand. +8H – ✿⊗ – (-20)	Foe attempts to break your arm lock by pushing himself backward. You move in the other direction. Foe breaks arm. +5H – 3✿ – (-20)	You decide to apply more pressure foe's arm and shoulder. He struggles against you and you toss him to the ground. He breaks his collarbone. +10H – 2✿⊗ – (-20)
66	As foe lunges toward you with his weapon, you deftly avoid the attack and catch his outstreached arm. Spinning gracefully you dislocate foe's shoulder. +5H – 3✿⊗ – (-50)	A simple thumb lock causes foe to fall to his knees in pain. He is totally immobilized. You take his weapon and decide what you want to do. (+25)	Foe attempts to strike you. You catch his outstreached hand and turn and throw him over your shoulder. Foe lands and manages to break both of his arms. +10H – 6✿⊗ – (-80)	You get angry at your opponent and decide to shatter his elbow. Foe drops his weapon and screams in pain. He is at your mercy. +10H – 12✿⊗ – (-40)	Crack. Foe's neck was not meant to move in that manner. Foe dies immediately. You look for your next opponent, this one was too easy. (+20)
67-70	Foe rushes you like a bull in a china shop. You step aside and trip him. Gravity does the rest. Foe stumbles and falls. Roll for a weapon fumble. +2H – ✿	Wrenching arm lock sends foe face down into the dirt. Foe is momentarily immobilized and strains his back fighting against your controlling hold. +3H – 2✿ – (-10) – (+10)	Foe trips, stumbles, and falls as you spin out from under his attack. Foe makes an attack against himself. You gain good position. (+10)	Foe's impulsive attack lands him in a near stranglehold. Foe's face turns red as he gasps for air. +2H – 2✿⊗ – 2(-30)	Foe must have a death wish. You disarm him easily. You may maneuver foe 5' in any direction this round. You have initiative for the next three rounds. +5H – 2✿ – 3(-30)
71-75	You catch the weapon arm of your foe. You have the initiative for the next 2 rounds. +2H – ✿ – (-10) – (+20)	Snap. You spin foe to the ground and break his leg with a brutal hold. Foe's leg is cleanly broken. +5H – 3✿ – (-20)	Cartwheeling throw dislocates foe's shoulder. Foe is unhappy. +7H – 4✿ – (-40)	Where did he go? Foe flails at empty air as you slide under his attack and grab his legs. Foe is upended and defenseless until he can break your hold. +3H – 2✿⊗ – (+20)	Controlling hold forces the foe in any direction you choose this round. Foe loses initiative for the next three rounds. You also sprain foe's neck. +5H – 2✿⊗ – (-50)
76-80	Foe is thrown off-balance as you suddenly release your hold and step back. Foe is confused. +4H – 3✿ – (+10)	Foe is confused by your technique and you gain a strong hold on him. You have initiative for the next 3 rounds. +3H – 3✿	You grab the back of your foe's head and throw him to the ground. Foe eats dirt. You twist his nearby leg into an uncomfortable position. +6H – 2✿⊗ – 2(-30)	You show your foe no mercy as you shatter his weapon arm with a brutal knee strike. Foe's arm is useless and he whimpers in pain. +6H – 2✿⊗ – (-30)	Your strong hold results in ripping the tendons in foe's wrist and arm. Foe's arm is useless. +8H (stunned 3 rnds, -40 to all actions) +8H – 3✿ – (-40)
81-85	Spin foe around with your controlling hold. Foe's defenses are down. You have initiative for the next 2 rnds. 2✿⊗ – (+25)	Sweeping throw sends foe rolling 10' in any direction. He strikes a hard object and injures his head. Foe is bleeding badly from his forehead into his eyes. +8H – ✿ – ♦ – (-50)	You grapple your foe and engage him in close combat. He is unsure what to do. You have initiative for the next 3 rounds. +2H – 2(×-40) – (+30)	Foe learns the power of gravity as he falls upon his own weapon. Roll for a weapon fumble. He also knocks the wind out of his lungs. +4H – 3✿⊗	You manage to throw foe into the attack of another combatant. Foe tries to untangle himself this round. He also breaks his arm landing on the ground. +8H – 4✿⊗ – (-20)
86-90	Foe attacks you with abandon. You sprain his weapon arm with ease. He is not going to last long. +4H – 3✿ – (-20)	You block foe's attack and take his weapon. You also decide to dislocate his shoulder for good measure. +4H – 2✿ – (-30)	Strong throw causes foe to break ribs. One broken rib penetrates a lung. Foe is not feeling well. +12H – 5✿⊗ – (-50)	With little apparent effort you block foe's attack and place him in an immobilizing hold. You have initiative for the next 6 rounds. +6H – 6✿⊗	You immbolize foe with a head lock. You can choose to choke him to unconsciousness or death if you so wish. (+10)
91-95	Foe is thrown hard to the ground by your attack. If he has no helm is knocked out. +8H – 9✿	You send foe flying 10' in any direction. Foe lands and fractures his ribs. +8H – 12✿⊗ – (-30)	Throw breaks both of foe's knees. Foe cannot move. +16H – 8✿⊗ – (-80)	Your attack pins foe's arms to his sides. The follow-up head butt to foe knocks him out cold. +12H	Tiring of your foe's attacks, you strike back. Foe is thrown 15' in any direction and knocks himself unconscious for the next 6 hours. +12H
96-99	Foe attempts a bizarre movement to free himself of your hold. You discover a new technique and immbolize the foe with one hand. Foe is helpless. —	Your attack pins foe with relative ease. You decide to go through foe's pockets while deciding what to do with him next. Foe is unable to defend himself. —	Foe back is broken as you tighen your hold. He is paralyzed from the waist down. +12H – 12✿⊗ – (-80)	Your arm hold on foe causes him to beg for mercy. You decide to break his neck instead. Foe dies instantly. You are mean. (+20)	Foe attempts to break your hold as you tumble while maintaining your hold on his head. You break his neck cleanly. Foe is dead. Who is next? (+25)
100	Careful hold on foe's shoulder pushes him to the ground. You strengthen your position and immobilize him. He is at your mercy.	You throw foe head over heels. Foe lands on his own weapon and impales himself. Foe dies immediately. Not a pretty sight. —	Your deadly throw results in foe breaking his neck. He dies immediately. You need to find a new opponent. —	You guide foe's attack against you into his own body. Foe can only watch helplessly as you slay him with his own weapon. Carry on. (+10)	Showing absolute mastery, you engage your foe and immobilize him. Your follow up strike breaks his neck. Foe dies immediately. You have half the round left to act. (+25)

Key: ß×=must parry ß rounds; ß⊗=no parry for ß rounds; ß✿=stunned for ß rounds; ß♦=bleed ß hits per round; (-ß)=foe has -ß penalty; (+ß)=attacker gets +ß next round.

19.2 NERVE STRIKES CRITICAL STRIKE TABLE

	A	B	C	D	E
01-05	Bad form on your strike. You almost hurt yourself. +0H	Feeble attempt. You are glad your teacher is not here to see that. +0H	Strong attempt is blocked by foe. Better luck next time. +1H	Glancing strike. Foe seems unconcerned. +2H	You see a wonderful opening in your foe's defenses but you mistime your strike. +3H
06-10	You strike weakly. Better luck next time. +1H	You are being too cautious. +2H	Weak follow through on strike. +3H	Foe jumps back and avoids most of the force of your blow. +4H	Light strike on foe's arm hits a nerve cluster. Foe winces at the flash of pain. +6H
11-15	Foe blocks most of your strike, but you gain initiative next round. +2H	Unexpected strike causes foe to retreat. You gain initiative next round. +3H	Your cunning strike forces the foe to backpedal wildly to avoid your blow. You gain initiative next round. +5H	You manage to land a solid nerve strike against the upper arm of your foe. He winces in pain. +5H – (✕-10)	Powerful strike to foe's sternum knocks the air out of his lungs. You gain initiative for the next 3 rounds. + 6H – ✿
16-20	You delieiver a glancing blow. You have initiative next round. +4H	Well-placed kick strikes foe in the thigh. He is can only move with half move and you have initiative next round. +4H	Double strike to foe's upper torso causes his arms to go numb. You gain initiative next round. +7H – (✕-10)	Forceful blow just misses its target. Foe retreats back wairily. You have initiative for 2 rounds. +9H – (✕-20) – 4(-20)	Foe manages to avoid most of your attack but you still land a painful blow to the lower back. + 10H – ✿ – (-10)
21-30	Foe blocks your attempt, and steps back. He attempts to parry your next strike. +5H – ✕	Powerful strike to foe's sternum leaves him gasping for air. You gain initiative next round. +6H – ✕	Penetrating strike to the side of foe's ribs leaves him doubled over in pain. +8H – 6(-10)	Gouging strike to foe's side causes him to gasp in pain. +6H – 2✿	Spinning kick lands in foe's midsection. Foe is knocked down by the force of the blow. +6H – ✿ – (-10)
31-40	You manage to pentrate your foe's guard and delieiver a quick strike to his ribs. He circles you cautiously this round. +6H – (✕-10)	Elusive footwork after your attack leaves foe swinging at air. Carry on. You gain initiative next round. (parry -20) (✕-20)	Deliberate strike to foe's unguarded leg causes the leg to buckle. You have initiative the next 3 rounds. +7H – (✕-20) – 3(20)	Hammerhand strike to middle of foe's chest. Crack. Foe's ribs are badly bruised. +8H – 3✿ – (-20)	Knife hand strike to foe's upper arm causes him to drop his weapon. He cannot move his arm for one round. +4H – ✿
41-50	You maneuver around your foe and manage to land a hard blow to his back. +6H – 3(-10)	Glancing throat strike. Foe eyes you with anger. +5H – ✿ – 2(-20)	Crane fist strike to the side of the foe's head disorients him. He stumbles into the path of your next attack. +4H – ✿ – (+10)	Pinpoint strike to foe's upper shoulder causes his arm to go numb. Foe is bewildered by the result of your attack. +5H – ✿ – 3(-30)	Snake fist strike to foe's lower back causes him to lose feeling in his legs. Foe is restricted to one-quarter of movement for the next three rounds. 3✿ – 3(-40)
51-55	A fast stabbing knife hand strike to the chest causes your foe to stumble back, almost losing his balance. +3H – ✿ – (+10)	Painful strike on weapon arm. The muscle is bruised. +8H – ✿ – (-10)	You strike deeply through your foe's defenses. Foe leaps back to avoid your deadly follow-up strike. +8H – 2✿⊗ – (+20)	Deadly strike to foe's chest causes him to stumble backward. He sees his death in your eyes. Press your advantage. +6H – 2✿✕	Jab to foe's eyes causes him to flinch, leaving him open for your brutal throat strike. +7H – 2✿⊗ – (-20)
56-60	Twisting strike to foe's weapon arm bruises him deeply. Foe almost drops his weapon. He looks around for someone else to fight. +3H – ✿ – 6(-10)	Wheeling open-handed strike to foe's ear dazes him. +3H – 2✿ – 4(-10)	Textbook strike to foe's chest knocks him down. You can see the pain in your foe's eyes. +5H – 3✿ – (-10) – (+10)	Fierce double-handed strike to foe hits a vital point. Foe does not look good. +8H – 3✿ – 6(-20)	Precise darting attack causes foe to momentarily freeze in midst of combat. Take your advantage. +8H (stunned no parry for 2 rnds) +8H – 3✿⊗
61-65	Jabbing strike to foe's stomach causes him to double over in pain. +5H – ✿ – 3(-20)	You evade foe's attack and strike hard. +5H – 3✿ – 3(-30)	Lightning-fast strike slips through foe's guard. with chest armor: +8H without chest armor: +8H – 5✿	Fluid evasion followed by devastating strike racks foe with pain. You have great position for your next attack. +10H – 3✿ – (+25)	Classic phoenix fist puch to the chest causes foe to experience slight numbness throughout his body. +8H – 3✿⊗ – (-20)
66	Violent attack strikes foe in the leg. He stumbles and falls as his leg buckles underneath him. Foe suffers permanent nerve damage in his leg. +8H – 2✿ – (-50)	Powerful crane fist to foe's chest leaves him short of breath. He drops to his knees as he struggles to breathe. +12H – 6⊗ – (-20)	Devastating throat strike damages foe's vocal chords, he cannot speak. He passes out due to shock. Carry on. +12H – (-20)	Your precise attack pentrates your foe's guard and strikes a vital point. You make strange noises as your foe drops to the ground unconcious for the next 6 hours. +15H	Lightning fast attack strikes several vital points. Foe is paralyzed for the next 5 hours. You are fearsome. (+20)
67-70	Well-timed strike hits foe just as he was about to attack. Foe must roll on the appropriate fumble table. +4H – 2✿	You manage to inflict serious damage on foe's shoulder with your punishing attack. +6H – 2✿ – 2(-40)	You anticipate your foe's attack perfectly. Foe is completely out of position as a result. +5H – 2✿ – (-20)	Clever strike numbs nerve in foe's leg and he nearly falls to the ground. Foe is restricted to walking pace while his leg is numb. +8H – 3✿ – 6(-25)	Foe leaves himself open to your attack. You take advantage with a devastating knife hand strike to the eyes. Foe is partially blinded. 5✿⊗ – (-50)
71-75	Vicious clawing strike against foe's lower weapon arm. If he is not wearing greaves, he drops his weapon to the ground. +4H – ✿ – (-40) – (+10)	You show no mercy to your foe as you rain precise strikes at his body. Foe suffers greatly. +5H – 2✿ – (-25)	Leaping snap kick catches foe under his shoulder. Foe's entire arm goes numb and he drops his weapon. +8H – 2✿ – 2(-30)	Open-handed blow to foe's temple connects. Foe staggers and drops to his knees this round. +10H – 3✿⊗ – (-20)	Lethal dragon-claw fist inflicts massive damage to foe's leg. If foe has no armor he suffers major nerve damage to his leg (all movement rates are halved). with leg armor: +9H – 5✿ w/o leg armor: +9H – 5✿ – (-50)
76-80	Precise strike to foe's heip causes him to lose most of his feeling in his leg. +4H – 2✿ – 6(-10)	Jab to foe's lower back numbs both of foe's legs for three rounds. +5H – 3✿ – 3(-50)	Phoenix fist strike to foe's lower back paralyzes his legs for 2 rnds Foe drops to the ground. +6H – 2✿⊗ – 4(-30)	Pain-inducing strike to his arm causes foe to drop his weapon. +12H – 3✿⊗ – 3(-30)	Suddenly the words of your teacher make sense. You try your newfound knowledge on your foe. He is at your mercy. +5H – 8✿⊗
81-85	Strike to foe's stomach causes him intense pain. Foe drops his weapon. +5H – ✿⊗ – (+10)	Foe lets his guard down and you attack. Your elbow strike to his face breaks his nose and causes him to stagger back. +6H – 2✿⊗ – (-20)	Your strike catches foe in the lower chest. Your followup attack causes him to loose feeling in his upper body. Foe must roll a Fumble for his weapon. 3✿⊗ – (-25)	Double fist strike to foe's back paralyzes both of his arms for 6 rounds. You have him at your mercy. +10H – 3✿ – 6(-80)	Devastating combination strike manages to hit all of the foe's vital points. The foe immediately drops due to pain overload. +90H
86-90	Wheeling roundhouse kick breaks foe's nose. Your followup elbow strike hurts him even more. 3✿ – (-20)	Knife hand to foe's ear causes major damage. He is now partially deaf in that ear. Foe screams in pain. +8H – 5✿ – (-30)	Glancing strike paralyzes foe completely. Foe freezes for 6 rounds as he tries to regain control of his muscles. +10H – 6✿	Sweeping kick connects with foe's temple. Foe drops immediately and dies in 12 rounds. Foe is also bleeding internally. You assume a dangerous stance. +10H – 6♦	Powerful strike to foe's chest causes damage to his heart. Foe suffers a major heart attack and goes into cardiac arrest. Foe dies in 9 rounds. (-50)
91-95	Jab to foe's leg causes it to become paralyzed. Foe suffers major nerve damage to his leg and is very unhappy. +12H – 2✿⊗ – (-30)	You execute your strike perfectly. Foe suffers total loss of feeling in all extremities for one hour. +10H – 6✿ – (-50)	Violent double-handed strike to foe's ears shatters his eardrums. Foe is now deaf. +12H – 12✿⊗ – (-80)	You strike with the skill of your teaches. Foe does not even have time to wonder what happened. Foe drops immediately and is in a coma for 2 weeks. +15H	You sense your foe's weakness and strike. Foe is completely paralyzed. You easily disarm him and kill him with his own weapon. Carry on. +25H – (+10)
96-99	You strike foe with his own weapon after you disarm him. Foe is completely bewildered. 2✿⊗ – (+20)	Jabbing hand strike destroys foe's vocal cords. Foe goes into shock and drops. +12H – 12✿⊗ – (-80)	Unrestrained strike to foe's sternum shatters bone and bruises his heart. Foe suffers a mild heart attack and collapses. +16H – 24✿⊗	Snake fist strike penetrates foe's stomach and destroys his liver. Foe drops and dies in 9 rounds. +18H	Terrifying strike through both of foe's eyes blinds him and continues into the brain. Foe goes into shock and drops immediately. Foe dies due to internal hemorrhaging of the brain in 3 rounds. +20H
100	Palm strike to foe's forehead. If the foe is not wearing a helm, he is unconcious. +20H – 6✿⊗	You easily evade your foe's clumsy attack and strike with terrifying precision. Foe is blinded. +15H – 20✿ – (-100)	One finger strike to foe's sternum paralyzes him completely. Foe is at your mercy. Do what you wish. +20H	Foe does not have a chance. Your strike causes his body to go into convulsions. Foe is helpless and dies in 6 rounds. +20H	You duck under foe's strike and lightly tap him in the chest, disrupting the natural flow of energy in his body and causing his heart to stop. He stands in amazement and drops dead the next round. (+25)

Key: ß✕=must parry ß rounds; ß⊗=no parry for ß rounds; ß✿=stunned for ß rounds; ß♦=bleed ß hits per round; (-ß)=foe has -ß penalty; (+ß)=attacker gets +ß next round.

BODY RENEWAL

1. **Flow Stoppage I** — Reduces caster's bleeding by 1, as long as the caster concentrates or is immobile. For example, this will take a wound that is bleeding at a rate of 4 hits per round down to 3 hits per round. If the caster is suffering from multiple bleeding wounds, this only affects one of them.

2. **Clotting I** — As *Flow Stoppage* I, except after 1 hour the stoppage is permanent. If the caster is unconscious, this spell will operate without concentration.

3. **Stun Relief I** — Caster is relieved of 1 round's worth of accumulated stun.

4. **Pain Relief I** — Heals 1 hit per minute for as long as the caster concentrates. If the caster is unconscious, this spell will operate without concentration.

5. **Cut Repair I** — As *Clotting I*, except the permanent stoppage occurs immediately.

6. **Fracture Repair** — Concentrating with this spell for 2 hours per day for 1-20 days (depending on the severity) will repair a broken bone (not a shattered or destroyed bone).

7. **Muscle/Tendon Repair** — As *Fracture Repair*, except cut or damaged muscles or tendons may be repaired.

8. **Clotting III** — As *Clotting I*, except bleeding wounds can be reduced by 3.

9. **Stun Relief III** — As *Stun Relief I*, except 3 rounds are relieved.

10. **Resist Poison** — Delays the effect of poison as long as the caster concentrates.

11. **Pain Relief II** — As *Pain Relief I*, except heals 2 hits per minute.

12. **Vein/Artery Repair** — As *Fracture Repair*, except repairs a vein or artery.

13. **Cut Repair III** — As *Cut Repair I*, except bleeding wounds can be reduced by 3.

14. **Fracture Repair True** — As *Fracture Repair*, except repair only takes 2 hours of concentration for 1 day.

15. **Muscle/Tendon Repair True** — As *Fracture Repair True*, except cut or broken muscles can be repaired.

16. **Minor Nerve Repair** — Repairs minor damage to one nerve. Requires a 1 day recovery period. Minor damage is defined as any nerve damage that results in penalties up to -20.

17. **Eye/Ear Repair** — Concentrating with this spell for 2 hours per day for 1-10 days (depending on the severity) will repair any external damage to caster's ear (including ear loss) or eye (including corneal scratch, foreign objects, etc.).

18. **Self Joining** — Allows the caster to reattach a severed limb; limb is fully functional after 1-10 days (caster must concentrate with this spell for 2 hours each day).

19. **Neutralize Disease/Poison** — Has a 50% chance of neutralizing one disease or poison (modified by the potency of the disease or poison) if the caster concentrates for 1 hour or is unconscious for 1 hour. In any case, it delays the disease or poison as long as the caster can concentrate.

20. **Self Keeping** — Upon receiving a death blow, the caster goes into a state of suspended animation, until he is cured or his brain is destroyed.

25. **Clotting True** — As *Clotting I*, except stop all bleeding and is permanent after 1 minute of concentration for each hit stopped.

30. **Neutralize Disease/Poison True** — As *Neutralize Disease/Poison*, except caster can neutralize one disease and poison with 100% chance of success (modified by the potency of the disease and poison).

BODY RENEWAL

Lvl	Spell	Area of Effect	Duration	Range	Type
1)	Flow Stoppage I *	caster	varies	self	U
2)	Clotting I*	caster	varies	self	Us
3)	Stun Relief I *	caster	—	self	Us
4)	Pain Relief I *	caster	C	self	Us
5)	Cut Repair I	caster	—	self	U
6)	Fracture Repair	caster	varies	self	U
7)	Muscle/Tendon Repair	caster	varies	self	U
8)	Clotting III *	caster	varies	self	Us
9)	Stun Relief III *	caster	—	self	Us
10)	Resist Poison *	caster	C	self	Us
11)	Pain Relief II *	caster	C	self	Us
12)	Vein/Artery Repair	caster	varies	self	U
13)	Cut Repair III	caster	—	self	U
14)	Fracture Repair True	caster	varies	self	U
15)	Muscle/Tendon Repair True	caster	P(C)	self	U
16)	Minor Nerve Repair	caster	varies	self	U
17)	Eye/Ear Repair	caster	varies	self	U
18)	Self Joining *	caster	varies	self	U
19)	Neutralize Disease/Poison *	caster	varies	self	Us
20)	Self Keeping *	caster	varies	self	Us
25)	Clotting True *	caster	varies	self	Us
30)	Neutralize Disease/Poison True	caster	varies	self	Us
50)	Renewal True	caster	varies	self	Us

50. **Renewal True** — While in a trance (from the *Self Keeping* spell on this list), the caster can use the lower level healing spells on this list to repair himself.

SPECIAL NOTES

See Section 7.2 in *Spell Law* for additional notes regarding healing.

Note: *This list is identical to the Monk Base list with the same name.*

MARTIAL
ARTS
COMPANION

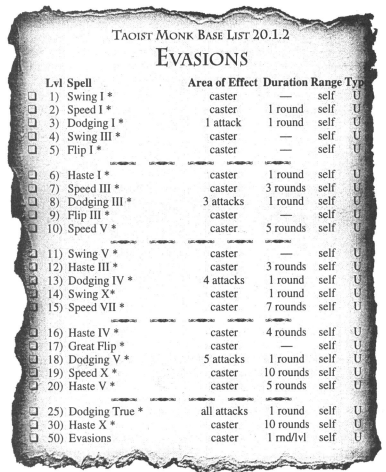

Taoist Monk Base List 20.1.2

Evasions

	Lvl	Spell	Area of Effect	Duration	Range	Typ
❑	1)	Swing I *	caster	—	self	U
❑	2)	Speed I *	caster	1 round	self	U
❑	3)	Dodging I *	1 attack	1 round	self	U
❑	4)	Swing III *	caster	—	self	U
❑	5)	Flip I *	caster	—	self	U
❑	6)	Haste I *	caster	1 round	self	U
❑	7)	Speed III *	caster	3 rounds	self	U
❑	8)	Dodging III *	3 attacks	1 round	self	U
❑	9)	Flip III *	caster	—	self	U
❑	10)	Speed V *	caster	5 rounds	self	U
❑	11)	Swing V *	caster	—	self	U
❑	12)	Haste III *	caster	3 rounds	self	U
❑	13)	Dodging IV *	4 attacks	1 round	self	U
❑	14)	Swing X*	caster	1 round	self	U
❑	15)	Speed VII *	caster	7 rounds	self	U
❑	16)	Haste IV *	caster	4 rounds	self	U
❑	17)	Great Flip *	caster	—	self	U
❑	18)	Dodging V *	5 attacks	1 round	self	U
❑	19)	Speed X *	caster	10 rounds	self	U
❑	20)	Haste V *	caster	5 rounds	self	U
❑	25)	Dodging True *	all attacks	1 round	self	U
❑	30)	Haste X *	caster	10 rounds	self	U
❑	50)	Evasions	caster	1 rnd/lvl	self	U

Evasions

1. **Swing I** — Allows caster to leap up to 10' vertically or laterally, grasp and swing from a fixed object, and land perfectly (up to 20' away from the object). The object could be a tree, branch, rafter, rope, chandelier, etc.

2. **Speed I** — Caster may act at twice his normal rate (i.e., 200% activity per round), but immediately afterwards, he must spend a number of rounds equal to the rounds speeded at half rate (i.e., only 50% activity per round).

3. **Dodging I** — Allows caster to dodge one non-spell attack (missile or melee) that occurs during the same round that this spell is cast. The caster must be able to see the attack (i.e. the attack cannot be from a foe to the rear or an invisible foe) and be must have room to dodge the attack; this results in the attack receiving a -50 modification.

4. **Swing III** — As *Swing I*, except three such maneuvers may be executed in rapid succession.

5. **Flip I** — Allows the caster to flip in any direction, landing up to 10' away (facing in any direction —no orientation roll required).

6. **Haste I** — As *Speed I*, except no half rate rounds are required.

7. **Speed III** — As *Speed I*, except duration is 3 rounds.

8. **Dodging III** — As *Dodging I*, except 3 attacks can be dodged.

9. **Flip III** — As *Flip I*, except the caster can execute three such maneuvers in rapid succession.

10. **Speed V** — As *Speed I*, except duration is 5 rounds.

11. **Swing V** — As *Swing I*, except five such maneuvers may be executed in rapid succession.

12. **Haste III** — As *Haste I*, except the duration is 3 rounds.

13. **Dodging IV** — As *Dodging I*, except 4 attacks can be dodged.

14. **Swing X** — As *Swing I*, except ten such maneuvers may be executed in rapid succession.

15. **Speed VII** — As *Speed I*, except duration is 7 rounds.

16. **Haste IV** — As *Haste I*, except the duration is 4 rounds.

17. **Great Flip** — As *Flip I*, except the total distance traveled is 1' per level.

18. **Dodging V** — As *Dodging I*, except 5 attacks can be dodged.

19. **Speed X** — As *Speed I*, except duration is 10 rounds.

20. **Haste V** — As *Haste I*, except the duration is 5 rounds.

25. **Dodging True** — As *Dodging I*, except all attacks can be dodged.

30. **Haste X** — As *Haste I*, except the duration is 10 rounds.

50. **Evasions** — Caster can use any one of the lower level non-*Speed/Haste* spells (on this list) each round.

Special Notes

See Section 7.1.24 in *Spell Law* for additional rules regarding *Speed* and *Haste* spells.

Note: *This list is identical to the Monk Base list with the same name.*

INNER EYE

1. **Meditation Trance** — Caster gains a special +25 modifier to all Meditation static maneuver rolls.

2. **Nightvision** — Caster can see 100' on a normal night as if it were daylight.

3. **Sidevision** — Caster has a 300 degree field of vision. The flank bonus for attacks against the caster is lowered to +5 and the rear bonus is lowered to +15.

4. **Sense Harmony** — Caster can sense if the "natural order" of the world is in harmony within the area of effect. The caster can determine if a man-made object is placed in a harmonious manner with the landscape, etc.

5. **Watervision** — Caster can see 100' in any water (including murky water) as if were daylight.

6. **Fogvision** — Caster can see 100' in any precipitation (including thick fog) as if it were daylight.

7. **Sense Disharmony** — Caster can sense if there is a disharmony in the "natural order" of the world within the area of effect. The caster gets an impression of something wrong, but not the reason why. For example, the caster could sense that magical effects were altering nature, or that some curse lay upon the area, etc.

8. **Darkvision** — As *Nightvision*, except any darkness can be seen through. Also no light is needed to make this spell work.

9. **Detect Invisible** — Detects any invisible object in the area of effect. Caster can concentrate on a different 5' radius each round.

10. **Detect Illusion** — Caster can check one object or place (up to 5' R) and tell if it is an illusion or has an illusion on it.

11. **Sense Spirits** — Caster can sense if spirits or elementals are within range. This spell does not give the caster the ability to communicate with the spirits or elementals,

12. **Disillusion** — One illusion within the area of effect ceases to exist.

13. **Awake** — Awakens caster from any unnatural sleep (e.g., *Sleep* spell, sleeping drug, etc.). Caster takes one round to awaken.

14. **Sense Disharmony True** — As *Sense Disharmony*, except for the duration and range.

15. **See Invisible** — Caster can see all invisible things anywhere that he can normally see. In addition, he suffers no penalties against invisible targets (as they are not invisible to him).

TAOIST MONK BASE LIST 20.1.3
INNER EYE

Lvl	Spell	Area of Effect	Duration	Range	Type
1)	Meditation Trance	caster	—	self	U
2)	Nightvision	caster	10 min/lvl	self	U
3)	Sidevision	caster	10 min/lvl	self	U
4)	Sense Harmony	1' R/lvl	1 min/lvl (C)	50'	U
5)	Watervision	caster	10 min/lvl	self	U
6)	Fogvision	caster	10 min/lvl	self	U
7)	Sense Disharmony	1' R/lvl	—	50'	U
8)	Darkvision	caster	10 min/lvl	self	U
9)	Detect Invisible	5' R	1 min/lvl (C)	100'	U
10)	Detect Illusion	5' R	—	100'	U
11)	Sense Spirits	5' R	1 min/lvl (C)	100'	U
12)	Disillusion	100' R	—	self	U
13)	Awake *	caster	—	self	U
14)	Sense Disharmony True	1' R/lvl	1 rnd/lvl	100'	U
15)	See Invisible	caster	10 min/lvl	self	U
16)	Woodsight	caster	C	self	U
17)	Long Vision	caster	10 min/lvl	self	U
18)	Illusionsight	caster	1 min/lvl	self	U
19)	Stonesight	caster	C	self	U
20)	Taovision	caster	10 min/lvl	self	U
25)	Conveyance	caster	1 min/lvl	self	U
30)	Metalsight	caster	C	self	U
50)	Taosense	caster	1 rnd/lvl	self	U

16. **Woodsight** — Caster can see through wood (up to 1" per level).

17. **Long Vision** — As any of the lower level *Vision* spells on this list but without a range limit (i.e., they allow the caster to see anywhere he could normally see).

18. **Illusionsight** — Caster cannot see any visual illusions. This does not affect any of the other senses.

19. **Stonesight** — Caster can see through stone (up to 1" per level).

20. **Taovision** — As all lower level *Vision* spells functioning at the same time.

25. **Conveyance** — Caster's awareness leaves his body (which is inactive for the duration of this spell) and may travel at a rate of 1 mile per minute. However, it can only travel 10' per round when moving through solid material or observing the real world. If the spell expires before the caster returns to his physical body, he will return to his body at the fixed rate of 500' per round and upon returning to his body, he must make a RR modified by -50 or die (the attack level is equal to the number of rounds overstayed).

30. **Metalsight** — As *Stonesight*, except any metal can be seen through.

50. **Taosense** — Caster may use any one of the lower level spells (on this list) each round.

SPECIAL NOTES

See Section 7.1.19 in *Spell Law* for more information on the environment's effects on vision.

MARTIAL
ARTS
COMPANION

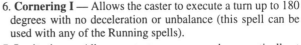

MONK'S BRIDGE

Lvl Spell	Area of Effect	Duration	Range	Typ
1) Leaping I *	caster	1 round	self	U
2) Landing *	caster	varies	self	U
3) Traction	caster	10 min/lvl	self	U
4) Edgerunning	caster	1 min/lvl	self	U
5) Leaping III *	caster	1 round	self	U
6) Cornering I *	caster	—	self	U
7) Levitation	caster	1min/lvl	self	U
8) Landing True *	caster	varies	self	U
9) Wallwalking	caster	1 min/lvl (C)	self	U
10) Great Leap *	caster	1 round	self	U
11) Cornering III *	caster	1 round	self	U
12) Wall Flip *	caster	—	self	U
13) Wallrunning	caster	1 min/lvl (C)	self	U
14) Fluidrunning	caster	1 min/lvl (C)	self	U
15) Breezerunning	caster	1 min/lvl (C)	self	U
16) Earthwalking	caster	1 rnd/lvl (C)	self	U
17) Fluidrunning True	caster	1 min/lvl (C)	self	U
18) Breezerunning True	caster	1 min/lvl (C)	self	U
19) Ceilingwalking	caster	C	self	U
20) Run True	caster	1 rnd/lvl	self	U
25) Ceilingrunning	caster	C	self	U
30) Earthrunning	caster	1 rnd/lvl (C)	self	U
50) Monk's Bridge	caster	1 rnd/lvl	self	U

MONK'S BRIDGE

1. **Leaping I** — Allows the caster to leap 50' laterally or 20' vertically in the round that the spell is cast.

2. **Landing** — Allows the caster to land safely in a fall up to 20' per level, and to take that distance off the severity of any longer fall.

3. **Traction** — Caster can run on even, unstable surfaces (sand, ice, etc.) as he would on a hard stable surface.

4. **Edgerunning** — Caster can run on even, narrow (at least 2" wide) surfaces as if he were on normal ground.

5. **Leaping III** — As *Leaping I*, except the caster can execute three "leaps" in succession. Each leap must be within 90 degrees of the last leap's direction.

6. **Cornering I** — Allows the caster to execute a turn up to 180 degrees with no deceleration or unbalance (this spell can be used with any of the Running spells).

7. **Levitation** — Allows caster to move up or down vertically at a rate of 10' per round. Horizontal movement is only possible by normal means.

8. **Landing True** — As *Landing*, except caster can land safely from any fall 99% of the time.

9. **Wall-walking** — Caster can walk on solid surfaces up to 90 degrees as if he were on normal ground.

10. **Great Leap** — As *Leaping I*, except limit is 10' per level laterally and 5' per level vertically.

11. **Cornering III** — As *Cornering I*, except caster may execute three such turns in one round.

12. **Wall Flip** — If the caster has a wall within 10', he can leap up to the wall, bounce off and land up to 25' from the wall (facing any direction – no orientation roll required).

13. **Wallrunning** — As *Wallwalking*, except caster may run.

14. **Fluidrunning** — Caster may run on any calm fluid surface as if on level ground.

15. **Breezerunning** — Caster can run on air if there is a wind blowing. However, he cannot run into the wind, and when running in any other direction, the wind's speed will modify his movement rate (i.e., like the effect of wind on a sail boat).

16. **Earthwalking** — Caster can walk just underneath the surface of the ground. Loosely packed ground will betray the caster's direction of movement. The caster cannot go deeper into the ground than his body height. In addition, this spell will not function in hard rocky soil.

17. **Fluidrunning True** — Caster can run on any fluid surface as if on level ground, regardless of turbulence.

18. **Breezerunning True** — As *Breezerunning*, except caster may run against the wind, and his movement rate is unaffected by the wind speed.

19. **Ceilingwalking** — Caster can walk on any solid surfaces as if he were on normal ground (includes ceilings).

20. **Run True** — Caster use any of the lower level *Running* spells once per round.

25. **Ceilingrunning** — As *Ceilingwalking*, except caster may run.

30. **Earthrunning** — As *Earthwalking*, except caster may run.

50. **Monk's Bridge** — Caster can use any one of the lower level spells (on this list) each round.

SPECIAL NOTE

See Section 7.1.12 in *Spell Law* for more information on encumbrance limits for spells.

Note: *This list is identical to the Monk Base list with the same name.*

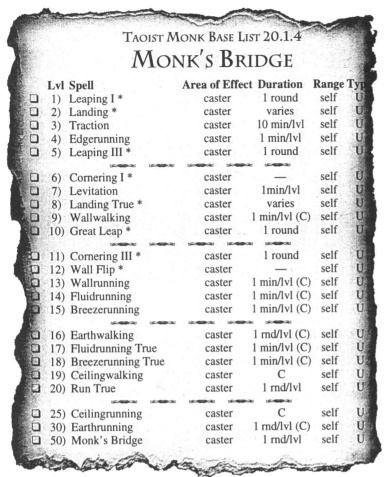

NATURE'S FORMS

1. **Fury of the Tiger I** — Caster gets a +5 bonus to all unarmed attacks.

2. **Cunning of the Fox** — Caster gains increased sense of hearing and smell like those of a fox. Adds +50 to Awareness maneuvers with only those senses; +20 to Awareness maneuvers using these senses combined with others.

3. **Coil of the Snake I** — Caster may roll one extra die for initiative and choose which ones he wants to use.

4. **Eyes of the Eagle** — Caster gains an increased sense of sight like that of an eagle. Adds +50 to awareness maneuvers using only sight; +20 if using sight combined with other senses.

5. **Lash of the Dragon I** — Caster can strike an inanimate object and deliver damage to it (taking no damage himself). Caster makes a normal Martial Arts Strikes attack against the object. In addition, there is a chance that the object will break if it has any flaws (e.g., cracks, fractures, etc.) in it. The chance is equal to 10% plus 1% per degree of severity of the critical delivered in the attack (i.e., 'A' critical = 11%, 'B' critical = 12%, etc.). This chance is modified by +10% to +50%, depending on the severity of the flaws.

6. **Coil of the Snake II** — As *Coil of the Snake I*, except caster may roll two extra die.

7. **Strength of the Bear II** — In melee, the caster does double normal concussion hits and his Strength stat bonus is doubled.

8. **Fury of the Tiger II** — As *Fury of the Tiger I*, except bonus is +10.

9. **Shell of the Turtle III** — For the duration of this spell, the caster's skin is treated as AT 3 (this is only effective if the caster is wearing no armor at all).

10. **Heart of the Tiger** — The caster may ignore the effects of the next critical strike made against him. At the end of this spell's duration, all effects apply normally. Only one wound can be ignored in this fashion at a time (i.e., the caster cannot have more than one *Heart of the Tiger* spell active at any given time).

11. **Coil of the Snake III** — As *Coil of the Snake I*, except caster may roll three extra die

12. **Lash of the Dragon II** — As *Lash of the Dragon I*, except chance of breakage is equal to 25% plus 3% per degree of severity of the critical delivered in the attack (i.e., 'A' critical = 28%, 'B' critical = 31%, etc.). This chance is modified by +10% to +50%, depending on the severity of the flaws.

13. **Precision of the Crane** — Caster's next attack this round becomes more precise. If the attack delivers a critical, the critical roll is modified by +/-5 by the caster.

14. **Strength of the Bear III** — As *Strength of the Bear II*, except caster does triple normal concussion hit damage and his Strength stat bonus is tripled.

15. **Fury of the Tiger III** — As *Fury of the Tiger I*, except bonus is +15.

16. **Shell of the Turtle IV** — As *Shell of the Turtle III*, except the caster's skin is treated as AT 4.

17. **Coil of the Snake IV** — As *Coil of the Snake I*, except caster may roll four extra die.

18. **Lash of the Dragon III** — As *Lash of the Dragon I*, except chance of breakage is equal to 40% plus 6% per degree of severity of the critical delivered in the attack (i.e., 'A' critical = 46%, 'B' critical = 52%, etc.). This chance is modified by +10% to +50%, depending on the severity of the flaws.

19. **Fury of the Tiger IV** — As *Fury of the Tiger I*, except bonus is +20.

20. **Wrath of the Dragon** — Caster's unarmed attack this round will do an additional elemental critical of equal severity (same roll) to the martial arts critical (if any). For purposes of special defenses, this attack will count as magical. The elemental

TAOIST MONK BASE LIST 20.1.5

NATURE'S FORMS

Lvl Spell	Area of Effect	Duration	Range	Type
1) Fury of the Tiger I	caster	1 rnd/lvl	self	U
2) Cunning of the Fox	caster	1 min/lvl	self	U
3) Coil of the Snake I *	caster	1 round	self	U
4) Eyes of the Eagle	caster	1 min/lvl	self	U
5) Lash of the Dragon I	caster	—	self	U
6) Coil of the Snake II *	caster	1 round	self	U
7) Strength of the Bear II	caster	1 round	self	U
8) Fury of the Tiger II	caster	1 rnd/lvl	self	U
9) Shell of the Turtle III	caster	1 rnd/lvl	self	U
10) Heart of the Tiger	caster	1 min/lvl	self	U
11) Coil of the Snake III *	caster	1 round	self	U
12) Lash of the Dragon II	caster	—	self	U
13) Precision of the Crane *	caster	—	self	U
14) Strength of the Bear III	caster	1 round	self	U
15) Fury of the Tiger III	caster	1 rnd/lvl	self	U
16) Shell of the Turtle IV	caster	1 rnd/lvl	self	U
17) Coil of the Snake IV *	caster	1 round	self	U
18) Lash of the Dragon III	caster	—	self	U
19) Fury of the Tiger IV	caster	1 rnd/lvl	self	U
20) Wrath of the Dragon *	caster	—	self	U
25) Fury of the Tiger True	caster	1 rnd/lvl	self	U
30) Strength of the Bear IV	caster	1 round	self	U
50) Master of Forms	caster	1 rnd/lvl	self	U

critical can be either heat, cold, lightning, or impact. The caster must chose one elemental effect when the spell is developed and cannot change it.

25. **Fury of the Tiger True** — As *Fury of the Tiger I*, except bonus is +30.

30. **Strength of the Bear IV** — As *Strength of the Bear II*, except caster does quadruple normal concussion hit damage and his Strength stat bonus is quadrupled.

50. **Master of Forms** — Caster can use any of the lower level spells (from this list) once per round.

MARTIAL
ARTS
COMPANION

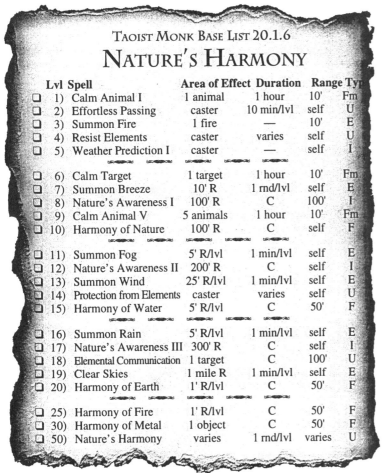

Nature's Harmony

Lvl	Spell	Area of Effect	Duration	Range	Typ
☐ 1)	Calm Animal I	1 animal	1 hour	10'	Fm
☐ 2)	Effortless Passing	caster	10 min/lvl	self	U
☐ 3)	Summon Fire	1 fire	—	10'	E
☐ 4)	Resist Elements	caster	varies	self	U
☐ 5)	Weather Prediction I	caster	—	self	I
☐ 6)	Calm Target	1 target	1 hour	10'	Fm
☐ 7)	Summon Breeze	10' R	1 rnd/lvl	self	E
☐ 8)	Nature's Awareness I	100' R	C	100'	I
☐ 9)	Calm Animal V	5 animals	1 hour	10'	Fm
☐ 10)	Harmony of Nature	100' R	C	self	F
☐ 11)	Summon Fog	5' R/lvl	1 min/lvl	self	E
☐ 12)	Nature's Awareness II	200' R	C	self	I
☐ 13)	Summon Wind	25' R/lvl	1 min/lvl	self	E
☐ 14)	Protection from Elements	caster	varies	self	U
☐ 15)	Harmony of Water	5' R/lvl	C	50'	F
☐ 16)	Summon Rain	5' R/lvl	1 min/lvl	self	E
☐ 17)	Nature's Awareness III	300' R	C	self	I
☐ 18)	Elemental Communication	1 target	C	100'	U
☐ 19)	Clear Skies	1 mile R	1 min/lvl	self	E
☐ 20)	Harmony of Earth	1' R/lvl	C	50'	F
☐ 25)	Harmony of Fire	1' R/lvl	C	50'	F
☐ 30)	Harmony of Metal	1 object	C	50'	F
☐ 50)	Nature's Harmony	varies	1 rnd/lvl	varies	U

Nature's Harmony

1. **Calm Animal I** — Caster can calm one animal to a passive, non-threatening state. The animal will remain calm until provoked, or until one hour passes. This spell ceases if the animal is provoked.

2. **Effortless Passing** — Caster can move through undergrowth and forested areas with little hindrance. Any attempts to track the caster are modified by -20 to represent the difficulty in finding his trail.

3. **Summon Fire** — Caster can summon a small flame. Once summoned, this fire acts in all other manners as normal, non-magical fire (e.g., it will go out if it runs out of fuel, etc.).

4. **Resist Elements** — Caster is protected from natural heat up to 170° F and natural cold down to 20° F (treat as if caster was in 70° F temperature). For temperatures above 170° F, subtract 100° F to determine the effective temperature for the caster. For temperatures below 20° F, add 50° F to determine the effective temperature for the caster. Caster also receives +20 to all RRs versus heat spells and heat attacks (+20 DB versus elemental fire and heat attacks); as well as +20 to all RRs versus cold spells and ice attacks (+20 DB versus elemental cold and ice attacks). The duration of this spell is 10 minutes per level of the caster if the caster does not move. If the caster moves, the spell will last as long as the caster concentrates.

5. **Weather Prediction I** — Gives caster a 95% chance of predicting the time, type, and severity of the weather over the next 24 hour period.

6. **Calm Target** — As *Calm Animal I*, except this spell may effect any one man-sized target.

7. **Summon Breeze** — Caster causes a breeze to come forth that will drive out any gaseous matter (cloud, etc.) Once set, the direction of the breeze will not change.

8. **Nature's Awareness I** — Caster can monitor animate activity in the area (e.g., he will be aware of subtle movements). For the duration of the spell, the caster cannot move.

9. **Calm Animal V** — As *Calm Animal I*, except this spell can effect 5 animals.

10. **Harmony of Nature** — Caster can attempt to influence environmental conditions (e.g., precipitation, wind, temperature, etc.) back to their natural state (GM's discretion).

11. **Summon Fog** — Caster causes fog to arrive that obscures all vision in and through the area of effect.

12. **Nature's Awareness II** — As *Nature's Awareness I*, except for area of effect.

13. **Summon Wind** — Caster can control the wind speed by 1 mph x his level. He can increase or decrease the wind speed as desired. By directing the wind speed against missile attacks, they receive a special -1 modifier per 1 mph of the wind speed. Note that the caster can also control the direction or flow of gases or clouds.

14. **Protection from Elements** — Caster is protected from any natural heat or cold (treat as if caster was in 70° temperature). Caster also receives +40 to all RRs versus *fire/ice* spells and *heat/cold* attacks (+40 DB versus elemental attacks). The duration of this spell is 10 minutes per level of the caster if the caster does not move. If the caster moves, the spell will last as long as the caster concentrates.

15. **Harmony of Water** — Caster can attempt to calm the activity of water within the area of effect.

16. **Summon Rain** — Caster causes rain or snow (depending on the temperature) to fall. The rain or snow obscures vision into the radius by 25% and modifies all missile attacks passing through any part of the area by -25.

17. **Nature's Awareness II** — As *Nature's Awareness I*, except for area of effect.

18. **Elemental Communication** — The caster can communicate with any elemental force within range. The elemental force must be able to communicate with the caster (i.e., this spell does not confer communication abilities upon the force).

19. **Clear Skies** — Caster can make the skies clear of haze, precipitation, clouds, etc. This spell will not affect the wind.

20. **Harmony of Earth** — Caster can attempt to influence the structure and properties of the earth within his area of effect. The caster can cause the earth to become packed/loose or dry/muddy. The caster may also attempt to strengthen walls/structures that have cracks or flaws within them.

25. **Harmony of Fire** — Caster can attempt to influence the activity of all fires within the area of effect. The fires can be influenced to burn hotter or to cool down (or extinguish).

30. **Harmony of Metal** — Caster can attempt to influence the structure and properties of one metal object. The object must be smaller than 10 cubic feet in volume. The metal object can be strengthened/weakened or made malleable if desired. Breakage numbers, reliability numbers, and/or strengths should be adjusted appropriately.

50. **Nature's Harmony** — Caster can use one lower level spell (on this list) each round.

Special Notes

All weather generating and environmental changing spells occur gradually over a period of one minute. In addition, those spells that affect weather have no effect in areas where there are not normally occurring weather patterns (e.g., inside buildings, etc.).

Body Renewal

1. **Flow Stoppage I** — Reduces caster's bleeding by 1, as long as the caster concentrates or is immobile. For example, this will take a wound that is bleeding at a rate of 4 hits per round down to 3 hits per round. If the caster is suffering from multiple bleeding wounds, this only affects one of them.

2. **Clotting I** — As *Flow Stoppage I*, except after 1 hour the stoppage is permanent. If the caster is unconscious, this spell will operate without concentration.

3. **Stun Relief I** — Caster is relieved of 1 round's worth of accumulated stun.

4. **Pain Relief I** — Heals 1 hit per minute for as long as the caster concentrates. If the caster is unconscious, this spell will operate without concentration.

5. **Cut Repair I** — As *Clotting I*, except the permanent stoppage occurs immediately.

6. **Fracture Repair** — Concentrating with this spell for 2 hours per day for 1-20 days (depending on the severity) will repair a broken bone (not a shattered or destroyed bone).

7. **Muscle/Tendon Repair** — As *Fracture Repair*, except cut or damaged muscles or tendons may be repaired.

8. **Clotting III** — As *Clotting I*, except bleeding wounds can be reduced by 3.

9. **Stun Relief III** — As *Stun Relief I*, except 3 rounds are relieved.

10. **Resist Poison** — Delays the effect of poison as long as the caster concentrates.

11. **Pain Relief II** — As *Pain Relief I*, except heals 2 hits per minute.

12. **Vein/Artery Repair** — As *Fracture Repair*, except repairs a vein or artery.

13. **Cut Repair III** — As *Cut Repair I*, except bleeding wounds can be reduced by 3.

14. **Fracture Repair True** — As *Fracture Repair*, except repair only takes 2 hours of concentration for 1 day.

15. **Muscle/Tendon Repair True** — As *Fracture Repair True*, except cut or broken muscles can be repaired.

16. **Minor Nerve Repair** — Repairs minor damage to one nerve. Requires a 1 day recovery period. Minor damage is defined as any nerve damage that results in penalties up to -20.

BODY RENEWAL

Lvl	Spell	Area of Effect	Duration	Range	Type
1)	Flow Stoppage I *	caster	varies	self	U
2)	Clotting I*	caster	varies	self	Us
3)	Stun Relief I *	caster	—	self	Us
4)	Pain Relief I *	caster	C	self	Us
5)	Cut Repair I	caster	—	self	U
6)	Fracture Repair	caster	varies	self	U
7)	Muscle/Tendon Repair	caster	varies	self	U
8)	Clotting III *	caster	varies	self	Us
9)	Stun Relief III *	caster	—	self	Us
10)	Resist Poison *	caster	C	self	Us
11)	Pain Relief II *	caster	C	self	Us
12)	Vein/Artery Repair	caster	varies	self	U
13)	Cut Repair III	caster	—	self	U
14)	Fracture Repair True	caster	varies	self	U
15)	Muscle/Tendon Repair True	caster	P(C)	self	U
16)	Minor Nerve Repair	caster	varies	self	U
17)	Eye/Ear Repair	caster	varies	self	U
18)	Self Joining *	caster	varies	self	U
19)	Neutralize Disease/Poison *	caster	varies	self	Us
20)	Self Keeping *	caster	varies	self	Us
25)	Clotting True *	caster	varies	self	Us
30)	Neutralize Disease/Poison True	caster	varies	self	Us
50)	Renewal True	caster	varies	self	Us

17. **Eye/Ear Repair** — Concentrating with this spell for 2 hours per day for 1-10 days (depending on the severity) will repair any external damage to caster's ear (including ear loss) or eye (including corneal scratch, foreign objects, etc.).

18. **Self Joining** — Allows the caster to reattach a severed limb; limb is fully functional after 1-10 days (caster must concentrate with this spell for 2 hours each day).

19. **Neutralize Disease/Poison** — Has a 50% chance of neutralizing one disease or poison (modified by the potency of the disease or poison) if the caster concentrates for 1 hour or is unconscious for 1 hour. In any case, it delays the disease or poison as long as the caster can concentrate.

20. **Self Keeping** — Upon receiving a death blow, the caster goes into a state of suspended animation, until he is cured or his brain is destroyed.

25. **Clotting True** — As *Clotting I*, except stop all bleeding and is permanent after 1 minute of concentration for each hit stopped.

30. **Neutralize Disease/Poison True** — As *Neutralize Disease/Poison*, except caster can neutralize one disease and poison with 100% chance of success (modified by the potency of the disease and poison).

50. **Renewal True** — While in a trance (from the *Self Keeping* spell on this list), the caster can use the lower level healing spells on this list to repair himself.

SPECIAL NOTES

See Section 7.2 in *Spell Law* for additional notes regarding healing.

> **Note:** *This list is identical to the Monk Base list with the same name.*

MARTIAL
ARTS
COMPANION

Zen Monk Base List 20.2.2
Evasions

Lvl	Spell	Area of Effect	Duration	Range	Typ
1)	Swing I *	caster	—	self	U
2)	Speed I *	caster	1 round	self	U
3)	Dodging I *	1 attack	1 round	self	U
4)	Swing III *	caster	—	self	U
5)	Flip I *	caster	—	self	U
6)	Haste I *	caster	1 round	self	U
7)	Speed III *	caster	3 rounds	self	U
8)	Dodging III *	3 attacks	1 round	self	U
9)	Flip III *	caster	—	self	U
10)	Speed V *	caster	5 rounds	self	U
11)	Swing V *	caster	—	self	U
12)	Haste III *	caster	3 rounds	self	U
13)	Dodging IV *	4 attacks	1 round	self	U
14)	Swing X*	caster	1 round	self	U
15)	Speed VII *	caster	7 rounds	self	U
16)	Haste IV *	caster	4 rounds	self	U
17)	Great Flip *	caster	—	self	U
18)	Dodging V *	5 attacks	1 round	self	U
19)	Speed X *	caster	10 rounds	self	U
20)	Haste V *	caster	5 rounds	self	U
25)	Dodging True *	all attacks	1 round	self	U
30)	Haste X *	caster	10 rounds	self	U
50)	Evasions	caster	1 rnd/lvl	self	U

Evasions

1. **Swing I** — Allows caster to leap up to 10' vertically or laterally, grasp and swing from a fixed object, and land perfectly (up to 20' away from the object). The object could be a tree, branch, rafter, rope, chandelier, etc.

2. **Speed I** — Caster may act at twice his normal rate (i.e., 200% activity per round), but immediately afterwards, he must spend a number of rounds equal to the rounds speeded at half rate (i.e., only 50% activity per round).

3. **Dodging I** — Allows caster to dodge one non-spell attack (missile or melee) that occurs during the same round that this spell is cast. The caster must be able to see the attack (i.e. the attack cannot be from a foe to the rear or an invisible foe) and be must have room to dodge the attack; this results in the attack receiving a -50 modification.

4. **Swing III** — As *Swing I*, except three such maneuvers may be executed in rapid succession.

5. **Flip I** — Allows the caster to flip in any direction, landing up to 10' away (facing in any direction — no orientation roll required).

6. **Haste I** — As *Speed I*, except no half rate rounds are required.

7. **Speed III** — As *Speed I*, except duration is 3 rounds.

8. **Dodging III** — As *Dodging I*, except 3 attacks can be dodged.

9. **Flip III** — As *Flip I*, except the caster can execute three such maneuvers in rapid succession.

10. **Speed V** — As *Speed I*, except duration is 5 rounds.

11. **Swing V** — As *Swing I*, except five such maneuvers may be executed in rapid succession.

12. **Haste III** — As *Haste I*, except the duration is 3 rounds.

13. **Dodging IV** — As Dodging I, except 4 attacks can be dodged.

14. **Swing X** — As *Swing I*, except ten such maneuvers may be executed in rapid succession.

15. **Speed VII** — As *Speed I*, except duration is 7 rounds.

16. **Haste IV** — As *Haste I*, except the duration is 4 rounds.

17. **Great Flip** — As *Flip I*, except the total distance traveled is 1' per level.

18. **Dodging V** — As *Dodging I*, except 5 attacks can be dodged.

19. **Speed X** — As *Speed I*, except duration is 10 rounds.

20. **Haste V** — As *Haste I*, except the duration is 5 rounds.

25. **Dodging True** — As *Dodging I*, except all attacks can be dodged.

30. **Haste X** — As *Haste I*, except the duration is 10 rounds.

50. **Evasions** — Caster can use any one of the lower level non-*Speed/Haste* spells (on this list) each round.

SPECIAL NOTES
See Section 7.1.24 in *Spell Law* for additional rules regarding *Speed* and *Haste* spells.

Note: *This list is identical to the Monk Base list with the same name.*

MARTIAL
ARTS
COMPANION

ZEN AWARENESS

1. **Sly Ears** — Caster gains double normal hearing. This results in +50 to Awareness maneuvers only involving hearing, +25 to Awareness maneuvers involving hearing and other senses.

2. **Meditation Trance** — Caster gains a special +25 modifier to one Meditation static maneuvers this round.

3. **Sidevision** — Caster has a 300° field of vision. The flank bonus for attacks against the caster is lowered to +5 and the rear bonus is lowered to +15.

4. **Inner Perception II** — Caster gains insight or facts by observing a person or thing with intense concentration. Gives the caster a +20 modification to applicable Awareness maneuvers.

5. **Intuitions I** — Caster gains a vision of what will probably happen within the next minute if he takes a specified action.

6. **Detect Illusion** — Caster can check one object or place (up to a 5' R) and tell if it is an illusion or has an illusion on it.

7. **Sense Hostility** — Caster is aware of any being within the area of effect that has hostile intentions towards him. The hostility must be directed specifically at the caster or the spell reveals nothing. The being's hostility must be active (i.e., driving the being to perform aggressive actions), not passive (i.e., hate exists, but no action is planned).

8. **Touch** — Caster gains extreme tactile sensitivity. This results in a bonus to all actions that require a sense of touch. For example, the caster might receive a +25 bonus for picking locks, disarming traps, opening secret doors, etc. In addition, this spell confers a +50 bonus to Awareness maneuvers involving only touch, +25 to Awareness maneuvers involving touch and other senses.

9. **Recall** — Caster gets a 25% chance of recalling some key fact or occurrence that he has experienced. This information should relate to the current situation (could be from his background or something that he has forgotten, GM's discretion). This spell gives the caster a +25 modification to his Memory stat bonus for one maneuver (e.g., the use of a Lore skill, one hand of a card game, etc.).

10. **Inner Perception V** — Caster gains insight or facts by observing a person or thing with intense concentration. Gives the caster a +50 modification to his applicable Awareness maneuver.

11. **Intuitions II** — As *Intuitions I*, except caster gets to gaze 2 minutes into the future.

ZEN MONK BASE LIST 20.2.3
ZEN AWARENESS

Lvl	Spell	Area of Effect	Duration	Range	Type
1)	Sly Ears *	caster	10 min/lvl	self	U
2)	Meditation Trance	caster	—	self	U
3)	Sidevision	caster	10 min/lvl	self	U
4)	Inner Perception III	caster	varies	self	U
5)	Intuitions I	caster	—	self	I
6)	Detect Illusion	5' R	—	100'	U
7)	Sense Hostility	10' R	—	10'	I
8)	Touch *	caster	10 min/lvl	self	U
9)	Recall	caster	varies	self	U
10)	Inner Perception V	caster	varies	self	U
11)	Intuitions II	caster	—	self	I
12)	Awake *	caster	—	self	Us
13)	Sense Hostility True	10' R/lvl	1 min/lvl (C)	10'/lvl	I
14)	Disillusion	100' R	1 min/lvl	self	U
15)	Inner Perception VII	caster	varies	self	U
16)	Detect Illusion True	5' R	1 min/lvl (C)	100'	U
17)	Intuitions V	caster	—	self	I
18)	Disillusion True	caster	1 min/lvl	self	U
19)	Meditative Sleep	caster	varies	self	U
20)	Inner Perception True	caster	varies	self	U
25)	Intuitions True	caster	—	self	I
30)	Total Recall	caster	varies	self	U
50)	Awareness True	caster	1 rnd/lvl	varies	U

12. **Awake** — Awakens caster from any unnatural sleep (e.g., *Sleep* spell, sleeping drug, etc.). Caster takes one round to awaken.

13. **Sense Hostility True** — As *Sense Hostility*, except for area of effect, duration, and range.

14. **Disillusion** — For the duration of the spell, one illusion within the area of effect ceases to exist (for the caster only). Caster must know that something is an illusion before this spell is cast.

15. **Inner Perception VII** — Caster gains insight or facts by observing a person or thing with intense concentration. Gives the caster a +70 modification to his applicable Awareness maneuvers.

16. **Detect Illusion True** — As *Detect Illusion*, except caster can check one object or place per round.

17. **Intuitions V** — As *Intuitions I*, except caster gets to gaze 5 minutes into the future.

18. **Disillusion True** — As *Disillusion*, except all illusions within range cease to exist for the caster. Caster need not be aware of any illusions within the range before casting this spell.

19. **Meditative Sleep** — During normal sleep, the caster may make Perception rolls (that are not based on sight), at no penalty.

20. **Inner Perception True** — Caster gains insight or facts by observing a person or thing with intense concentration. Gives the caster a +100 modification to his applicable Awareness maneuvers.

25. **Intuitions True** — As *Intuitions I*, except time limit extends 1 minute per level into the future.

30. **Total Recall** — As *Recall*, except recall is nearly automatic and, in effect, gives the caster a photographic memory. Memory stat bonus modification is +50.

50. **Awareness True** — The caster can use one of the lower level spells on this list each round.

MARTIAL
ARTS
COMPANION

Zen Monk Base List 20.2.4
ZEN FOCUS

Lvl	Spell	Area of Effect	Duration	Range	Typ
☐ 1)	Body Weaponry I	caster	1 rnd/lvl	self	U
☐ 2)	Nerve Strike I *	1 target	1 rnd/10 fail	touch	F
☐ 3)	Quick Strike III *	caster	1 round	self	U
☐ 4)	Crushing Blow I	caster	—	self	U
☐ 5)	Stunning Strike *	1 target	1 rnd/10 fail	touch	F
☐ 6)	Nerve Strike II *	1 target	1 rnd/10 fail	touch	F
☐ 7)	Quick Strike V *	caster	1 round	self	U
☐ 8)	Body Weaponry II	caster	1 rnd/lvl	self	U
☐ 9)	Shadow Strike *	1 target	1 round	self	U
☐ 10)	Stunning Strike True *	1 target	5 rnd/10 fail	touch	F
☐ 11)	Crushing Blow II	caster	—	self	U
☐ 12)	Nerve Strike III *	1 target	1 rnd/10 fail	touch	F
☐ 13)	Body Weaponry III	caster	1 rnd/lvl	self	U
☐ 14)	Paralysis Strike *	1 target	1 rnd/10 fail	touch	F
☐ 15)	Distance Strike	1 target	—	25'	F
☐ 16)	Crushing Blow III	caster	—	self	U
☐ 17)	Find Weakness	1 target	—	50'	I
☐ 18)	Nerve Strike V *	1 target	1 rnd/10 fail	touch	F
☐ 19)	Body Weaponry IV	caster	1 rnd/lvl	self	U
☐ 20)	Paralysis Strike True *	1 target	5 rnd/10 fail	touch	F
☐ 25)	Body Weaponry True	caster	1 rnd/lvl	self	U
☐ 30)	Slaying Strike	1 target	—	touch	U
☐ 50)	Distance Strike True	1 target	—	50'	F

ZEN FOCUS

1. **Body Weaponry I** — Caster gains a +5 bonus to all martial arts attacks.

2. **Nerve Strike I** — Target suffers a -10 penalty to all actions for the duration of this spell. If the caster inflicts a critical on the strike the RR is modified as follows: 'A' -10; 'B' -20; 'C' -30; 'D' -40; 'E' -50.

3. **Quick Strike I** — Caster may roll one extra die for initiative and choose which ones he wants to use.

4. **Crushing Blow I** — Caster can strike an inanimate object and deliver damage to it (taking no damage himself). Caster makes a normal unarmed attack against the object. In addition, there is a chance that the object will break if it has any flaws (e.g., cracks, fractures, etc.) in it. The chance is equal to 10% plus 1% per degree of severity of the critical delivered in the attack (i.e., 'A' critical = 11%, 'B' critical = 12%, etc.). This chance is modified by +10% to +50%, depending on the severity of the flaws.

5. **Stunning Strike** — Target is stunned for the duration of the spell.

6. **Nerve Strike II** — As Nerve Strike I, except modifier is -20.

7. **Quick Strike II** — As Quick Strike I, except caster may roll two extra die.

8. **Body Weaponry II** — As Body Weaponry I, except bonus is +10.

9. **Shadow Strike** — Caster's next attack during this round does not appear to be forceful, but it is resolved as a normal attack.

10. **Stunning Strike True** — Target is stunned for the duration of the spell.

11. **Crushing Blow II** — As Crushing Blow I, except the base chance of breakage is equal to 25% plus 3% per degree of severity of the critical delivered in the attack (i.e., 'A' critical = 28%, 'B' critical = 31%, etc.).

12. **Nerve Strike III** — As Nerve Strike I, except modifier is -30.

13. **Body Weaponry III** — As Body Weaponry I, except bonus is +15.

14. **Paralysis Strike** — Target is paralyzed for the duration of the spell.

15. **Distance Strike** — Caster can strike the target from a distance through the use of this spell. The strike is resolved as a normal melee strike made by an "unseen" foe. The caster must have a clear line-of-sight to the target.

16. **Crushing Blow III** — As Crushing Blow I, except the base chance of breakage is equal to 40% plus 6% per degree of severity of the critical delivered in the attack (i.e., 'A' critical = 46%, 'B' critical = 52%, etc.).

17. **Find Weakness** — Caster knows the weaknesses of his target. This spell must be successfully cast on the target before the Slaying Strike spell can be applied to the target.

18. **Nerve Strike V** — As Nerve Strike I, except modifier is -50.

19. **Body Weaponry IV** — As Body Weaponry I, except bonus is +20.

20. **Paralysis Strike True** — Target is paralyzed for the duration of the spell.

25. **Body Weaponry True** — As Body Weaponry I, except bonus is +30.

30. **Slaying Strike** — The next attack made by the caster in this round or next round is treated as a Slaying attack against its target. This spell may only be cast after a Find Weakness spell has been cast. No other spell may be cast after Find Weakness (or the Find Weakness must be cast again).

50. **Distance Strike True** — As Distance Strike, except caster can strike through intermediate objects. The caster can ignore any line-of-sight restrictions with regards to his target, providing he knows where his target is located. If the target is wearing armor, he is treated as if he was AT1. Natural ATs are not affected.

MIND'S SHADOW

1. **Minor Presence** — Caster is aware if there are thinking/sentient beings within 20' but does not know their number or approximate location.

2. **Empathy** — Caster learns the target's basic feelings. The caster can concentrate on a new target each round.

3. **Focus Chi II** — This spell adds +20 to any one Self Control skill or Chi Powers skill maneuver.

4. **Major Presence** — Caster is aware of the presence of all sentient/thinking beings within 20'. He knows the general number and approximate location of the beings.

5. **Cloaking I** — [RR Mod = -50] Target makes a RR. Failure results in the caster being invisible to the target; others see the caster normally. If the caster makes an obvious action (e.g., talking, moving an object, etc.), the target may make another RR (the GM may deem it appropriate to apply modifiers to this RR based on the action the caster takes). If the caster attacks the target, the target may make another RR with a +50 modifier. The caster can extend the duration of this spell indefinitely as long as he concentrates.

6. **Read Emotions** — Caster learns targets emotions in detail. The caster can concentrate on a new target each round.

7. **Suggestion** — Target will follow a single suggested act that is not completely alien to him (e.g., no suicide suggestions, no blinding himself suggestions, etc.).

8. **Cloaking III** — As *Cloaking I*, except the caster can affect 3 targets (the caster makes one BAR that applies to all targets).

9. **Focus Chi IV** — As *Focus Chi II*, except bonus is +40.

10. **Cloaking Sphere I** — As *Cloaking I*, except every target in the area of effect must make an RR (one BAR every round for all targets). Once a target makes a successful RR, he need not make another RR against this spell.

11. **Cloaking V** — As *Cloaking I*, except the caster can affect 5 targets (the caster makes one BAR that applies to all targets).

12. **Thoughts** — Caster receives surface thoughts from target. If the target makes his RR by more than 25 he realizes that someone is trying to read his thoughts. The caster can concentrate on a new target each round.

ZEN MONK BASE LIST 20.2.5
MIND'S SHADOW

Lvl	Spell	Area of Effect	Duration	Range	Type
1)	Minor Presence	20' R	C	self	U
2)	Empathy	1 target/rnd	1 rnd/lvl (C)	10'	Pm
3)	Focus Chi II *	caster	1 round	self	U
4)	Major Presence	20' R	C	self	U
5)	Cloaking I	1 target	10 min/lvl	10'/lvl	Fm
6)	Read Emotions	1 target/rnd	1 rnd/lvl (C)	50'	Pm
7)	Suggestion	1 target	Varies	10'	Fm
8)	Cloaking III	3 targets	10 min/lvl	10'/lvl	Fm
9)	Focus Chi IV *	caster	1 round	self	U
10)	Cloaking Sphere I	10' R	C	self	Fm
11)	Cloaking V	5 targets	10 min/lvl	10'/lvl	Fm
12)	Thoughts	1 target/rnd	1 rnd/lvl (C)	100'	Fm
13)	Leaving I	caster	None	self	U
14)	Cloaking X	10 targets	10 min/lvl	10'/lvl	Fm
15)	Unpresence	caster	C	self	U
16)	Cloaking Sphere II	20' R	C	self	Fm
17)	Focus Chi VI *	caster	1 round	self	U
18)	Cloaking XX	20 targets	10 min/lvl	10'/lvl	Fm
19)	Leaving III	caster	None	self	U
20)	Psychic Voice *	caster + 1 target	C	500'	Fm
25)	Cloaking Sphere III	40' R	C	self	Fm
30)	Focus Chi True *	caster	1 round	self	U
50)	Zen Enlightenment	caster	1 rnd/lvl	varies	U

13. **Leaving I** — Caster teleports up to 100' away. There can be no intervening barriers in a direct line between the caster and the point. A barrier is defined as anything the caster could not physically go through (e.g., a closed door is a barrier, a pit is not).

14. **Cloaking X** — As *Cloaking I*, except the caster can affect 10 targets (the caster makes one BAR that applies to all targets).

15. **Unpresence** — For the purposes of mental or magical detections, the caster appears to have no presence (e.g., he cannot be detected by Presence spells).

16. **Cloaking Sphere II** — As *Cloaking Sphere I*, except for the area of effect.

17. **Focus Chi VI** — As *Focus Chi II*, except bonus is +60.

18. **Cloaking XX** — As *Cloaking I*, except the caster can affect 20 targets (the caster makes one BAR that applies to all targets).

19. **Leaving III** — As *Leaving I*, except range is 300'.

20. **Psychic Voice** — Caster can mentally speak to another thinking being. Caster and target must be able to see each other or the caster must know the exact location of the target.

25. **Cloaking Sphere III** — As *Cloaking Sphere I*, except for the area of effect.

30. **Focus Chi True** — As *Focus Chi II*, except bonus is +100.

50. **Zen Enlightenment** — Caster may use one of the lower level spells on this list per round.

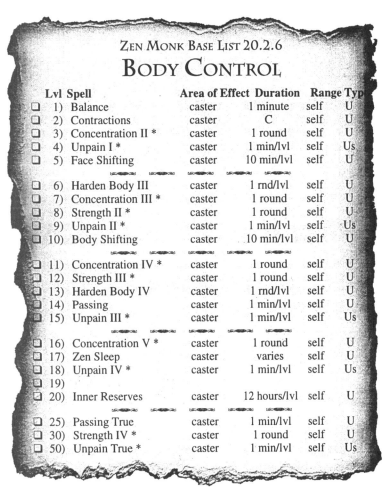

ZEN MONK BASE LIST 20.2.6
BODY CONTROL

Lvl	Spell	Area of Effect	Duration	Range	Typ
☐	1) Balance	caster	1 minute	self	U
☐	2) Contractions	caster	C	self	U
☐	3) Concentration II *	caster	1 round	self	U
☐	4) Unpain I *	caster	1 min/lvl	self	Us
☐	5) Face Shifting	caster	10 min/lvl	self	U
☐	6) Harden Body III	caster	1 rnd/lvl	self	U
☐	7) Concentration III *	caster	1 round	self	U
☐	8) Strength II *	caster	1 round	self	U
☐	9) Unpain II *	caster	1 min/lvl	self	Us
☐	10) Body Shifting	caster	10 min/lvl	self	U
☐	11) Concentration IV *	caster	1 round	self	U
☐	12) Strength III *	caster	1 round	self	U
☐	13) Harden Body IV	caster	1 rnd/lvl	self	U
☐	14) Passing	caster	1 min/lvl	self	U
☐	15) Unpain III *	caster	1 min/lvl	self	Us
☐	16) Concentration V *	caster	1 round	self	U
☐	17) Zen Sleep	caster	varies	self	U
☐	18) Unpain IV *	caster	1 min/lvl	self	Us
☐	19)				
☐	20) Inner Reserves	caster	12 hours/lvl	self	U
☐	25) Passing True	caster	1 min/lvl	self	U
☐	30) Strength IV *	caster	1 round	self	U
☐	50) Unpain True *	caster	1 min/lvl	self	Us

BODY CONTROL

1. **Balance** — Caster gains +50 to any moving maneuvers performed at a walking pace (e.g., walking a 3" beam).

2. **Contractions** — This spell allows the caster to slightly alter his muscles, limbs and torso. This facilitates escaping from bonds and small places. Gives a +25 to +50 bonus to maneuvers utilizing the Contortions skill.

3. **Concentration II** — This spell adds +20 to any one maneuver. No other action can be performed the round this maneuver is resolved.

4. **Unpain I** — Caster is able to sustain an additional 25% of his total concussion hits before passing out; hits are still taken and remain when the spell lapses.

5. **Face Shifting** — Caster is able to alter the form of his face to resemble someone else.

6. **Harden Body III** — For the duration of this spell, the caster's skin is treated as AT 3 (this is only effective if the caster is wearing no armor at all).

7. **Concentration III** — As *Concentration II*, except bonus is +30.

8. **Strength II** — In melee, caster does double normal concussion hits and his Strength stat bonus is doubled.

9. **Unpain II** — As *Unpain I*, except an additional 50% of the caster's total hits may be sustained.

10. **Body Shifting** — As *Face Shifting*, except the form and the body can be altered slightly to the general shape and size of the desired humanoid race (must be within 25% of the caster's normal mass).

11. **Concentration IV** — As *Concentration II*, except bonus is +40.

12. **Strength III** — As *Strength II*, except caster does triple normal concussion hits and his Strength stat bonus is tripled.

13. **Harden Body IV** — For the duration of this spell, the caster's skin is treated as AT 4 (this is only effective if the caster is wearing no armor at all).

14. **Passing** — Caster can move through any inanimate material up to 1' per level; it takes 1 round to pass through 2'.

15. **Unpain III** — As *Unpain I*, except an additional 75% of the caster's total hits may be sustained.

16. **Concentration V** — As *Concentration II*, except bonus is +50.

17. **Zen Sleep** — This spell halves the normal amount of time needed for rest. For example, after a normal day, instead of needing only 8 hours of sleep, the caster will need only 4. This spell will remain in effect for the duration of the sleep.

18. **Unpain IV** — As *Unpain I*, except an additional 100% of the caster's total hits may be sustained.

20. **Inner Reserves** — Caster can go without sleep for the duration of this spell without any penalties. When this spell expires, caster must make up the amount of sleep he missed (assume 8 hours of sleep per day).

25. **Passing True** — As *Passing*, but caster can pass through as much material as the duration allows at a rate of 10' per round.

30. **Strength IV** — As *Strength II*, except caster does quadruple normal concussion hits and his Strength stat bonus is quadrupled.

50. **Unpain True** — As *Unpain I*, except caster ignores all pain. Caster ignores all penalties (i.e., negative modifiers to actions) due to wounds and his concussion hits total is double his normal hits plus his Constitution temporary stat (on a 1-100 scale). When he exceeds this limit, he dies from system shock.

OTHER CHARACTER INFORMATION

This section gives specific advice for handling other issues regarding characters.

◆ 21.1 ◆
CHARACTER CONVERSION

If you want to convert characters from the RMSR to the new rules from the Martial Arts Companion, the best advice is to "re-create" the character from scratch. Converted characters will not be as effective as characters created from scratch, but if you want a fast way to convert, follow these guidelines for a quick and painless upgrade to *Martial Arts Companion*!

STEP I

If the character has any skill ranks in Martial Arts Strikes Degree 1 or Martial Arts Sweeps Degree 1, take the skill ranks and move them to Martial Arts Striking or Martial Arts Sweeping.

STEP 2

If the character has any skill ranks in the following skills (which are no longer used), he may use the development points that he spent developing these skills to develop other skills in the Martial Arts skill group.

• Martial Arts Strikes Degree 2
• Martial Arts Sweeps Degree 2
• Martial Arts Strikes Degree 3
• Martial Arts Sweeps Degree 3
• Martial Arts Strikes Degree 4
• Martial Arts Sweeps Degree 4

STEP 3

If the character has any ranks in any Special Defense skills, a small number of development points will be available since the total cost for these skills has been reduced for all professions. Figure the difference between the old cost and the new cost and then multiply by the number of ranks the character has in these skills. This is the total number of extra development points that the character will have available.

The character should spend these bonus development points in martial arts related skills, subject to the following guidelines.

• The normal rules for development must be followed just as if the character had attained a level (i.e., if a skill costs 2/6, it will cost 8 DPs to get two new ranks in that skill).
• Any modifiers for Everyman, Occupational, or Restricted skills are applied normally.

◆ 21.2 ◆
MODERN CHARACTERS

The rules presented in this book will work fine for using martial arts in the modern (or pulp) genres. However, it is suggested that the two new professions not be used in either of these genres. The new training packages may be used (with the GM's discretion), but certain skills may or may not be appropriate.

The Core rules from this book will apply to all modern and pulp genre characters. The heroic rules will probably work fine in most games (though the GM should examine them carefully). The fantastic rules should probably be left out (though the GM should examine them to see if they fit any flavor issues that might be appropriate). Other than that, all rules from this book apply to modern characters.

		WEAPON LISTING										
Weapon	**Attack Table**	**Armor Type Modifications**					**Length**	**Weight**	**F**	**B#'s**	**Str**	**Range Modifications**
		20-17	**16-13**	**12-9**	**8-5**	**4-1**						
1-H Concussion Weapons												
Fan	Club						1-2	1-2	1-2	5	47-53w	10' (-20)
Flute	Club	-5	-5	-5	-5	-5	1-2	1-2	1-3	5	47-53w	10' (-10); 25' (-30)
Hammer Copper	Mace	-10	-5	+0	+5	+5	1.5-2.5	4-5	1-3	8	74-80w	10' (-35)
Jitte	Club	-10	-10	-5	-5	-5	2.5-3.5	5-6	1-5	8	74-86w	—n/a—
Jo Stick	Club	-5	-5	-5	-5	-5	3-4	2-3	1-3	6	65-75w	—n/a—
9-Section Whip	Metal Whip	+0	+0	+0	+0	+0	5-8	3-7	1-6	6	75-86	—n/a—
Tonfa	Club	-15	-10	-10	-5	-5	1.5-2	2-3	1-2	8	65-75w	—n/a—
1-H Edged Weapons												
Butterfly Knife	Dagger	+5	+0	+5	+10	+15	1.5-2	2-4	1-5	6	74-86	10' (-30)
Chinese Sword	Broadsword	+0	+0	+0	+0	+5	2-3.5	3-5	1-3	7	75-86	—n/a—
Circular Knife	Scimitar	-10	-5	+0	+5	+10	2-3	4-6	1-5	7	65-76w	—n/a—
Kris	Dagger	-5	-5	+0	+5	+5	1.5-2.5	2-4	1-4	6	65-76	10' (+50)
Nine-Ring Sword	Falchion	+0	+0	+0	+5	+5	2-3.5	3.5-5	1-5	7	74-86	—n/a—
Sai	Main Gauche	-5	+0	+0	+0	+5	1.5-2	2-3	1-3	5	65-76	10' (-20)
Spring Sword	Rapier	-5	-5	+5	+5	+5	5-7	4-6	1-8	7	65-76	—n/a—
Willowleaf Knife	Scimitar	+0	+0	+0	+0	+5	2-3	3-4	1-4	5	56-64	—n/a—
2-Handed Weapons												
Bo Staff	Quarterstaff	+0	+0	+0	+0	+0	5-7	3-5	1-4	7	65-75w	—n/a—
Kusari-gama	Chigiriki						4-12	4-7	1-8	7	75-86	10' (-20)
Manriki-gusari	Chigiriki						2-3	2-3	1-4	6	75-86	10' (-10); 25' (-30)
Ring Metal	Club	+0	+0	+5	+5	+5	2-4	2-4	1-2	5	74-86	—n/a—
Thorn Staff	Quarterstaff	+0	-5	-10	-10	-15	2.5-4	4-8	1-5	8	68-74w	10' (-35)
Missile Weapons												
Dai-kyu	Long Bow	+10	+10	+10	+10	+10	5-7	3-4	1-5	Auto	54-66	10' (+25); 100' (+0); 200' (-30); 300' (-40); 400' (-50)
Han-kyu	Short Bow	+0	+0	+5	+5	+5	2-3	1.5-2	1-4	Auto	54-66	10' (+10); 50' (+0); 100' (-40); 180' (-70)
Polearm Weapons												
Tiger Fork	Spear	-5	+0	+0	+5	+5	5-8	3-7	1-5	5	47-53w	10' (-30)
Naginata	Polearm	-5	-5	-5	-5	-5	6-8	5-10	1-6	7	65-76	—n/a—
9-Dragon Trident	Polearm	+0	+0	+0	+5	+5	6-8	18-25	1-10	7	65-75	—n/a—
Yari	Spear						5-7	3-6	1-5	5	47-53w	—n/a—
Thrown Weapons												
Dart	Dagger						1.5-3"	2 oz	1-4	6	74-86	10' (-10); 25' (-20)
Flying Claw	Bola	-5	-5	-5	-5	-5	20	2-3	1-6	5	47-53s	10' (+0); 20' (-20)
Rope Dart	Dagger	-5	+0	+0	+5	+5	20	2-3	1-6	5	47-53s	10' (+0); 20' (-20)
Shuriken	Dagger	+5	+5	+0	+0	+0	2-3"	2 oz	1-5	5	74-86	10' (+10); 25' (+0); 50' (-30)
Martial Arts Attacks												
Fingernail Razor	MA Strikes	+0	+0	+0	+0	+5	1"	n/a	1-2	5	65-76	—n/a—
Shuko	MA Strikes	+0	+0	+5	+5	+5	n/a	1	1-2	6	65-76	—n/a—

NOTES

MARTIAL
ARTS
COMPANION

ROLEMASTER STANDARD SYSTEM ™

Core Titles: These titles are 3-hole punched and perfed for your binder!

5500 Rolemaster Standard Rules™ $30

The *Rolemaster Standard System* is a detailed, state-of-the-art FRP system that adds realism and depth to your campaign without sacrificing playability. The *Rolemaster Standard Rules (RMSR)* is the cornerstone of this system and provides all the guidelines and rules needed to play *Rolemaster*. Its primary parts are concerned with character definition, character design, and performing actions. These rules are designed to provide both the Gamemaster and the players with tremendous detail and flexibility in character development and the resolution of a wide variety of actions and activity. *Rolemaster Standard Rules* are essential for tying together and using the Standard versions of *Arms Law, Spell Law,* and *Gamemaster Law*. Experience *Rolemaster* and experience the ultimate in fantasy roleplaying! 3-hole drilled and perforated.

5520 Arms Law™ (Standard System) $16

Feel the thrill of melee, brace against a monster's charge, master the martial arts, let your arrows fly—do battle with the best combat system around! In *Arms Law* you get a fantasy/ medieval melee and missile combat system with attack tables. Plus you get a dozen different critical strike tables for 29 different weapon types including Slashing, Puncture, Unbalancing, as well as tables for brawling, martial arts, fumbles, weapon breakage, and more!

Arms Law features one weapon attack table per page for ease of use during fast and furious combat, with the corresponding critical hit table right on the back! *Arms Law* is one of the four cornerstones of the *Rolemaster Standard System*; however, it is fully compatible with the earlier editions of *Rolemaster*.

5521 Gamemaster Law™ (Standard System) $20

Gamemasters, learn how to use the system to its fullest potential! *Gamemaster Law* provides a wealth of guidelines and details that a Gamemaster needs to run a RMSS or any other FRP game. Also provided are tips and guidelines on group dynamics, player motivations, and story presentation that will prove invaluable to GMs of all systems.

This book is perfect bound with perforated pages and is 3-hole punched for use with 3-ring binders if desired. Yes, you can master *Rolemaster,* as long as you have *Gamemaster Law!*

5522 Spell Law™ (Standard System) $25

Feel the crackling flow of Essence course through you as you repel the soul-tearing power of a dark cleric! Stand firm against the insidious power of the mentalist, and loose the ravening elemental force of nature against your foes! Cast your lot with the best spell system around—*Spell Law!*

Spell Law is the highly acclaimed magic system that improves any game. This is a mighty tome that can add realism and depth to your campaign without sacrificing playability. A must for your favorite characters, be they Magicians, Clerics, or Mentalists!

Spell Law provides over 200 spell descriptions, critical strike tables for attack spells, spell failure tables, and everything else needed to provide a fully detailed magic system adaptable to any FRP game. *Spell Law,* one of the four cornerstones of the *RMSS,* is fully compatible with older versions of *Rolemaster*.

Other Titles Currently Available:

5510 Rolemaster 3 in 1™ $65

Special packaging of three of the four *Rolemaster Standard System* primary books. Get *Arms Law, Spell Law,* and *Rolemaster Standard Rules* together for a savings of $6.00. This should prevent the headaches of finding only one or two of the titles in the store, when you are looking for all three of them!

5502 Rolemaster GM Screen™ $12

This screen is a useful game aid for every *Rolemaster* Gamemaster and player. Each 25.5" x 11" stand-up screen is actually two screens (with three faces each) and has many of the most frequently used *Rolemaster* tables along with the modifiers for those tables. Included with the screens is a 48 page booklet containing all of the encounter tables from *Creatures & Monsters* as well as a master listing of creatures (not available in any other product).

5504 Rolemaster Character Records™ $12

Filling out a character sheet from scratch can take a long time.... Now, for each profession you can use a customized skill development sheet that will efficiently organize all skills (and categories). *Rolemaster Character Records* features customized pages for each of the 16 races/cultures in *RMSR*, a weapons skill sheet that provides a master listing of all weapons & their categories, and a spell skill sheet that provides enough space to list all levels of spell development.

5505 Rolemaster Annual 1996™ $10

Rolemaster Annual 1996 provides replacement pages for certain sections of the *RMSS* (to reflect 1996 additions to the system), as well as providing master tables for many areas of the system. In addition, the *Rolemaster Annual* also provides character record sheets for the new races and professions in the *RMSS* (these sheets are not available in any other product). All pages provided in an easy-to-use, 3-hole drill, perforated format.

5523 Talent Law™ $18

From the ranks of the paupers comes the champion of kings! Now you can explore the incredibly diverse possibilities of options available to characters through their backgrounds. *Talent Law* provides Gamemasters and players with a new system of customizing characters through background options. In *Talent Law* you get a point-based system for background options that allow characters to select from Special Training, Special Abilities, Physical Abilities, and Mystical Abilities and a corresponding system for determining flaws, to make the characters even more interesting! Gamemasters, you will find complete guidelines for customizing the background options to your own game worlds, as well as a system for creating brand new races.

5524 Weapon Law: Firearms™ $18

Now you can run combat for the *Rolemaster Standard System* in post-medieval settings! *Weapons Law: Firearms* provides all of the tables and information you need to resolve combat involving firearms from any era, from the Renaissance to the modern day. Now the thrust, parry, and assassin's dagger can be met with hot lead as much as cold steel! In *Weapon Law: Firearms* you get more than 40 attack tables covering all firearms through the modern day, new critical strike tables, and a new weapon failure table. You'll find complete statistics for over 500 specific weapons covering all major areas and times from medieval to modern, and rules for incorporating firearm combat into your role playing game. All material is presented in a convenient 3-hole drilled, perfed format.

5540 Creatures & Monsters™ $30

A bestiary of epic proportions! Inside, you will find hundreds of animals, monsters, and races. Many are culled from myth, others are staples of fantasy fiction, and many more are completely original—unlike anything you have ever seen in a role playing game before! *Creatures & Monsters* includes monsters that can fly, swim, and terrorize the land. You'll also find many pages devoted to animals of all types, ranging from those that characters can protect and befriend to those that can threaten their very lives. *Creatures & Monsters*: it's all the bestiary that you will ever need for hundreds of *Rolemaster* adventures.

5541 Races & Cultures: Underground Races™ $16

Come to the depths of the worlds and explore these fully detailed cultures! Each of the underground races in this volume, including Dwarves, Gnolls, Gnomes, Goblins, Halflings, Hobgoblins, Kobolds, five different kinds of Orcs, and Troglodytes, has pages of specialized weapons, lifestyle and religious notes, training packages, spell lists, adolescent development tables, and much more!

5542 Castles & Ruins™ $20

In *Castles & Ruins* you get new training packages and spell lists that represent the vocations and lifestyles of the folks who build and live around castles, and details on the processes used in castle construction, along with cost guidelines. Details on staffing of castles, as well as notes about the day-to-day operations of these bastions of power are also included. Plus, you get new attack tables for besieging castles: Ballista, Catapult, Ram, and Trebuchet, along with rules for siegecraft and castle defense. Finally, learn how castles age, becoming ruins, often the sites of lost treasure and adventure.

5600 Arcane Companion™ $18

Since the dawn of time man has struggled to understand the nature of magic... Now you can probe the origins of the most powerful, but hardest to control, type of magic: Arcane. This companion explores the dangerous world of Arcane spells, the professions adopted by the Arcane spell users, and the ancient and powerful Arcane spells themselves.

In *Arcane Companion* you get four new professions, 46 Arcane spell lists, and new spell attack and critical strike tables. A Spell Failure table unveils the risks and perils of using Arcane magic. For Gamemasters, we include a discussion of the concepts and premises behind Arcane magic as well as rules for controlling the acquisition of Arcane magic.

5601 Treasure Companion™ $18

Treasure Companion is designed to allow Gamemasters to quickly generate normal and magical treasures to be discovered and won by the characters in their games. For players, the long awaited Alchemist profession is now added to the *Rolemaster Standard System*. Inside this book are full discussions on the nature of wealth and magic in a FRPG, including guidelines for the buying and selling of the items that characters might find.

In *Treasure Companion* you get complete item descriptions for over a hundred unique magic items, as well as tables for generating all types of treasure (including a detailed system for creating gemstones and jewelry). Three new Alchemist professions and 22 Alchemist spell lists bring these creators of magic items to life.

5700 Black Ops™ $16

Want to experience the dark, mysterious world of espionage, mercenaries, and counter-terrorists? Then you need to explore the realm of *Black Ops*—the first genre book for the *RMSS! Black Ops* brings you into the complex, and often dangerous world of modern day covert operations with new rules for creating characters and handling combat.

Inside this genre book you'll find 3 new professions, training packages for modern characters, and guidelines for using *Weapon Law*™ in the modern world. You'll also get equipment lists, guidelines on terrorism and counter-terrorism, a timeline of major world events, and sample adventures that will allow your character to experience the adrenaline rush of covert operations.

5701 Pulp Adventures™ $16

In *Pulp Adventures* you will find three new professions for characters in the Pulp World, equipment lists, and more than a dozen new training packages. Also included are guidelines on how to use *Weapon Law*™ in the Pulp era, plus details on using magic. And as a bonus, you'll get a timeline of major events, and lists of major motion pictures, radio shows, popular series, popular dances, and personages of the Pulp era.

6303 Curse of Kabis™ $18

It all begins with a murder and a mysterious toy... Visit cities of hope and peril. Explore eerie islands, rugged caverns, and forgotten ruins. Encounter exotic cultures, deadly creatures, and fiendish plots. All while confronting layers of opposition on a journey with an unknown destination. A Rolemaster adventure in Shadow World.™